Reproductive Restraints

Reproductive Restraints:
Birth Control in India, 1877–1947

Sanjam Ahluwalia

University of Illinois Press
Urbana and Chicago

© 2008 by Sanjam Ahluwalia
All rights reserved
Manufactured in the United States of America
1 2 3 4 5 C P 5 4 3 2 1

♾ This book is printed on acid-free paper.

Library of Congress Cataloging-in-Publication Data
Ahluwalia, Sanjam
Reproductive restraints : birth control in India, 1877–1947
/ Sanjam Ahluwalia.
p.   cm.
Includes bibliographical references and index.
ISBN-13 978-0-252-03240-0 (cloth : alk. paper)
ISBN-10 0-252-03240-3 (cloth : alk. paper)
ISBN-13 978-0-252-07480-6 (pbk. : alk. paper)
ISBN-10 0-252-07480-7 (pbk. : alk. paper)
1. Birth control—India—History.
I. Title.
HQ766.5.I5A713   2008
304.6'66095409034—dc22   2007037074

For Aeka and Sanjay

Contents

Acknowledgments ix

Introduction 1

1. Demographic Rhetoric and Sexual Surveillance: Indian Middle-Class Advocates of Birth Control, 1877–1947 23

2. Global Agenda and Local Politics: Western Advocates and Discourse of Birth Control in Colonial India, 1920s–40s 54

3. Polyvocality, Ambivalence, and Negotiations: Indian Middle-Class Feminism and Debates on Birth Control in Nationalist India, 1920s–40s 85

4. A Fractured Discourse: Colonial Attitudes on Birth Control in the Twentieth Century 115

5. Untrained "Professionals": Medical Practitioners and the Politics of Birth Control in Colonial India, 1920–47 143

Epilogue 173

Notes 187

Bibliography 219

Index 241

Acknowledgments

In the time it has taken me to complete this book, I have accumulated many professional and personal debts and it gives me great pleasure to acknowledge the support and help I have received over the years. Archival and ethnographic research for this project was conducted across three continents. In London I found archival and library staff at the British Library, the Wellcome Institute for the History of Medicine, and the London School of Economics to be very helpful. In Delhi the staff at the National Archives of India, the Nehru Memorial Museum and Library, the Marwari Library, and the National Medical Library made documents available to me and at times pointed me toward other sources that spoke to my project. Mr. Gupta at the Marwari Library was generous in allowing me to photocopy materials on short notice, as was the staff at the National Medical Library. I would also like to express my gratitude to the staff at the Uttar Pradesh State Archives in Lucknow where I did some work for this project. Library staff and interlibrary loan services both at the University of Cincinnati (UC) and Northern Arizona University (NAU) helped me procure important documents for which I am immensely grateful.

I would also like to acknowledge the important research support I had from the Society for the Integrated Development of the Himalayas (SIDH) and in particular from Anuradha Joshi and Pawan Gupta. Savitri (Sabu) Tamta gave generously of her time and provided important contextual information about the area based on her many years of involvement and work with the Jaunpur community, especially its womenfolk. My deepest respect and thanks also to the women in Jaunpur who accommodated my intrusions into their daily chores. I would especially like to thank Rukhma Devi, Shanti, Bhura Devi, Leela Devi, and Padma Devi. I would also like to thank Jayant Gokhale for introducing me to his grandmother Pamella Gokhale, whom I interviewed in Kanpur, and through whom I got to meet and interview Chandrika Rohtagi, Surendra Rohtagi, and Lakshmi Sehgal.

The initial research for this project was undertaken as part of my doctoral work. At UC I was fortunate to have received important grant support from the Taft Foundation, the Department of History, and the Friends of Women's Studies, which enabled me to undertake necessary research in London and India. Further research was made possible with an intramural grant at NAU. The generous support of the Women's Studies Department and the Department of History has made it possible to present my work at various forums, where I received extremely useful feedback on my project.

I cannot list all the teachers and mentors who have shaped my scholarship, especially my undergraduate and postgraduate teachers and mentors at Delhi University. All I will say is that they were foundational in shaping my intellectual trajectory and in providing me with the best training to further pursue and explore my academic interest. At UC I was very fortunate to have found another set of the most amazing and wonderful mentors and teachers, especially my adviser Barbara Ramusack, who has gone out of her way to provide necessary direction and support, both professionally and personally. As a token of my appreciation for her encouragement over the past decade, it gives me great pleasure in acknowledging her as my very special mentor, guide, and friend. I have, of course, learned a great deal from her work, and hope to emulate her enthusiasm for continued archival research, writing, and publishing—not to mention her general panache!

Antoinette Burton, Mrinalini Sinha, and Lesley Hall have all read many different versions of the chapters in this book. They have, at different times, provided invaluable feedback, helping me push my argument further; in addition, they have all provided important bibliographic references. I would like to thank them for their intellectual generosity and support over the years. Also, as will be evident from this work, I have been greatly influenced in my own thinking on global transnational histories and gender histories by their rich and pioneering research. I would also like to thank David Arnold for sharing his work and providing many useful references for my study.

Rukun Advani at Permanent Black initially read and approved of this project. It was his approval that gave me the confidence to convert this work from a dissertation into a book manuscript. I have also enjoyed working with Kerry Callahan, Joan Catapano, Rebecca Crist, and Anne Rogers at the University of Illinois Press. I would also like to thank the two anonymous readers from the Press for their very thoughtful and generous comments.

Friends made the entire process much less strenuous than it may have been otherwise. At NAU, Susan Deeds and Sheryl Lutjens have read chapters from this study and provided necessary reassurance and feedback, especially at times when I felt frustrated with a particular line of argument I was trying to tease out! I have come to rely on them both for their wisdom, mentorship, and warm friendship over the years. NAU has provided me with a wonderful community of cohorts and friends who have, through their own vibrant and prolific intellectual production, provided a conducive environment in which to teach and pursue research goals. I would especially like to thank Judith Giesberg and Jennifer Denetdale for their warm friendship and intellectual camaraderie. Besides them, Cindy, Eric, Geeta, Irene, John, Karen, Leilah, Monica, Nancy, and Scott have provided much support and encouragement over the years. A special thanks to my colleague and friend Heather Martel, who closely read and commented on parts of the manuscript, providing useful and encouraging comments. Shelly and Marybeth both provided significant administrative support, making work life that much more manageable and pleasurable, besides being indulgent listeners in times of stress.

I cannot mention friends without thinking of my oldest and dearest friends, Kamalam and Indira, who have been a significant source of support since my days in high school. Friends from Delhi University, while not always staying in touch regularly, have over the years provided a strong community of support—Smita, Ravikant, and Geetanjali have allowed me the luxury to pick up on conversations even after months of total silence. Anshu and Charu have been friends with whom I have continued to share discussions about work and fun. Outside of India, Sarah and Anne have been great cohorts with whom to share my work. In Cincinnati, Sarah, Chirp, and Bob adopted me as part of their family, making sure I was never alone on Thanksgiving or Christmas. Sumita has provided sane and wise advice even as we exchanged notes on comparative gender and women's histories. Stephy and Patricia have provided a strong community and support system in Flagstaff, complete with much-welcomed breaks for walks and coffee, while Peggy was generous with her time, providing useful editorial feedback for which I am very grateful. In London, Uma Maitreyan provided a home away from home, and Shalini, Rashmi, and Subir have helped make research trips a lot of fun.

I have been most fortunate to have found loving and caring in-laws. I thank Aija and Babu for their understanding and love. I regret that Babu will not see this book. Given his love for books, he would have taken special joy in seeing this study in print. In Meenu I have found a wonderful friend, and we have had many long conversations about work and family. It was largely through her and Kaku's support that I was able to undertake a short research trip to Jaunpur. I have greatly benefited from their long years of work and research in the area.

My own family has been a pillar of support that I have come to rely on at all times. Ma and Dad have, over the years, come to appreciate my unconventional tastes and take pride in what I do, even while not always agreeing with my choices. For that I am deeply grateful and eternally thankful. They both provided crucial support in the last stages of this work, freeing me from household chores as well as babysitting for my newborn daughter. Also, I don't know if a sister could do more than Shalu has for me.

How do I even begin to thank my spouse Sanjay? Despite looming deadlines and demanding schedules of his own, he has found time to closely read and comment on my written prose, always to my initial dismay but ultimate relief. If it were not for his love, intellectual companionship, and "gentle" nagging, this work would have taken longer to complete. He has been my strongest supporter and harshest critic, and it is to him I owe the most, more than I can say.

My little daughter Aeka Vinod Joshi made sure she arrived before I sent off the manuscript to the publishers. She came a couple of weeks early, adding tremendous joy and happiness to our lives, not to say an appropriate point of closure for a study about reproductive restraints! I am very happy to dedicate this work to Sanjay and to her.

Reproductive Restraints

Introduction

> The myth of overpopulation is destructive because it prevents constructive thinking and action on reproductive issues. Instead of clarifying our understanding of these issues, it obfuscates our vision and limits our ability to see the real problems and find workable solutions. Worst of all, it breeds racism and turns women's bodies into a political battlefield. It is a philosophy based on fear, not on understanding.
> —Betsy Hartmann, *Reproductive Rights and Wrongs: The Global Politics of Population Control*

When I first began to think of working on this project many (too many!) years ago as a graduate student at the University of Delhi, I wanted to write a history of the birth control movement in India. As a feminist and a historian,[1] and with my interest in feminist activism, I had hoped to write a narrative to document how women wrested control of their own bodies, sexuality, and fertility in a patriarchal world. Even then, though, I was a little troubled by the fact that all around me, birth control was rhetorically more a critique of less-privileged sections of Indian society rather than the glorious march toward women's emancipation I wanted to relate. Since that time, and after plowing through reams of archival data, engaging in many intellectual debates, and much agonizing, I have finally produced a work that reveals how it is that birth control, a subject so many feminists believe to be inherently empowering for women, became part of an elitist agenda that actually restrained women from exercising control over their own reproductive capacities. In doing so, this book highlights not only the specificity of the Indian case, but also serves as a cautionary tale for feminists who would universalize their own parochial histories to reify "birth control" as an always already feminist issue.

A recent show on Indian television perhaps best captures the elitist nature of the discourse on birth control in India. Between December 17 and 20, 2004, NDTV, one of India's premier news channels, hosted a passionate discussion on the question of "Do We Need Compulsory Birth Control in India?" Transnational respondents from Abu Dhabi, Bangalore,

Chennai, Goa, Gurgaon, Kolkata, Kuwait, Ludhiayana, Melbourne, Mumbai, New Delhi, Patna, Riyadh, and Rome weighed in on the discussion via Short Message System (SMS) messages on their mobile phones.[2] Most responded in the affirmative, arguing that "population explosion" was the cause for unemployment, low literacy rates, terrorism, and separatism in contemporary India.[3] Elite immigrants and resident Indian elites agreed that India's demographic "explosion" was one of the leading challenges to the nation's development and economic modernization—compulsory birth control, they suggested, was therefore the logical and necessary solution.

Advocates of compulsory birth control are, unfortunately, not limited to the world of television, SMS, or the Internet and, even less fortunately, do not represent isolated individual opinions. In fact, it would be fair to argue that such opinions reflect a dominant contemporary view on the subject of birth control and its relationship to national demographic management. In contemporary India, this commonsense understanding was reflected in a recent Indian Supreme Court decision that upheld a state government law prohibiting a person from contesting village-level elections if she or he had more than two children. It was argued that such a disqualification did not contravene any fundamental rights of the individual, but rather was "a disqualification conceptually devised in the national interest."[4] A former member of the Indian cabinet deemed having more than two children was an act of "sedition," and advocated the disenfranchisement of those guilty of such "anti-national" acts. "Evaluating the ethics of all other methods of family planning," the former minister in charge of India's environment argued, "the one of losing adult franchise is the most appropriate," asking rhetorically, "How can one have the right to vote for a nation after having been convicted of anti-national activity against that very nation?"[5]

These contemporary examples capture both the "top-down" approach on fertility control and exemplify the long-standing Malthusian and elite nationalist concerns that have shaped public discussions on the subject. They express an underlying elite anxiety to deploy national fertility as a measure of the social, political, and economic well-being of the nation. There is a strong desire to manage the population not only through technoscientific means, but also through a selective denial of civic rights that most modern nation-states promise their citizens. The use of contraceptives is represented as a national duty in India. Procreative and sexual behaviors are understood to be closely tied to national well-being, and as such become legitimate sites of state interrogation and management. Unfortunately, these opinions also evoke the horrific specter of the Emergency days, which within the Indian context has become a trope for forced sterilization and suspension of all democratic safeguards to promote the larger abstract ideal of national well-being.⁶ The Mainstream discourse on birth control in India does not incorporate ideals of justice, choice, freedom, sexual autonomy, or reproductive rights.

The construction of demography and contraceptive usage as markers of national well-being unfortunately do not reflect a departure from the past; rather, this particular position has a long history. This study seeks to inquire into the intellectual and political genesis of such an articulation and to highlight its underlying problematic assumptions. The key to understanding this position, I would argue, lies as much within the intellectual traditions of Malthusianism, eugenics, demography, and sexology as it does within the larger history and politics of feminism in the early twentieth century. Dominant feminist thought has linked control over one's body as essential to the constitution of modern selves and viable individuals. However, this premise of a normative and universal feminist subject draws upon specific histories, rooted within bourgeois Western thought and experiences. Within the dominant feminist understanding, birth control and contraceptive technologies are largely represented as necessarily empowering for all women at all times. The history of birth control in colonial India, however, did not empower all women to control their bodies and determine their fertility. In *Reproductive Restraints* I examine the historical genesis for the demand for birth control within India, moving between empirical history and postcolonial feminist theory while seeking to find new ways of thinking about the subject.

This study takes as its starting point the need to fill a glaring lacuna for a historically nuanced narrative, one that traces the intellectual, political, and social genealogy of the demand for birth control as it emerged from the late nineteenth century in colonial India. As a historical investigation, this work highlights the political and intellectual legacy, whereby reproduction has long been identified as "simultaneously very private and highly public."⁷ From the late nineteenth century onward, numerous intellectual and discursive traditions shaped the discussions on India's population and its health. Debates on population size and health of Indians generated a demand for wider dissemination of contraceptive information and usage. Various intellectual and political currents of Malthusianism, eugenics, demography, Western biomedical discourse, sexology, and mainstream nationalism, as well as middle-class feminism, framed the reproductive script in colonial India. In mapping the trajectory of the birth control movement in India, *Reproductive Restraints* interrogates the multiplicity of logics and intellectual traditions that shaped the writings and work of Indian advocates.

Instead of a singular point of origin, this work recognizes the scattered and multiple production sites that simultaneously delivered and sought to possess fecund subaltern bodies during the nineteenth and twentieth centuries. Numerous proponents of bourgeois nationalism, middle-class feminists, Western birth control enthusiasts, and some biomedical and alternative medical practitioners, along with a few colonial representatives, identified lower-caste and working-class Indian women as primary targets of contraceptive technologies—both chemical and mechanical. The various historical actors examined in this study emphasized women as primary users/consumers of contraceptive devices, and in so doing turned women's bodies into embattled sites for control. Birth control enthusiasts sought to contain what they identified and labeled as fecund bodies, whereas those opposed to birth control, such as Mahatma Gandhi, the moral nationalist reformer, sought to wipe out all traces and expressions of nonprocreative sexuality from the realms of monogamous heterosexual patriarchal conjugality.

As a critical narrative of the history of birth control in colonial India, this work carefully locates the unfolding of this history at the nexus of a complex web of local, nationalist, and international initiatives. Historically, intellectual concerns and ideas have been tested, debated, adopted, and discarded within a geographical context that is usually larger than that defined by national boundaries. Indian advocates in the colonial period were not thinking and writing in a cultural or political vacuum. The work of Western advocates formed a significant part of the intellectual capital that shaped the intertextual discourse of birth control in colonial India. Early Indian male proponents of birth control belonged to the emerging Western-educated middle class, conversant in Western intellectual traditions, employing Western ideas selectively to further their political agendas. To legitimize public discussions and obtain funding for this controversial subject, early advocates in India sought support from their contemporaries in the West such as Margaret Sanger, Marie Stopes, Edith How-Martyn, and Eileen Palmer. Western enthusiasts performed important labor in propagandizing the issue of birth control in public debates and discussions within India. In turn, Western advocates found in countries like India an opportunity to experiment and extend their subjective locations in ways not necessarily available to them within their own national boundaries. Deploying a transnational framework, *Reproductive Restraints* is interested in understanding how global, national, and local initiatives influenced each other and continue to do so, though from highly unequal power positions.

Ironically, despite the dense public discourse promoting contraceptive use among Indian women, reproductive technologies were very much in their infancy during the early twentieth century. There was a gap between rhetorical gestures of liberating women and viable technology that would make it feasible for women to control their fertility at will. Although many advocates of birth control highlighted the aim of liberating women from their biological destiny, a closer examination of the history of birth control in colonial India demonstrates that the concern with empowering women and ensuring better reproductive health facilities for Indian women were not the guiding principles in the debates on birth control. Politics of gender, class, caste, race, sexuality, community, demography, and nation shaped the discourse of birth control in colonial India. This study is interested in unraveling how the various proponents and opponents of birth control selectively deployed these multiple variables to produce an essentially elitist, nondemocratic, and oppressive politics of reproduction. As a feminist project, this empirical and theoretical study is engaged in what Jane Flax refers to as the "thinking of thinking," particularly on the subject of birth control and women's reproductive rights in colonial India during the late nineteenth and early twentieth centuries.[8]

Reproductive Restraints attempts to restore the contested history of birth control to the ongoing feminist battles within contemporary India for better, safer, and more reliable contraceptive technologies in the wake of the recent liberalization of the markets. Providing the missing and unfamiliar narrative on the struggle for women's reproductive rights makes this at once both a historical and a political inquiry, following in the footsteps of Linda Gordon's seminal work on the history of the birth control movement in the United States.[9] While recognizing the importance of filling gaps and lacunae in our accounts of the past, this work methodologically implements the suggestion of feminist theorists to adopt a "narrativizing strategy in addition to a deconstructive one."[10] In addition, while providing the missing narrative of the history of birth control in India, this work scrutinizes the underlying political lexicon and agenda of multiple proponents and opponents of contraceptive technologies. Moreover, this study also critically interrogates the assumptions with which we approach the subject and history of birth control and contraceptive usage.

Historiographical Engagements and Contributions of this Study

Examining the history of birth control in colonial India necessarily leads this study to engage with a wide range of historiographical issues that currently animate Indian and Euro-American scholarships. In constructing the genealogy of birth control discourse in colonial India, the recent shift within history writing—exploring the possibilities of constructing "multi-sited" historical narratives—has been particularly instructive. Barbara Ramusack, Antoinette Burton, Kumkum Sangari, Mrinalini Sinha, and Nancy Rose

Hunt, among other feminist scholars, have been calling for an interrogation of the narrow national boundaries within which we locate our work.[11] This study draws upon the work of these scholars to argue that the history of birth control in colonial India can only be understood as interrelated to larger transnational birth control movements.

This work draws much from existing feminist scholarship, which has called for a rethinking and redrawing of the conventional geographical boundaries within which historical accounts are largely located. Constructing interactive and relational histories of birth control allows us to challenge national historical narratives that assume splendid isolation in mapping a script for the past. Identifying national histories as interacting across cultures and across narrow national boundaries also enables us to escape the trap of constructing colonial histories as essentially "derivative" gestures. Interconnecting national narratives will, moreover, allow us to better represent the larger intellectual context within which debates on issues such as birth control took place in the early twentieth century. This approach helps demonstrate the complex relationship of intellectual and commodity exchanges that take place within a globally connected economy. *Reproductive Restraints*, therefore, argues that although the birth control movement in India drew sustenance from a few Western birth control activists, simultaneously it had important contributions of its own to make to the global community and politics of birth control. Indian presence was important in shaping the emergence of an international body of thought on the subject as these ideas were materializing in the twentieth century. Aliyappin Padmanabha Pillay, a birth control activist, started an international journal, *Marriage Hygiene,* which contemporaries such as Havelock Ellis judged as one of the leading English language journals on sexology.[12] Indian enthusiasts participated in international conferences, invited Western activists to India, and visited birth control clinics in London. Indian activists participated in an emerging transnational birth control movement and India became important as a newly emerging market for contraceptive technologies.

Although recognizing the transnational movement of ideas, personnel, and technologies of birth control within a globally connected economy, this work is not an unproblematic celebration of globalization. Instead, through a close analysis of transnational exchanges, it highlights the underlying inequality of power relations that determined interactions. While being cautious about the dangers of celebrating globalization, the emphasis on relational histories allows us to disrupt the all-encompassing metanarrative of nationalism (and its other in the Indian context—communalism) from subsuming other narrative possibilities. Besides providing a counter to narrow hypernationalist narratives, interactive histories also serve as important corrective to Eurocentrism—forcing us to recognize the constitution of the West as historically contingent upon its interactions with the non-West. Transregional historical narratives effectively call into question the historical mythologies that represent the West as the site of origin for politics, technology, discourse, and interest on topics such as birth control. Finally, an interactive lens better reflects the complex phenomena of intellectual debates and currents, which, much like weather patterns, do not abruptly come to a halt at historically constructed national, ethnic, or racial boundaries.

This study also engages with a significant debate within Indian history, the nature of middle-class feminist politics. Feminist historians such as Tanika Sarkar, Barbara Metcalf, Gail Minault, Uma Chakravarty, Prem Choudhry, Anshu Malhotra, Charu Gupta, Partha Chatterjee, Dipesh Chakrabarty, Faisal Devji, and Mytheli Sreenivas have demonstrated the centrality of gender politics in shaping the agenda of Indian reform movements, arousing community consciousness and influencing Indian nationalism in different regions in colonial India.[13] These scholars have highlighted the contested nature of gender politics that shaped Indian politics in the late nineteenth and early twentieth centuries. I draw from their works as much as from that of an earlier generation of scholarship that has examined and written extensively on the first wave of organized Indian women's politics. Writing as a third-generation feminist scholar, my work obviously benefits enormously from the rich scholarship of my predecessors.

The early writings of historians of women, such as Barbara Ramusack, Aparna Basu, Kumari Jayawardena, Vina Majumdar, Gail Minault, Gail Omvedt, and Gail Pearson, to name just a few, have been instrumental in highlighting an alternative archive to that of the colonial records.[14] Their books and articles examine the emergence of Indian feminist politics and its troubled relationship with the dominant "malestream" nationalist politics in the early twentieth century. Their pioneering work has made it possible for the next generation of scholars to construct narratives distinct from the malestream nationalist storyline with only men as actors and agents. Drawing upon the existing literature, this study seeks to push the boundaries, critically interrogating the fractured relationship between feminism and nationalism, to highlight the tensions and contradictions that marked the negotiations between these two sets of political impulses in colonial India.

Using birth control as a lens, *Reproductive Restraints* critically reviews dominant Indian feminism to understand how variables of class, caste, community, and nation shaped its politics. Indian middle-class feminism emerges on its own terms, both as simultaneously acting and being acted upon by mainstream Gandhian nationalism. Instead of adopting the simplistic betrayal script that some scholars have deployed to read the interaction between middle-class feminism and bourgeois Indian nationalism, this study identifies the radical limitations of Indian feminists to lie in their middle-class subject positions, and for the majority of the women in their upper-caste identity. As members of the social elite, Indian middle-class women leaders in colonial India were as invested in preserving their privileges as in calling into question the inequitable distribution of resources or challenging existing power relations. In many ways, the early Indian women leaders were complicit with the modernist bourgeois project of nation building that perpetuated power inequities based on class, caste, and community identities.

Geraldine Forbes, Pearson, Omvedt, and Jayawardena have all argued that the central paradox of Indian feminism, the claim to speak on behalf of women and the inability to fully articulate and further the interests of their constituents, was a result of its troubled alliance with Gandhian nationalism. According to Forbes, the early women activists insisted that their "commitment to India's freedom was compatible with their concern for women's rights. It was strategically important to do so."[15] This pragmatic and strategic move made it hard for the women leaders to confront basic socioeconomic issues. Directly confronting gender issues would have been unproductive, bringing the women leaders in confrontation with patriarchal oppression, attitudes, and institutions in the midst of a nationalist struggle.[16] Forbes argues that women leaders "espoused a feminist ideology but time and again put it aside in favor of the broader struggle," adding that "they did not think it possible to raise women's consciousness about politics and women's rights at the same time."[17] For Forbes, the limitations of the women's movement in India lay in its alliance with the nationalist movement. The Gandhian nationalist movement allowed women to "come out" only because the house was on fire, but it expected that once the fire was out, women would go back inside the house.[18]

Gail Pearson argues that the claims of the universalism of the Congress-led bourgeois nationalist movement rested on the participation of women. Gandhian nationalism used women for its political goals to project itself as a mass movement, but women themselves gained very little from their participation.[19] This argument is similar to Gail Omvedt's critique of Gandhi. Omvedt asserts that Gandhi recruited women to channel the energies of an emerging women's movement into the nationalist political movement he controlled.[20] Kumari Jayawardena also finds that women were deployed to enhance the cause of nationalism. "While Indian women were to participate in all stages of the movement for national independence, they did so in a way that was acceptable to, and was dictated by, male leaders and which conformed to the prevalent ideology on the position of women."[21]

Some of the more recent feminist theoretical work, such as that of Deniz Kandiyoti and Anne McClintock, argues that male nationalist discourses represent women as repositories of traditional and "authentic" national culture. According to Kandiyoti, "feminism is not autonomous, but bound to the signifying network of the nationalist context which produces it," and concludes that "women, who were also active participants in nationalist movements, felt compelled to articulate their gender interests within the parameters of cultural nationalism, sometimes censoring or muting the radical potential of their demands."[22] Anne McClintock also argues that women within the nationalist narrative figured as "the conservative repository of the national archaic." In her assessment, "nowhere has feminism in its own right been allowed to be more than the maidservant of nationalism."[23] Like Lata Mani, these scholars argue that within nationalist debates, women become the sites on which the conflict over tradition was constructed.[24]

The above explanatory frameworks locate the limitations of feminist politics within malestream nationalism and as such fail to recognize women as subjects of their own history. Historical agency is assigned to male nationalists with their agenda as the object of investigation while women's utterances and politics are marginalized. What these readings suggest is an idealization of feminism as an always already radical political intervention, and any disarticulations from this position are read as a betrayal of feminism by its ally, which in most instances is nationalism. *Reproductive Restraints* treats Indian feminist politics as a subject of history, complete with its own sets of contradictions and ambiguities, arising from its situated class, caste, community, and national bearings. Locating feminist politics within its historical context and recognizing its conditions of constitution allows us to challenge a linear understanding of feminist politics and reflect instead on the messy terrain its practitioners mapped. What this work seeks to do is tease out the "subject-ing" of women, in a Foucauldian manner, with the analytical lens focused on feminist utterances and politics.[25]

This work seeks to understand how middle-class feminism in colonial India simultaneously affirmed and challenged the bourgeois national project. While agreeing with Mrinalini Sinha's assessment of middle-class feminist politics in colonial India and its appropriation of the language of modernity to forward its agenda as representatives of the Indian nation and its women, this study interrogates both the possibility and limits of Indian feminists' imbrication with the discourse of modernity and particularly the ways in which it attenuated their politics of empowerment.[26] Even while acknowledging the ways in which modernity was used to further the political agenda of feminist politics, *Reproductive Restraints* is interested in understanding how the deployment of the modernist discourse also fortified the elitism of middle-class women's politics, allowing them to forward their particular class and caste interests at the expense of subaltern Indian women.

My own location and training has determined my historical reading of the first wave of organized Indian feminism. Intellectually, the writings of women of color, postcolonial, and lesbian feminists provide important insights to critically review dominant feminist politics within Indian history through a focus on the debates on birth control in colonial India.[27] This impressive body of critical literature has called into question the hegemonic tendencies within mainstream Western, white, middle-class, and heterosexual feminist politics and theorizing. I write in the presence of and as a participant in these ongoing conversations, as this study interrogates critically the historical past of Indian feminism and questions its lack of a democratic agenda. Within Indian historiography, I think it both necessary and appropriate to move beyond hagiographic accounts of Indian feminists and analyze the elitism that framed the politics of early organized Indian feminism.

Rather than privileging either the metropolis or the periphery, the colonial or the national, the "public" or the "private" sphere, this work suggests that the history of birth control in colonial India is best located within the folds of discursive loops spread across national boundaries,[28] linking international, national, and local politics, "public" as well as "private" concerns. Moreover, in placing gender as one of the important variables in understanding the history of birth control in colonial India, this study draws much from feminist literature, which has argued that gender as an analytical category "cannot but undergird *any* attempt at a historical reconstruction which undertakes to demonstrate our sociality in the *full* sense, and is ready to engage with its own presuppositions of the social moments and movements it sets out to represent."[29]

Archival Silences, Voices from the "Field"

Early Indian male birth control advocates, such as A. P. Pillay, Narayan Sitaram Phadke, Pyare Krishan Wattal, and Radhakamal Mukherjee, wrote passionately on the need to disseminate birth control technology and information in colonial India. For most of these men, the use of birth control came to signify a desirable sociosexual modality for attaining modern, scientifically managed and progressive family units that in turn positively impacted the project of nation building. Their writings comprised of numerous monographs, journals, journal articles, and conference papers and proceedings, many of which are extensively referenced in this study.[30]

The ideas of these Indian advocates did not emerge in a political or intellectual vacuum. Indian men and middle-class women, from the early twentieth century, were in close communication with Western advocates in countries such as Britain and the United States. Western advocates such as Margaret Sanger, Edith How-Martyn, Eileen Palmer, Marie Stopes, C. P. Blacker, and E. F. Griffith exchanged correspondence with Indian supporters. Some of them made multiple visits to India to undertake propaganda work, build global alliances, market their brands of contraceptives, render financial support to the work being done in India, and, at times, seek financial support for the work they did in their respective countries. Some Western advocates also entered into joint intellectual projects with Indian enthusiasts; for instance, during the 1930s, E. F. Griffith and Norman Himes served as editors for Pillay's international journal *Marriage Hygiene*. The private papers of Western advocates such as Marie Stopes, C. P. Blacker, and E. F. Griffith, housed at the Contemporary Medical Archive Center, at the Wellcome Institute in London, in the Eileen Palmer Collection at the London School of Economics, and in the Margaret Sanger Papers, help trace the intellectual and political exchanges of Western supporters of birth control with Indian activists. Moreover, these collections are also useful to capture the interrelated and relational histories of birth control in colonial India with similar movements in Britain and United States.

The literature on women's history, while emphasizing the significance of gender as an analytical category in understanding the past, has pointed to some of the problems in working with conventional sources/archives to present women as active subjects of historical research. This literature has argued convincingly for the need to locate and identify new sources and archives that would speak to our concerns about putting women back into our stories of the past and integrating gender into our historical narratives.[31] My work closely examines the more accessible colonial state records together with the less conventional sources of historical writings by women. Here it is important to acknowledge the intellectual debt to feminist scholarship of the past two decades for locating and identifying the writings of middle-class Indian women from the early twentieth century. This study is able to draw upon a wide range of writings and records of elite Indian women

Introduction 11

housed in various repositories within and outside India, on account of the intellectual labor and commitment of feminist scholars who have restored these records and voices to our archival collection.[32]

This study relies upon an array of historical sources and archives to integrate women's voices into the narrative on the history of birth control in colonial India. The majority, if not all, of these records render the opinions of "named" middle-class Indian women and focuses on the debates among these women.[33] The records of the All India Women's Conference (AIWC) are one such important source. Unfortunately, the files and private papers of the AIWC housed in its New Delhi head office are in a state of disorder, and large bodies of these records are badly damaged. Despite missing and damaged files, the Margaret Cousins Library at the AIWC houses a full collection of its yearly reports and copies of its journal *Roshni*. These are important sources that present the voices of Indian middle-class women to help us understand the debates within AIWC on birth control and other issues such as franchise and struggles over the nature of women's education. Middle-class women leaders did not articulate a homogenous position on the controversial subject of birth control. Differences among individual women leaders and internal variations within their positions on birth control comes through in the private papers of women leaders, such as Kamaladevi Chattopadhyaya, Rameshwari Nehru, and Muthulaskhmi Reddi housed in the Nehru Memorial and Museum Library in New Delhi.

The biomedical establishment and its practitioners also participated in the public debates on contraceptive usage in the early twentieth century. Men and women doctors debated the many tangled medical and moral issues related to the use of birth control, without necessarily coming up with a consensus. The contentious debates among biomedics found expression in the numerous twentieth-century volumes of Indian regional and national medical journals. Many of these journals carried full-page advertisements on the biomedical contraceptives marketed in India and those available in foreign markets that could be mail-ordered by those who could afford to pay for the product and its postage costs. The Indian Medical Library in New Delhi is a rich and largely untapped repository of these medical journals, which are useful sources for assessing the engagement of the biomedical establishment in the public debates on the subject of birth control.

Vernacular magazines, especially *Stri-Darpan, Madhuri, Sudha,* and *Stri-Dharma,* provided middle-class women an important platform to voice their opinions on the controversial subject of birth control. In order to specify what methods of contraceptives were in circulation in the early twentieth century, the many advertisements on contraceptives carried in these magazines are useful. Many of the advertisements in these vernacular magazines were placed by indigenous practitioners of medicine such as *vaids* and *hakims,* many of whom happened to be women. Some individual Indian women *vaids* and *hakims* also wrote pamphlets on the subject, discussing some of the available methods along with a list of their potential benefits and harmful side effects. One such pamphlet, titled *Garbh Nirodh* [Birth Control] and written by Vimla Devi Vaidya in 1940, is still in limited circulation.[34]

The colonial state represented itself as an agent of modernity in colonial India and, as such, many advocates, Western and Indian, called upon the state to shoulder the burden of disseminating contraceptive technology and knowledge to its colonized subjects. The colonial state was instrumental in generating encyclopedic information on Indian demographics. The Census Report of 1931, for instance, became a standard document that various state agencies and individual advocates cited while making a case for overpopulation, and demanded state intervention to deter an impending Malthusian dread or environmental disaster. There were other times in the twentieth century that state-generated inquiries, committees, and studies raised the issue of birth control; most prominent were the Age of Consent Committee Report, 1929; the Famine Commission Final Report, 1945; and the Health Survey and Development Committee Report, 1946. Together, these reports convey the various political and intellectual stands that different state representatives adopted on the issue of birth control. In the absence of a shared understanding among its various administrative levels, the state chose not to pursue a consistent policy of institutional support to advance the use of birth control in colonial India. What the colonial archives reveal is how the state apparatus, especially its various representative bodies, were being compelled to deliberate on acceptable modalities for intervention and dissemination of contraceptive knowledge and usage in colonial India during the early twentieth century.

The range of these historical sources captures the multiple locations of the dense discourse on birth control, interrupting any simplistic recognition of a singular site or historical actor associated with the project of "manufacturing consent" on the use of contraceptives in colonial India. The sources used to craft this historical narrative are made visible to readers as part of feminist methodological imperative that informs this work. The sources are highlighted and presented above with the intent of foregrounding the "data"—especially the textual data that inform the historical script of this work. The information will also allow interested readers to peruse the documents/records referenced in this study for projects different from the one undertaken here.

Although drawing upon important theoretical insights of feminist scholarship shaped by the recent linguistic turn in history writing, this work would not have been possible without extensive reliance on numerous archival records, many of which are housed in scattered locations across India. While recognizing that archival information housed in numerous repositories in India does not necessarily present better or even fuller information on our subjects of research, nevertheless, an argument needs to be made for engaging in committed research and study of a region and culture one seeks to represent in academic publications and scholarship.[35] This is an argument removed from one made against simplistic positivism or fetishistic tendencies that hinder imaginative readings of historical records. I fully recognize the dangers of a narrow focus on conventional archives, which, for the most part, render elite phallocentric subjects as legitimate objects of historical investigation, given their disproportionately high visibility in conventional archives. Nor do I wish to present a myopic or chauvinistic territorial argument about turf battles either, about who can and who cannot legitimately research a topic or work on a specific region or culture.[36] However, I would like to advance both an intellectual and ethical argument about requiring scholars to commit time and resources to an area they wish to represent in their academic work. I am mounting a "call for a return to the archive—conventionally understood as an institutional site in a faraway place that requires hotel accommodation and a grueling nine-to-five workday."[37] An intellectual, ethical, and physical engagement with a "faraway place" does not necessarily entail the historian's "breaking into a sweat, if not a fever."[38] Instead, an argument favoring research from a "safe" distance, advocating the ability of scholars to publish studies on non-Western areas without engaging with these regions or ever visiting these locations, I would have to argue, replicates troubling colonial gestures of cultural arrogance. Moreover, the fact that scholars located in non-Western parts of the world rarely reciprocate this intellectual gesture underscores the highly unequal power dynamic that shapes the project of knowledge production in the contemporary global academic and publishing world.

Most of the archival and literary sources listed above do not provide any understanding of how the subaltern groups in India received these debates. For the most part, their views are absent and silent in the elite sources. This study confronts questions related to the vexed issue of retrieving subaltern agency and subjugated knowledge, interrogating whether Pillay/Phadke, Gandhi, Sanger/Stopes, or even the voices of Indian middle-class women leaders such as Kamaladevi Chattopadhyaya or Rameshwari Nehru constitute the complete history of birth control in India. What are some of the possible ways of compensating for the archival absence of Indian subaltern women's voices? How can we retrieve subaltern agency that simultaneously allows for both the recognition and the questioning of mainstream ideas of family, reproduction, sexuality, and also that of the nation? Is there a way of deauthorizing the script of elite politics?—especially as it represented desirable "reproductive futurism" in specific caste, community, class, and race terms. How can one best challenge elite constructions of the reproductive practices of socially marginal groups in India as nationally disruptive and undesirable?

Although presenting an empirically grounded narrative, this work recognizes that no discipline is a completely trustworthy resource, nor is any singular set of disciplinary tools comprehensive. Following Nancy Naples's recommendation, *Reproductive Restraints* does not reify any singular disciplinary methodology. Instead, the research that informs this study is grounded in an interdisciplinary, intercultural, and interconnected study of the history of birth control.[39] Most of the conventional elite archival and literary sources I examined for my work did not provide any understanding of how subaltern groups in India received the dominant debates on birth control. For the most part, their views were absent and silent in the elite sources. If elite sources do not allow the subalterns to speak, can one remedy this by searching for nonelite sources that record alternative stories? Yes and no. I agree with Kalpana Ram, who argues that although there is a profound social distance between the women writing and the women written about, it is unlikely that there would ever be a feminist enterprise if it was robbed entirely of the impulse to reach out to the other woman, who will necessarily never occupy a subject position of utter identity with the feminist subject. As Ram argues, relations of utter identity cannot be made the prerequisite for writing and speaking.[40] Despite Ram's careful positive assertions, feminist ethnographers working and writing about women in different sociocultural settings from their own have expressed a sense of unease and self-doubt in representing the "other" woman. Feminist scholars worry that their work might consciously or even unconsciously end up reinforcing colonial caricatures of the non-Western women as victims or stressing the existence of female subcultures of resistance to extend their notions of what constitutes agency to their subjects.[41]

The unease and self-doubt among practicing anthropologists is also the result of the recent writing back from the margins by postcolonial critics, who have called into attention the tendency of imposing liberal enlightenment paradigms to understand non-Western subjectivities and worldviews.

Liberal humanism constructs a universal rights-bearing autonomous subject and postulates the possibility of this individual's achievement of "sovereignty, self-knowledge and self-mastery."[42] Western liberalism celebrates and highlights the autonomous as opposed to a relational view of self. This perspective allows for little or no recognition of the place of community or family relations in determining an individual's identity and subjective location within a specific cultural and historical context. My study employs historical research, postcolonial feminist insights, and subaltern Indian women's voices from the local fringes of a tribal block in Tehri Garhwal District of Uttaranchal in North India to challenge the liberal ideal of universal individualism, unambiguously embracing an autonomous rational subjectivity. From their subaltern location, Jaunpuri women refuse to ascribe to liberal feminist ideas of individualism and empowerment, revealing for us the possibilities of alternative conceptions of self and embodiment, grounded in discursive differences. In analyzing the oppressive historical trajectory of birth control in colonial India, this study presents a critique of the universalist and hegemonic project of liberal feminist humanism, particularly for its inability and unwillingness to recognize and embrace an alternative worldview.

By now, the much-quoted rhetorical Spivakian question "Can the subaltern speak?" has drawn attention to "moments of reflexive anxiety" within the postcolonial feminist project.[43] Commenting on her own work and how it has come to mean "all things to all men," Spivak has pointed out that her concern was not with constructing the subaltern as the absolute other, but more to ensure a "politics of demanding and building infrastructure so that when the subalterns speak they can be heard."[44] A possible modality of building such enabling and supportive infrastructures, Spivak suggests, is moving from the official/conventional archival spaces to spaces of subaltern dwellings, laying great stress on the importance of face-to-face work with the subaltern.[45] This study moves from colonial and national archives to the "field" in Jaunpur to simultaneously reflect on the politics of birth control as a technology of power as well as on local modes of resistance.

Conversations with *dais* (midwives) were highly instructive in my efforts to understand what "reproductive freedom" means to women in Jaunpur. Unlike the frustrations of working with the official archives and elite sources, field conversations with practicing Jaunpuri *dais* present direct challenges to the arrogant perceptions of subaltern fertility behaviors. These conversations highlighted why, despite a rather long history of birth control in India, contraceptive usage has received limited enthusiasm in this region. The argument in favor of birth control in India has, for the most part, been made from within a liberal tradition that represents abstract and self-fulfilling individuality as normative.[46] This universal representation of contraceptive technologies as always already desirable for rational and autonomous individuals, is a highly inadequate conceptual model for understanding the cultural imperatives that have shaped, and continue to shape, Jaunpuri women's reproductive and procreative experiences. There is a gap between the elite agenda represented in universal and abstract terms of individualism and Jaunpuri women's local understandings of their reproductive bodies through a predominantly "communal interpretative grid." Instead of identifying themselves as autonomous individuals making independent decisions and choices about their reproduction, Jaunpuri women for the most part recognize themselves as members of multigenerational family units and also as members of their patrilocal village communities. Their binding emotional, cultural, and economic reliance on familial and community ties shape Jaunpuri women's reproductive decisions and choices. Ultimately, it is this cultural and political gap in the conceptions of embodied subjectivities that simultaneously accounts for the limits of elite hegemony and subaltern resilience in the context of birth control.

This study does not investigate the overlaps and continuities between the colonial and the postcolonial worlds of Jaunpuri *dais* because Rukhma Devi and Gunda Devi in Bhatoli village, Bhura Devi and Leela Devi in Bhediyan, and Padma Devi in Sainji village were for the most part interested in narrating their stories of the present. These women spoke of time in relation to seasonal change and local festivals; most of their memories were constructed around births and deaths rather than around clock time or wall calendars. Interviews with gynecologists in Kanpur, an industrial urban center in U.P., were much more conducive to questions of change and continuity within the biomedical establishment on birth control and related reproductive health issues. These "professional" doctors were eager to recall the methods they recommended to their patients during the 1940s, 1950s, and 1960s, stressing that it became increasingly easier for them to recommend contraceptives in the postindependence period as these became more accessible.

When evaluating notes from the field, the works of feminist ethnographers such as Cecilia Van Hollen, Kamran Asdar Ali, Nancy Scheper-Hughes, and Ruth Behar were important for recognizing the need to pay closer attention to the subtle differences in the understanding of female bodies, reproductive functions, and sexualities among Jaunpuri women. The works of these anthropologists are set in Tamil Nadu, Egypt, Brazil, and Mexico, respectively. Through a close and engaged study of these different regions, these authors enable readers to see the inadequacy of deploying Western categories and experiences in trying to grasp the complexities of women's lives within these different non-Western cultures. Their work, as much as my own experiences in the field, helped highlight one of the serious

Introduction 17

limitations of the assumptions with which my own fieldwork began, where I had hoped to "discover" traditional modes of contraceptives circulating within the Jaunpuri female subcultures.[47]

In using oral testimonies of rural midwives, and of their clients, this study seeks to examine the lack of fit between state objectives and subaltern aspirations of "ideal" family size. The younger Jaunpuri women are opting for surgical sterilization because some of the more recent contraceptive technologies have not found their way into rural India as a result of their high cost and the lack of medical expertise required for administering them to clients. Safer and better technologies remain a privilege of the upper-class, urban-educated elites in India today. Abortion is strongly discouraged, and most Jaunpuri women regard it as a sin against god. Despite the distance between my agenda and theirs, the voices of women from the fringes of Jaunpur present counternarratives that disinvest popular and historical mythologies associated with birth control as an always already feminist issue.

Organization of the Study

Reproductive Restraints constructs the genealogy of birth control discourse in colonial India. In doing so, it pays close attention to how advocates of birth control, in seeking to rationalize procreation, worked to regulate women, working classes, and other subaltern groups. Chapter 1 examines the writings of early middle-class male advocates of birth control in colonial India, primarily Goplajee Ahluwalia, Pillay, Phadke, Karve, and Wattal. It argues that in advocating the use of contraceptives, these men for the most part promoted an elite agenda, one that sought to limit the size of India's population along eugenic and Malthusian models. There was little in their writings that sought to empower subaltern women in making important decisions about sex, maternal health, and family size. The subject of birth control also gave these male advocates a platform from which to invent "truths" about sex and sexuality. Through their writings, Indian male advocates produced and naturalized gender- and class-derived articulations of sexuality. This chapter, therefore, highlights the underlying eugenic patriotism of the early Indian male advocates of birth control who outlined national procreative imperatives in specific class, caste, and community terms. As will be evident from the discussion of their writings, these men valued certain reproductive futures over others, yet presented their specific class, caste, and gender interests as universally beneficial to an emerging nation.

Chapter 2 investigates the interrelated histories of birth control in colonial India, Britain, and the United States to understand the historical outcomes of these connected histories. Instead of presenting Western advocates as "world citizens," this chapter examines how hierarchies of race and class played off one another in the writings and work of Western birth control advocates. Sanger and Stopes competed for leadership positions within India from the 1930s onward. They deployed different political modalities, which included wooing Indian advocates to their organizations, by placing advertisements for their books, products, and organizations in important Indian journals such as *Madras Birth Control Review*. Juxtaposing the ideas and writings of Gandhi with those of Western enthusiasts, this chapter seeks to highlight how Gandhi's alternative understandings of sex, conjugality, and reproduction challenged universal and normative liberal humanist feminist positions. Western advocates sought to impose their universal conception of embodiment and sexuality, thus failing to appreciate that cultures and societies could be differently gendered. Sanger, Edith How-Martyn, and Eileen Palmer made many visits to India to undertake propaganda work and also to try to "convert" Gandhi into a supporter of birth control. In placing the work of Sanger and Stopes within an international discursive framework rather than exclusively within the narrow confines of national U.S. or British histories, this chapter makes a case for historical connectivity, which allows us to recognize that Europe and the colonial worlds were entangled in circuits of knowledge and practice that mutually constituted these worlds.

This book argues that even the advocacy of birth control by Indian feminists did not succeed in ameliorating the elitist and oppressive trajectory of the birth control movement in India. Chapter 3 examines how Indian middle-class women negotiated, and eventually reproduced, patriarchal nationalist images of Indian women. While claiming to be the representatives of all Indian women, these elite women redeployed essentialist images of women as mothers and moral guides of the nation. The chapter locates the limitations of the middle-class feminist movement in colonial India within the historical context of Indian nationalism, especially as it was shaped under the dominant leadership of Mahatma Gandhi. Gandhi was strongly opposed to all mechanical and chemical contraceptives, and in his view, "good" sex was no sex at all. In seeking nationalist credentials for themselves, Indian feminist articulations moved in and out of Gandhian nationalist representations of femininity and family, accepting gender polarities and presenting women as biological reproducers of the nation and motherhood as a national duty. However, even while recognizing the contextual limitations and the matrix of power within which these elite women operated, this chapter highlights their inability to make cross-class/caste alliances within their politics, rarely transcending their social and cultural privileges.

The last two chapters look at institutions we may have expected to play a large role in promoting birth control in colonial India. Chapter 4 looks at the response of colonial authorities to birth control advocates. The colonial state generated important information on Indian demographics, information that invigorated public debates among Indian and Western elites about the need to promote contraceptive usage in colonial India. However, despite gathering the information and making it available through its numerous reports, by looking at the colonial state from the perspective of the history of birth control in India, it is fair to argue that, far from being an all-encompassing presence, colonial authority is revealed as internally fractured and limited. Various state agencies were conflicted about the role of the state in supporting and disseminating contraceptive information. Although the colonial state arrogated to itself the role of modernizing Indian society, it was reluctant to act out this role in the context of birth control and make contraceptive information available to Indian women through its maternal and infant health care system. Though seeking to locate the role of the state in shaping the history of birth control in India during the early twentieth century, this chapter brings to the fore the conflict and gap between colonial rhetoric and policy.

The last chapter evaluates the role of the biomedical community and of indigenous practitioners of medicine in the debates on birth control in colonial India. Many advocates of birth control looked toward biomedical science to provide the essential services to advance the use of contraceptives. Traditional or alternative medical practitioners advertised their expertise on this subject in various vernacular journals such as *Sudha* and *Madhuri*. A close reading of the writings and debates among biomedical and traditional practitioners of medicine such as the Ayurvedic *vaids* and *hakims* reveals the internal divide among both these groups not only on the basis of their medical training, but also on the question of the moral impact of wider dissemination of contraceptive information. There was also no consensus among these "professionals" on the issue of providing specialized training on birth control to medical students. This chapter also examines the writings of alternative practitioners to demonstrate that they too did not have much to offer to their patients on this subject.

Together, these five chapters demonstrate the elitist politics of Indian nationalists, middle-class feminists, Western activists, colonial authorities, and the medical establishment in shaping the history of birth control in colonial India. The historical trajectory of birth control discourse traced in this study demonstrates how health, sexuality, and reproduction were significant concerns that nationalists, Western enthusiasts, middle-class feminists, demographers, and members of the medical establishment selectively drew upon to promote their specific agendas. These agendas for the most part had precious little to do with safeguarding women's reproductive rights, and were mostly concerned with regulating and restraining women's reproductive capacities. This study therefore challenges the dominant assumptions that birth control was natural and basic to Indian women's empowerment. It argues that, historically, birth control within India has had an oppressive rather than liberatory trajectory since colonial and postcolonial supporters of birth control framed the issue in a way that left most people out, failing to address their concerns and needs.

1 Demographic Rhetoric and Sexual Surveillance: Indian Middle-Class Advocates of Birth Control, 1877–1947

> And if you could brave a visit to the dark, dusty, dingy slums of the mill operatives you will find that almost in *every family* the woman is either carrying or in confinement. And when our eyes fall on street loafers who find their food on the dunghill and make their bed in the gutter we find them bearing more children than the rags with which they cover their shame and are *reminded of the bitch that breeds kennelfuls of puppies four times a year.*
>
> —Narayan Sitaram Phadke, *Sex Problem in India*, 1927 (emphasis added)

Narayan Sitaram Phadke, making a case for wider dissemination of contraceptive knowledge and usage in colonial India, conjured up a highly negative animalistic imagery of working-class subaltern procreative practices and of their domestic dwellings. From his elitist location, national goals of development, progress, and modernization were understood as being endangered on account of irresponsible sexual "breeding" among India's poor and marginal social groups. Phadke's words reveal blatant elitist condemnation of subaltern lifestyles and sexuality. However, as will become evident later in this chapter, his was not an isolated position among early middle-class and upper-caste Indian male advocates for birth control. In mapping the historical trajectory of the birth control in India, this chapter examines various intellectual and political currents that shaped and influenced the writings and work of Indian male advocates of birth control.[1] The writings of Indian male proponents in calling for wider dissemination of contraceptive information, this chapter argues, were driven as much by science as by nationalism, blending together different discourses of Malthusianism and eugenics, demography and nationalism, sexology, and morality. This chapter critically examines the discourse of birth control that Indian male advocates produced in the early twentieth century, setting in motion a long historical tradition of evaporating feminist concerns for reproductive rights and, instead, deploying contraceptive technologies as modalities for subaltern surveillance and further marginalization.

Given the colonial context of this demand for the introduction of birth control in India, it should come as no surprise that the early Indian male advocates of birth control reflected their hybrid intellectual and cultural positions as colonial subjects. They selectively drew their arguments from a variety of positions, borrowing both from indigenous and Western systems of knowledge. In assessing the writings and works of these male advocates in colonial India, this chapter, very much in keeping with the argument of this work, recognizes the larger geopolitical and intellectual context within which the discussions and conversations on the subject took place from the late nineteenth to the early twentieth century.

The movement for propagating the knowledge of contraceptives in colonial India can be traced back to the early discourse on "overpopulation." In what appears to be the prehistory of birth control, urban-educated middle-class and predominantly upper-caste men played a significant role, articulating the issue of demographic numbers as a cause for concern. These early male actors can be credited with laying down a lasting legacy, one in which demographic numbers became a central focus of debates on population and later fueled the advocacy for contraceptive use to control human fertility. In the early phase, middle-class actors were concerned with determining the rise in India's population, with neo-Malthusianism guiding their understanding of population as a problem rather than an asset. This was a short phase and unfortunately there are few remaining sources to reconstruct the nature of debates among the participants of this period. In the later phase, middle-class actors combined Malthusian dread with eugenic concerns; however, in both the phases the nationalist concern of ensuring healthy male bodies/citizens was one of the dominant underlying issues.[2] Participants in the later phase, more clearly closely tied reproduction and procreation to nationalist imaginations. The emphasis on fertility control in the later phase called for a close inspection of sexual practices and expressions within the intimate domain, destabilizing the divisions between the private and the public and revealing the interconnectedness of these two domains.

An elementary introduction to Malthusianism and eugenics, which played such an important role in the concerns of Indian and Western advocates of birth control in India, may not be out of place here. In his *Essay on Population,* published anonymously in 1789, Thomas Malthus turned the prevalent ideas of population on their head. Departing from the opinions of his contemporaries, he questioned the eighteenth-century notions of "power of population." He argued for checking the growth of population to ensure it did not exceed the levels of subsistence. Malthus claimed that if the population grew unchecked, it would double itself every twenty-five years or increase in a geometrical ratio.[3] He asserted that poverty and unemployment were a direct outcome of a lack of exercising prudent restraint on the size of the family. However, Malthus advocated moral restraint, rather than the use of birth control, to check the size of the population. Francis Galton coined the term "eugenics" in his book *Human Faculty,* published in 1883. He later defined it as "the science which deals with all influences that improve the inborn qualities of a race; also with those that develop them to the utmost advantage." The aim of his science was to "bring as many influences as can be reasonably employed, to cause the useful classes in the community to contribute *more* than their proportion to the next generation."[4]

In India, the eugenicist rhetoric of "improving the race" found ready acceptance along with the neo-Malthusian emphasis on absolute numbers. The historical moment of nationalist aspirations and anxieties in colonial India allowed the advocates to deploy arguments from both camps without necessarily finding them internally inconsistent or hostile. However, it is important to remind ourselves that the Indian middle-class/upper-caste discourse of birth control was not simply a mimetic gesture, involving a mindless derivation or borrowing of ideas from the West. Intellectually, it would be more appropriate to identify their discourse as hybrid, for while these men drew upon the intellectual capital available from the West, they radically transformed and redeployed it for specific political projects such as bourgeois nationalism and family reforms within the context of colonial India.[5]

The proponents of birth control in colonial India also relied heavily upon state-generated statistical information to make a case for India's growing population and declining national health and prosperity. Indian advocates employed quantifiable data to make a convincing case about an impending Malthusian gloom in order to support their demands for wider dissemination of birth control. Examining the discourse on birth control in colonial India and its deployment of statistics enables us to recognize what Appadurai and others have called the "political arithmetics" of colonialism and nationalism.[6] Middle-class advocates argued that a large population, particularly of subaltern groups, was incommensurate with national goals of a fit and healthy male citizenry, born of healthy fit mothers. Information, particularly from the decennial census, although created for colonial consumption, was often used by middle-class Indians to support their elite hegemonic projects of nationalism and community-based politics.[7] Indian advocates deployed the census information to construct an argument of "overpopulation" as a national problem. In their discourse on overpopulation, Indian proponents, like others in different parts of the world, drew upon statistical information as a "uniquely privileged way of 'knowing' the social body, and as a central technology in diagnosing its ills and managing its welfare."[8] Relying on numerical data, elite male advocates in colonial India constructed a rhetorical trope of India being overpopulated and argued that it was necessary to manage the reproductive practices of women and men, particularly of those from the subaltern classes, to ensure national well-being.

The census data also made it possible to construct comparative numerical analyses on a global scale. National figures could be compared and nations could be placed on a hierarchy based upon respective birthrates and death rates. Increasingly, the census came to be regarded as an essential part of the equipment of every political and social worker. The 1871 census inaugurated an uninterrupted series of decennial censuses in the Indian subcontinent. However, the 1911 census was the first to systematically cover most of the subcontinent. A noticeable increase in population was recorded only in the 1911 census, but even this increase was not substantial enough to mark a trend. The 1921 census showed a net decline in the Indian population because of an influenza epidemic. It was in 1931 that the census figures first demonstrated a substantial demographic increase of 10.6 percent.[9] Although the census showed a significant demographic increase only in 1931, as we see below, the "population explosion" script was being written in India well before demographic "facts" were available to support such a thesis.

The Early Phase—Population Increase Becomes a Subject of Public Concern: 1877–1900

The beginnings of the discussions and debates on the size of India's population, in fact, occurred in the late nineteenth century. Unfortunately, the early organizations and leading proponents left few records, and their initiatives have not been duly credited in the writings of the later wave of birth control activists. Consequently, only a short descriptive account of the early wave, gleaned from the fragmentary information available in primary sources and secondary literature, is possible at this time.

Edith How-Martyn, a British suffragist, joined the British Malthusian League in 1910 and was active in the birth control movement in England.[10] In the 1930s, she worked closely with Margaret Sanger to promote the cause in India.[11] In How-Martyn's brief essay on the "History of the Birth Control Movement in India," she mentioned that from its very inception, the Neo-Malthusian League in Britain had some members and correspondents in India.[12] Much of the early organizational activity of the Neo-Malthusian

League in India appears to have taken place in southern India, although correspondents of the League were also to be found in Calcutta, Ahmedabad, Lahore, Delhi, Lucknow, and Patna. In 1880, Murugesa Mudaliar from Madras became the vice president of the London Neo-Malthusian League and published a journal, *The Philosophic Inquirer,* in Madras. There were other Indians among the early vice presidents of the league, such as Dr. V. V. Naidu, Dr. Muthiah Naidu, and Dr. K. Banerjee. Among the earliest leaders concerned with the population question in India was Dewan Rangacharlu of Mysore, a princely state in south India. Rangacharlu was known for being socially progressive, and he raised the question of population and development in the Mysore State Legislative Assembly as early as October 1881. He expressed concern at the rapid population growth and claimed that it hampered production and increased poverty.[13] A Hindu-Malthusian League was formed in Madras as early as 1882 by a section of Madras elites including Muthiah Naidu, Lakshmi Narasu, and Mooneswamy Naiker.[14]

In north India, Swami Rama Tirtha, a religious and political leader in the early years of the twentieth century, blamed the growing population for India's poverty. He wrote that "no country on the face of this earth is so poor and so populous as India," adding that "if the population problem is to be left unsolved, all talk about national unity ... will remain a utopian chimera."[15] Rama Tirtha constructed an unambiguous connection between poverty, national well-being, and the size of the population. A Malthusian paradigm appears to have informed his understanding of the issue; however, given the paucity of sources, it is difficult to make a conclusive evaluation of the nature of these early initiatives or to demonstrate the extent of their affiliations with the movement, ideas, or personalities of birth control in other parts of the world, especially in Britain or the United States.

In the early phase of public debates, the focus appears to have been on highlighting the inherent dangers of unrestrained fertility growth, especially for a nation struggling under colonial control, seeking to come into its own. The debates in this period witnessed a shift in the way population was understood; it was no longer regarded as an important national resource, but as a cause for concern, one that demanded public attention. It is to this early phase of public discussions on population that we can trace back the long legacy of constructing demographic increase as a mark of national poverty, backwardness, and overall economic, social, and cultural underdevelopment. It was left to birth control advocates, who emerged on the public scene from the 1920s onward, to articulate a modality for public intervention to reverse or arrest the trend of demographic increase through an active adoption of contraceptive technologies.

The Later Phase—Advocacy of Birth Control: 1910–47

It is from the 1910s onward that we have clear evidence of the influences and concerns that drove the birth control movement in India and gave it its oppressive trajectory. There was probably a short lull between the two phases, or so it appears from the available sources. S. Anandhi has argued that the activities of the early Hindu-Malthusian League in Madras were revived in the 1930s, after it was renamed the Madras Neo-Malthusian League under the aristocratic patronage of the Maharaja of Pittapur. Sir P. S. Sivaswami Aiyer was the president of the league and its vice presidents included Sir C. P. Ramaswami Aiyer and Justice Sir Vepa Ramesam. The league had a medical advisor, Dr. M. S. Krishnamurthi Aiyer, and published a journal, *The Madras Birth Control Bulletin*.[16] Following on the trajectory that activists established during the initial phase, birth control advocates of the later phase tied reproduction and procreation to nationalist imaginations. However, a greater emphasis on fertility control meant that the advocates in their writings now called for a close inspection of sexual practices and expressions within the intimate domain. Reproduction could no longer be regarded as a private practice that could be allowed unmonitored expressions within the privacy of one's home. Instead, procreative practices and behaviors now became a legitimate subject of public debates, and middle-class male advocates called for policy initiatives and resource allocation for its scientific and rational management, in keeping with what they understood to be the desirable goals of national development and well-being.

Among the prominent male advocates of birth control during the later phase were Gopaljee Ahluwalia, Aliyappin Padmanabha Pillay, Raghunath Dhondo Karve, Narayan Sitaram Phadke, Pyare Krishan Wattal, and Radhakamal Mukherjee. Although they all espoused the need for wider dissemination of biomedical contraceptive information, it is important to point out that they did not constitute an invariant, homogeneous group. A closer analysis of their writings demonstrates the differences in their positions while revealing certain overlaps.

Gopaljee Ahluwalia, a professor of biology at Ramjas College, Delhi, was instrumental in establishing the Indian Eugenic Society in Lahore and Simla in 1921. He issued a leaflet, "Eugenics a Bird's Eyeview" in July 1921. It opened with Sir Francis Galton's definitions of eugenics followed by Ahluwalia's own definition. Ahluwalia borrowed Galton's definition, but he added elements of moral and spiritual components as being important to any project of "racial improvements." While enumerating the "Aims and Objectives" of the Indian Eugenic Society, Ahluwalia emphasized "the importance of a critical study of problems relating to race improvement, from an Indian point of view and having regard for Indian traditions and present conditions."[17] In January 1922, Ahluwalia moved to Delhi where he started a new organization, the Indian Birth Control Society. In the same year, he began corresponding with Marie Stopes, the well-known British birth control activist.[18] Ahluwalia joined the international birth control circuit, presenting papers at the International Birth Control conferences held in London in 1922 and in New York in 1923. His paper on the "Indian Population Problem: Selective Lower Birth Rate, a Sure Remedy of Extreme Indian Poverty," was printed in the November 1923 issue of Margaret Sanger's journal *Birth Control Review*.[19]

During the late 1920s, other eugenic societies were established in Bombay and Sholapur. The Bombay branch was formed in 1929. Among its most important aims was the encouragement of constructive birth regulation clinics for married persons, especially for the poorer masses. The Sholapur Eugenic Society functioned from 1929 to 1934. A. P. Pillay was the honorary director of this society and he was in frequent contact with the London office, asking them for films and propaganda material. He wanted to set up a small museum of all contraceptives that had been used in the past and those in current circulation. Pillay asked the London office to send him prices for contraceptives along with addresses for possible suppliers.

Ragunath Dhondo Karve, though formally trained as a mathematician, was widely read in social science literature. He was the eldest son of Dhondo Keshav Karve, an eminent upper-caste social reformer from Maharashtra and founder of the first women's university in India, in Bombay. Ragunath Karve published a pamphlet on birth control as early as 1921. In the same year, he established a birth control clinic in Girgaum, Bombay, the first of its kind in India and quite possibly in all of Asia. Malati, his wife, helped in spreading his birth control message, especially among women. Karve, as did Phadke later, lost his position as a university professor because of his views on birth control. Colonial authorities prosecuted Karve for publishing what was referred to as "obscene" literature on birth control, prostitution, nudity, venereal diseases, and abortion.[20]

Narayan Sitaram Phadke, an upper-caste Brahman from Maharashtra, was a professor of philosophy, but his writings on birth control made it difficult for him to find a teaching job. He first wrote on the subject of birth control in *Birth Control Review* in 1924. His most important work was *Sex Problem in India,* published in 1927.[21] Contributing a foreword, Sanger regarded Phadke's arguments in favor of eugenics as inspired by a patriotic desire for his country to progress on sound biological principles.

Pyare Krishan Wattal, an upper-caste Kashmiri, was trained in statistics and economics and was a fellow of the Royal Statistical Society and the Royal Economic Society. In 1912, he joined the Indian Audit and Accounts Service.[22] Wattal's disciplinary training determined the way in which he framed the issue of population in his writings. In 1916, Wattal wrote *The Population Problem in India: A Census Study,* and, as the title suggests, census records were the main sources Wattal examined to make a case for overpopulation in India.[23]

Radhakamal Mukherjee was a renowned economist interested in the subject of population; he convened the First Indian Population Conference in Lucknow in February 1936. He compiled *Population Problem in India,* a volume of papers presented at the conference. These essays reflect how some of the leading economists in India framed the issue of population during the 1930s.[24] According to Mukherjee, India's *most basic* problem was overpopulation. He argued that India's growing population introduced the Malthusian law of diminishing returns, operating "not only by the soil but also by water acting as a limiting agent in agricultural development."[25] The language employed to articulate the issue revealed an attitude dismissive of people as individual human beings. "Population" was seen as representing faceless numbers who constituted a "problem" that needed to be "combated" and "attacked." Advocates understood population studies or an institute set up for evaluating the question of population as being responsible for examining issues of "vital statistics and food supply, crops and agricultural practice and productivity, standards of living and the cost of living, dietary and nutrition, migration within India and overseas, overpopulation and its results on unemployment, pauperism, vagrancy and crime."[26] This list did not include issues of women's health or an analysis of the existing class and social structure. In a more contemporary vocabulary, this was not a "people-friendly" approach to population issues.[27] The socially disadvantageous groups were reproached for "mindless" procreation and blamed for creating a "population problem."

Ideological Alliances: Neo-Malthusianism and Eugenics

Middle-class male advocates of birth control in colonial India combined neo-Malthusian and eugenic arguments to support their demands. Because these two intellectual currents were available in India at the same time, they were found acceptable in providing urgency to the cause of birth control. The proponents of birth control in India moved freely between these two ideologies. The title of Ahluwalia's 1923 essay, "Indian Population Problem: Selective Lower Birth Rate, a Sure Remedy of Extreme Indian Poverty," amply demonstrates my argument of an alliance between Malthusian and eugenic ideas in the thoughts of Indian birth control activists, especially those who were writing during the later phase. For the birth control enthusiasts, the class and caste composition of India's population amplified the problem of rising demographics.

In his article, Ahluwalia claimed that the primary cause for India's poverty was "thoughtless, irresponsible and extensive breeding, particularly among the middle and poor classes."[28] The root cause for people's depravation is population growth, made that much worse, in his analysis, because of the eugenic composition of this population; he lamented that "racial defects and poisons are multiplying from day to day. The physique of the people was surely deteriorating. The tall, stout and strong is being fast replaced by persons lean, lanky and bony—objects fit and proper for the study of a student of medicine. The extent and pace of growing degeneration justify anxious and speedy cure." The cure was to be found in spreading knowledge about sex hygiene, eugenics, and birth control. Eugenic concerns of racial degeneration coupled with Malthusian dread of an ever-increasing population were what fueled Ahluwalia's advocacy of birth control. He complained how "India resembled a vast garden literally choked with weeds, fine roses being few and far between."[29] His was an alarmist construction of population as a problem in both numerical terms and in its caste and class composition; he, like his other contemporaries, gave little to no thought to issues of unshared prosperity or increasing inequality.

Pillay organized the Sholapur Eugenic Society, which ran a "Wives Clinic" giving advice on contraceptives, venereal disease, sterility, sex problems, marriage problems, heredity, and eugenics.[30] Socially, Pillay argued, the use of birth control would prevent prostitution and promiscuity, reduce housing congestion, overpopulation, destitution, and the resulting need for charity. The traditional Malthusian dread of charity resurfaced in Pillay's articulation of the need to impart birth control information in colonial India.[31] The society's leaflet combined eugenicist and Malthusian arguments in promoting birth control, unlike the eugenic organization in Britain, which initially shied from embracing birth control.

Pillay's eugenicist ideas were clearly stated in his article "Eugenical Birth Control for India," published in *Birth Control Review* in November 1931. This article also reflected his Malthusian disdain for philanthropy. Pillay argued that the indiscriminate efforts of welfare workers to keep alive all who were born were helping the unfit to survive. He complained that philanthropy was being practiced with very little regard to racial safeguards; as a result, the "unfit" were "allowed" to survive, multiply, and leave behind "tainted descendants."[32] Guided by eugenic principles, Pillay called for the prevention of the "unfit" from leaving any descendants and for the encouragement of the multiplication of the more "fit" and useful citizens. He defined the category of those he considered to be "unfit" in physical and moral terms, such as those who were careless, foolish, feeble, inefficient, or insane. Like Ahluwalia, he advocated differential fertility behaviors based on his definitions of "fit" and "unfit" citizens, and suggested the sterilization of the "unfit" either voluntarily or through compulsory means. A large population of the so-called unfit people was considered to be incommensurable with nationalist goals of a healthy male citizenry. Those recognized as "unfit" were therefore to be denied procreative expression and liberties in the name of national well-being.

In an early article on birth control, Phadke presented an environmentalist plea, common among neo-Malthusians, arguing that even though *swaraj* (self-rule) could achieve a lot of things, it would not be able to neutralize the dreadful consequences of "foolish procreation indulged in by its subjects without regard to the natural resources of the land."[33] For the most part, in the writings of birth control advocates, reproductive issues were addressed in isolation from the wider context of social and gender inequality; the vision for change was not grounded on a plea for equal access to resources such as education, health care, ownership of land, or other economic opportunities.

Quite like Ahluwalia, Phadke also emphasized the need for "improving" Indians to become physically stronger, for he believed that "stalwart physiques of the people is one of the greatest assets of a country and an important instrument of its uplift."[34] Combining eugenic and neo-Malthusian positions, Phadke made a case for spreading the knowledge of birth control to improve Indian physiques. He believed that the use of new contraceptive technologies would ensure healthy males for the development and modernization of the embryonic nation. In a chapter of his book entitled "The Mother of the Race," he assigned women the sole responsibility of producing and parenting healthy sons for the nation. "Like the sun from which all light radiates the mother is the root source of the strength or weakness of the race."[35] According to Phadke, women as mothers were important for the success of the eugenicist project; hence, it was important to focus on the need to improve women's health to stem their physical decline and, in turn, that of the nation's.

Writing in 1927, Phadke articulated a eugenicist position that was different from the classic eugenicist position, which argued for increasing the "fit" as opposed to the "unfit" by encouraging the fit to multiply while controlling the population of the unfit. For Phadke, in the India of 1927, the problem of a eugenically unfit population was compounded by the Malthusian problem of overpopulation. As a eugenicist in India, he could not rest content with merely providing for the mating of fit men and women.[36] In his writings, Phadke stressed the need for "fit" married couples to adopt birth control methods to limit their progeny because any increase in population now had a deleterious effect. In the 1920s and 1930s, overpopulation became a culturally constructed problem that led to an increasing concern with managing reproduction; reproduction was now understood to have important consequences for the well-being of the country. Conjugal sexuality was no longer regarded merely as belonging to the "private sphere"; instead, it was viewed as directly impacting the public life and prosperity of the nation. This new understanding of marital sex called for its "scientific" management within the discourse on birth control in colonial India. We return in a later section to a more detailed analysis of the politics of sexual management that Indian male birth control advocates espoused, both for their own class as well as for other subaltern groups.

While espousing eugenic ideals, Phadke argued strongly that eugenics was indigenous to Indian thinking and intellectual traditions. He asserted that eugenics was not a Western importation into India. He traced the genealogy of eugenicist thought to the Aryans when, he argued, the necessity of breeding a race of "warriors" was impressed upon men and women. According to Phadke, the *Upanishads* and *Sutras* (ancient Hindu philosophical and prescriptive texts) provided elaborate discussions of methods that, if practiced, would make women mothers of warriors.[37] Incidentally, all the examples he cited were taken from Brahmanical canonical texts in which women figured merely as mothers of warrior sons. The invocation of this sort of "Indian" tradition while writing about eugenics was important for men such as Phadke who had been active in the Gandhian civil disobedience movement, exhorting college students in Poona to boycott foreign education and foreign goods. Within the Gandhian nationalist context, Phadke did not want to be accused of importing "foreign" ideas such as eugenics or birth control from the West. The middle-class ambiguity vis-à-vis projects of improvement that drew as much from "Western" as from indigenous traditions is evident in Phadke's writings and in the writings of other proponents of birth control in colonial India.[38]

In both the first and the second editions of *Population Problem,* Wattal deployed the Malthusian paradigm to argue that in India rising population numbers were a major impediment to any progress. Malthusian doctrine was "as essential to a correct understanding of social problems as Newton's law of Gravitation is to Astronomy."[39] In the 1916 edition, Wattal suggested that the only remedy for "poverty and other evil effects of the principle of population is moral restraint or abstinence from improvident marriages."[40] To make a convincing case for overpopulation in India, Wattal compared Indian birth and death rates with those of France and Britain. In the 1934 edition, he shifted his emphasis from abstinence to use of birth control, arguing that the practice of abstention placed "too much strain on human nature . . . [and] if practiced for any length of time, . . . would destroy their health and would lead to irregularities of sex relations, perversions and eccentricities."[41] The second edition carried a section on birth control, presenting arguments both in favor and in opposition to the use of contraceptive devices. This added section can be read as an indication of the shift that took place within the debates on the population question from the 1910s to 1930s in colonial India. By the 1930s, the discourse had become much more focused on demographic control, with contraception seen as the solution to India's "population explosion."

The social agenda of the speakers at the first All India Population Conference in February 1936 in Lucknow indicated both an alteration in the traditional Malthusian position along with an acceptance of some of its tenets. For instance, Malthusian prudery and reluctance to advocate birth control was absent in the lectures at the conference. In his introduction and also in a paper at the conference, Mukherjee asserted the importance of "the diffusion of knowledge of birth control." What was needed, he said, were "appropriate and cheap devices of birth control derived by the rural population from materials in its own domestic surroundings . . . so that contraception can be applied until the man has attained the age of say 21 or 23 and the woman the age of 20 or 22 in India."[42]

Debendra Nath Ghoshe, one of the participants at the Lucknow population conference, argued in his presentation "Social Background to Pauperism in India" for curbing welfare measures toward the poor. Like Pillay, Ghoshe also echoed the traditional Malthusian position on charity.[43] Although the poor needed to be given some support, Ghoshe cautioned that "humanity should not be carried too far" and advocated a formula to deal with paupers where "liberty was regulated by law, rights by discipline and leniency by rigor." Ghoshe elaborated a scheme of helping the poor whereby the "hopeless destitutes" would be turned into "normal" men capable of helping themselves and the society. He suggested that arrangements should be made with tea gardens or coal fields so that able-bodied paupers be sent there to work.[44] Operating under Malthusian paranoia, Ghoshe recommended that the poor be denied control over their own bodies and labor, and in the name of "reform" they be transported to some of the most extreme sites of labor exploitation in colonial India, the tea garden and coal mines.[45] The middle-class birth control advocates exhibited an apathy toward the plight of subaltern groups and sought mainly to safeguard the values and interests of their own class. Indian middle-class/upper-caste male advocates of birth control in the name of the nation and also the Hindu community attempted to institute various "reforms" aimed at further marginalizing subaltern groups while simultaneously preserving the existing structures of the elite privileges.

National Demography and Partial Citizenship: Politics of Class, Caste, Community, and Gender

Birth control activists were keen on projecting a "modern" image of India. *Swaraj* was imagined as an inauguration of the new modern era in India. Phadke argued that for India to be a free nation, it needed strong, sturdy, well-clad men and women. This could only be achieved if scientific thought was given to procreation so as to not have a single unwanted child. Although Phadke wrote of the exploitation of Indian resources by foreign imperial forces, he also lamented the "foolish procreation indulged in by its subjects."[46] The need for birth control was far greater under colonialism, he argued, because there was a danger of the "foreigners" exploiting India's population for their own imperialistic use. By bringing forth more children than they could take care of, Indians were only creating a "race of slaves who will too readily fall a prey to the designs of the foreign rulers and exploiters."[47] In the emerging middle-class politics of empowerment in colonial India, individual sexual functions were seen as directly affecting society and nation. The logical extension of an argument that tied national well-being to sexual practices was to call for a strict surveillance of reproductive functions, particularly of those represented as undesirable national citizens—the working class, lower castes, and, in some instances, Muslims.

In their debates on birth control, middle-class male advocates established the parameters for defining the rights of citizens in independent India. The social aggregate whose interests they defended and promoted through such constructions were upper-caste, middle-class, Hindu men. The discourse on birth control is therefore a useful lens for understanding how the intersecting politics of class, caste, community, gender, and sexuality shaped political rhetoric in colonial India. It is important to recognize that the advocates of birth control were not writing in a political or cultural vacuum. Their own elitist vantage positions clearly marked their discourse on the subject of birth control and population.

It is helpful to locate the middle-class and upper-caste call for wider dissemination of contraceptives in colonial India, within the larger political and social context of the 1920s–30s. The larger context will also enable us to understand why these elite men were successful in deploying numerical and statistical information to present a scenario of declining national health, increasing poverty, and arrested social, cultural, and political development? What was the wider context that provided their negative assessments legitimacy in public debates, making room for their alarming articulations of overpopulation? The tumultuous political climate of these years in colonial India provided a rather receptive backdrop for their writings and work. The impact of World War I on Indian economy and society, Sumit Sarkar has argued, sharpened the "numerous contradictions between Indian and British interests . . . the war affected Indian life through massive recruitments, heavy taxes and war loans, and a very sharp rise in prices."[48] The war also sharpened class divisions within Indian society in the differential economic impact it had on the various sections of India's population. For instance, although during the war the price rise "meant misery and fall in the living standards for majority of India people . . . it also contributed to fabulous profits by business groups taking advantage of the war demand."[49] There was massive recruitment of Indians in the war, according to Judith Brown: "[B]y the end of December 1919 nearly 1½ million Indians had been recruited into combatant and non-combatant services."[50] The travel to western Europe, according to Stanley Wolpert, gave birth to new aspirations and a new consciousness among Indians because "for the first time in history, large numbers of Indians had gone to western Europe, where they saw how French and English 'peasants' lived in comparison to Indians and found themselves treated as social equals rather than mere natives or coolies. . . . Most of them returned home with strange, dreadful, and wonderful tales of the world of Europe and Africa, their minds opened, their visions and aspirations for their children—if not for themselves—irreversibly altered."[51]

According to Sarkar, one of the important ideological currents that many Indians were exposed to in Europe was the socialist ideas of the Russian Bolshevik revolution of 1917. Even when definite news about the domestic changes in Russia was not available, "there were many rumors about a total change, a world being turned upside down with the dispossessed coming into their own."[52] There was certainly increased labor unrest during the early 1920s. The All India Trade Union Congress was formed in 1920 and there were 396 labor strikes involving 600,351 workers and a loss of 6,994,426 workdays in 1921.[53] Along with labor, there were also many peasant movements; the best-known early *kisan* or peasant movements developed in 1920–21 in the Pratapgarh, Rae Bareli, Sultanpur, and Fyzabad districts in the Avadh region of U.P.[54]

Added to this situation of economic unrest during the war years and the intellectual influences of socialism was the increased popular participation of Indians in the 1920s–30s in a newly emerging mass-based Gandhian nationalist movement. Even while there was great enthusiasm about freedom among Indians in the 1920s–30s, there was also a heightened environment of anxiety about the future and the outcome of the nationalist movement. Among the middle classes there were public debates on the desired nature of "*swaraj*" and anxieties about the necessary reforms that needed to be implemented to ensure freedom from British colonial rule. At the same time, leaders such as Gandhi presented self-introspective critiques of the bourgeois nationalism and Western modernity while constructing "Indian-ness" in contrast to Western liberal ideals of individualism, industrialization, and biomedical traditions.[55] During this period, India witnessed unrest among peasant, labor, and lower-caste groups along with eruption of communal tensions along religious lines. These conflicts disrupted and challenged the existing social and cultural fabric from within, questioning many of the privileges based on class and caste distinctions.

There were strong lower-caste movements that emerged in Maharashtra and Tamilnadu. Many of the upper-caste birth control advocates such as Phadke, Karve, and Pillay came from these regions. Phadke and Karve were Maharashtrians, and Pillay, although a Tamil Brahman, was located in Bombay during the 1920s–40s. The caste movements in these regions were strongly anti-Brahmanical; the Satyashodhak movement in Maharashtra and the Self-Respect movement in Tamilnadu challenged the caste privileges of Brahmans and other upper castes. In both these areas there were incidents of public burnings of the Brahmanical canon, *Manusmriti*.[56] Phadke in his work *Sex Problem in India* quoted extensively from this text to support his claims about eugenics being indigenous to Indian intellectual tradition.

There were also communal tensions rising between Hindus and Muslims in many parts of India. There was a violent millenarian outburst in 1921 among the Moplahs of Malabar. Hindu communal opinion read this violence as an expression of Muslim aggression against Hindus, instigating the Arya Samaj to begin its projects of conversions and reconversions, popularly known as *shuddhi* (purification) and *sangathan* (forging Hindu unity). These movements were particularly strong in the Punjab and in parts of western U.P.[57] In response, there were similar movements among the Muslims, *tabligh* (propagation) and *tanzim* (organization), to reassert the hold of Islam among the poorer groups.[58] Dayanand Saraswati, one of the leaders of the Arya Samaj movement in Punjab, wrote extensively on what he perceived to be a decline in Hindu masculinity and health in his book *Satyarthprakash* (*Light of Truth*).[59] U.P. was the stronghold of Madan Mohan

Malaviya's Hindu communal organization—the Hindu Mahasabha started in Hardwar (U.P.) in 1915.[60] Wattal and Mukherjee, both brahmans, raised the issue of high fertility among aboriginal tribes, lower castes, and Muslims. The communalization of demographic issues, one can argue, was an outcome of the dominant communal rhetoric from the 1920s onward.[61]

During this same period, India witnessed an increasing communalization of organized politics. The Government of India Act of 1919 heightened divisions and tensions based on community affiliations. These reforms, as Sarkar argues, considerably extended communal representation and reservations. The extension of electorates based on one's religious affiliations sharpened social fissures, providing the anxiety of numbers a new lease of life within Indian public sphere politics. The politics of numbers also underlined caste conflicts; the Justice Party in the Madras presidency made demands for separate electorates and reservations for non-Brahmans.[62] It was within this overall chaotic and unstable political, social, and economic context that the Indian middle-class and upper-caste men articulated their agenda for population control with both a Malthusian emphasis of reducing the size of the population along with emphasizing eugenicism aimed at improving the racial/caste composition of the Indian population. As becomes evident in the section below, the advocates' language was ideologically loaded, negating subaltern subjectivities.

Wattal's analysis of the "population problem" betrayed the communal, caste, and class biases of an upper-caste man. According to Wattal, high fertility among the Indian aboriginal tribes was an indication of lack of civilizational dignity and low worth of individual life among them. Similarly, the high fertility rate among Muslims was, for him, a sign of that community's being intellectually less advanced than Hindus. Because Muslim "cerebral development is so much less (compared to the Hindus)," Wattal argued, that "as a consequence their fecundity is so much greater."[63] Likewise among Hindus, the lower castes had greater fecundity than the higher castes. Unfortunately, Wattal the statistician could not locate the data to support his "thesis" about the lower castes or Muslims from the Indian census. For his correlation between class, intellectual ability, and fecundity, therefore, he had to cite figures from the census of Scotland for 1911. Deploying these data from Scotland, Wattal could "prove" that the laboring classes, the agricultural and fishing occupations, the workers in mines and quarries, and transport workers had higher fertility than those in legal, medical, and teaching professions.[64] This comparative analysis, moreover, was extended to prove that the intellectual civilizational hierarchy did not exist only between communities, classes, and castes, but also between nations. Citing figures of average life expectancy for men and women in England and India, Wattal claimed that "it is generally accepted that the Englishman possesses greater vitality than the Indian."[65] He presented Western bourgeois reproductive regime as a desirable universal, one that Indians should emulate in order to limit their population in proportion to the means of subsistence.

Male upper-caste Hindu proponents such as Wattal, Mukherjee, Phadke, and Pillay failed to address issues of social inequity based on variables of class, caste, gender, or community. Instead, they perpetuated social stereotypes of the working classes, lower-caste Hindus, and Muslims as sexually irresponsible subjects. In the analyses of the birth control advocates, subaltern groups created their own poverty through irresponsible procreation. In their estimation, national prosperity and well-being rested on attending to matters of the womb. Mukherjee and other participants at the first population conference presented an alarmist projection of India's population growth and argued that this demographic increase placed a tremendous burden on the national resources.[66] Documenting his case with statistics that were assumed to tell an "objective" story, Mukherjee stated that "the outstanding feature of the population situation is India's chronic and increasing food shortage. By 1941 India's population will number 400 million, while her population capacity, estimated on the basis of her present food supply, cannot exceed 330 million."[67] At the Lucknow conference, the "experts" did not discuss the uneven distribution of resources based on class, caste, community, and gender privileges. The discourse of population problem extended the hegemonic project of the Indian elites, giving them a legitimate reason to police reproductive behaviors of subaltern groups.

Citing data, Mukherjee, as had Wattal, made a case for the higher fertility of lower castes and among Muslims, representing both groups as sexually degenerate, arguing:

> As in the West, the *most fertile social strata in India are inferior* but nowhere is the disparity between fecundity and culture greater than in Northern India. In the United Provinces the Brahmins and Rajputs have diminished by about 5 and the Kayastha and Kurmis by about 10 and 12 per cent while the Chamars and Ahirs now aggregate more than the total number represented by the four upper castes, who have increased by 6 and 2 per cent respectively. Among other lower castes, the Pasis, Gadarias and Lodha have increased by so much as 18, 9 and 5 per cent respectively.[68]

Deploying statistical numbers was intended to ensure "objectivity." As Urla has argued, statistics came to be regarded as a "uniquely privileged way of 'knowing' the social body, becoming a central technology in diagnosing its ills and managing its welfare."⁶⁹ In discussing the case of Indian Muslims, Mukherjee once again deployed a communal alarmist numerical narrative:

> The Muhammadan, who is less literate than all upper caste Hindus everywhere and in Bihar and Bengal less than even some of the backward castes such as the Santhals, Mahisyas and Namasudras, increased by 51 per cent in Bengal and Punjab during the last 50 years while the Hindu has declined by 6 in the Punjab and increased by about 7 per cent in the United Provinces and 5 per cent in Bihar and 23 per cent in Bengal. . . . The enormous growth of the Muslims is no doubt due to widow remarriage, to polygamy, and later consummation of marriage than among most Hindus and probably also to the differences of food and economic habits.⁷⁰

Mukherjee represented "Muhammadans" as a homogenous social group who were universally less literate than *all* upper-caste Hindus. Low literacy levels, the practice of widow remarriage, polygamy, and later consummation of marriage were identified as the causes for high fertility within the Muslim community, and the community as a whole was castigated for their backward rather than modern controlled reproductive behavior. As suggested by Lynn Thomas in the case of colonial Kenya, in India too, politics of the womb came to be closely tied to modernistic ideal of national body politics and its overall well-being and viability.⁷¹

Ridicule was also heaped on the overwealthy aristocratic families and their lifestyles; they were reprimanded for not fulfilling their eugenic duty of producing "fit" sons for the nation. According to Phadke, "[T]he prospect of a child is as impossible as the nut tree yielding an apple in the case of those over-wealthy people whose daily life is divided only between eating and sleeping and who have no other occupation than rolling in knee-deep cushions all day long and who visit the beach in the evening, as if with the object of giving exercise, not to their own bodies but, to their horses or automobiles."⁷² The middle-class advocates were anxious to define themselves in opposition to social classes both below them and above them.⁷³

Indian male advocates of birth control further analyzed fertility behavior through a class-based prism in demonstrating how the greater "nervous energy" of the male middle-class intellectuals made for lower fertility. "Nervous energy" was distinguished from ordinary physical strength. Phadke clad his class prejudices in scientific garb, claiming that nervous energy was high among men whose professions involved mental labor, or brain work, and "since nature has decreed an inverse relation between nervous energy and fertility, progeny is prolific amongst the manual workers and shows a slower rate as we move on to rich people."⁷⁴ He enumerated five basic conditions that would ensure the proper development of nervous energy in a man: a complex environment leading to incessant mental activity; a moderate amount of physical labor; a plentiful diet, rich in proteins; a dry, bright, and bracing climate; and cheerful surroundings.[75] In a distinctly class-biased discourse, the middle-class man was credited with exercising his high nervous energy to ensure a eugenically prudent family size.

In the 1934 edition of *Population Problem in India,* Wattal articulated similar ideas about high fertility among the working classes. Wattal too viewed high fertility as a reflection of lower intellectual level and heightened sexual life among the working classes, which, in his opinion, differentiated them from the upper classes. He asserted:

> Communities and occupations which are concerned with intellectual pursuits and have a relatively high standard of living show a smaller rate of fertility than occupations connected with manual labor and communities whose standard of living is relatively low or whose outlook on life is more material and physical than intellectual and spiritual. The well to do have many interests in life and more than one outlet for their nervous energy; but the poor have few. Sex life for the poor means much more than it does for the well to do.[76]

According to Wattal, nothing in the working-class lifestyle could be identified as either cultural, intellectual, or spiritual because these were traits preserved solely for the "well to do."

Sharing Wattal's and Mukherjee's analysis of working-class fertility patterns, Ghoshe suggested forced sterilization to ensure that "propagation of pauper species may not be possible."[77] Nowhere in the literature of these early writers on population is there any trace of a critique of social relations and the need for land reforms or more equitable distribution of resources. The existing hierarchical social structure came under scrutiny only to express middle-class anxiety about its possible displacement. Great effort was placed on ensuring the perpetuation of privileges based on class, caste, community, and gender, even if it meant exercising control over subaltern bodies, particularly their reproductive functions. Ghoshe's "solution" betrayed his blatant disregard for individual rights. Advocates who framed the issue mainly in economic terms completely overlooked the element of human agency. Employing Malthusian slurs, Mukherjee rebuked people of the subaltern groups for "breeding like field rats, rabbits and fruit flies."[78]

Disciplining Sexuality

Roy Porter and Lesley Hall, in their essay "Good Sex: The Rhetoric of Conjugal Relations," have argued that Marie Stopes's writings were instrumental in constructing a new understanding of sexuality, particularly of sex within marriage.[79] Indian male advocates, especially Pillay and Phadke, as sexologists, were also interested in rethinking ideas of sexuality and in presenting strict prescriptions of normative sexual practices, for working classes and other subaltern groups, the declining aristocracy, and the emerging middle classes. The subject of birth control presented a legitimate platform for the articulation of new discourses on sexuality and conjugality. Here it is important to stress that colonial India during the 1920s and 1930s witnessed heightened public interest and veritable discourses on the body and sexuality. Issues of the "private domain," unlike Partha Chatterjee's contention, were neither repressed, resolved, nor absent from public-sphere debates in colonial India during the twentieth century.[80] Instead, it would be fair to argue, as does Burton, that the "imperial public sphere was saturated with the 'woman question,' in these heady and tumultuous decades."[81] These decades witnessed some of the anxieties of late-nineteenth-century social reformers who had called for the need to build stronger, masculine bodies in the face of colonial onslaught and violation of Indian life.[82] With the emergence of strong nationalist sentiments in the 1920s, there was a renewed search for ways of empowering Indians and of overthrowing the burdens of imperialism. It was argued that for India to be free, it had to be strong, robust, and masculine. Issues of sexuality and its associations with physical well-being of individuals and, by extension, the social body were becoming an acceptable subject for public debates among Indian middle-class men. A closer scrutiny of the public discussions on birth control in colonial India during the 1920s and 1930s illuminates how sexuality was related to the physical well-being of individuals and of a nation in the making. In the process, the public and the private spheres were braided more closely together.

In the writings of Indian male birth control activists, Hindu, upper-caste, middle-class men were allowed to enjoy full rights over their bodies and sexuality while other social groups were denied the same rights and represented as sexually irresponsible subjects. The demands for wider dissemination of birth control information and technology allowed middle-class men to examine the intimate domain of procreation and conjugal relations of subaltern groups. Middle-class advocates expressed great suspicion toward working-class sexuality. Phadke argued that it had been scientifically proven that "specific types of environments were productive to prolific progeny, and it had also been shown that this peculiar type *naturally obtained* in the homes of the poor."[83] In the chapter "Higher Living," Phadke elaborated his views on the hypersexuality of the working class as reflected in the high fertility of this socioeconomic group. He represented the private spaces of working-class homes as breeding sites, and his middle-class observer's gaze was hostile, impatient, and incriminating. His distinctly middle-class discourse represented working-class sexuality as animal-like,

> And if you could brave a visit to the dark, dusty, dingy slums of the mill operatives you will find that almost in *every family* the woman is either carrying or in confinement. And when our eyes fall on street loafers who find their food on the dunghill and make their bed in the gutter we find them bearing more children than the rags with which they cover their shame and are *reminded of the bitch that breeds kennelfuls of puppies four times a year.*"[84]

As a sexologist, Pillay saw himself as a guardian of middle-class sexual well-being, defining and labeling appropriate sexual expectations for men and women of this class within matrimony. He laid down that the sex urge varied in women just like it did in men, but that desire in middle-class women had a definite periodicity. Pillay contrasted the periodicity of desire in middle-class women with daily copulation among lower-class women. The working class and the rural poor (and, in this case, also Western women) were represented as the "other," possessing hypersexualities. According to Pillay, "[T]he poor women are ordinarily robust and though they have much manual labor to do are not tired out by the evening. Their husbands are also robust and do not suffer from lack of virility. It has therefore to be assumed that they enjoy sexual intercourse, according to their interpretation of the term. I may as well mention here that the *majority of these people copulate almost daily.*"[85] As a middle-class observer, Pillay glossed over the exploitative labor conditions of working-class men and women. His observation captured well his bourgeois disdain for heavy physical labor, which he believed could be performed endlessly without fatigue! He extended his analysis of working-class life to interrogate subaltern sexuality, arguing that even though the rural poor copulated daily, their sexual relations did not provide emotional satisfaction either to the husband or the wife. Pillay regarded sexual relations among the poor as a mere monotonous physical act, and as such incapable of capturing expressions of "real" intimacy. Sexual pleasure in its "true" essence as "recreation, mentally stimulating and physically invigorating," Pillay believed, was the preserve of the educated middle classes.[86] It is interesting to note that in the emerging discourse of birth control, sexual pleasure itself was tied to a definite class character.

Besides being suspicious of what they regarded as subaltern sexual excesses, middle-class male advocates were anxious to locate sexual expressions strictly within the confines of heterosexual matrimony. In the Sholapur Eugenic Society, Pillay ran a "Wives Clinic," giving advice on contraceptives, venereal disease, sterility, sex problems, heredity, and eugenics.[87] In this clinic, Pillay laid down certain rules whereby contraceptive information was only to be imparted to married women under the following criteria. To receive birth control information, a woman had to be under eighteen years of age, ill, or very weak. Birth control was also to be made available to a woman whose husband suffered from venereal diseases or other conditions such as insanity, idiocy, epilepsy, moral imbecility, sexual perversion, criminality, or pauperism, which it was feared he could transmit to their offspring. Pillay asserted that if the knowledge of contraceptives was imparted with discretion, it would ensure that every wife attained a fully developed body and mind before becoming a mother and would allow for sufficient intervals between childbirths to recoup the mother's health. Use of birth control, he argued, would enable the wife to keep her husband's happiness and preserve harmony in the home. The "Wives Clinic" emphasized maternal well-being and divorced marital sexuality from reproduction, but at the same time perpetuated the stereotype of gendered sexuality whereby the wife was required to provide sexual services to ensure "her husband's happiness."

Phadke presented statistical evidence from colonial records, such as the report of the Department of Health, Bombay, 1921, to document high maternal mortality in India. He linked the "decline of India" to the "fact" of high maternal mortality, arguing that it would be useless to look for a strong and fit race "when those to whom the function of procreation is assigned by nature are hopeless and helpless souls."[88] He argued that "the true starting point of eugenics in India, and everywhere, must be the *improvement of the mother*."[89] According to Phadke, only marriage gave Indian women the "lawful rights of motherhood," adding that motherhood outside of marriage either for virgins or widows would shatter the institution of marriage, leading to immorality and social anarchy.[90] Phadke presented sexual union within marriage as natural and acceptable, in contrast to other sexual relations that he viewed as illegitimate and unacceptable. The subtext within the writings of Indian male birth control advocates disclosed their attitudes toward sexuality, demonstrating their approval only of "compulsory heterosexuality," strictly located within the confines of matrimony. Sexual norms in colonial India were being articulated and constructed through the writings on eugenics and neo-Malthusianism.

"In marriage lie the ultimate springs from where the race rises and maintains a steady flow," wrote Phadke.[91] Because marriage was regarded as the "most important eugenic instrument," it was subjected to close scrutiny.[92] Phadke stressed a need to promote eugenically prudent marriage between a man of twenty-five and a woman of at least sixteen years of age, based on the principle of "love marriage." Love marriages were defined in opposition to traditional marriages where the couple, instead of being deeply attached to each other, were more like two disparate beings who came together merely for the sexual act, producing children of "inferior stuff." While advocating love marriages, Phadke cited examples from the Hindu epics, the *Ramayana* and the *Mahabharata,* to demonstrate that the idea of compatible conjugality was part of Indian traditions and as such was indigenous to India. Love marriages, according to Phadke, were popular in ancient India, without causing widespread immorality or destructive influences. On the contrary, he claimed, Indians of that time were stronger and healthier than those in the present day. Addressing what was evidently a controversial subject, Phadke reiterated that love marriages in the West failed not because of any inherent problem with love marriages, but because of the nature of Western culture. Because "Indian" culture was distinct from, and presumably superior to, that of the West, Phadke insisted that love marriages would prove to be eugenically prudent for Indians.[93] The emphasis on "quality" as opposed to "quantity" was clear in his discussions on the goals of eugenic couples. The eugenic couple was assigned the social responsibility of producing "fit" male children for the nation and asked to exercise eugenic considerations on their procreative act, through birth control. The act of procreation was sacred and holy, with far-reaching effects on the welfare of society. Because it was understood that procreation determined the good of the society in a very large measure, lending it stability and cohesion, procreative practices warranted strict surveillance and control.[94] Advocates of birth control such as Phadke and Pillay evaluated and promoted specific contraceptive technologies, but in doing so they also reevaluated ideas of sexuality, constructing what they believed to be the "ideal sexual behavior." As noted above, their constructions of sexuality were marked by their class, caste, and gender affiliations.

Gendered biases were very evident in Phadke's descriptions of male/female physiologies and in his analysis of male and female contraceptives available in the early twentieth century. While writing about male/female generative organs and about sex, Phadke shifted back and forth between evoking "scientific" arguments and popularly held beliefs, depending on which better supported his argument. He stated that because the structure of the male genitals was comparatively simpler and evident on the surface, he would only explain the structure and functioning of the female generative organs. As opposed to the simple and evident male genitals, the female organs, according to Phadke, were "*considerably intricate,*" and the inner parts were "*hidden from common view.*"[95] On the basis of his "biological/scientific" observation, he labeled what he called the various "internal" and "external" female generative organs. Such an exclusive concentration on the female body, it has been argued, perpetuated the concept of the female as "other" or "exotic" and as such a legitimate object of scrutiny.[96] Phadke provided a functionalist description of the female genital organs to argue that female bodies were biologically adapted for mothering. The uterus was described as "the house of the embryo almost from the moment of conception to the moment of birth"; this was understood to be the sole "useful" function of the uterus. Similarly, the vagina was defined in terms of its reproductive functions: "the main function of the vagina is that it is the place where sexual intercourse takes place. It receives the male organ (penis) during the sexual act, and serves as a temporary repository for the male semen. After the sperm of the male has reached the uterus, the vagina has no further function to perform."[97] Within the sexual act, women's bodies were coded as passive and receptive. In his discussion of the generative organs, Phadke argued for the necessity of undertaking knowledge in a "healthy spirit of scientific inquiry." Interestingly, this "healthy spirit of scientific inquiry" did not allow any discussion of the male generative organs. An ideal body type was constructed through a "scientific" explanation of how the female generative organs function. Because the "external sex organs" of women were seen as outside the reproductive economy, there was only a brief definition of these organs that were regarded as presumably nonfunctional and therefore nonutilitarian body parts.

Phadke inconsistently synthesized scientific principles with popular beliefs to explain the process of procreation. For instance, he deployed the metaphors of seed and soil in order to explain how conception took place within the human species. He critiqued eugenically unfit marriages that he argued resulted in "seeds which contain a positive promise of a rich and exuberant harvest" to be "foolishly scattered on uncongenial soil, a well furrowed fertile field is wastefully sown with rotten seeds and hence instead of a fit race a herd of unfit humans hobbles into existence."[98] The agricultural metaphors of "seed" for male sperm and "soil" for the female womb continue to be used in parts of rural India even today when talking of human conception.[99]

The advocates' discussion of various contraceptive technologies reflected their understanding of sexuality. Abstinence as a method of contraceptive, Pillay argued, "may be adopted by those who can practice it without physical or moral or mental decline." He added that while advising this method to young couples, one needs to bear in mind that sexual appetite, after hunger, was the most dominating influence in the life of human beings. Sex was constructed as a "natural instinct." Constructing the truth of sex biologically and as timeless, Phadke wrote, "Hunger and love are the two great mother impulses, the ultimate source of all other impulses. Why, we may go a step further and assert that . . . in the ultimate analysis of things the impulse of love—or what is vulgarly described as the impulse to reproduce—will be found to be more primary."[100]

Although Pillay and Phadke constructed sexual impulses as "natural," they were quick to limit the expression of this natural instinct to men, tying women to maternity and tying their sexual expression to maternity. The ambiguity about sex and its role within marriage is amply demonstrated when Pillay and Phadke described various contraceptive technologies. Abstinence as a method of birth control was rejected out of hand because, according to Phadke, "considering the common course of sexual desire and the control to which it can be ordinarily subjected, the sexual act *has to be allowed at least once a week*."[101] Abstinence was regarded as self-denial, something that could not be asked of mortal men because it would be as "ridiculous as asking the mountain tree tops not to wave when in a storm, or a lump of butter not to melt before a fire."[102] Male sexual instincts were treated as a natural biological given akin to hunger, thirst, and sleep; therefore, preaching abstinence as a method of birth control was believed to be a denial of "the *natural rights* of the married man."[103] Even though sex was constructed as a "natural" instinct, Phadke warned against "sexual extravagance" within marriage. He wrote, "It should be deeply impressed on the minds of all that none but the married have the right to sexual intercourse and that illicit intercourse is a heinous guilt, bound to spell the ruin not only of the individual but also the family and the nation. Every married person must conscientiously believe that even in the married state sexual excess is a breach of duty, that is an unnameable sin to use marriage as a permit for sexual intemperance."[104]

The emerging middle-class discourse on sexuality was anxious to impose its own norms of morality even while challenging the utilitarian ideas of sex merely for procreation. Sexuality was located within the discourse of national destiny, and in order to safeguard national well-being, sexuality had to be placed under a strict regime of surveillance even within bourgeois households. The practices of the private domain were clearly understood as overflowing and impacting the public life of the nation, and as such they could not be left unsupervised. Sexual acts performed in the privacy of middle-class bedrooms and working-class homes became a legitimate subject of interrogation because these could impact a nation's well-being, health, and its overall ranking among modern nations in the world.

Phadke briefly described some male contraceptive methods such as *coitus interruptus* and use of the condom, especially because he considered these to be harmful and unreliable. *Coitus interruptus,* he argued, could cause a harmful local effect on the male organ and in the woman it could cause sacral pain and weakness, a sensation of pain and dragging in the pelvis, and general neurosis. Phadke argued that the absorption of seminal and prostatic fluids was highly beneficial to the whole system of the woman, which would be impossible in a method using external ejaculation. The interruption of seminal and prostatic fluids is what prevents conception, and because Phadke was a birth control advocate, the above critique of the withdrawal method seems curiously misplaced. The male condom was rejected as a contraceptive because it was considered unreliable and, like *coitus interruptus,* did not permit the woman to absorb the seminal and prostatic secretions and was thus detrimental to her health. Phadke argued that male condoms were unacceptable, particularly for men who did not have a "very strong sex capacity," since its constant use "may reduce his potency for consistent erection and proper ejaculation."[105]

With male contraceptives discarded as unreliable, the focus during this period shifted to analyzing female contraceptive devices. In their discussion of female contraceptives, there was an uncomfortable disjuncture in the writings of birth control advocates such as Pillay and Phadke. Both these men generally addressed other men as their readers because women's sexual knowledge was considered to be inadequate, if not completely lacking. Yet both promoted female contraceptives as more reliable than male contraceptives. Placing contraceptive responsibility on women created an interesting tension; it required women to be active sexual participants in sexual acts at the same time that the dominant patriarchal understanding constructed women as sexually innocent. The advocates sought to resolve this tension through indirectly imparting contraceptive information to women via their husbands. Therefore, even though the onus of contraceptive use fell on women, women were not entrusted with this sexual knowledge. Men alone were trusted with the important knowledge and task of determining the family size and of ensuring national well-being by exercising sexual control over their wives.[106]

Phadke discussed female contraceptives such as douching, pessaries, and sponges. He recommended the cervical cap that Norman Haire introduced as the Dutch Cap or Mensinga Pessary, as opposed to Stopes's Pro-Race Cap. Phadke referred to the disagreement between Haire and Stopes regarding which was the preferable method and added that his own inclination was toward the Dutch Cap because the "possibility of sliding out of place is eliminated in its case and hence it looks like a *surer weapon* than the Pro-Race Cap."[107] Without basing his statements on any specific clinical tests, Phadke stated that people feared that the use of the Dutch Cap might cause injury to a woman's womb; however, according to him there was no cause for fear because no one had complained about the product.

Marie Stopes's journal, *Birth Control News*, reporting Phadke's opinion on the Dutch Cap, stated that Phadke's "uninstructed prejudice" caused a lot of harm, because not only did the Dutch Cap slide out of place, but it also lost its shape and left a large gap between itself and the vagina on one side or the other.[108] Clearly, the issue of which method of birth control was best suited was one that vexed the advocates as much as it must have the consumers.

Birth control advocates in their writings articulated a strict prescription on acceptable sexual behaviors. For instance, Pillay wrote extensively on the need for sex education that could be incorporated within the school curricula. Within the rubric of sex education, he argued that "character or moral training" and "sex education proper" should be included. Pillay asserted that character or moral training should start at home, inculcating notions of "regularity, obedience, conscience, personal cleanliness and reverence for the body, temperance, self control, proper sense of shame, and an initiation to helpful play."[109] It was the responsibility of parents to ensure that these "qualities" were inculcated at home. Besides character training, Pillay stressed that education also required "proper" sex instruction that covered a wide range of subjects such as maternity, paternity, the significance of marriage, fertilization and development, physiology and functions of sex organs, changes in adolescence, health rules, venereal diseases, hygiene of married life, prostitution, preparation for marriage, principles of heredity, preparation for parenthood, family life, and "mothercraft."[110] While never questioning the institution of marriage itself, Pillay addressed the need to reform and recast certain practices in order to uphold the new modern bourgeois ideals of conjugality, emphasizing both sexual and mental compatibility. The twentieth-century emphasis on "good sex" within matrimony was in sharp contrast to the nineteenth-century male reformers' emphasis on female education as the principal ingredient for producing compatible companions for educated middle-class men. Nineteenth-century reformers, for the most part, did not address issues of sexual compatibility or of the importance of sex within marriage.[111] By the twentieth century, procreative sex became a critical component of conjugal relations, closely tied to bourgeois understanding of national well-being.

Pillay's later works, *Ideal Sex Life* and *Birth Control Simplified*, reveal how birth control advocates deployed the new "scientific" discipline of sexology to articulate the need for promoting the spread of birth control knowledge.[112] These are important texts for understanding the narratives on sexuality as these circulated among the Indian middle classes during the early twentieth century. Pillay became interested in the subject of birth control as an essential tool for promoting "marital bliss" because, according to him, it made it possible to divorce sex from reproduction. As a sexologist, Pillay argued that a satisfactory sex life within marriage was one of the components of the utopia that he visualized.[113] Pillay laid great emphasis on a "satisfactory sex life" within matrimony. Sex, he argued, was a biological function; like hunger, it was a "natural" bodily response. Yet at the same time he lamented that India, unlike Germany, did not have organized marriage consultation centers where people could be "educated" and made "sex conscious." Pillay's own understanding of sexuality appears to be interestingly split, at once constructing sex as a natural bodily response and also calling for its "scientific" management.[114] This fragmentation was even more pronounced in his discussions on female sexuality and working-class sexual practices.

According to Pillay, frigidity among women was a social myth and not a reality. He argued that women would respond to sexual urges just like they would to hunger. Pillay asserted that response to sexual stimulation in women resembled the "natural" response of sneezing when appropriate stimulation was applied to their nostrils, just as the eyes watered when chili powder was applied to them.[115] The only woman who would not respond to sexual stimulation by a man was a woman "who is a fool or a liar or so ugly that no one wants to rouse her." The danger with the "deformed and ugly" woman, according to him, was that she would turn to homosexuality because of the lack of heterosexual stimulation. In the same text, Pillay claimed that homosexual tendencies within women would cause frigidity in heterosexual life. The idea that a "normal" woman would "naturally" respond to any male sexual stimulation, along with a negative representation of the homosexual woman, needs to be recognized as a patriarchal construct, defining female sexuality strictly in its relation to male sexuality. In seeking to represent a homosexual woman as the "other" and "sexual deviant," Pillay deployed the ultimate rhetorical maneuver of displacing her onto the West. According to Pillay, homosexuality among women was not common in India as it was in the West, where in big towns, many working girls were setting up homosexual relationships.[116] As a sexologist, Pillay was anxious to define situations under which women might turn to homosexual relationships, since for him these warranted social caution.

In *Ideal Sex Life,* Pillay discussed many issues related to female sexuality. He emphasized the need for married women to be sexually satisfied by their husbands, or else he warned that they might take up a lover.[117] Sexually unsatisfied women, Pillay warned, would "in course of time become a bag of nerves, develop menstrual disorders and may experiment with masturbation."[118] While recognizing the need for mutual sexual satisfaction within matrimony, Pillay advised that if there was no sexual satisfaction for a woman in marriage, she should learn to "bear up and cheer up" and "take up social activity."[119]

In constructing his image of a "sexual utopia," Pillay emphasized the importance of mutual sexual attraction within marriage, and thereby he recognized that women were not merely passive objects of male desires within matrimony. But he was quick to add that, for a woman, raising a family was necessary for her emotional satisfaction. A woman's emotional satisfaction *would never* be complete without having at least one child.[120] Women's sexuality was in the ultimate analysis always tied with maternity. Interestingly, even when the more traditional ideals of female sexuality were being questioned, they were never completely discarded. Women were allowed sexual expression exclusively within marriage, yet within marriage, maternity circumscribed the parameters of feminine sexuality.

Even while Pillay sought to repudiate certain negative traditional associations of sex, he inadvertently ended up reinforcing them. This is particularly clear in his discussions on masturbation. *Ideal Sex Life* states in many places that masturbation was not a sexually harmful practice, adding that "it does not produce insanity or any nervous disorder or sexual weakness, and it is not sinful or immoral, judged by the tenets of any religion."[121] In other places in the same book, masturbation was represented as a practice that would make boys self-centered and averse to marriage, and a masturbator "is not likely to be ambitious as he would be content with whatever he could get without effort."[122] When discussing masturbation in girls, Pillay argued that the practice would affect a girl's facial appearance and cause menstrual disorders, leukorrhoea, and dislike for society and companionship.[123] Pillay advised that this practice should be avoided, and if one was tempted, the remedies he suggested were early dinner and a strict routine of exercises. Someone fighting the habit was also advised to avoid reading "sentimental four anna novels and thrillers," for these, according to Pillay, made a person think more of sex than was good for them.[124] Middle-class parents were warned to protect their wards from the corrupting influences of servants who might initiate the children into the autoerotic techniques of masturbation and other "forbidden" sexual activities.[125] The verdict was against masturbation, despite the author's overt claims that masturbation was not harmful and that sex was as natural a bodily sensation as hunger.

Anxious middle-class projects of self-improvement allow us to better comprehend the internal contradictions and inconsistencies that marked the discourse of birth control and sexuality in twentieth-century colonial India. Just when sexual compatibility was constructed as an important component of conjugality, middle-class activists also encoded strict, oppressive sexual norms to ensure "legitimate" sexual expressions. The writings of middle-class/upper-caste male birth control activists capture for us their understanding of the relationship between intimate private sexual practices and national progress. The activists in their surveillance of sexual practices linked together the affairs of the home/hearth with that of the emerging nation.

Conclusion

This chapter examined the writings of some early elite male advocates of birth control to understand and map the public life and presence of this issue in colonial India. It delineates the various ideological alliances and influences that these advocates drew upon to make a convincing case for the need for wider dissemination of contraceptive information during the decades from 1920 to 1947. Numerous competing intellectual, social, and political currents—such as eugenicism, neo-Malthusianism, demography, sexology, and nationalism—shaped the birth control movement in colonial India. Most of the elite male proponents of birth control belonged to new categories of social experts such as demographers, sexologists, and economists who in the name of national welfare argued for strict surveillance of sexual behaviors, linking sexual practices to the health and prosperity of the nation.

In trying to understand the trajectories of the birth control movement in colonial India, it is important to recognize the distinct political, social, and cultural interests that determined the discourse on birth control. The early advocates of birth control, as this chapter has demonstrated, linked the issue of birth control to what they argued was the problem of overpopulation and the physical and racial decline of Indians. The articulation of the issue of birth control as one intimately linked to demographic concerns served a variety of political interests and purposes. For one, it gave the call for wider dissemination of contraceptive information social and economic urgency that would have been hard to gain and sustain had the issue been constructed solely as one of sexual reforms, divorcing marital sex from its utilitarian function of reproduction. The middle-class/upper-caste discourse of demographic crisis fed into and fueled as much as it drew upon the overall climate of social and political anxieties of the 1920 onward. It also drew upon existing caste and community tensions and in turn provided these politics with statistical ammunition, as seen in Mukherjee's and Wattal's writings. Their complaints of a decline in Hindu upper-caste numbers in comparison with Muslims and the lower castes deepened communal and caste tensions with seemingly "objective" evidence.

This chapter also argued that Indian middle-class men during the 1920s and 1930s deployed the issue of population control as a new modality of class, caste, community, and gender privilege and power. Birth control provided Indian elites with a new technology to exercise control over the bodies of men and women belonging to the working classes, lower castes, and minority communities, as well as the aristocracy. The sexual practices of subaltern groups and the declining aristocracy were placed under strict surveillance under the pretense of "improving" national bodies and population. The social aggregate the advocates were invested in was the middle-class, upper-caste Hindu male, and their politics were aimed at safeguarding the privileges of this social group. These advocates made distinctions between the "animal-like" sexual gratification of the lower classes and the "higher" plane of sexual satisfaction enjoyed by the more "cultured" social groups. Despite the lip service paid to women's sexual desires, women's sexual needs were not only seen as secondary to that of men's, but it was also believed that they found their ultimate expression in maternity and mothercraft. The emphasis and contest over reproduction within the debates on birth control blurred distinctions between the private and public domains, demonstrating the overflow of these two spheres instead of the strict separation that Partha Chatterjee suggests.

A close examination of the public-sphere debates on birth control reveals that responsible and modern citizenship within an embryonic nation came to be defined in terms of reproductive restraint. In the writings of upper-caste, middle-class Indian male advocates of birth control, numerical abstractions of national demography came to prevail over issues of reproductive health and sexual well-being. Their elite agendas inflected and shaped their espousal of contraceptive technologies. The evaporation of personal and human concerns from the early-twentieth-century discourse of birth control unfortunately created a lasting legacy in the marginalization of debates on women's reproductive rights, especially in the zealous policies of the postcolonial Indian state aimed at reducing national birthrates.

While evaluating the writings of middle-class Indian male advocates, it is important to keep in mind that many of these men were in conversation with birth control enthusiasts in the West. Indian advocates operated on an international circuit; the next chapter, therefore, shifts its focus to examine the involvement of Western advocates in promoting the cause of birth control in colonial India, to reflect closely on their contributions to the debates within India and the many different alliances they entered into, and to frame the issue in the twentieth century.

2 Global Agenda and Local Politics: Western Advocates and Discourse of Birth Control in Colonial India, 1920s–40s

> In my coming campaign I hope to do the preliminary work for realizing two aims—first, to bring to the *poorer and biologically worse endowed stocks the knowledge of birth control* that is already prevalent among those who are both genetically and economically better favored, and secondly, to bring the birth rates of the East more in line with those of England and the civilizations of the West.
> —Margaret Sanger to C. P. Blacker, 1935 (emphasis added)

The previous chapter demonstrated the history of the birth control movement in India as inextricably tied to the project of nationalism and nation building. This chapter demonstrates how this is a history that cannot be adequately grasped strictly within national boundaries or nationalist constructs. The chapter is also a critical appraisal of the involvement of Western birth control advocates such as Marie Stopes, Margaret Sanger, Edith How-Martyn, and Eileen Palmer in promoting contraceptive usage in colonial India during the early decades of the twentieth century. In 1921, Stopes, along with her husband Humphery Verdon Roe, opened the first English birth control clinic in Holloway, a working-class district in north London.[1] Although Stopes would prescribe contraceptive techniques to Indian sympathizers, she never visited India. The other women did. Sanger, an American birth control activist who claimed to have coined the phrase "birth control" in 1915, went to prison in 1917 for distributing contraceptives to immigrant women from a makeshift clinic in Brooklyn, New York. Sanger first visited India in December 1935.[2] How-Martyn, a British suffragist, joined the British Malthusian League in 1910 and was active in the birth control movement in England. She was the director of the Birth Control International Information Center (BCIIC) in London during the 1930s, when Sanger was the president of this organization. Eileen Palmer was the honorary secretary of BCIIC during the 1930s. How-Martyn and Palmer made many trips to India from 1934 to 1939 to promote birth control and contraceptive use.³

In assessing the participation of these proponents' politics of birth control in India, I focus on the symbiotic relationship of Western activists and their Indian allies, patrons, and opponents. Western proponents of birth control faced opposition from Indian political leaders such as M. K. Gandhi. There were also intense rivalries among the activists themselves. Despite sympathetic support from a few individual colonial officials, these women received no sustained support from the colonial state for the project of birth control.⁴ In seeking to unravel their interventions within the Indian birth control debates, I locate these Western actors within a complex historical web of relations with different Indian groups as well as with various constituencies in the West. The interactions and exchanges between and among Western advocates and Indian proponents and opponents of birth control provide a useful entry point to examine how global concerns, as much as local and parochial interests, varyingly contended and collaborated in shaping the historical discourse and practices associated with contraceptive usage and knowledge.

This work argues that birth control in colonial India was necessarily linked to global movements of ideas, technology, and personnel. Indian advocates were influenced by ideas that had a global reach. Mainstream bourgeois understanding on the subject of birth control derived as much from ideas of Malthus and Galton as from new mentalities about sexuality that, in turn, borrowed from indigenous traditions as from those that had origins outside India. While recognizing that altruism as well as feminism (albeit of the imperial variety) was no doubt an important part of Sanger's, Stopes's, How-Martyn's, and Palmer's orientation, at the same time, India was more than just a site for their disinterested philanthropy.⁵ India was, instead, as this chapter demonstrates, an important location where these Western advocates contended to accumulate cultural and economic capital, prestige, and patronage, as well as markets for their newly developed contraceptive technologies.

This chapter argues for understanding the politics of birth control in colonial India and its overlaps with the politics and discourses in Britain and United States as a phenomenon of cross-continental discursive loops or as interrelated histories.⁶ Such an examination of the history of birth control, as globally interconnected, allows us to question national absolutisms, emphasizing instead the conjunctural and relational aspects of our understandings of the past. Viewing political and intellectual movements as interactive enables us to recognize the complex historical agencies of non-Western societies and also helps to dismantle Western or nationalist parochialism within scholarship. Analyzing the history of birth control in India as interrelated with developments in the West also enables us to discard simplistic historical readings of the Indian movement as either a mindless mimetic gesture or as a derivative and flawed copy of its Western counterpart. Through the focus on the presence and participation of British and American birth control activists in the debates on the subject in India, this chapter constructs the histories of birth control in these countries as locked in argument and debate rather than being hermetically sealed. I argue for the need to comprehend the politics of birth control in the early twentieth century as a "shared commitment of multiple worlds and individuals to the production of new knowledge and the consumption of new techno-scientific products and interventions."[7] I find this approach more productive than a simple binary perspective of thinking about the historical moments in the West and the non-West as exclusively, or more simplistically, as a one-way traffic lane of ideas and initiatives flowing from the West to the non-West. The history of reshaping reproductive practices in colonial India is best understood as a collaborative endeavor bringing together multiple advocates from various geographical locations.

For the most part, Eurocentric accounts and Indian nationalist historiography have been reluctant to acknowledge what Fernando Coronil and others have identified as the "process of mutual historical constitution of European and colonial worlds."[8] On the one hand, Eurocentric and colonialist writers overplayed the polarized and hierarchical conception of the West and its others. On the other hand, the Indian nationalists were overly enthusiastic in underplaying the relational aspects of political, cultural, and social exchanges between the West and India. In their work they focused on the "natural revulsion against foreign rule" to argue for the success of Indian nationalism under the leadership of Gandhi. According to Sumit Sarkar, nationalist historians such as Tarachand and R. C. Majumdar understood the interests of all Indians as simplistically "always opposed to alien domination."[9] These common interests of Indians, the nationalists argued, did not coalesce into a mass movement before the 1910s because India lacked a charismatic leader. The nationalist narrative concludes that Gandhi filled in the leadership gap, ultimately leading India to freedom and independence.[10] This narrow and unitary history of Indian nationalism allows no room for conflicts and tensions within Indian society, nor does it permit a serious examination of the interactions between India and the West beyond the simple binaries of colonizer/colonized or exploiter/exploited.

The scholarship on Sanger and Stopes within American and British history has paid little attention to their international activities and exchanges.[11]

The work of Sanger and Stopes is located primarily within Western history and in isolation from the rest of the world. Richard Soloway and Peter Neushul[12] have pointed out the sharp professional rivalries that emerged between Sanger and Stopes, but neither have examined the presence of non-Western countries such as India or South Africa and their importance in shaping the work and politics of these two women. More recently, scholars have begun to interrogate the exchanges and presence of these Western proponents of birth control in the colonial world.[13] By locating the work of Sanger and Stopes within a larger historical/geographical field than the West, my work builds upon recent historiography that simultaneously challenges the bracketed domains of European/Western history as well as expands the national boundaries within which conventional narratives of Indian history are traditionally located.[14]

Scholars have warned that globalization works to simultaneously deny and universalize difference.[15] Therefore, while calling for an emphasis on relational histories of the West and the non-West, I am also acutely aware of what Kaplan and others identify as the calculated ideological maneuvers of global politics.[16] Globalization is not an inherently inclusive endeavor; its agenda is marked by a complex process of inclusion and exclusion of group interests and is inflected by gender, race, class, and national politics. An overemphasis on globalization does not allow for differences to surface and challenge Western universalisms such as liberal individualism, modernity, development, and progress. Uncritical use of global/world historical paradigms can reinstate colonial power relations, once again failing to recognize the transnational circulation of goods, information, technology, people, and ideologies. To avoid some of the pitfalls of globalization, I pay close attention to the power structures that shaped transnational interactions, but in doing so also challenge the construction of the world through margins and centers. This chapter seeks to destabilize the metropole/nonmetropole or center/margin binary by historicizing and contextualizing the interactions between Indian and Western birth control enthusiasts from the 1920s onward.

Through a close evaluation of the intervention of Western advocates in India, I argue that the global agenda of foreign enthusiasts such as Sanger, Stopes, and How-Martyn and their elite Indian cohorts, such as Ahluwalia, Pillay, Phadke, and Karve, failed to take into account the wide spectrum of reproductive experiences and needs of people, on whose behalf they claimed to be speaking. Although Sanger and Stopes did bring a feminist agenda to debates on birth control in India, their feminism was tempered by their deployment of racist, eugenicist, and class-specific logic in seeking to advance their program to determine and control fertility. They emphasized the need for initiating a global procreative imperative, one marked by definite class, race, and national interests. The interactions and exchanges between Western activists and Indian enthusiasts detailed in this chapter demonstrate how birth control in colonial India while allowing for new forms of freedom also enforced new sets of sociocultural controls. The advocacy and promotion of birth control by Western and Indian elites during the 1920s and 1930s unleashed new modalities of surveillance and social control. This chapter, therefore, reinforces the larger argument of this work: that the history of birth control in colonial India can at best be understood as simultaneously emancipatory and regulatory, at once constrictive and expansive, inhibiting and liberating.

Sanger and Stopes: Competing for Global Influence

The community of Western birth control activists was not a homogeneous group of people working together to promote a common cause. Stopes and Sanger devoted time and energy to propagate and promote the cause of birth control in India and in other parts of the British empire. Both women also campaigned hard to get the state to promote birth control in their respective home countries. Despite sharing a common cause, there were significant personality differences and important issues of power, linked with competition over gaining influence and greater patronage in India as well as other parts of the non-Western world, that created fissures among the Western advocates.

Stopes had support at home from a political lobby comprised of the Eugenic Society and the Neo-Malthusian League, along with other birth control organizations such as BCIIC.[17] The economic crisis of the late 1920s and early 1930s made birth control a somewhat acceptable topic of public discussions in Britain. The dominant public discourse in Britain argued that rising unemployment and population had led to the country's economic hardships after the war. The Workers Birth Control Group and the National Union of Societies for Equal Citizenship in 1929 apparently submitted questionnaires to potential political candidates to determine if they would support birth control instruction in the welfare centers.[18] In 1929, according to Soloway, "newspapers and journals were filled with articles discussing the relationship of over-population to the parlous state of the economy, and there were favorable commentary" on birth control.[19] The Royal Institute of Public Health in Britain acknowledged that birth control was medically important, and instruction on the subject was introduced in 1930 to senior medical students with Stopes and C. P. Blacker among the few lecturers.[20] In the same year, the Ministry of Health in Britain, under pressure from various groups, introduced a memorandum that allowed for limited access to contraception through maternal and child welfare centers.[21] However, recent scholarship has highlighted that after the 1930s, Stopes's influence within the British birth control movement began to wane, leading her to turn her attention to new areas of influence such as the colonies.[22]

In the United States, Sanger had to contend with court orders and arrests. The United States had conservative legislation in place since the late nineteenth century, particularly the infamous Comstock Laws (1873) that forbade any public exchange of contraceptive information. In the late 1920s and early 1930s, Sanger faced many political defeats when lobbying for birth control legislation in the U.S. Congress. In America, the Depression was linked to the decline in birthrates. Economists such as Louis Dublin argued that the country's economic collapse was a "result of an insufficiency of purchasing power brought on by . . . the static rate of national population growth."[23] It was argued that economic recovery would be achieved through encouraging American workers to have more babies. Within this intellectual understanding of the economic problem in America in the 1920s and 1930s, there was obviously little room for public support for birth control. Moreover, during this same period, the U.S. Catholic Church became a powerful lobby and, as a result, as Sanger's biographer put it, "birth control was denied a place in the social welfare and public health of the triumphant New Deal."[24] By the end of President Franklin Roosevelt's first term in office, birth control reforms in the United States had lost momentum. For instance, in 1935, birth control bills before the Seventy-fourth Congress were tabled in committee without so much as a hearing.[25] In keeping with the overall hesitant acceptance of birth control in the United States, it was only in 1937 that the American Medical Association conceded that birth control as a subject should be taught in medical schools.[26] All these hurdles made it politically more compelling and possibly emotionally rewarding for Sanger to work with advocates internationally and to win support for birth control abroad, with the hope of thereby gaining greater respectability for her cause at home. Ellen Chesler, in her biography of Sanger, points out that in her meeting with Gandhi in Wardha, Sanger was aware of the "potential publicity value of such an encounter."[27] Moreover, Sanger "understood that from the standpoint of her American audience, the glamour of her personal association with the legendary Indian nationalist far outweighed any real philosophical differences between them."[28] Her visit with Gandhi was widely reported in the U.S. press, giving her and her cause much-needed publicity at home.

There were also other less tangible but equally important considerations, such as fame and prestige, as well as a range of material and affective benefits, that accrued to famous white women doing social work in the colonies during this time. In her letter from India, Sanger mentioned the exclusive treatment she was accorded by Indian princes and elite members. After a visit with Maharaj Sayaji Rao of Baroda, she wrote, "I had a lovely car and spiffy chauffeur all the time at my disposal night and day. Everything most luxurious and glorious." Describing the reception after her lecture, she wrote, "Flowers and garlands and cheers. Red carpet spread to the car . . . and all this makes you feel very important."[29] Sanger wrote to her husband exoticizing India and passionately consuming it: "[Y]ou would like India for one thing anyway. . . . You would not be allowed to carry a package not even a small one. My watchful bearer looks up and takes from my hand my coat and everything I bear. . . . I am falling in love with India. Life is so easy and charming and warm and bright for those who have money. The poor are horribly poor but the large intellectual population just middle class are very lovely. The women are beautiful!"[30] More generally she wrote about India and Indians: "[i]ts dazzling colors everywhere. Then the people are so gentle and kind and happy and leisurely. It is just restful to watch them. Their temples are filthy but that's nothing as I don't have to live in them. The dogs and pigs and bullocks and goats run about the streets with the people."[31] While Sanger enjoyed what she saw as a leisured way of life, there were others in her team who found the pace of work and the work ethos among Indians frustrating. One of her companions whined that "they don't seem to know the meaning of the word hurry here."[32] To the Western enthusiasts, India at once represented the idealized "other" to the mechanized Western world as well as a "backward" and unmodern culture that had little appreciation for the discipline of clock time.

Stopes, like Sanger, wrote in an overwhelmed tone about her trip to Japan where she had the opportunity to meet Japanese elites: "I am quite in 'High Life' Barons, Counts, Ambassadors, Military attaches, etc. . . . Isn't it a change from the days of my early youth when fossils were the staple article? I am rather a lioness here, as there is no single scientist in this place among the foreigners." She was invited to parties at the Akasaka Palace, writing, "[I]t is frightfully select and I am awfully pleased to go."[33] There were clearly multiple logics of power that drove the early Western advocates to widen their area of influence on a global scale.

Western and Indian Advocates: A Symbiotic Relationship

Indians and Western advocates alike attempted to create a strong international support for birth control in order to win greater public acceptance for their controversial agendas domestically. Early Indian advocates corresponded regularly with their counterparts in the West. To engage wider public interest, Sanger organized international population and birth control conferences during the 1920s to which she invited prominent advocates from various countries. Ahluwalia presented papers at the International Birth Control conferences held in London in 1922 and in New York in 1923.[34] He corresponded with Stopes and contributed articles to Sanger's journal, *Birth Control Review* (BCR),[35] as did Pillay. The latter also communicated with C. P. Blacker, the secretary of the British Eugenic Society, from the 1930s onward.

At times, Western activists and their Indian counterparts shared an uneasy, even acrimonious, relationship. The tensions became particularly sharp when Indian advocates favored one Western personality over another within the birth control movement. Phadke, for instance, sought support from Sanger and extended his own support to her and her products, advocating the Dutch Cap as the more appropriate contraceptive instead of Stopes's favorite Pro-Race.[36] Phadke remained in Sanger's camp and asked her to write an introduction to his influential book. Generally, however, Indian advocates simultaneously corresponded with both Sanger and Stopes, trying not to antagonize either of them.

Indian intellectuals such as Rabindranath Tagore expressed support for birth control as early as 1925, sending open letters to Sanger and Stopes. Stopes wrote to Tagore, including membership forms, in the hope that he would accept her invitation to join the Society for Constructive Birth Control and Racial Progress (CBC) as one of its vice presidents.[37] In 1925, Tagore wrote to Sanger stating that he considered the birth control movement significant because it "saved women from enforced and undesirable maternity and helped the cause of peace by lessening the number of surplus population scrambling for food and space."[38] He asked Sanger to send him copies of her journal and complimented her commitment to the cause of birth control. On her first visit to India in 1935, Sanger solicited an appointment with him in Calcutta. Although Tagore recognized the importance of women exercising control over their own bodies and fertility, he regarded poverty and world strife as an effect of overpopulation. He did not question the unequal class distribution of resources and wealth.[39] Tagore, unlike Gandhi, was less suspicious of the enlightenment's project of modernity seeking to enhance control over life. For Tagore, the humanist position was acceptable because he expressed faith in the culture of modern science that aimed at providing greater control over "natural" phenomena such as reproduction. Tagore's position on population and on women's rights made him an acceptable ally of middle-class Western advocates who also did not question the social structures of class and race differences either at home or abroad.⁴⁰ Given class and caste oppressions in colonial India, as well as class and race stratification within British and American societies, speaking in the abstract about women's rights over their bodies was in keeping with an elite liberal position that sought to alter sexual and procreative behaviors while maintaining the status quo regarding inequalities based on class, caste, and race. Such articulations simplistically abstracted gender from other overlapping and intersecting axes of marginalization, failing to recognize how sexual procreative codes are constructed in very specific class, caste, and race contexts.

Western advocates selectively interacted with Indian political and social figures whom they identified as prominent players both within the Indian political landscape and abroad. For instance, Western enthusiasts did not woo Subhas Chandra Bose⁴¹ or B. R. Ambedkar, despite the early endorsement of birth control by these men. Western advocates selectively built alliances within India to make sure they did not engage themselves with the political debates within and among various contending nationalist factions, who were all throwing up their different imaginations for a free and independent nation. Both Bose and Ambedkar, unlike Gandhi, supported birth control. Deploying a Malthusian perspective, Bose argued that Indian population was expanding at a rate that could not keep pace with India's production levels: "[A] nation that lives in a state of chronic starvation is nevertheless multiplying at a rate that puts animals to shame. Is it right? What is the maximum population that India should have considering the food supply and industrial potentialities? If India has already reached that point, how should we check the further increase of population? Should artificial birth control be adopted as a public policy, seeing that birth control through self control has failed completely?"⁴² Ambedkar, leader of the untouchable Mahars in Maharashtra, espoused the cause of birth control from 1938.⁴³ He argued that it was not economically viable for lower-caste Indians to procreate limitlessly.⁴⁴ Ambedkar stressed the importance of survival rate rather than birthrates for his constituency, the Dalits, whom Gandhi later labeled *Harijans,* or children of God. Ambedkar argued that birth control would improve the health and financial condition of the Dalits. Moving a resolution on birth control in the Bombay Legislative Assembly on November 10, 1938, as leader of the Independent Party, he mentioned that the Indian poor, despite being illiterate, were intelligent enough to know where their interests lay and would fully utilize the invention of various contraceptives. He called for the government and municipal hospitals to provide vasectomy operations for poor men. It is important to note that Ambedkar was not interested in increasing the numbers of his constituency, unlike the upper-caste Hindu nationalist forces. Ambedkar asserted that

"Bombay is the gate-way of India and this movement [birth control] also entered this country through that very gate. It would be in the fitness of things, therefore, that it should also be nurtured in this very province."[45] His resolution was defeated; only eleven members voted in favor of it and fifty-two opposed it.

Despite articulating their support of the cause of birth control, neither Bose nor Ambedkar became important allies of Western advocates. One can speculate about the reason for the absence of these men within the rank of allies. On the one hand, it may well have been a result of the limited knowledge among foreign advocates about prominent players within Indian politics. Although there was one letter that Sanger's secretary sent to Ambedkar prior to Sanger's trip to India acknowledging his position on birth control, there are no records of Sanger meeting him while in India or of How-Martyn and Palmer making any contact with him during their numerous tours to India.[46] On the other hand, this absence of contact with Bose and more particularly Ambedkar may be revealing the limits of their one-point agenda for social transformation tied to the use and dissemination of contraceptive technology and information. Even while these Western advocates espoused somewhat radical ideas about gender politics, their class affiliations and political program were clearly middle class. Ambedkar's social base and his radical program of social transformation would have made him an unsuitable ally. Unlike the foreign advocates who were driven by eugenicist concerns, he was seeking to empower marginal social groups within Indian society and politics. From a socialist position, Bose too spoke to a diverse socioeconomic political constituency. Given the narrow and singular focus of their agenda, Western activists in India avoided being embroiled in public debates that did not focus exclusively on birth control.

Race politics also undermined the facade of international cooperation. Although there were working alliances between Indian and Western birth control activists from the early twentieth century, it is important to point out that within the international alliance, there were always differences between Sanger and Stopes. There were also significant differences between Western advocates and their Indian counterparts based on professional rivalry and race locations. Men and women in the West tried to ensure that they retained leadership of organizations and international forums on birth control. This was exemplified by the efforts to move the headquarters of the quarterly journal *Marriage Hygiene,* which Pillay began in 1934 in India, to either Britain or the United States. Pillay personally financed the journal during its initial period between 1934 and 1936. The correspondence exchanged between Norman Himes, the U.S. editor, and Edward Griffith, the British editor, reveals the antipathy of Western advocates toward Pillay. The correspondence between the editors in Britain and United States also clearly reflects their discomfort at having an Indian be the editor of a prestigious international journal. Havelock Ellis rated this journal as one of the best on the subject in English.[47] Ellis suggested that the journal should ultimately aim at becoming the literary organ of all organizations in the world working on family and sex.[48] Himes expressed reservations about the journal being published in India. He and the editor in Britain complained and grumbled to each other about Pillay. In his letter to Griffith, Himes wrote, "Pillay is obviously not the ablest man in the world; yet he is actually doing what others are talking about. I suppose it is true that we might get more support if the editor-in-chief were English. While I am an internationalist in spirit both in politics and certainly in science, I am willing to recognize practical obstacles."[49] Himes also complained that the cost of the journal was too high because it was being published in India, where the problem, according to him, was one of "cheap labor but low productivity." This problem, he argued, would be resolved if the site of publication shifted either to the United States or Britain.[50] C. P. Blacker of the Eugenic Society wrote to Griffith suggesting that his society would be willing to adopt a more-or-less friendly attitude toward the journal if it was published in England.[51] Because of the lack of international support, Pillay encountered financial difficulties that forced him to close down the journal in 1938. This journal would certainly have enjoyed a longer life if it had been published from somewhere in the West.

Different Western organizations and individuals supporting the project of birth control gave up aspirations of addressing diverse global concerns and limited themselves to what, by the 1940s, was understood as the real problem—the problem of too many colored folk! When Pillay wanted to restart the journal in 1947, Blacker, in a letter to Griffith, suggested that his organization would be willing to provide financial support to the journal, but only if it altered its "focus to solving specific Asiatic problems of religious and social mores affecting that continent's very high fertility." If that happened, Blacker continued, "then I would be very much in favor of the enterprise. There is now a widening opinion that the very high fertility rates of Asiatic countries must be lowered."[52] For Blacker, birth control in India was narrowly linked to population control rather than a mode for exploring more complex social and cultural issues related to family, marriage, sexuality, or women's empowerment. Although the Western advocates of birth control were eager to extend the use of contraceptives into India and were willing to work with Indian activists, they were not ready to relinquish leadership or control of the movement, or even of a prominent journal in the field, to individual Indians such as Pillay. Western activists and players also sought to dictate the terms of the work that needed to be undertaken in India in return for any financial or institutional help they were willing to extend to their Indian cohorts.

Competing Technologies

The issue of the "appropriate" contraceptive during the early twentieth century became a subject of contention among Western advocates, creating divisions even within the ranks of Indian advocates based on which method they were willing to support. Even though all advocates spoke urgently about the need for contraceptive information to be imparted to people, they were not certain about the most appropriate and suitable method to recommend. Although Sanger was trained as a medical nurse, she did not have the qualifications to develop contraceptives. Stopes, a paleobotanist, was not qualified for this job either. Contraceptive technology became an issue that created tensions between them and this was played out in their interactions with Indians with each trying to promote her preferred product over that of her rival.[53] Both Sanger and Stopes were anxious to introduce a universal contraceptive technology that they could claim as appropriate for subaltern groups across the world, be it poor Indian mothers, poor white and black women in South Africa, African American women in the United States, or working-class women in Britain. The lack of sensitivity toward introducing and promoting culturally appropriate technologies seems to have a long legacy, one that the interconnected history of birth control helps to bring to the fore most clearly.[54]

Stopes wrote to the editor of the Indian journal *Madras Birth Control Bulletin* (MBCB) asking him to publish her article on a method of contraceptives for Indian women, in which she claimed she would protect Indian women "from commercialism and enable them to obtain for themselves an absolutely simple and safe method of contraception which their circumstances require; not boosting commercial firms like the Holland-Rantes as Mrs. How-Martyn does."[55] In this same letter, Stopes also expressed her disagreements with How-Martyn and her International Center, demonstrating how tensions and disagreements in London were being played out in India. Stopes asked in her letter whether the editor of MBCB had inquired about How-Martyn's credentials in Britain, and then went on to give her assessment of How-Martyn's work. Stopes advised that "perhaps you do not know that her so-called 'International Center' was founded in 1930, the year when we accomplished the great events recorded in the enclosed *Birth Control News* for that year. Mrs. How-Martyn has not taken any part in our work; is not a member of our Society and the information given by her organization is very biased and incomplete as perhaps you will be able to judge for yourself in leaving out all mention of my books in the list of books supplied by 'International Center' on the subject."[56]

Western advocates also sought to test and introduce experimental contraceptive technology in India. Sanger and How-Martyn carried assorted technologies with them on their trips to India. They distributed contraceptives to Indian advocates and also tried to market them through specific chemists in the country. Stopes relied on correspondence and her books to express her preference for certain contraceptives over others. Visits to Stopes's clinic in London by Indian advocates were also a way by which the technology traveled from London to India. Both Sanger and Stopes had specific chemists in India through whom they supplied their preferred products. Indian journals such as the *Madras Birth Control Bulletin* and *Marriage Hygiene* carried advertisements for their products and as such became another site of competition for greater publicity for Stopes, Sanger, and How-Martyn.

Contraceptive technology, even in its initial, inadequately tested stages, had become a highly contested field of knowledge among Western advocates seeking to widen their clientele. Even though the stated purpose of the advocates was to provide cheap, accessible contraceptives to the poorer sections of the population in the world, they failed to share their "discoveries," competing instead for a larger market for their respective products. The CBC, in the postindependence period, sought agents in India who would be willing to stock a small supply of the special sponges and occlusive caps designed by Stopes and used in the London clinic.[57] Gandhi foresaw the contraceptive war between the early advocates, and wrote that the opposition to his advice was based on the loss that his simple method, abstinence, would cause to the birth control clinics and propagandists who would find their *trade* gone.[58]

Birth control advocates challenged Gandhi's opposition to birth control by highlighting the importance of new mechanical and chemical contraceptive technologies that they sought to introduce. Although the advocates made grandiose claims, there were serious limitations in terms of what they had to offer as contraceptive technologies during the early twentieth century. Competition between the advocates, and market concerns, drove them to make claims that were simply not borne out by scientific tests and empirical consumer data. A second and even more serious problem of the technological solutions advocates offered was the near-total disregard for the health of the women who were the intended consumers of this technology. The tension between the rhetoric and agenda of birth controllers was quite apparent, as the urgent call for disseminating contraceptive usage was not really matched with any viable technological innovation to realize this demand.

Sanger and How-Martyn supported the use of Duo-Foam as the most "suitable" contraceptive for India, apparently on the grounds of India's hot climate. According to How-Martyn, "[T]here is little doubt in my mind that it is the introduction of the foam-powder in India which has so stimulated the formation of clinics."[59] In Bombay, Stella and Company packaged and marketed Duo-Foam powder, and a year's supply cost about two rupees. Mr. Stevens of Stella and Company sent his agents to sell this product in Madras, Punjab, Calcutta, Karachi, and Gujarat. He insisted that to obtain a larger market, the product should not only be directed toward the mill workers, but toward clerks and some educated people too. He also proposed that in order to raise the sale of this product, there should be a fully trained nurse who would be a saleswoman conducting a door-to-door campaign trying to sell the product to potential consumers.[60] Clearly, Stevens was interested in capturing a large market for his product. Securing the Indian market for their respective contraceptive became an issue of contention among Western advocates.

During her visit to India in 1938, How-Martyn had an interview with Stevens. From this interview, it appears that Duo-Foam was introduced in India in 1937, but it drew complaints from some consumers from the very outset. From 1937 to 1938, within one year, the sales of the product had declined from 1,911 packages to 1,621. Most of the sales were to medical doctors, who ordered in bulk and distributed it to their patients. In their interview, Stevens mentioned that he had received many complaints from doctors about the product. In a letter to Stella and Company, Dr. (Mrs.) Sen from Calcutta complained that many of her patients suffered from a "terrible burning" caused by the use of the powder.[61]

Other complaints that the Bombay company received were about the shape and size of the sponge—essentially, the sponge was not large enough. Stevens thought of introducing circular sponges instead of the square ones that were in use, but that raised financial issues because the cost of the circular sponges would be more than those already in use. The company also had trouble advertising the product because it did not have enough literature and information on Duo-Foam and was reluctant to translate the advertisement into the vernacular. Moreover, the company gathered that the powder was not doing too well in the market because medical doctors were recommending pessaries and jelly to their patients rather than the powder.[62] Eileen Palmer and How-Martyn, in their interviews with Pillay, heard additional complaints about the powder. Pillay reported that his private patients found this method of contraception unsatisfactory, and in the clinical tests done for this product, patients complained about irritation caused by its use.[63]

In How-Martyn's meetings with other medical doctors who gave out contraceptive information and provided their patients with contraceptives, some spoke of the success they had with the foam powder. Dr. Rose Beals, a missionary who worked in Wai Hospital in western India, reported that she had fitted fifty cases and followed up on all of them. Only one pregnancy was reported in a woman who did not always use it, and two cases of complaint were from women who had put on too much powder.[64] According to Beals, physicians needed to instruct their patients in the use of foam powder, and this was certainly not a method that required no medical supervision, as Sanger and How-Martyn had suggested. Dr. S. Pandit of Dufferin Hospital in Calcutta reported that she had recommended the powder to her patients and was satisfied with its success rate. She kept detailed records of the number of patients to whom she recommended birth control, and there was a steady rise in the number of cases from 1935 to 1938. The total number of patients in 1938 was 138, with the majority between twenty to thirty-five years of age. Their reasons women sought contraceptive advice varied: family spacing, medical, and financial were cited. Dr. Pandit recommended foam powder to 88 of the 138 women who visited her clinic. Women complained about the foam method being messy, whereas those using a jelly and cap were satisfied. There had also been two complaints of failure, which Pandit argued may well have resulted from the patient's failure to carry out the instructions properly.[65]

Sanger, writing from Calcutta, mentioned that for a contraceptive to be successful in India, it would need to be of the "simplest and cheapest kind." Primary concern was with the efficacy of contraceptive technology rather than with its safety. In December 1935, she recommended what she then called the Duponol foam powder and sponge method for India, which would cost only U.S. 10 cents for a year's supply.[66] This method had not been adequately tested in the United States, and by 1936 there were complaints about this method in the United States. In a confidential letter to Margaret Sanger, Helen Countryman wrote, "The colored people said that Duponol made too much foam and was messy in some instances. Mrs. Boggs said that this was true since colored people carry on coitus for one half to two hours while white persons generally have a much shorter relation. I think this is interesting and essential in giving out material. As a result Fem-Foam or Dr. DeVilbiss' powder is better for colored people and Duponol for white people."[67] From the above illustration, one can conclude that appropriate contraceptive technology was decided on the basis of cultural assumptions and ideas of racialized sexualities of men and women. Somewhat similar assumptions about race informed the advocacy of contraceptive technologies in India.

Although the foam powder was not a clinically tested and approved contraceptive method, Sanger and How-Martyn, during their tour in India in 1935–36, were promoting it as the most appropriate and suitable form of contraceptive for Indians. One example of the many problems women had with using the powder is evident from the report about a "woman who came to the clinic with very severe inflammation since she had emptied nearly half the container on to the sponge because her housing condition was so bad that she could not see how much powder she was putting on."[68] As more consumers reported dissatisfaction, Sanger sought cooperation from Indian advocates seeking information on the formula of the powder being used in India and requesting the completion of a questionnaire about the product by its users and by Indian doctors who were recommending it to their patients. Sanger wanted to know the number of women who had complained about the product because she claimed that at least 100,000 people were using this method in various parts of the world and while there were "a few scattered complaints, they do not amount to any more in numbers than those who complain of other methods, such as boric acid, lactic acid, quinine and other chemical ingredients which sometimes proved irritating to those who have a particular idiosyncrasy for those drugs."[69]

Like Sanger and How-Martyn, Stopes claimed that after considering the specific conditions of Indian women, she had "thought out a special substitute adapted for the poorest Indian Women." This method, Stopes stressed, had the advantage of not costing anything and the woman did not need to go to any special shop or person to buy anything, for she could make what she required herself in her own house from materials available there. The method was mainly for poor Indian women, Stopes argued, because they could not afford the price of a rubber cap and she also doubted if they could be relied upon to place the rubber cap accurately each time.[70] What Stopes was promoting as an "ideal" contraceptive for working women in India consisted of cotton waste dipped in bland cooking oil to form a barrier past which the fertilizing spermatozoa would not be able to enter. However, such rough-and-ready methods were, of course, class specific. "For the well-to-do Indian woman, educated, and with sufficient money to spend on hygienic requirements, some *scientific and precise method may be better suited*," she said.[71] Stopes argued that poor Indian women could not be relied upon to use the more scientific and precise methods. What was being offered to the poorer Indian women, while certainly more economical, was a method whose efficacy Stopes doubted herself.

In her books, Stopes also promoted the use of the Pro-Race Cap. A few Indians used this method but it failed to prevent conception. S. N. Datar in Gujarat wrote to Stopes that his wife had become pregnant despite using the Pro-Race Cap. He also mentioned that he received advice from R. D. Karve in Bombay to use the Dutch Cap rather than Pro-Race. Datar was confused by this conflicting advice and by the failure of the Pro-Race pessary to prevent conception. Frustrated, he added that now he did not believe in birth control methods, neither the Pro-Race nor the Dutch pessaries. Stopes's reply to his letter was terse: "A woman cannot wear a cap if she is lacerated."[72]

Although market considerations were important to Western advocates in their work in countries such as India, they were not necessarily the guiding principles of their work. Sanger and Stopes masked their differences and relations of ruling among women to espouse an imperial feminist sentiment grounded in shared biological experiences of pregnancy and motherhood. They both supported a eugenicist understanding of the population issue; for them, India represented a dysgenic population that needed to have lower fertility rates than the white races of the Western nations. Sanger, in requesting funds from C. P. Blacker of the London Eugenic Society for her international trip, constructed her agenda in eugenic and racist terms. She wrote, "In my coming campaign I hope to do the preliminary work for realizing two aims—first, to bring to the *poorer and biologically worse endowed stocks the knowledge of birth control* that is already prevalent among those who are both genetically and economically better favored, and secondly, to bring the birth rates of the East more in line with those of England and the civilizations of the West."[73]

The limits of the universalism of science and technology that the Western advocates claimed for their agenda were also revealed through the racial prejudices so evident in their writings about India and their relations with their Indian "allies." In a letter to Sanger from India written in February 1935, How-Martyn indicates her intolerance and racist attitude toward the people on whose behalf the Western advocates claimed to be working. She wrote, "But how humanity breeds here. No registration of deaths, so infanticide, abortion and even stealthy murders can go on unchecked. *Sanitation they will not understand.* Cows and other animals wander almost anywhere unmolested. They bathe in the Ganges. Yet for the most part they are attractive good looking, quiet and *have the animals unquestioning acceptance of life as it is and its surroundings.* So far as we have been there has been no beautiful scenery and nothing like the colour and glamour I expected."[74] Adding to the condescending representations of Indians, when writing to Mrs. Elmhirst in England for funding to continue the work in India, Sanger wrote, "[A]ll the prognostications concerning what the Indian women would and would not do have been unjustified. All that they need is encouragement, a little stimulation from authoritative sources and a general educational campaign on sex hygiene and birth control, such as we have had to do in America and other countries."[75] Clearly, despite her claim that birth control would give Indian women more control over their lives, Sanger's attitude remained patronizing at best and in many ways paralleled colonial representations of Indians as passive subjects in need of authoritative figures from the West to guide and provide a civilizing influence.

Political Contentions: Gandhi and Western Advocates

From 1915 onward, Gandhi emerged as a prominent figure on the Indian political landscape, making him one of India's most popular leaders. Western advocates of birth control were quick to recognize Gandhi's importance in shaping Indian popular opinion. Given his reluctance to espouse chemical and mechanical contraceptives, Sanger in particular sought to "convert" him into a supporter of the birth control cause. Sanger and Stopes both claimed that contraceptives would allow women freedom from unwanted pregnancies and believed that birth control would liberate and free women. Yet on these issues in particular they failed in their task and came up against Gandhi.

Gandhi strongly advocated *brahmacharya,* by which he meant control over all senses, including the sexual. Because he believed that women were sexually passive and apathetic, he primarily addressed men while speaking of the ideal of attaining control over one's senses, betraying an underlying masculinist premise that informed his understanding. Gandhi wrote:

> I do not believe that woman is prey to sexual desire to the same extent as man. It is easier for her than for man to exercise self-restraint. I hold that the right education in this country is to teach the woman the art of saying *no* even to her husband, to teach her that it is no part of her duty to become a mere tool or a doll in her husband's hands. She has rights as well as duties. . . . To ask India's women to take to contraceptives is, to say the least, putting the cart before the horse. The first thing is to free her from mental slavery, to teach her dignity of national service and service to humanity.[76]

In his interviews with How-Martyn, Gandhi further articulated his objection to the use of contraceptives. "Contraceptives are an insult to womanhood. The difference between a prostitute and a woman using contraceptives is only this that the former sells her body to several men, the latter sells it to one man. Man has no right to touch his own wife so long as she does not wish to have a child, and the woman should have the will power to resist her own husband."[77] Gandhi feared that birth control would lead to heightened expressions of nonprocreative sex within marriage. His strong opposition to birth control, therefore, was based on his larger distrust of sexuality, particularly male sexuality. He idealized femininity, regarding women to be sexually passive, and therefore argued that the advocacy of birth control on their behalf would only further degrade them because it would make it possible for men to use women for lust. Gandhi regarded male sexuality as aggressive and argued that men had to exercise control over themselves if they meant to liberate women: "It is not she who tempts. In reality man being the aggressor is the real culprit and the tempter."[78] He celebrated feminine virtues of sexual restraint over what he regarded as masculine sexual excesses. For Gandhi, it was the masculine that invoked phantoms of social disruption and required regulation and restraint. Male sexual excesses, Gandhi argued, led to weak bodies and weak minds, which in turn resulted in social and national disruptions. Gandhi emphasized the need for strict sexual discipline of the self, particularly for men. He warned against sexual dangers, not allowing any room to explore sexual pleasures even within matrimony—the otherwise traditionally accepted legitimate space for such expressions.

For Gandhi, the site for legitimate expressions of even limited sexual desires was matrimony. However, even sex within marriage was to be strictly confined to the act of procreation. It was, he claimed, a "sacred" rite "to be performed prayerfully," and not something "designed to provide sexual excitement or pleasure." If there was no desire for progeny, there was no need for marriage, Gandhi said, as he did not believe in "platonic marriages."[79] Elimination of pregnancy as a physical consequence of sex, Gandhi feared, would lead to moral and social corruption and chaos. Gandhi sought to write out all nonprocreative sexual expressions, while Sanger and Stopes sought to claim sexual expression equally for women and men, divorcing marital sex from procreation. Despite the differences of opinions among them, both Gandhi and the birth control advocates were seeking to alter and manage sexual expression within heterosexual conjugality.

Gandhi believed in the "uncleanliness of sex," seeking and preaching ways to overcome sexual passions through fasting, because the principle of self control had to be extended to all senses including the organ of taste.[80] Besides fasting, the reading of the *Ramayana* or a similar religious text was considered the most powerful ally in conquering animal passion.[81] Sex was akin to "animal passion."[82] He advocated the need for sex education, with the objective of conquest and sublimation of the sexual passion. The right kind of education, he argued, would bring home to children "the essential distinction between man and brute, to make them realize that it is man's special privilege and pride to be gifted with the faculties of head and heart both; that he is a thinking no less than a feeling animal.... In man, reason quickens and guides feelings." Gandhi evoked religious idioms to convey his meaning, arguing that all "great religions have rightly regarded '*kama*' [lust] as the arch enemy of man, anger or hatred coming only in second place."[83] Sexual restraint as one of the basic Gandhian principles was clearly spelled out in the context of the birth control debates in colonial India.

Engaging with Gandhi, Sanger entered into a long dialogue with him in December 1935 while she was in India. How-Martyn also made time to speak with Gandhi in February 1935, seeking to convince him of the need for the use of contraceptives in India. They both tried to influence Gandhi by talking about the issue with some of his close friends, especially Charles F. Andrews and Jawaharlal Nehru. Although Sanger spent time speaking with Gandhi and claimed that he made concessions to her point of view in accepting the adoption of a "safe period" as the method of birth control, she was disappointed in Gandhi's refusal to regard the propagation of birth control knowledge as the "solution" to Indian women's problems.

Stopes, instead of trying to gain Gandhi's approval, wrote a scathing review of his book *Self-Restraint versus Self-Indulgence* in 1930 and asked Indian editors of national journals to publish her review of the book.[84] In her review, Stopes accused Gandhi of writing on birth control without having read the available literature on it, and claimed that he had not heard of her "medical" textbooks nor of the results of the thousands of cases at the CBC and other clinics. Questioning Gandhi's leadership, Stopes wrote that it was the "generosity of the British people" who had "pampered the egotism and disruptive folly of Gandhi, treating him as though he were a simple saint."[85]

Stopes argued that it was Gandhi's opposition to birth control that was responsible for the increase in India's population. "Even if we gave half of our too meager rations we could not feed that one decade of Indian increase insufficiently." Her remedy for what she called the "flood of undesired and unhappy births" was to allow her to broadcast repeatedly in every Indian language so as to reach all Indians. She claimed she had help and enlightenment to offer to the unhappy women of India whose cries of help often reached her, but in turn her response to those cries was diverted and therefore she warned that the peace of the world was at stake![86]

In Stopes's critiques of Gandhi, the major difference was their divergent understanding of sexuality and of sex within marriage. Stopes was an ardent advocate of sexual liberation and called for divorcing sex from reproduction. She argued that sex within marriage was an integral part of matrimony and was important for both men and women. Stopes questioned the notion of passive female sexuality to highlight what she called the "periodicity of recurrence of desire in women."[87] She celebrated female sexual desire as positive. When asked about the effects of masturbation on a widow of sixty-eight, she replied, "That she does have sex feelings is a sign of strength and vitality and she is to be congratulated and encouraged."[88] Stopes embraced and celebrated female expressions of sexual desires. Gandhi essentially regarded women as sexually passive. The two therefore brought their very different understandings of sex, especially female sexuality, to defend their opposing articulations on the subject of birth control.

Indian men sent numerous letters to Stopes seeking birth control information and also sexual advice. Stopes answered with information about Indian chemists who sold contraceptives or references to one of her books for more information regarding their particular sexual problem. As early as 1921, A. R. Bustani from the Bombay General Traffic Managers office wrote to request a dozen copies of *Letters to Working Mothers* and information on firms that sold the "gold pin" or "wish bone" pessaries that Stopes wrote about in her book *Wise Parenthood*.[89] She also received letters seeking specific information on sexual matters. For instance, T. V. Venkateswara Aiyar from Vellore also wrote to her in 1921, asking about how best to ensure sexual satisfaction of the woman, referring to Stopes's writing that sexual satisfaction for a woman was as important as it was for a man.[90] In 1931, C. P. R. Ayyar inquired about how best to ensure the woman reaches "complete satisfaction."[91] In her reply, Stopes suggested he read her book *Enduring Passion*. For these correspondents, Stopes functioned as a sexologist who provided answers to their intimate sexual problems in an unconventional manner—through overseas post.[92]

Stopes was greatly influenced by sexologists and the feminist movement that was beginning to assert female sexual impulses as "natural" and therefore inherently "good."[93] In contesting some of Gandhi's views on sex, Stopes asserted that sex was a "beautiful mutual relation between man and woman immeasurably higher than anything which appears to have yet entered his mind as a human possibility." The use of contraceptives, she argued, made it possible for "parents to have the God-given need for mutual coitus satisfied wholesomely and properly."[94] Claiming that sex was "God-given" was a rhetorical device aimed at naturalizing it, seeking to blunt any negative associations of human sexuality. In complete contrast, using the language of sexology allowed Stopes to speak in an authoritative tone of a discipline newly claiming, and in large measure being granted, decisive authority in social and cultural issues.[95] Both Sanger and Stopes were products of the modernist project that sought to enhance control over life through rationalizing reproduction with the adoption of new technologies—technologies that they claimed could be mass-produced and distributed. Gandhi, in turn, was deeply suspicious of modernity and technology, and he conceived the world from a moral perspective—in which, though, the body was also equally deeply implicated.

According to Stopes, Gandhi's opposition to the use of contraceptives on the grounds that their use would cause "imbecility and nervous prostration" was "complete and arrant nonsense" stemming from his ignorance on the subject of both human sexuality and the use of artificial contraceptives.[96] Gandhi's position on sex and his opposition to the use of contraceptives were, according to Stopes, those of an ascetic calling upon people to lead "unnatural lives of deprivation and consequent deterioration" and based more on superstition rather than on science.[97] From Stopes's perspective, a modern subject of desire was a natural subject, a subject that the force of modern science of sexology had sanctioned and acknowledged. For a modernist such as Stopes, "science" represented an incontestable truth based on sound principles of experimentation and observation and as such was understood to be above human intervention and subjective biases. In her estimation, any contestation of the given "scientific" truth reflected a flawed understanding based on superstition—the "other" of science.

Sanger, although not as aggressively as Stopes, questioned some of Gandhi's ideas on sex within marriage and the use of contraceptives in "Does Gandhi Know Women? What He Told Me at Wardha," an article based on interviews with him.[98] She challenged Gandhi's claim that he knew "tens of thousands of women in India," adding that she was better placed to "know their experiences and aspirations" than Gandhi, writing, "I have discussed it [family relations] with some of my educated sisters but I have questioned their authority to speak on behalf of their unsophisticated sisters because they have never mixed with them. The educated ones have never felt one with them. They have regarded me as half a woman because I have completely identified myself with them.... I feel I speak with some confidence because I have worked with and talked with and studied many women."[99] According to Sanger, Gandhi did not have the "faintest glimmering of either the experiences or the aspirations, or the inner workings of a woman's mind, heart, or being." Sanger asserted that she knew more than Gandhi about what women in India wanted through her work with tens of thousands of women in twenty years. She claimed to have had private talks and intimate confessions from thousands of women of all nations, all religions, and all classes. These women, she said, had "shared their sorrows and their joys, as well as their hopes and longings. And I believe firmly that the heart of the Indian woman is not different from the heart of the American, Chinese, Italian, or European woman where love is concerned." Sanger's celebration of "universal sisterhood" obliterated differences among women and failed to see gender identities as being inflected by social stratifications such as class, caste, community, or race.[100] While evoking a sentiment of "universal sisterhood," Sanger allowed for *no* recognition of power differentials between herself as an enfranchised Western elite woman and the colonized Indian woman on whose behalf she claimed to be speaking and acting.

The Gandhian emphasis on sexual restraint within marriage, Sanger claimed, would lead to the breakdown of Indian family structures because "there would be no loving glances, no tender good night kisses, no gentle words of endearments lest such attentions, such natural expressions of affection might excite the sexual emotions." Gandhi's advice would create "calamity in Indian life" because "no husband could or would remain devoted very long if his emotions and instincts were continually denied expression by the wife he loves." By resisting their husbands, Indian women would bring "dissension into their happy home." According to Sanger, the solution to their problem "lay in the simple birth control methods which science has brought forward." Interestingly, in critiquing Gandhi's position, Sanger was upholding Indian men's conjugal rights. Women were being advised not to resist their husbands sexually, but rather to adopt the use of contraceptives and be sexually accommodating to maintain peace and tranquility within the family. Sanger was calling for a liberal feminist accommodation within patriarchal heterosexual conjugality rather than make an argument for women's right to sexual expression without the fear of pregnancy. As we see in the next chapter, Indian feminists too were careful not to link contraceptives to female sexual freedom. Within the context of Gandhian nationalism, celebration of female sexuality could not be deployed as a significant organizing frame without some serious negative political implications.

In contesting Gandhi's views on sex, Sanger stressed the difference between "sex love" and "sex lust." For her, sex was a positive force that could be "transmuted from lust into beauty." "Women in their own lives and relationships with men transmuted this force into one of the most stimulating, beautifying, spiritual acts of human experience," she said. Sanger was a product of the "new morality" of the early twentieth century, where questioning Victorian values about sexuality was becoming more prominent among middle-class and elite women. Sanger, like Stopes, was also a liberal feminist who argued that control over one's own body was the most basic and inviolable fundamental aspect of being an individual. She argued that "no woman can call herself free who does not own and control her own body. No woman can call herself free until she can choose consciously whether she will or will not be a mother." As Carole McCann argues, for Sanger, "self-possession of the body and self-regulation of its processes were the grounds of political autonomy."[101]

Gandhi was one of the few prominent Indian male political leaders who wrote extensively on related issues of female and male sexuality, sex within marriage, and on the use of contraceptives. His was, then, an important voice shaping the sexual landscape in colonial India in the early twentieth century, even as he challenged the assertions of birth control advocates. As a political leader and social thinker, Gandhi was one of the most complex and contradictory personalities within modern Indian history. Some scholars have sought to understand the multivalence of Gandhian discourse, speaking of him as one man with many personalities.[102] For the purposes of this chapter, Gandhi's articulations on the women's question and on subjects of sex and conjugality capture well the productive paradoxes in his positions that simultaneously challenged and reaffirmed the patriarchal sexual code.

Gandhi's opposition to contraceptive use can be better understood within his larger views on the role of women. Gandhi naturalized a sexual division of labor, arguing that equality of the sexes did not mean equality of occupations. Unraveling patriarchal assumptions, Gandhi essentialized gendered divisions, writing that although "there may be no legal bar against woman hunting or wielding a lance . . . she instinctively recoils from a function that belongs to man. Nature has created sexes as complements of each other. Their functions are defined as are their forms."[103] He held women, as mothers, largely responsible for shaping future Indian citizens: "The future of India lies on your knees, for you will nurture the future generations. You can bring up children of India to become simple, God-fearing and brave men and women, or you can coddle them to be weaklings, unfit to brave the storms of life and used to foreign fineries which they would find difficult in after-life to discard."[104] Gandhi naturalized motherhood for women, and in his worldview, Indian women remained associated with maternal attachments. The Gandhian definition of the category of "woman" was in part shaped and produced as an effect of patriarchal power. Gandhian insistence on normative gender dualism did not allow for a historical recognition of the internal fluidity and complexities of women's and men's experiences, especially as these were shaped through their different class, caste, race, or sexual locations.

Historians of Indian women have argued that Gandhi was instrumental in making it possible for large numbers of Indian women to participate in public-sphere politics in the early twentieth century. His personality, and his political modalities of *satyagraha* and nonviolence, made it possible for women to join in the public struggles against British imperialism.[105] Gandhi saw in women the necessary "qualities" for being *satyagrahis* because, according to him, women were inertly passive and nonviolent by nature. "All the evidence in my possession goes to show that it is man who lacks the power of self-restraint more than woman."[106] Gandhi regarded women as "mother of man and trustee of the virtue of her progeny."[107] Gandhi stripped women of sexual desires and reaffirmed motherhood as the natural vocation for women.

In the celebration of sex and of bodily pleasures, Gandhi saw reflections of what he called the "curse of modern civilization." He argued that modern civilization had taken hold of Europe and, as a result, Europeans lacked real physical strength or courage because they were seeking to increase bodily comforts. The basis of this civilization was to make bodily welfare the object of life.[108] Overindulgence of the human body, according to Gandhi, was the curse of modern civilization, and the use of contraceptives was just another instance of such bodily indulgence. In his analysis, contraceptives left the human body and mind weak and exhausted. Overindulgence of bodily pleasures in the name of "civilization" only resulted in depriving people of self-control and making them effeminate.[109] Of course, Gandhi celebrated manhood based on moral strength rather than on brute physical force and he argued that "a man devoid of courage and manhood can never be a passive resister."[110] Simultaneously, though, he maintained that Indians needed to "improve our physiques by getting rid of infant marriages and luxurious living." And the way to become a strong passive resister was through observing perfect chastity, adopting poverty, following truth, and cultivating fearlessness. Gandhi argued that without chastity, "the mind cannot attain requisite firmness. A man who is unchaste loses stamina, becomes emasculated and cowardly. He whose mind is given over to animal passions is not capable of any great effort."[111] In Gandhi's estimation, sex was a lowly animal instinct, an instinct that man should strive to overcome and control. In Gandhian sexual imagery, therefore, liberation, particularly male/masculine liberation, was tied to desexed corporeality.

Gandhi regarded sex as an unclean negative force that utterly emasculated the body and the mind.[112] He wrote, "I can affirm without the slightest hesitation, from my own experience as well as that of others, that sexual enjoyment is not only not necessary for, but is positively injurious to health. All the strength of body and mind that has taken long to acquire is lost all at once by a single dissipation of vital energy."[113] Writing from personal experience, Gandhi maintained that "I am not aware of having derived any benefit, mental, spiritual or physical. [from sex]. Momentary excitement and satisfaction there certainly was. But it was invariably followed by exhaustion. And the desire for union returned immediately the effect of exhaustion had worn out."[114] Further, he went on to add, "[i]t is being said that restraint and abstinence are wrong and free satisfaction of the sexual appetite and free love is the most natural thing. There was never a more ruinous superstition."[115] Reversing Sanger's and Stopes's construction of sex and sexuality, Gandhi suggested their opinions were based on mere superstition rather than reflecting some scientific "regimes of truth" about human beings.

According to Gandhi, sex within marriage had to be strictly functional and restricted to procreation. Gandhi posed a direct challenge to the celebration of sexuality and conjugal love that birth control advocates espoused in the early twentieth century. Because Gandhi believed that to have more than three or four children was immoral, sexual union within marriage was to be confined to three or four times.[116] Quoting a fourth-century treatise attributed to Manu,[117] Gandhi claimed that only the firstborn child could be described as born of *dharma* (duty or religion); the rest, as born of *kama*—lust.[118] Gandhi's "solution" for married people was that the husband and wife should make a fixed resolution never to share the same room or the same bed at night.[119] In this one injunction, Stopes seems to have shared Gandhi's views, although for completely opposite reasons! Stopes advised married couples to have separate bedrooms because, according to her, this practice preserved "modesty and romance" within marriage.[120] Gandhi, in turn, advised husbands to avoid privacy with their wives, adding that "whenever they [husband and wife] feel a craving for sexual indulgence, they should bathe in cold water, so that the heat of passion may be cooled down, and be refined into the energy of virtuous activity."[121] Although Gandhi shared the interest that the birth control advocates had in mapping the intimate and managing the domestic space, his understanding of conjugality differed dramatically from Sanger's and Stopes's idealization of compatibility, friendship, and sexual and romantic love.

Unlike some of the birth control advocates both in India and abroad, Gandhi did not argue for the need to limit procreation from a Malthusian understanding. "If it is contended that birth control is necessary for the nation because of over-population, I dispute the proposition. It has never been proved. In my opinion, by a proper land system, better agriculture and a supplementary industry, this country is capable of supporting twice as many people as there are in it today."[122] Gandhi presented an oppositional counterdiscourse, making a case for distributive justice. His was a lone voice that called for land reforms and argued that the "solution" to poverty and population lay in equal distribution of resources rather than on any inherent principle underlined by Malthus.

Unlike Western and some prominent Indian advocates, Gandhi tied his critiques of sexuality to imperialism. He argued that sexual self-control was particularly necessary for India under colonialism, once again framing sexuality as an object of nationalist gaze and inquiry. "Is it right for us" he asked,

> who know the situation to bring forth children in an atmosphere so debasing as I have described? We only multiply slaves and weaklings, if we continue the process of procreation while we feel and remain helpless, diseased, and famine stricken. Not till India has become a free nation, able to withstand avoidable starvation, well able to feed herself in times of famine . . . have we the right to bring forth progeny. I must not conceal from the reader the sorrow I feel when I hear of births in this land. . . . India is today ill-equipped for taking care even of her present population, not because she is over-populated, but because she is forced to foreign domination whose creed is progressive exploitation of her resources.[123]

He argued against the president of the Indian Medical Board, who claimed that famines in India were the result of high birthrates. Gandhi asserted that the argument of high birthrate was a way of diverting the attention from the real cause of recurring famines in India. A famine, Gandhi said, was not a "calamity descended upon us from nature but is a calamity created by the rulers whether through ignorant indifference or whether consciously or otherwise does not matter."[124]

Nowhere in their writings did the Western advocates speak of repeated famines in India or present a critique of colonialism. On the contrary, it can be argued that they represented themselves as agents of empire. While Sanger and Stopes spoke of the need for Indian women to determine their own sexuality and control over their bodies as the basis of liberal subjectivities, they did not stop to consider the political and economic consequences of colonialism, which denied basic rights of personhood to its colonized populations. These advocates, and their Indian counterparts, abstracted sexual rights, privileging discussions on sex, leaving out other social, political, and economic determinants shaping the lives of women on whose behalf they claimed to be speaking.

Ironically, despite Gandhi's emphasis on celibacy and its importance for regenerating national health, he shared an understanding about the profound power of sexuality with the birth control advocates—together their different voices engendered a productive discourse on sexuality and opened up private issues for passionate public debate and discussion. Sanger and Stopes became popular among Indian middle-class men and women, who associated these two women not only with birth control but also sex reforms. Indian men and women wrote to them seeking advice on suitable methods of contraceptives and on private sexual problems. Stopes in particular received letters from Indian men seeking information on how to improve their marital sexual life. In their letters, middle-class educated Indian men represented sex within marriage as an important component of marital bliss. The early-twentieth-century focus on sex within marriage was an extension of the ideal of compatible conjugality as articulated in the late nineteenth century, with its emphasis on intellectual compatibility. Throughout the debates on birth control in the early twentieth century, physical and sexual compatibility within marriage were presented as important components for happy and successful marriages. The use of birth control, it was argued, would ensure happier families. This argument sought to "domesticate" the use of contraceptives, countering those who asserted that contraceptives subverted the main purpose of marriage; that is, procreation.[125]

Patriarchal understanding shaped Gandhi's ideas of gender relations, whereby he deployed rather than questioned gender polarities. His representations of feminine and masculine characteristics affirmed gendered identities. For instance, Gandhi represented sexual passion in negative masculine terms. Masculinist mythologies and assumptions underlined his constructions of female sexual passivity, renewing social pressures on women to be sexually virtuous and modest. There was a dangerous split in his gendered representation of sexuality, whereby he projected all negative values onto men and masculinity. Despite these limitations in Gandhian sexual politics, Gandhi challenged the Western advocates, questioning the teleology of birth control as necessarily liberatory and empowering. Moreover, his recalcitrance to modernity posed important questions for which we have no ready answers.

Conclusion

Even though this chapter pointed out the rather precarious interactions among Western advocates, their Indian contemporaries, and their potential Indian consumers, it argued for the need to place the history of birth control in India within a larger geographical framework. The emphasis on interconnected histories helps to situate the historical dynamics of the debates and the development of contraceptive technologies. While focusing on the activities of Western women advocates, the chapter at the same time emphasized that their global agenda of birth control can only be understood in the context of local politics. Sanger and Stopes, despite their significant differences, were no doubt driven by domestic politics in their respective home countries. For their Indian allies, the support—moral, financial, and institutional—that an alliance with these prominent figures offered was of considerable significance.

However, the ways in which local concerns inflected these global movements are brought home very clearly through examining, first, the discussions on contraceptive technology. Even while the Western advocates were competing for international influence and promoting their respective contraceptive technologies as most "appropriate" for use in India, these technologies were still very much at an experimental stage. What these early birth control advocates, both Indian and Western, had to offer was strong rhetoric supporting the need for wider knowledge of the possibility of fertility control. Safe technology to make the use of contraceptives more popular and accessible was not available; instead what was available were very rudimentary methods that consumers found largely unsatisfactory during the 1920s and 1930s.

Even when the global inadequacy in technological developments limited the grandiose claims of the Western advocates, a closer examination of their rhetoric and politics shows that other, more parochial concerns, including the quest for fame, status, and power, significantly fueled the politics of the Western advocates. Racial and class prejudice, however, was probably the most evident example of the limits of a truly inclusive global agenda. Although Western advocates, particularly Sanger, were eager to get feedback on their products in India, they were unwilling to relinquish any aspect of the intellectual leadership of this movement to Indians as is evident through the exchanges between Himes and Griffith and between Pillay and Blacker. They were keen to maintain their intellectual hegemony over the movement, and when they could not do so, they did not support the work being done in India. British and American editors wanted Pillay to transfer *Marriage Hygiene* either to Britain or the United States. When Pillay was unwilling to do so, they preferred to let the journal cease publication as a result of lack of funds rather than continue to support publication in India.

Ultimately, perhaps, nothing reveals the connections and contradictions between the local and global better than the sorts of debates on sexuality that ensued, although the intervention of Western birth enthusiasts Stopes and Sanger posited a universalist notion of female sexuality and maternal corporeality and deployed that to justify the introduction of contraceptive technology. They claimed that sexual desire was a positive physical and psychological phenomenon and an important component of modern compatible conjugality. Through introducing contraceptive technologies, these advocates in effect claimed to be "liberating" Indian women who were, however, perceived as not being able to represent their own true desires. This universalist notion of sexual desire successfully concealed more parochial feminist concerns, limited not only through race but class and national politics as well.

In contrast to this, Gandhi offered an alternative vision that demonized sexual desires, linking the untrammeled gratification of sexual desires to his larger critique of Western civilization. For Gandhi, sexual control was the real problem; in his vision of matrimony, there was no room for sexual pleasures because he regarded these as subverting social values. Sexual desire, in his view, was far from liberating; rather, it was disruptive, dissipating not just individual bodies but also the larger social body. Therefore, Gandhi stressed the importance of sexual self-discipline, particularly for men. What Gandhi presented in place of the new ideal of sexual compatibility was the rationalist limitation of sexual expression within matrimony to its functionalist purpose of procreation. Taking this local, though undoubtedly patriarchal, critique of the universalist notions of sexuality into consideration reveals the extent to which universalist notions of sexuality were, in fact, parochial and products of a specific culture that served to conceal provincial agendas.

At best, Gandhi's legacy is ambivalent. It is not easy to dismiss his views, like Stopes did, or to assume that his perspective was uninformed by women, as Sanger asserted. He operated within a dualistic gendered understanding, but simultaneously he challenged the gendered creation of the public domain, with the "rational man at the center and embodied woman at the periphery."[126] Gandhi's antimodernist cultural nationalism posed an important challenge to the dominant Western definitions of the self. However, despite differences between Gandhi and the Western advocates, there were some important overlaps in their perspectives, which allowed for little to no variations on feminine experiences and desires in either of their articulations. While Western advocates evoked a universal category, "woman," in making a case for contraceptive dissemination, in his strong opposition to contraceptive technology and usage, Gandhi was locked within an essentialist patriarchal dualism that denied women sexual expression even within matrimony.

As is evident from the discussion in this chapter, Western advocates made a case for contraceptive use in the name of the Indian woman, and Gandhi opposed the introduction of these technologies, also in the name of the Indian woman. For the most part, they allowed little room for real

Indian women's voices in their deliberations on the subject, and neither of their positions served to promote women's reproductive freedoms. To remedy this, in part, the next chapter focuses on the writings of Indian middle-class women leaders to render the complexity of their positions visible on the subject and explores how their interventions shaped the public debates on birth control in colonial India.

3 Polyvocality, Ambivalence, and Negotiations: Indian Middle-Class Feminism and Debates on Birth Control in Nationalist India, 1920s–40s

> [M]ere indulgence devoid of its highest moral object of procreation cannot but have harmful effects upon the individuals concerned.
> —Muthulakshmi Reddi, 1932

> Mere breeding adds neither to the quality nor the greatness of a nation, it merely lowers vitality, spreads diseases and brings unsound citizens into the world. Those who would have a healthy clean nation must submit to scientific regulation and stop indiscriminate reproduction. The deadly scourge of venereal disease today is eating into the vitals of 47% of our people and if we would prevent its spreading birth control is indispensable.
> —Kamaladevi Chattopadhyaya

Elite nationalist concerns, particularly with limiting population, attenuated the agenda of India's early male advocates of birth control. Race (as well as class) played a role in limiting the possibilities articulated by Western women advocates of birth control in colonial India. It is logical to expect that when Indian women themselves took up the issue, especially those we consider to be at the vanguard of the feminist movement in India, that birth control would come into its own as a feminist issue. This chapter examines the debates on birth control among Indian middle-class feminists from the 1920s to independence in 1947 and seeks to understand the contributions that Indian middle-class feminists made to the public debates and understandings on the issue.

In evaluating the contributions of Indian feminists to the debates on birth control in colonial India, it is important not to allow our feminist lens to be directed entirely on the current pro-choice/antichoice politics in the United States. Such a focus would not only tie our understanding of the issue into a simple dualistic reading, but also tie it to one derived from a very different political and discursive context from the one in which Indian feminists worked and debated the issue. As becomes evident through this chapter, the debates within colonial India were framed more broadly than whether middle-class feminists supported or opposed the issue of wider dissemination of contraceptive usage and knowledge. A closer attention reveals a whole range of concerns and overlaps that animated the debates in India. Indian feminists operated in a complex historical milieu, one that espoused not only different notions of individuality, but also different understandings of femininity, motherhood, and sexuality; they were also distinct from those framing the debates in the United States and elsewhere. Indian feminists also operated under specific circumstances of colonial modernity and an emerging anticolonial Gandhian nationalist movement, which together rendered the situation in India complicated, making it particularly resistant to endeavors that sought to neatly contain it within categories and experiences derived from the West.

This chapter recognizes Indian feminist politics as a product of specific time, place, and location, and highlights its historically shifting and heterogenous character. Although there were some women leaders who argued that contraceptive technologies were important for women's progress, there were others who opposed it on the grounds that their introduction within matrimony would challenge "traditional" familial relations. As we see later in the chapter, feminists such as Rameshwari Nehru were highly ambivalent about advocating changes within domestic gender arrangements, and many others kept reassuring their audience and readers that theirs was not a radical agenda seeking a complete overhaul of existing traditional familial arrangements. In their public utterances and writings on birth control, Indian feminists did not present an internally coherent or sustained commitment to "modernity."[1] On the specific issue of birth control, it would be fair to argue that Indian feminists were caught between a contradictory impulse of simultaneously representing Indian women as repositories of national traditions and as embodiments of modernity in an emerging nation. The discussion below analyzes the nature of feminist interventions on the subject of birth control to reveal internal tensions and fissures that marked the dominant feminist discourse in colonial India. While examining Indian middle-class feminist texts/utterances, I pay close attention to how their elite subject locations shaped their advocacy and understanding of contraceptive usage.

Most of the existing literature exploring the relationship between the politics of feminism and nationalism has argued that the primary dominance of anticolonial struggles and of nationalism made it difficult for women to assert their own agendas. Kumari Jayawardena's early work *Feminism and Nationalism in the Third World* indicated that in India it was the nationalist movement that made women's participation in public-sphere politics possible. She explained the constraints within the women's movement in terms of the boundaries the dominant nationalist movement laid down. Jayawardena suggests that "Indian women participated in all stages of the movement for national independence, they did so in a way that was acceptable to, and was dictated by, the male leaders and which conformed to the prevalent ideology on the position of women."[2] Nationalist politics dictated the women's agenda and, in Jayawardena's analysis, feminist politics is merely regarded as derivative of and an appendix to hegemonic nationalism. Deniz Kandiyoti, in an analysis of women's politics in the Middle East and South Asia, has pointed out that "feminism is not autonomous, but bound to the signifying network of the national context which produces it." The national context and the metadiscourse of Islamic cultural nationalism in the Middle East made it difficult for women to articulate their independent agendas because doing so would have meant "changing the terms of this discourse" and "extract[ing] a heavy price: alienation from the shared meanings which constitute a language of identity, affiliation and loyalty."[3] Nationalism as a dominant and effective ideology of modern times is recognized as enabling feminist politics to emerge; however, it is also argued that the genesis of this politics set boundaries within which feminism was historically forced to rework and reimagine possible futures. The limitations of feminism are placed on the altar of nationalism. Sharing Kandiyoti's assessment of the constraints on feminism, Anne McClintock has suggested that "nowhere has feminism in its own right *been allowed* to be more than the maidservant of nationalism."[4] In this chapter I argue that it was an alliance with patriarchal nationalism and an engagement with modernity as well as the privileged class and caste locations of Indian women leaders that determined the feminist agenda in colonial India.[5]

In contrast to Kandiyoti's and McClintock's assessment, Margaret Jolly has argued that the images of women as "mothers of the nation" cannot be understood merely as masculinist creations. Jolly calls for the recognition that women themselves authored the maternal script of feminine representations.[6] In a similar vein, Ellen Fleischmann has called to assess women's involvement in a more nuanced way, situating women "simultaneously as actors, symbols and authors—using, being used by, and constructing nationalism on their own terms."[7] Debates on birth control in colonial India reveal the problematic alliances between Gandhian nationalism and middle-class feminism to suggest that middle-class Indian women were not mere victims or objects of nationalist politics. A few middle-class women leaders reinforced the patriarchal nationalist stress on women's principal identity as mothers and wives. They deliberately deployed the trope of maternity to do the political labor of legitimizing women's presence and involvement in public politics. The debates on birth control in colonial India are helpful in interrogating the rhetorical, tactical, and strategic maneuvers of first-wave Indian feminism. A close examination of the utterances and politics of middle-class feminists allows us to better appreciate the historically tangled encounters and exchanges between Gandhian nationalism, colonial modernity, and feminist politics. Far from arguing for an inherent incompatibility between nationalist and feminist political impulses, I agree with Sinha that this relationship is shaped differently under specific historical conjunctures.[8] For the purposes of this chapter, I foreground an analysis of this tangled relationship within the context of public debates on birth control.

In order to evaluate the feminist interventions in the debates on birth control in colonial India, I examine the writings and activities of Rameshwari Nehru, Dr. Muthulakshmi Reddi, Margaret Cousins, Rani Laxmibai Rajwade, Lakshmi Menon, Begum Hamid Ali, and Kamaladevi Chattopadhyaya.[9] These women were active members of leading national women's organizations in colonial India, and were important participants in the debates within their organizations in the 1930s and 1940s on the subject of birth control. Their articles, books, letters, and private papers indicate the differences and fissions among feminists themselves on the subject of disseminating contraceptive information in colonial India. Some of these women revised their positions on the subject later, all of which indicates that feminist politics was not homogeneous or static, nor did it articulate the issue of birth control from a singular unified perspective. This chapter argues that feminist rhetorical trajectory on the topic of birth control was messy rather than following a neat and linear story line. Even as Indian feminists borrowed from liberalism to make an argument for rationality and progress, they reworked its principal premise of individualism. Within liberalism, the individual as a basic unit of society maintains a sense of an autonomous self closely tied to an integrated and uninterrupted experience of embodiment. In this sense, it is fair to argue that the individual is largely defined as a masculine subject rather than feminine subject. For a feminine subject, maternity and childbirth disrupt, discontinue, and disallow the luxury of maintaining stable boundaries of embodiment. Interestingly, although some Indian feminists incorporated ideals of attaining bodily integrity for women into their discussions on birth control, there were others who simultaneously evoked the necessity of maintaining women's maternal and familial responsibilities. Highlighting the attachment to women's maternal and familial role is not presented as a critique of Indian feminists' political platform in the early twentieth century; instead, it is presented with the intent to convey the discursive parameters of their transformative political agendas.

Before examining the different positions on birth control that Indian women activists articulated, it is important to locate these women within their specific socioeconomic, cultural, and political backgrounds. Rameshwari Nehru was born in 1886 in Lahore and was the daughter of Raja Narendra Nath. Through marriage to Pandit Brijlal Nehru, a nephew of Pandit Motilal Nehru, Rameshwari came to be related to the elite Nehru family, which came to play an important political role in India. Nehru served as the editor of *Stri-Darpan,* an early Hindi woman's journal published from Allahabad between 1909 and 1924. In 1928, Rameshwari Nehru served as the only Indian woman member on the Age of Consent Committee, which examined witnesses throughout India to ascertain the conditions of married life and maternity and to recommend amendments to the laws relating to the age of consent for sexual relations.[10] In 1940, she acted as the president of the AIWC. In independent India, Rameshwari Nehru became the adviser to the Ministry of Relief and Rehabilitation, which was responsible for forcefully rehabilitating displaced women across the national borders of India and Pakistan.[11] In 1955, the government of India awarded her the Padma Bhushan, the third-highest certificate of honor awarded to civilians, and in 1961, she won the Lenin Peace Award.[12]

Muthulakshmi Reddi was born to middle-class parents in the small princely state of Pudukottah in 1886. She was the first female student to join the Madras Medical College on a state scholarship and received her medical degree with distinction in 1912. For a time she served as house surgeon in the Government Maternity Hospital in Madras, and later she started her own private medical practice. In 1925 she went to Britain on a Government of India scholarship to specialize in diseases of women and children. A year later, Reddi became the first woman legislator in Madras when she was nominated as a member of the Legislative Council; but she resigned from this post in 1930 to protest against the imprisonment of Gandhi during the Civil Disobedience Movement. Reddi served as the president of the AIWC in 1930 and in a similar role in the WIA from 1933 to 1935; she also edited *Stri-Dharma,* the WIA journal, from 1931 to 1940.[13]

Margaret Cousins was one of the pioneers in the Irish women's suffrage movement. She came to India in 1917 at the invitation of Annie Besant. In India, Cousins worked closely with the two national women's organizations, the WIA and the AIWC. Cousins was the honorary secretary of the WIA branch of Madanpalle. Later, she edited the *Stri-Dharma,* which was published in four languages: English, Tamil, Telugu, and Hindi. At the first AIWC conference in Poona in 1927, Cousins was the honorary secretary; later, in 1936, she served as president of the AIWC. Cousins arranged for an invitation to Sanger to address the AIWC on the issue of birth control in 1935.[14]

Lakshmi Menon was born into a well-known Brahman family in 1899 in Trivandrum. Educated in Trivandrum, Madras, Lucknow, and London, she taught in Queen Mary's College in Madras from 1922 to 1926 and, after marrying Professor Nandan Menon of Lucknow, she taught at Isabella Thoburn College in Lucknow from 1930 to 1932. One of the founding members of the AIWC, she also served as its president and edited its journal *Roshni*. In 1949–50, she was chief of the United Nations (UN) Section on the Status of Women and Children. In 1952, Menon was elected to the Rajya Sabha, and was also the alternate delegate from India to the United Nations General Assembly. In 1957, she, like Nehru, was awarded the Padma Bhushan.[15]

Kamaladevi Chattopadhyaya was born in 1903 to a wealthy Saraswat Brahman family of South Karnataka. Educated in a Catholic school and then at Queen Mary's College in Mangalore, she later studied at Bedford College and the London School of Economics. An early first marriage left her a widow while in school, and she later married Harin Chattopadhyaya and traveled widely with him in Europe. A founding member of AIWC, Chattopadhyaya was the first woman to stand for elections in Mangalore in 1926, losing by a narrow margin. A socialist nationalist, Kamaladevi was often at odds with both British official and Indian nationalist leaders, and was jailed several times for her anticolonial protests. She was awarded the Magasaysay Award in 1966 for community leadership.[16]

Unfortunately, there is little biographical information on Begum Shareefah Hamid Ali and Rani Laxmibai Rajwade.[17] Begum Hamid Ali was the daughter of Abbas Tyabji, the grandson of the Muslim merchant-prince Bhai Mian Tyabji. She was appointed to the Women's Sub-Committee of the National Planning Committee in 1939 and served as president of the AIWC. Rani Rajwade was the chair of the subcommittee of the National Planning Committee. She also served as the president of the AIWC. Rajwade, as a member of the AIWC, actively supported and campaigned for female suffrage in the 1920s.

As is evident from the brief biographical sketches above, these women came from socially elite, upper-caste, upper-class backgrounds; were Western educated; and a few of them were well-connected through marriage to politically influential families in colonial India. Many of these women received some of the most prestigious civil awards for their social services that the government of India bestowed. These women spoke from highly privileged locations, even as they claimed to represent "Indian" women's needs and requirements.[18] In their framing of the subject of birth control, Indian middle-class feminists were not "receptive" listeners in sustained dialogue with working-class or any other group of subaltern women they claimed to be representing. It would be fair to argue that it was the privileged and elite articulations of middle-class Indian women (even though these were internally fractured) that became part of the public debates on birth control, which did not allow much room for subaltern concerns or agendas to shape and determine these debates in the twentieth century.

Divided Ranks: Opponents and Proponents of Birth Control

Indian middle-class women began addressing the issue of birth control a few years after some of the leading Indian male advocates. Some possible reasons for the delay in their responses might be that the earliest national women's organizations, the WIA and the AIWC, only emerged between 1917 and 1927. Several of the women leaders were young girls in the 1910s, and emerged on the political platform later. Besides, given the highly controversial nature of the subject of birth control, women's organizations, which were just beginning their work in the late 1920s, may not have felt confident enough in their early stages to debate a highly contentious subject such as birth control and female sexuality. Even in the 1930s, women activists in support of birth control encountered opposition from within their organizations. The initial resolutions on the subject failed in AIWC meetings because members were not willing to adopt it as a woman's issue. Only after heated debate could AIWC pass the resolution in 1932, and even then it was not adopted unanimously.

Annie Besant was the first president of WIA in 1917. She had been one of the earliest advocates of birth control in Britain. It was her trial with Charles Bradlaugh in 1877 that placed the issue of birth control before the public in Britain and led to the establishment of an early birth control organization in Britain, the Malthusian League.[19] In an article, "The Social Aspects of Malthusianism," written in 1879, Besant argued for the need to expand the avenues of expression for woman beyond those of motherhood and wife society accorded to her. She indicated that "[w]oman is not only for man; she also has a right to her own life, and to condemn her to constant childbearing to consume the prime of her life in continual illness and recovery, is an injustice to herself and a grave injury to society.... Regarded in her completeness as woman, she will be nobler and more beautiful when her intellectual life is fuller and stronger, when she recognizes her duty to the world as well as her duty to the home."[20] Besant was clearly calling for more access to public spaces for women rather than their confinement within the homes in their primary domestic roles as wives and mothers. The traditional gendered boundaries of the private home and national public spaces, Besant argued, needed to be rethought and renegotiated. Women needed access and exposure to wider political and intellectual exchanges to ensure that they served as better mothers and citizens at the same time. Besant was not challenging gendered differences or calling for equality between the sexes; instead, hers was a reformist agenda calling for patriarchal concessions.

Given Besant's support for the cause of birth control in Britain, she would have been an obvious person to introduce the issue within WIA. However, she had completely revised her position on birth control after joining the Theosophical Society in 1891, and advocated self-control as the ideal method for reducing population. In "Theosophy and the Law of Population," written in 1896, she opposed the use of contraceptives, presenting a strong critique of uncontrolled human sexuality. Like Gandhi, as noted in the previous chapter, she too was particularly suspicious of male sexuality.[21] Besant considered sexual expressions within marriage divorced from reproduction as acts of self-indulgence. Representing sexual passions in purely masculine terms, she asserted, "Now the sexual instinct that he has in common with the brute is one of the most fruitful sources of human misery, and the satisfaction of its imperious cravings is at the root of most of the trouble of the world.... The excessive development of this instinct in man far greater and more constant than in any brute has to be fought against, and it will most certainly never be lessened by easy-going self-indulgence within the marital relation, any more than by self-indulgence outside it."[22]

Besant's positions on sex and sexuality were later echoed in Gandhi's injunctions against any expressions of sexual pleasures. Besant frowned upon sex, considering it to be physically degenerative, intellectually exhausting, and culturally deleterious, and argued that sex within marriage should be strictly confined to procreative functions. Other members of WIA, such as Cousins, despite Besant's opposition to the issue of birth control, addressed the need to promote debate on the subject by the early 1930s. Some concerned members used *Stri-Dharma* to express their opinions. AIWC also debated the issue of birth control during the 1930s. The views of individual activists amply demonstrates the tensions among women within their organizations on the controversial issue of birth control.

Rameshwari Nehru was unequivocally opposed to any propagation of birth control information. Nehru adopted a staunch Gandhian advocacy of self-control as the only viable method of regulating fertility. In "Family Planning and Gandhiji," she outlined her position on the use of birth control. She feared that the use of artificial methods of birth control would give people an "open passport to do what ever they please." As a member of the Kasturba Gandhi National Memorial Trust, she argued that the only acceptable method that could be advocated was the Gandhian ideal of self-control and *brahmacharya*. The only concession she was willing to make, following the Gandhian discourse on sexuality and reproduction, was the rhythm method, which also required some degree of self-control. Although Nehru supported the adoption of the rhythm method, she did question its efficacy, publicly wondering how many people would be able or willing to adopt this as a method of family planning.[23]

Besides Nehru, there were other women within the AIWC who were also opposed to birth control. In countering the birth control resolution within the AIWC in 1932, Miss Khadijah Begum Ferozuddin, a professor of history and Oriental language at Women's College in Lahore, also argued that the emphasis should be on self-control as a method of restricting population because the quality of self-discipline was necessary to develop character. She deployed religion as grounds for opposing the use of artificial methods of control, arguing that "when religion is cast aside every thing is lost. The teaching of Gita is as much opposed to this resolution as Quran. Why should we cast out the ideal of self-control which is so plainly the teaching of both religions?"[24] Even though Ferozuddin evoked religion as grounds for her opposition to birth control, there were no specific Muslim or Hindu textual injections that forbade the use of contraceptives.[25]

In the debate on birth control in the 1936 annual conference of AIWC at Travancore, Miss Watts, Miss Rosemeyer, and Miss Ouwerkerk, all of them Christian women from Travancore, opposed the resolution.[26] Miss Watts argued that the spread of birth control would "revolutionize married and unmarried life and break up the family."[27] In promoting the spread of birth control, the AIWC, Miss Watts cautioned, would be introducing "slavery into the homes."[28] She quoted the examples of Greece, Rome, France, and Great Britain, where the population was decreasing as a result of birth control. Miss Ouwerkerk also mentioned that if "birth control was accepted there was a danger of race suicide."[29] She quoted statistics to argue that there was no indication that the population had outstripped the means of production.[30] Some women opposed to birth control cited medical arguments, suggesting that the use of contraceptives could lead to sterility.[31] What is evident from the above statements is that there seems to have been no consensus among middle-class women about population increase necessarily signaling a decline in national well-being, unlike the argument that Indian male and Western advocates presented so forcefully.

In commenting on these views, Sanger, in her address to the women at the AIWC conference in 1936, mentioned that those who had expressed opposition to birth control were mostly single Christian women who had no children and knew little of the impact of repeated pregnancies on women. Even though Sanger reflected on the religious identities of the AIWC women who opposed birth control, it is important to point out that within the women's movement, there were few signs of communal divisions, which were much more apparent within male-dominant nationalist politics. In the 1920s, India witnessed an increasing process of reification and enumeration of religious communities. The category "Hindu" was being constructed as electoral politics began to make numbers count.[32] But within the birth control debates among the AIWC and WIA in the 1930s, there were few communal undertones. It would be safe to conclude that the issue of birth control within women's politics was not communalized; although some opponents argued that use of contraceptives was against their religion, for the most part, organized women's politics was not divided and fractured along religious lines.[33] It was not until later, in 1939, that there may have been differences among women leaders such as Begum Hamid Ali and Rani Rajwade based on religious tensions.[34]

Despite evidence of some opposition, it is important to remember that there were also some proponents of birth control among Indian middle-class feminists. Few Indian women could directly confront Gandhi, as did Margaret Sanger who asked if Gandhi knew Indian women or as Marie Stopes did when accusing him of being a mere charlatan.[35] Indian middle-class feminists such as Kamaladevi Chattopadhyaya supported birth control and they suffered politically for their opposition to the Congress/Gandhi line. According to Cousins, Chattopadhyaya had to pay "for her championship of Birth Control and other social reforms by being denied inclusion in the Working Committee of the Congress."[36] In the face of Gandhian opposition to the use of mechanical and chemical contraceptives, Indian women activists were particularly cautious in expressing their support for birth control.

For instance, Muthulakshmi Reddi formulated an ambivalent response. The physician articulated her opposition to indiscriminate propaganda on birth control through her articles in *Stri-Dharma* and in the debates within the AIWC. She voted against the resolution on birth control within the AIWC in 1931, but a year later she remained neutral during the voting because her suggestions were not added to the resolution on birth control. Her principal objections were that the "knowledge of birth control should not be indiscriminately broadcasted through the platform of the press to the *ignorant lay public* but should be imparted by medical people only to those mothers and fathers who really need or deserve them, on account of ill health or chronic infective conditions or extreme poverty of the parents which compels the limitation of the family within *reasonable* bounds."[37] Reddi stressed that fertility management should not be left to the "ignorant lay public," but should be placed in the hands of medically trained professionals. Instead of supporting a blanket need for fertility control, she argued that eugenic ideals and financial considerations should guide limiting families within "reasonable bounds."

Despite Gandhi's opposition to birth control, AIWC passed a resolution on the issue in 1932 at its Lucknow session. The resolution framed the demand for birth control in pro-natal and economic terms. It stressed marital status as an important and necessary qualification for contraceptive consumers. Moreover, it specifically identified the biomedically trained professional as ideal for providing birth control information. "This conference feels that on account of the low physique of women, high infant mortality, and increasing poverty of the country, married men and women should be instructed in methods of birth control in recognized clinics. It calls upon all municipalities and local bodies to open such centers and invites the special help of the medical authorities towards the resolution of this important problem."[38] The resolution was passed by a large majority, with ninety-nine voting for and seven against it.[39] In the 1936 AIWC session the resolution on birth control was carried through with eighty-three voting for and twenty-five against it. At the Nagpur session of the AIWC in 1937, the resolution was passed with only one dissenting vote. Clearly, there was lively debate on this subject within the AIWC and sizable shifts in the opposition. A quick review of the positions of some of those who supported the resolution will allow us to understand how middle-class women framed the issue within their organization.

There were a few individual women who were strong supporters of contraceptive usage; important among these were Rani Laxmibai Rajwade, Lakshmi Menon, Begum Hamid Ali, Kamaladevi Chattopadhyaya, and Margaret Cousins. These women participated in debates on the subject and wrote articles in magazines and journals articulating their positions. As stated above, Indian middle-class women found politicizing the patriarchal ideology of motherhood helpful in defending the controversial demand for the use of birth control and contraceptives. After expressing their fundamental commitment to women's more traditional roles as mothers, they used the health script, relying heavily on medical vocabulary to blunt any potentially subversive or radical nature of their demand. Defending the demand for birth control, Laxmibai Rajwade argued "that child and maternal mortality are directly related to frequent child birth. The mothers grow anaemic, emaciated, are easy victims to disease while the offspring of such mothers are none better."[40] To popularize contraceptives in India, Rajwade highlighted the need for cheaper and simpler methods that would make it easy for women to use them, especially for working-class women whose economic and domestic conditions were such that available methods could not be freely used.[41] Rajwade was one of the early advocates who suggested that there might be some indigenous methods that should also be investigated and might prove to be helpful in providing effective contraceptive methods to the masses. Although advocating on behalf of working-class women, Rajwade condemned their reliance on indigenous *dais* for midwifery services, and lamented the fact that these native *dais* were the principal health care providers for the majority of the working-class Indian women. In condemning Indian *dais,* Rajwade was merely following the long line of colonial and nationalist criticism of indigenous midwifery practices.

Lakshmi Menon spoke at the 1936 AIWC session in Travencore where she emphasized the necessity of propaganda work on birth control. She argued that only through birth control could India hope to control its population and improve the lives of its peoples. In her pamphlet on *The Position of Women* written in 1944, Menon emphasized what she saw as a problem of the ever-increasing population, which was leading to low levels of national health.

Begum Hamid Ali advocated birth control in a report she authored in February 1940, titled "Marriage, Maternity and Succession," which might have been a part of the National Planning Committee Report.[42] Ali strongly supported the use of birth control to improve future social hygiene. "The Indian mother burdened as she is with too frequent, ignorant and custom ridden maternity which reduces her expectation of life to less than 22 years, will find in birth control a solvent for her difficulties."[43] Having placed birth control as an acceptable method for "rationalizing marriage," Ali called for the need to make available safe and cheap contraceptives in the market:

> [P]art of our national research must be directed towards the tasks of finding a safe and really cheap type of contraceptive which may be popularized or even given free at clinics, established for that purpose. Industry and research between them ought to devise a cheap and safe contraceptive which can be effectively used against over-population. . . . Because it is a costly method we are witnessing a state of affairs in which those who ought to practice birth control cannot afford it and those who should not or have no need to practice it do so assiduously.[44]

Kamaladevi Chattopadhyaya, like Rajwade, found medical/health arguments persuasive and effective in making an argument in favor of birth control. She argued that "from the point of national benefit birth control is necessary for reasons of health, social and economic considerations."[45]

Contesting an argument that birth control would lead to a drastic fall in population, Chattopadhyaya contended, "This is a most misleading statement. Mere breeding adds neither to the quality nor the greatness of a nation, it merely lowers vitality, spreads diseases and brings unsound citizens into the world. Those who would have a healthy clean nation must submit to scientific regulation and stop indiscriminate reproductions."[46]

Besides medical and health reasoning, middle-class women, as seen above, employed eugenic logic to frame the issue in terms of national racial benefits. Framing the demand in eugenic and medical terms gave these women a respectable vocabulary with which to address the issue in public.[47] Despite sharing the eugenic and national health concerns of Menon and Ali, Chattopadhyaya, unlike these women, stressed the benefits of sexual well-being that the use of contraceptives would ensure.

Chattopadhyaya revised her position on birth control and family planning later in the postindependence period. In her earlier writings she wrote from a socialist perspective, quoting Lenin and citing the example of Russia as an ideal for free India; this too changed in her later writings. In her previous work, she presented an analysis of intersecting gender and class politics, explaining that "while the millions of toiling women are being sealed up in darkness and hunger, the rich are being sealed up in luxurious prisons of marble and precious stone equally doomed only to pompous idleness. Overwork and under-work henceforth go hand in hand in the process of degrading women and shaping their history. Sex is no more so binding as class." In recognizing the differential positions and experiences of women based on their class situations, Chattopadhyaya, unlike some of her contemporaries, provided a more complex picture of women's location in society. Yet in her postindependence writing, Chattopadhyaya displayed a surprising lack of sensitivity to the question of how class determined people's lives. Her later writings exhibit a crude politics of "othering" the working class on the basis of their fertility patterns. Chattopadhyaya portrayed the working classes and the poor as the "Other" whose sensitivities were blunted as a result of their poverty. Her work indicated a crystallization of a conscious sense of "us" versus "them," reflecting how considerations of class shaped elite women's politics.

> Their [working-class] standard [of living] is so low that for them nothing can be worse.... To them a few more or less don't seem to have a difference. Their resources are so precarious that they seemed to have ceased to be haunted by the menace of hunger, to us [middle class] a calamity, and the very thought of which undermines us.... Another equally significant fact is that while they beget large number of children their survival rate is very low. It is not so easy

to convince them that they can save more children from fatalities if they had fewer ones. To them it makes simply no sense. To them they must have as many as possible since only a few will survive.[48]

The middle-class women proponents of birth control espoused an exclusive rather than an inclusive agenda, in that they did not address the wide spectrum of reproductive experiences or needs of Indian women. Instead, middle-class women leaders used the public spaces to further their own elitist hegemonic agenda. Even though they evoked women as a group, using women as a totality, they mainly spoke and represented the interests of middle-class, Hindu upper-caste or Muslim *ashraf* (high-born) women. Instead of empowerment and emphasizing the liberating influences of birth control, Begum Hamid Ali was presenting it as an additional modality of sexual-social control over people, particularly over the lower classes.

Tracing the Discursive Contours of Middle-Class Indian Feminism

How do we read this messy trajectory of feminist oppositions and demands for wider dissemination of contraceptive information in colonial India? To begin with, we need to abandon and challenge any argument that suggests a neat and linear thrust for feminist narratives and politics. I would like to propose that just as nationalism was not an inherently inclusive endeavor, nor was feminism, especially as it was represented by the early-twentieth-century middle-class women in India. In this chapter I examine the poetics and politics of middle-class feminism on its own terms. Feminist demand for wider dissemination of contraceptive information in colonial India was intertwined with other strands of thoughts, such as eugenics, Malthusianism, nationalism, and bourgeois ideals of domesticity. The demand for birth control displayed at once the underlying hegemonic and oppositional thinking among Indian feminists, allowing us to recognize that this politics was divided against itself. In charting feminist agency, it is important not to elide or bracket off questions of agency when Indian middle-class, upper-caste women leaders act as accomplices of bourgeois nationalist politics. In that instance, these self-appointed women leaders extended the vigilant reach of middle-class nationalism into the domestic sphere as much as they resist it. It is also important to recognize that in the context of anticolonialism, many of the women leaders were invested in the viability of the nationalist project and did not necessarily see nationalist citizenship in tension with feminist selfhood.

Birth control became an important concern for some elite middle-class women leaders who ideologically spearheaded the early feminist movement in colonial India. Middle-class women projected themselves as leaders and spokespersons for Indian womanhood, carefully integrating within the images of "Swaraj," images of the new modern Indian woman. Elite Indian women had access to the media through the numerous women's journals such as *Stri-Darpan, Stri-Dharma,* and *Roshni*. Through these journals and speeches in public forums, middle-class educated women were able to project themselves successfully as leaders and spokespersons for Indian women. In some senses, theirs was a dominant discourse and we need to analyze the power these elite women had in deciding and laying down the agenda for "Indian women" and in constructing a commanding ideology of womanhood. Middle-class feminist politics needs to be understood as much as a quest for power as it was a battle for rights.[49]

Since organized feminism emerged in the context of Indian nationalism, the feminist leaders during the 1930s and 1940s were intermeshed with middle-class politics of building a nation-state. Despite disagreeing with Gandhian politics at times, these women were careful never to advocate a complete break from mainstream politics. In fact, they claimed political legitimacy for their agenda on the grounds of its broad-based national character. They constructed feminism as an agent of national progress. They were careful not to represent their gender concerns as overriding national concerns. Women activists wrote from a certain self-consciously feminist position, seeking new identities for women as well as reinforcing women's role as moral agents of the nation, quite in keeping with Gandhi's projections of women's role within the national movement. The relationship between feminism and nationalism was at best brittle and unresolved. Middle-class women leaders were anxious to reiterate the significance of national consciousness in shaping feminism while also asserting that feminism worked as a catalyst for national progress.

Rameshwari Nehru identified nationalism as "the most universally legitimate value in [Indian] political life." Instead of prioritizing feminism over nationalism or subsuming the woman's question under the national question, she insisted on braiding the two: "India at present is engaged in her fight for freedom which means life and death to her. At this point she cannot afford to neglect any section of her people, however insignificant. The awakening of women means redoubled reenforcement of her resources. The fear that other activities besides the political may divert attention from real issues and thus weaken them is not right. . . . The battle of swaraj has to be fought and won by men and woman alike."[50] Nehru saw in the nationalist movement an opportunity to dispel the social and political apathy toward the feminine half of the nation. She carefully emphasized the mingling of "nationalist" politics with women-centered politics, neither conflating the two nor prioritizing one over the other. Moreover, she was anxious to integrate women's politics into mainstream national politics because she was concerned about it being negatively perceived as an exclusively gender-conscious politics. She did not want women's demands for freedom and sex equality to be mistakenly read as a declaration of a sex war, or as professing antimale sentiments. Nehru and other contemporary women leaders were invested in the viability of the Indian nationalist project. Reassuring the (male) public about the character of the women's movement, she wrote, "[W]e shall not fail you, nor lose our balance. . . . There can be no war between the father and daughter, brother and sister, husband and wife. And if there can be no war between them, there can be none between men and women. We have no bitterness in our movement. None is likely to come in."[51] Through her deployment of the familial imagery, Nehru was eager to convey her commitment to protect the family rather than interrogate the gendered familial power dynamics. The cultural script shaping her understanding and that of some other women leaders did not seek to undermine the family unit as a social institution, even though they may have suggested some revisions and alternations within its structure of patriarchal power dynamics.

It was not only Rameshwari Nehru who adopted a defensive position while expressing the objectives of the women's movement; Kamaladevi Chattopadhyaya and other women were also conscious of sending correct signals about the political philosophy and goals of their movement. Anticipating intense public scrutiny, these women leaders expressed their strong commitment to preserving familial bonds. Writing about women's politics retrospectively, Chattopadhyaya emphasized that women articulated their agenda as responsible citizens and members of society who were interested and invested in improving the society as a whole, instead of advancing a divisive agenda that would threaten social equilibrium. Feminist selfhood was presented as complementary rather than as contradictory to a nationalist self or citizenship. "Women's problems were never sought to be treated on a sex basis, but as social maladies of a common society to be cured by the efforts of all members of society, men and women alike. This kept the women free from tensions of sex confrontation and the violence of a sex war. While they were assertive and determined in their struggle, they were never physically aggressive or violent. One may say it was a civilized strain, and no yielding on principles."[52]

Middle-class women leaders were particularly sensitive and anxious about the way their movement and their demands were popularly perceived within the anticolonial nationalist backdrop. It was important for them not to be judged as socially disruptive, professing antifamily or antimale sentiments. Historians have pointed out that the emerging women's movement in Britain, the United States, colonial Syria and Lebanon, and in France all stressed the regenerative roles women would play as responsible citizens and national subjects.[53] Women leaders in these countries, as in India, were anxious to emphasize the idea of equality with a difference, articulating unproblematically contradictory agendas that sought to empower women in the public domain, without necessarily questioning or challenging the normative hetero-patriarchal roles of women as wives and mothers. Begum Sultan Mir Amiruddin, in her article in *Roshni* entitled "The Women's Movement and Its Implications," reiterated the noncombative social agenda of the women's movement; this was a continuous theme reappearing in many women's writings. Begum Amiruddin wrote about the direction of the women's movement: "The maintenance of equilibrium and eschewing of excesses are vital for the progress of the woman's cause.... The women's problem is not merely a sex problem, it is a human problem; and their demands are based upon faith in the unique value of human personality, for liberty of expression and development of one's faculties are as much necessary for woman as for man.... Their [woman's] movement has not been militant; it has not been anti-male."[54]

Women carefully qualified their demands for changes by constantly reiterating their faith in the traditional feminine roles; that is, as wives and mothers. In her article published in *Roshni,* Begum Amiruddin emphasized that the women's movement was neither militant nor antimale. She, like Nehru and Chattopadhyaya, wrote that Indian women in politics had not lost their "sense of proportion and balance . . . in their enthusiasm to rise to their full stature, had not allowed their judgement to become warped by a feeling of sex antagonism."[55]

The middle-class women's efforts to accommodate their politics within the nationalist movement may be related to their subject positions within the binds of nation, class, gender, and colonialism. For instance, it was Gandhian nationalist philosophy that supported women's political mobilization on the grounds that women were the "incarnation of *ahimsa*."[56] Gandhi demanded women's entry into the public sphere because, according to him, "it is given to her to teach the art of peace to a warring world thirsting for that nectar. She can become the leader of satyagraha which does not require the learning that books give, but does require a stout heart that comes from suffering and faith."[57] Gandhi singled out women as the true incarnation of self-sacrifice and self-abnegation. Given the context under which Indian women leaders worked, they could not easily overthrow these gendered conditions of entry into the nationalist public domain. It would be fair to argue that their modes of self-expression were, therefore, fraught with contradictions and tensions, seeking pragmatic egalitarianism rather than a radical feminist overthrow of existing sociocultural traditions.

Although I agree with Mrinalini Sinha's assessment that Indian women leaders were invested in making the nationalist project a viable one, I would argue that middle-class women constantly struggled to negotiate and reconcile their subject positions as feminists and nationalists.[58] Given the matrix of power within which Indian feminists operated and exercised their agency, they carefully traversed fuzzy boundaries of tradition and modernity while staying committed to their middle-class agenda of reform and empowerment. For Indian feminists in the early twentieth century, their gender identities were neither autonomous of nor subsumed within national politics, and this particular position created interesting pulls and pressures on women's agenda. Women strategically defended "little feminism" by emphasizing "little connubiality."[59] They qualified their demands with assurances of their commitment to feminine roles of mothers, wives, and daughters. As noted above, the issue of birth control was initially expressed as a concern with rising maternal deaths and the declining reproductive health of women and, as such, was grounded within the dominant ideology of "national mothers." It was argued that women had to be physically strong to be able to act as nurturing moral models to their children and also to keep their commitment to the family and, through it, to the nation. The special attention on the physical well-being of mothers should be placed within the cultural discourse of nationalism. There was a renewed emphasis on strong, healthy, and masculine national bodies.[60] Women, in analyzing the issue of "the Indian mother and her problems," in turn utilized some of these arguments to make a case for healthy mothers, healthy communities, and a strong nation.

However, once again in keeping with the competing heterogeneous positions within middle-class feminist politics, even when some Indian feminists such as Nehru expressed their commitment to maternal roles, there were others, such as Rajwade, who simultaneously tried to subvert the (male) nationalists' rhetorical glorification of motherhood. For instance, recounting motherhood and maternal experiences from a woman's perspective, Rajwade wrote, "Motherhood might have inspired poets to sublime flights of fancy or led theorists to philosophise but to the human race, it means existence and growth, *and individually to the mother the crises in her life—her greatest sacrifice for the family, the nation and the race; very much like the candle which burns itself to give light unto others.*"[61] Rajwade questioned the myth of motherhood and challenged its representation as a "natural" phenomenon, highlighting instead what historians have identified as maternal fears among women, especially during times when maternal mortality was high and birthing was a near-death experience for women.[62]

Ideals of sexual puritanism and sexual radicalism espoused by Nehru and Chattopadhyaya, respectively, shaped Indian middle-class feminist understanding. For instance, in her writings, Nehru reinforced patriarchal normative structures of self-sacrifice and self-effacing femininity foreclosing other possibilities—especially those that might have allowed for female sexual expressions within or outside matrimony. Nehru wrote reinforcing marital commitments and duties for women: "Let the wife not expect too much from the husband—instead of expecting from the husband, let the wife give and give freely without wanting any return for it. . . . The desire to give unreservedly must be cultivated. The husband's tastes and desires maybe studied in small details and complied with as far as possible. Interest should be taken in his affairs and things looked at from his point of view. In fact the wife should make the husband feel that his will and pleasure is her joy."[63] Given that discussions on sexuality for the most part remained extraneous to middle-class women's writings and public speeches, the above quotation could well be read as an implicit instruction for women's submission and discipline within marital sexual relations. Women were asked to purge and subordinate their sexual interests/desires in favor of an overriding concern for home and family. Nehru's advice to women could be read as an imposition and a rearticulation of the traditional understanding of appropriate female sexual response as derivative rather than autonomous.[64] Women were being instructed not to be resistive subjects but rather to develop sexual responses within matrimony that would fulfill male needs. The social script organizing Nehru's understanding of marriage and sex allowed no room for equality of sexual pleasures for men and women. Reinscribing patriarchal stereotypes of women as wives, mothers, and loving nurturers, Nehru claimed that "the more she purifies herself, the more she perfects herself, the happier will be the family of which she the wife and mother is the life and center."[65] Nehru romanticized women's conjugal and maternal responsibilities, instructing them to abandon ideals of bodily integrity and self-possessions. She called upon women to embrace their gendered roles within familial arrangements, roles that reinforced rather than challenged patriarchal discourses of power and social order.

Although not advocating for sexual liberty, women leaders such as Reddi challenged the dominant sexual double standards within Indian society. In her speech at the AIWC meeting in 1932, Reddi spoke of the need to raise the age of marriage, to teach the ideals of self-control in sex relations both to boys and girls, to educate the public on the importance of continence or self-control, and to emphasize that both men and women could develop and practice self-control to ensure "good health, long life, and the production of a virile and robust race."[66] Reddi recognized the need to address the double standards within the dominant Indian sexual culture whereby only girls were taught and trained in the values and principles of self-control, and boys were taught that sexual indulgence was not a sin. According to Reddi, birth control was an "unnatural method of limiting the family . . . mere indulgence devoid of its highest moral object of procreation cannot but have harmful effects upon the individuals concerned."[67] The Gandhian emphasis on self-control and a utilitarian reproductive perspective on sex, where sex is closely tied to procreation, resurfaced in Reddi's arguments. Her arguments also echoed Gandhi's overall distrust of sex, where it was seen as having a largely deleterious effect not only on the personal life of men and women but also on the overall well-being of the nation. However, it should be pointed out that not all middle-class women agreed with the Gandhian emphasis on self-control. Some women argued that if women practiced self-control, it might lead their husbands astray and lead them to prostitutes![68] Although this line of argument was certainly not an affirmation of female sexual expression, nor did it regard sex within marriage in rigidly utilitarian terms.

Within organized Indian feminist politics, Kamaladevi Chattopadhyaya advocated the use of contraceptive and birth control devices to enable women to control their sexuality. She lamented how "few have stressed the immorality of 'Property Rights' of man over the body of women."[69] She suggested that "the crusaders in the cause of freedom must destroy that dead hand of the past which seeks to reach out to the present in its attempts to extinguish the flame of new idealism and crush the fingers who would carve out the new woman, new society and a new world."[70] She linked the demand for birth control to women's control over their bodies and sexual desires. Her argument, therefore, was at a remove from women who demanded the use of birth control on grounds of declining women's health, degeneration of national race, or Malthusian dread of overpopulation.

As noted earlier in the chapter, for the most part, discussions about female sexuality remained extraneous to Indian middle-class feminist utterances on birth control. Chattopadhyaya was one of the few women leaders to address the issue of female sexual freedom that the use of birth control would allow women.[71] In her article "Future of Indian Women's Movement" in *Our Cause* and in her edited book, *The Awakening of Indian Women,* Chattopadhyaya argued that the use of birth control allowed women to gain control over their body and sexuality:

All imperialistic minded rulers encourage large families.... The other reason is because women freed from the penalty of undesired motherhood will deal a death blow to man's vested interest in her. He can no more chain and enslave her through children. And therefore this war which woman is waging today against man, against society, against nature itself, is against her sexual dependence. For as long as woman cannot control her body and escape the sentence that nature seems to have decreed upon her, her social and economic freedom would be innocuous. It is for the same reason that man strives desperately to thwart her efforts through religious canons, legal statues and social codes.[72]

In an essay in *Our Cause,* Chattopadhyaya identified feminine bodily integrity with the need for economic independence as necessary ingredients for women's liberation.[73] "No woman can call herself free who cannot own and control her body and can be subdued and enslaved through that very quality of fertility which once raised her to the altar as a deity in the dawn of early civilization.... A free nation cannot be born out of slave mothers."[74] Chattopadhyaya called for disengaging female sexuality from reproduction, although calling for women's rights over their own bodies and sexuality, she was careful not to represent her position as one professing that women should forgo motherhood. Enforcing maternal embodiment, she wrote, "motherhood is one of the most sacred and unique functions of womanhood and should not be left to the mercy of exigencies of accidental circumstances or allowed to be determined by ignorance. It must be a conscious task undertaken with joy and a full sense of its responsibilities, controlled and regulated according to the emotional urge and physical capacity of the woman."[75] Chattopadhyaya strongly refuted the popular myth that the use of birth control would lead to women abandoning their "natural" function of motherhood. She was careful to combine her ideals of feminine self-possession with an endorsement of women's familial responsibilities, thereby situating women both as individuals and as members of their family, community, and nation.

I do not want to suggest that Chattopadhyaya's position was entirely divorced from that of her contemporaries. For instance, in advocating the use of birth control and in demanding that it be made available to the working classes, Chattopadhyaya too reinforced the national benefit that the use of birth control would bring in terms of health, eugenics, and social and economic considerations. "Birth control is not curtailing of births but *scientifically regulating* them."[76] She saw in the use of birth control a viable technology that would enable the reduction in congenital diseases through allowing for "selective breeding." Contraceptives would make it possible to divorce sex from reproduction and free women from the burdens of repeated and early pregnancies. Yet at the same time she also believed that contraception facilitated "selective breeding" and promoted eugenic ideals into the nation-building project. She embraced both feminist and eugenic arguments for birth control. Chattopadhyaya's position, as well as that of other women leaders promoting the cause of birth control, reflects the internal tensions of a politics that spoke on behalf of Indian women, yet was limited in its emancipatory potentials by the very middle-class positioning of these women. The political, cultural, economic, and ideological fields of the times shaped Indian middle-class feminist politics.[77] Far from undermining the dominant hegemonic structures, these feminists strove to preserve these structures to further their own privileged class and caste interests.

Other middle-class women leaders who supported birth control, such as Margaret Cousins (Cousins invited Sanger to come to India to propagandize with Indian women about birth control), also saw in contraceptive technologies a way to "uplift" and "save" subaltern women. For instance, Cousins asserted that "I saw in Sanger's propaganda the beginnings of the fulfillment of a dream of mine of the prevention of misery to delicate and poor women."[78] Supporting the dissemination of contraceptive information, Cousins wrote bluntly and condescendingly, "[H]elpless mothers needed to be liberated physically and economically from too frequent and unwanted child-bearing. . . . [W]e must save by all health schemes a large proportion of 200,000 Indian mothers who are yearly victims of maternity and millions of babies who are unnecessarily born only to die in their first year of birth." In making a case for birth control, Cousins spoke in her middle-class voice deploying a health script. She contrasted the myth of glorified motherhood with the "mundane reality of women's ill health, ignorance of hygiene and over-production of babies."[79] Cousins's representations of subaltern women as mute and silently suffering objects denied these women full subjecthood. Disdain and condescension toward the very constituents on whose behalf she claimed to be speaking was unfortunately to become the dominant mode of representation of subaltern women within the first wave of organized elite Indian feminism.

Presenting birth control as a "solution" to Indian women's health problems gave middle-class women leaders an acceptable and effective vocabulary, one that made their demands seem less socially disruptive. At the 1932 AIWC session, several women physicians spoke in favor of disseminating contraceptive information. These women physicians drew upon their experiences of working with female patients who went through early and repeated pregnancies to present a medical argument in favor of birth control. Dr. Ratnamma Isaac, a physician in Mysore State service, mentioned that the contraceptives available in the market were too expensive for the poor people who, according to her, were the most significant section of the population who needed to have access to easy and cheap methods of birth control. Isaac mentioned that in her clinical practice in Mysore, she had seen middle-class people who came in for contraceptive advice and were using the available methods.[80] The unmet contraceptive need among the poor could be addressed, according to Isaac, if the "lady" doctors improvised some cheaper appliances and made these easily available to poor women. Dr. Sukhtankar from Bombay also spoke in favor of birth control and stressed that there were no sanctions against the use of contraceptives in the Hindu Shastras. She presented the increase in population as a cause for India's increasing poverty. India needed a strong and sturdy race for the future, she said, and that could only be ensured if the "vitality of the mother is not stopped by frequent child-birth."[81] These women were anxious to reclaim motherhood as central to women's liberation; for them, motherhood was a social function, tied closely to the welfare of the newly emerging nation-state. Dr. Sukhtankar spoke in favor of wider dissemination of information and methods for the "poor hard-working" women. In representing birth control as essential for the liberation of working-class women, middle-class women advocates were eager to stamp out any possible public association of birth control with free sexual expression among women. Although the discussions on birth control were limited by the class and caste location of middle-class women actors, at the same time these women managed to politicize the issues of the so-called domestic sphere. In linking motherhood to the well-being of the nation, elite Indian women actors challenged the traditional cultural dichotomy between private and public, personal and political domains. It would be fair to argue that, within the first wave of Indian feminism, like elsewhere, maternity and motherhood were highly embattled ideological issues that shaped women's theories and their agendas for liberation.[82]

In another AIWC session, women doctors who gave their support to the cause of contraceptives emphasized the need for doctors alone to give out such advice. For instance, in the discussion on the subject at the 1937 session at Nagpur, Dr. Isaac argued that only medical people could conduct clinics of birth control because they studied carefully each individual case and then prescribed. She warned against the improper use of the various appliances that could endanger the health of women.[83] Some doctors also demanded greater state involvement in the distribution of free birth control appliances to working-class poor women who could not afford to purchase them.[84] The medicalization of the issue of birth control provided much-needed legitimacy to the agenda of middle-class women doctors while simultaneously protecting and ensuring their professional monopoly over a newly emerging field of women's health.

Rajwade, in her article titled "The Indian Mother and Her Problems," also framed the demand for wider dissemination of contraceptive information within the health script, arguing that it would lead to lowering of maternal mortality.[85] Emphasizing the health and medical benefits of contraceptive use for Indian mothers, Rajwade stated that it would ensure national welfare and reduce maternal mortality, which she saw as "one of the tragic absurdities of our national life.... Frequent child-birth emaciates the mother, makes her a victim to diseases while the children are invariably underfed and neglected. Rickety from childhood they develop into weaklings—a hindrance to the growth of a *better race*."[86] Rajwade argued that "both pregnancy and child-birth are *natural conditions* and the after effects ought not to be so tragic."[87] Rajwade apparently did not find it contradictory to present childbirth as natural and motherhood as a social construct in the space of a single article!

For the great mass of people in India, Menon argued that the lack of birth control compounded the rate of high maternal mortality. The "unfortunate thing, however is that what is denied to the poorer classes is more or less within the reach of the well-to-do classes who have the wherewithal to bring up fair-sized families."[88] Menon complained about the lack of birth control advice for working classes, who, in her mind, were the ideal target consumers for contraceptive technology. She also lamented the easy access to this knowledge among middle classes in India who were using it to limit the size of their families. Contraceptive technology was being "wrongfully" used in dysgenic ways to limit the size of the "better stock" at the expense of the working classes raising their numbers, Menon said. The class pattern of contraceptive usage was of some concern to middle-class women because they argued that it was not working in favor of improving levels of national health, but on the contrary was lowering it by adding larger numbers of working classes to the national population. It is important to note that although Menon spoke of population increase as a major concern, she simultaneously disapproved of the middle classes limiting their family sizes through the adoption of contraceptive methods available in the market. According to Menon, procreative liberty required restriction on the basis of class and caste positions of Indian women.

Menon unambiguously stated her eugenic ideals in an earlier article, "The Woman's Burden," published in the *Twentieth Century*. According to her, emancipating the nation would become easier if its citizens would imbibe eugenic ideals and embrace rationality in education.[89] Clearly, for some middle-class feminists, demographic numbers per se were not the problem; the real cause for concern instead was the rise in the numbers of working class and other subaltern social groups. Subaltern fertility patterns were identified as the problem that needed to be closely monitored and policed to ensure national well-being and progress. It is important to point out that this line of argument was not unique to Indian feminists, but one that they shared with Indian male advocates such as Pillay and Phadke, as discussed in chapter 1.[90]

In her report titled "Marriage, Maternity and Succession," Begum Hamid Ali advocated the need to sterilize the "unfit." This measure, she argued, "needed to be counted among those compulsions which are necessary for the larger social interest especially in a country like India where perhaps the most fundamental of all problems is that of improving racial breed."[91] Here Ali was concerned with what she identified as "the rationalization of marriage." It is within this category that she discussed the subject of abortion. This procedure, according to her, could only be favorable where childbirth would mean grave danger to the mother's life or health. Even in that situation, conditional abortion would be acceptable only if it was performed under the most scientific conditions. The ultimate criterion for abortion to be permitted had to be eugenic necessity. The solution to counteract the practice of abortion, she argued, lay in the "popularization of birth control, the establishment of rescue homes."[92] Overpopulation was constructed as a "problem" that required combined efforts of industry and national research to ensure its containment. Ali also identified the working classes as "ideal" consumers of contraceptives, once again lamenting the dysgenic effects of contraceptive usage among the middle classes. Like Menon, despite claims of "over-population," Ali was not simply concerned with rising numbers, but with the rising numbers of "undesirable" dysgenic groups within the national population, which she feared would be detrimental for national welfare and the national body.

Rameshwari Nehru, in an article titled "Family Planning and Gandhiji," also emphasized India's rising population as a national problem.[93] Nehru argued that political leaders had rightly identified rising population as a problem and understood its dangers in Malthusian economic terms because available resources, especially land, grain, and clothing, would be hard to provide for an ever-increasing number of people. Even though Nehru reaffirmed Gandhi's opposition to chemical and mechanical biomedical contraceptives, she did not adopt his call for resource redistribution as a "solution" to India's growing poverty. Like the Indian middle-class male advocates and Western feminist cohorts, Indian feminists like Nehru also exonerated social institutions and structural inequalities in their analysis of poverty in colonial India. It is also important to point out that even while seemingly adopting a Gandhian perspective, Indian women leaders were selective in their appropriation of the Gandhian agenda.

Nehru asserted that it was not just a rising population but also the invasion of "modernity" and the shift in people's lifestyles that was leading to national physical decline. Echoes of the Gandhian antimodernist agenda are once again apparent in Nehru's articulations. Nehru argued that it was the rise in consumerism that was the main cause for the decline in the overall health of people. Increasing levels of consumerism was not a sign of progress, she claimed, but instead reflected a backward move in moral terms. Nehru asserted that high levels of consumerism in people's lives, particularly the middle class, had made them so weak that "just two drops of rain water falling on them brings them down with a cold or pneumonia. Walking in the sun leads to heat stroke or sun stroke. If they work just a little in the cold their hands and feet freeze."[94] Rameshwari Nehru's concern was with the decline in the health of the middle classes, whom she regarded as primarily composing the national citizenry. Those supportive of contraceptives also used a similar argument about declining national health but with a slightly different orientation. Nehru asserted that although the increasing population was a real menace and the nation had to deal with it in some way or the other, the use of artificial methods was definitely not the right answer to India's population problem.

While analyzing the internal polyvocality and ambivalences that marked Indian middle-class feminist discursive trajectory, especially on the subject of birth control, it is equally important to flesh out the parameters of a developing antifeminist backdrop. From the very moment of its inception, the women's movement in colonial India had to contend with an emerging antifeminist backlash. Some of the more conservative and reactionary sections within Indian society attacked the women's demands for contraceptives. In a 1936 article titled "The Indian Woman's Movement for Emancipation," published in the *Twentieth Century,* Richard Chinnathamby chastised the women's movement in general, labeling the demand for birth control as creating a prejudice against motherhood. According to him, the women's movement in India was a bid for downright occidentalism; the ideals of the movement were seen as unabashedly the "time-models of the West." He emphasized the "need for women to adhere to the integrity of the family unit and devotion to the motherhood ideal."[95] Feminist attempts to rethink the home, the private domain, and familial relationships were clearly recognized as political acts with the potential of transforming the national culture. In another article in the same journal, there was a hysterical outburst against the "feminist movement." Traditionalists such as Dharam Bir Vohra, in a 1938 article titled "Woman's Revolt against Man: An Analytical Study," argued that the women's movement was an "artificial" phenomenon for Indian women because it was "derived purely from the West" and was alien to the spirit of their own country.[96] Presenting a blistering critique of the women's movement in India, he argued that the movement smacked of Western feminism, espousing contempt for motherhood and as such was antifamilial. These antifeminist critiques were couched in what Lila Abu-Lughod calls "the language of cultural authenticity versus foreign influence."[97] For instance, Vohra identified modern education and science as the corrupting influence. Articulating an intense nationalist masculine anxiety about the profound social and cultural changes in the gender system, Vohra wrote:

> Masculine education develops masculine interests in women and leads them to disdain motherhood and its associated activities. This results in widespread use of contraceptives and in the avoidance of large families. . . . Since this is a result that can hardly be desired by anyone, it is clear that we must set about making a determined attempt to check the spread of feminist ideals. The need for this is all the more urgent when it is realized that the rapid development of biological sciences bids fare to provide a most formidable ally to the women's movement of the future. . . . For how could woman possibly have encroached upon the preserves of masculine endeavor if she had been obliged to labor under the handicap which natural married life entails? *How could she have found it possible to stand up as man's rival without evading the responsibilities which Nature imposed upon her?* It was science and science alone which enabled woman to emancipate herself from maternity and bring to fruition her devilish schemes against man.[98]

In upholding gendered traditionalism and in his critiques of modern science, Vohra lamented a lost Indian world through its colonial encounters with the West. From his countermodernity perspective, Vohra outrightly rejected science, contraceptive technology, and feminism as unoriginal and inauthentic cultural transplants from the West. I have taken the liberty to quote extensively from these antifeminist reactions to the women's movement that expressed fear over the possible increase in the use of contraceptives among middle-class women because they allow us to understand the context within which women's leaders were working and writing. Even though the backlash against the demand for birth control by Indian women was unlike what women in the United States had to endure, this restrictive environment called for cautionary expressions of political goals and measured support for change and modernization by women leaders.[99] The intellectual and political backdrop within which the women's movement in colonial India sought to articulate its special demands on behalf of Indian women set limits to their agenda. Women were always careful in navigating the available space for expressing their critiques of dominant social structures, particularly Indian patriarchal values and practices. Highlighting the intersectional politics of gender, class, and caste of feminist activists, this chapter has sought to carefully chart the nature of Indian colonized feminism rather than present an ahistorical narrative of its failures. While investigating the rhetorical maneuvers of middle-class feminists in colonial India, this chapter explores the internally fissured and complicated political platform these women adopted. The chapter looks closely at the dense polyvocality with its constant back and forth among Indian women on issues of change and modernity and their commitment to Gandhian nationalist ideals during the early twentieth century. Therefore, readers are cautioned not to mistakenly read the argument in this chapter as one about the failure of Indian feminism to come into its own—a position that I would argue is itself besieged by a distinct notion of an "ideal" feminism—rather than a historical examination of its discursive and strategic possibilities.

Conclusion

This chapter closely examined how some Indian middle-class women leaders shaped the public discourse on birth control in colonial India. While recognizing that specific middle-class, upper-caste, and *ashraf* positions of women leaders such as Nehru, Reddi, Menon, Hamid Ali, Rajwade, and Chattopadhyaya marked their discourse on birth control, this chapter also demonstrated internal differences among these women on the controversial subject. Some women activists were opposed to promoting birth control as a feminist issue, while there were others who selectively deployed the dominant discourses of Malthusianism, eugenics, and nationalism to make a public case for supporting birth control. There were still others who used the debates as a platform to bring greater public attention to women's maternal health issues as a reason for promoting contraceptive usage. It is therefore important to keep in mind the heterogeneity and polyvocality that marked Indian women's politics in the early twentieth century.

Hamid Ali and Menon made a eugenicist argument while lending their support to birth control, with the former going so far as to call for the sterilization of the "unfit." Nehru represented India's demographic increase as a problem in Malthusian terms and argued that unfettered consumerism and a modern lifestyle had weakened the Indian body. Although not an enthusiastic supporter of birth control, she was willing to promote the rhythm method as a form of acceptable contraceptive. Rajwade and Chattopadhyaya both supported birth control and regarded it as a solution for improving women's maternal health. These two women also made a cautious case for allowing women to have control over their bodies—this particular line of argument, though, was not dominant in the overall case that Indian women advocates made for birth control.

From our contemporary twenty-first-century perspective, these feminist activists might appear to be disappointing "foremothers" who were unable to transcend their limits to provide a truly egalitarian vision for social transformation—some of their ideas seem hopelessly trapped within elite ideals of patriarchal heteronormitivity. However, instead of quickly dismissing them and their political enterprise, we need to understand the larger matrix of political power under which these women leaders operated. Their feminism had to contend with the demands of Gandhian anticolonial nationalism, reassuring the wider public of their national authenticity. The internal ruptures, limitations, and tensions that shaped their utterances were the outcome of trying to accommodate their demands and visions for change within the dominant cultural script of Indian womanhood—one that closely tied women's identities to a self-effacing, self-sacrificing motherhood. Gandhian nationalism enabled women's public participation while simultaneously setting limits to their potential for rewriting the cultural script for gender transformations. Although Indian women leaders did not completely dismiss the traditional ideal of womanhood, there were some who did articulate changes in the roles and identities assigned to women. In assessing the discursive parameters of Indian feminism in the early twentieth century, it is apparent that Indian women leaders were both compliant and resistive subjects of patriarchy.

The contradictory and internally fractured politics of Indian middle-class feminism in the twentieth century also needs be understood within the larger context of colonial modernity. Colonial modernity generated public anxiety about transforming gender relations, as noted above; even as Indian women were beginning to make their voices heard, there were strong antifeminist sentiments that sought to discredit women's public utterances and participation as inauthentic mimicry of the West.

While teasing out the larger context within which Indian women leaders operated, it is equally important to acknowledge their privileged class and caste positions. Although Indian women activists contested some gender-specific discriminations and prescriptions, they were unwilling or unable to disentangle the complex social equations where gendered identities were inflected by those of class, caste, or community locations. It would be safe to conclude that both opponents and proponents of birth control among middle-class women in colonial India claimed to speak on behalf of Indian women rather than create what Alcoff suggests are "conditions for dialogue."[100] Elite women leaders positioned themselves as authoritative and knowledgeable subjects, writing out the experiences of subaltern women and imposing their middle-class ideals of conjugality, motherhood, and feminine respectability. In this chapter, a close reading of dominant feminist politics and rhetoric on birth control in colonial India reveals that it was not a movement of and for all women; it espoused an exclusivist rather than an inclusive agenda. The public debates on birth control reveal that Indian middle-class feminists in colonial India were plagued with similar limitations as those shaping the dominant nineteenth-century feminist politics in imperial Britain or late-twentieth-century feminist politics in postcolonial Egypt.[101] Hegemonic feminisms in colonial India, imperial Britain, and postcolonial Egypt imposed agendas for reform while claiming to represent and speak on behalf of their less-privileged "sisters."

In the resolutions passed within women's organizations on birth control, Indian middle-class feminists called upon the state to provide the necessary resources through its maternal and child welfare centers to disseminate contraceptives. Presenting an argument based on improving women's health, Indian feminists were demanding that the colonial state deliver on its self-assigned and self-proclaimed role of a modernizing agent, favorably disposed to promoting native women's well-being. The next chapter, therefore, explores the role and presence of the colonial state in the public debates to ascertain its position on the controversial issue of birth control.

4 A Fractured Discourse: Colonial Attitudes on Birth Control in the Twentieth Century

> I am wondering how far I shall feel able to tell India that the overgrowth of population is the factor limiting the standard of living, someone has warned me that I may come to be known as the 'Contraceptive Viceroy.' I think I should be rather proud of that epithet if it carried the sense that I had persuaded India to go in for fewer but better babies.
>
> —Viceroy Linlithgow to Malcolm Darling, 1936

> ... a deliberate state policy with the objective of encouraging the practice of birth control among the masses (e.g., by the free distribution of contraceptive devices) is impracticable. For religious reasons, the public opinion is not prepared to accept such a policy. Further, the economic condition of the poorer classes and their lack of education, together with the factor of expense, seem to make the widespread encouragement of birth control a practical impossibility.
>
> —Famine Commission Report, 1945

The two official statements above, nearly a decade apart, capture well the colonial disarticulations on the subject of birth control. In 1936, Viceroy Linlithgow expressed a keen desire to manage Indian fecundity to confront what he considered to be an "over-growth of population." According to him, the increase in population led to stunted growth and progress in colonial India. He also believed that policing fertility in India would ensure eugenically "better babies." Nearly a decade later, the Famine Commission Report in 1945 expressed colonial reluctance to regulate Indian sexual and reproductive practices out of a fear of public hostility. Together these quotes communicate competing perspectives on the role and extent of state intervention into the lives of their colonized subjects. Linlithgow called for colonial intervention, while the Famine Commission articulated the unwillingness of colonial authorities to commit resources to birth control, deemed a culturally and socially controversial project. The quotes also capture the temporal shifts in colonial tone and confidence, allowing us to recognize the change in the nature of colonial authority and presence in India, especially as the Indian nationalist movement strengthened and British imperial authority faced increasing pressures from various quarters. Moreover, the quotes convey a general lack of consensus on the controversial subject of birth control within and among the different levels of colonial administration, highlighting internal stratifications, splits, and divisions within colonial structures of authority, which were accentuated during the interwar period. Interestingly, even while colonial authorities lacked consensus on the subject of birth control, they generated a large body of data and information on Indian demography and fertility behaviors. This chapter draws upon rich archival information to argue that dense colonial discursive practices did not necessarily translate into policy initiatives or state directives that aimed to make contraceptive information available to its colonial subjects. The evidence in this chapter challenges theories of a totalizing British colonial power, uncovering the fissures within colonial discourse and the gaps between colonial discourse and practice on the matter of birth control in India.

Recent scholarship helps us grapple with the complex and contradictory character of the British colonial state, enhancing our understanding of the fragility of the state's position on the subject of birth control. Indeed, for one, the colonial state in India was far from a monolithic seamless entity that articulated clear policy initiatives on such conflictual subjects as birth control. Colonial participants engaged in discursive endeavors not of their own making, as various birth control enthusiasts willy-nilly pulled different levels of the colonial bureaucracy and representatives into their discussions. In fact, the colonial state, when examined through the lens of birth control, appears to have been far from a homogenous all-encompassing presence within the Indian political, social, economic, and cultural landscape. Colonial authorities and representatives did not generate or control the public debates that took place within India. Many times the state was a latecomer, responding to the demands of different constituents for the state to legitimize particular issues, formulate policies, and provide institutional support.

The state's apparent lack of will to act on the issue of birth control in India, however, cannot be read as a consistent position of nonintervention in social, cultural, and political practices that colonial representatives deemed sensitive or delicate. Some scholars have asserted that the post–1857 period was one of conservatism in British policy in India, and "official opinion was unanimous in thinking that local customs were best left to themselves."[1] Thomas Metcalf has argued that after the 1857 rebellion, "radical reform was not just dangerous, it had ceased to be fashionable."² Despite a stated policy of noninterference following the revolt of 1857 and the British fear of upsetting indigenous patriarchal traditions, there were many instances in the late nineteenth and early twentieth century in which the colonial state inserted itself into the lives of Indians. The colonial state undertook evaluative studies, promulgated laws, and initiated reforms that impacted the lives, as much in the public as in the private spheres, of its colonized population. For instance, the state took steps to introduce vaccination in different regions, despite strong resistance from various indigenous groups.³ The state introduced the Female Infanticide Act of 1870, despite strong opposition from many Rajput groups.⁴ Revenue systems and numerous forest laws the colonial state introduced altered customary land ownership and forest rights among the rural peasantry in the post–1857 period. Traditional birthing and midwifery customs of Indian women also came under close and critical inspection from various colonial authorities who sought to replace these with what were regarded as "scientific" biomedical birthing practices.⁵

At the most prosaic level, it is fair to state that the British colonial state lacked consensus on the issue of birth control in India. Colonial state representatives did not actively promote the dissemination of contraceptive information nor did they seek to hinder it in ways that Comstock Laws and Canadian laws did in North America.⁶ An extensive archival search did not yield evidence of coherent and consistent colonial policy initiatives on the topic. The lack of policy directives on the subject raises important questions about the obvious absences and gaps in colonial politics. The colonial state and its various representatives did not articulate clear policy directives on birth control; instead, they engaged in a deliberate practice of "foot dragging." On the one hand, the colonial records are replete with historical moments when different levels of state representatives addressed the topic of birth control. On the other hand, there are no archival traces of colonial policies either of institutional support or opposition toward birth control, even when the subject was addressed within the overall colonial agenda for the development of India.⁷ Finally, therefore, in trying to reconstruct the presence of colonial authorities in shaping the history of birth control, I find it useful to concede to Thomas's cautionary warning of assigning, "too dogged an attachment to 'colonialism' as a unitary totality and to related totalities such as 'colonial discourse.'"⁸

Various colonial authorities generated encyclopedic information on Indian fecundity and population in their official reports and surveys. The information in these documents served colonial officials and Indians as important statistical building blocks to shape their argument on the controversial topic of demographic increase and its correlation with national development and economic progress. Examined closely, these documents highlight the layered colonial administrative apparatus and competing understandings of state responsibility for making birth control available to Indians. While many individual colonial representatives articulated a desire to manage population and reproduction, the state remained cautious and hesitant to institute policies or invest in any schemes that would control and police Indian bodies, especially as reproductive bodies in the twentieth century. A chronological and thematic analysis of moments when various colonial authorities addressed the subject of birth control highlights the lack of clearly articulated state policy of either support or censorship of the subject under investigation.

Fecund Indian Bodies: Objects of a Colonial Gaze

From the 1920s onward there were numerous instances when Indian bodies in their sexual and reproductive capacities became objects of colonial scrutiny. In a few of these instances, birth control was presented as the solution for resolving India's social and economic ills. The Child Marriage Restraint Act of 1929, more popularly known as the Sarda Act, after Rai Sahib Harbilas Sarda, identified birth control as the answer for improving maternal and infant health.[9] In its final report, the Sarda Committee suggested the use of contraceptives as one of the alternatives for achieving the objective of the proposed law. The census of 1931 identified Indian bodies as overly fecund. J. H. Hutton, the census commissioner, argued that the high fertility rates required the use of contraceptives to keep the Indian population from expanding at an alarming rate. Senior British officials such as the Marquess of Zetland and Lord Pethick Lawrence, who served as secretaries of state in 1935 and 1946, and Viceroy Linlithgow in 1936, made a case to support birth control. These men understood contraceptive technology as providing an acceptable solution to what they presumed to be the "vast problem of over-population of India."

While some colonial officials called for interventions to control Indian bodies, overall, the colonial state appears to have been reluctant to undertake too many interventions, as exemplified by the age of consent issue in the 1920s. This reluctance stemmed in part from the strong opposition to a proposed Age of Consent Bill in 1891.[10] While still hesitant in 1927, the state was forced to appoint a committee in the face of rising Indian pressures and international critiques of the practice of child marriage in India. In June 1928, the Age of Consent Committee was formed, composed of ten Indians and one British woman doctor. This committee compiled a long questionnaire, sent out 8,000 copies, and toured all provinces except Assam between 1928 and 1929.[11] The committee compiled nine volumes of evidence, containing both oral and written statements from witnesses all over the country. It interviewed prominent Indian citizens and received numerous responses to their questionnaire. The debates around the Age of Consent deprivatized issues such as marital sex, maternity, family size, and the age of marriage. Many respondents represented these social issues as having direct consequences for the well-being of the nation. Some Indians, such as Miss Khadijah Begum Ferozuddin, were eager to invite the colonial state to legislate and intervene into the intimate reaches of their lives. In her written statement Begum Ferozuddin asserted that:

> It [higher age of marriage] will recognize the duty to motherhood not only from the ethical standpoint, but as an important factor in national regeneration. It must be kept in view that the degradation of motherhood is the degradation of society, of the race, and of the country. Any nation that disregards motherhood and fails to shelter its much needed mothers pays a penalty in mental and moral decrepitude, disease and racial decay as India has paid. Our race and country is suffering from maternal exhaustion and the remedy is in the hands of the committee, and the government.[12]

Ferozuddin not only opened up the sexual reproductive domain to the incriminating colonial gaze, but also called upon the state to act on behalf of Indian women. She, along with many other Indians, was willing to make maternal sexual politics a part of the processes and practices of governance, although without explicitly advocating for the use of birth control as a solution to a perceived problem. While the colonial state was hesitant to intervene, Indian demands, such as those captured in the quote above, to alter child marriage practices and to put an end to early and repeated teenage pregnancies among Indian girl-wives were pressurizing the state to act on behalf of Indian women.

In compiling its report and suggesting ways to achieve the objective of the proposed law, the committee cited contraceptives as one alternative for countering the negative consequences of early marital consummation. According to the committee, "the primary object of promoting legislation fixing the age of Marriage or raising the age of Consent in marital cases is to minimize the risks of maternal and infantile mortality and to increase the chances of a longer and healthier life of the citizens."[13] This goal, it was suggested to the committee, could be achieved by making the married couple realize that the spacing of births should be at longer intervals and the state or the enlightened section of the public ought to take steps to teach contraceptive methods and the benefits of birth control to young couples.[14]

However, after endorsing the use of contraceptives, the committee's report noted that the use of artificial methods to control the births of children would not work in India because people would find the idea both "entirely new and revolting." The committee stated that the dominant belief among Hindus about the son ensuring the spiritual salvation of the father would make the use of contraceptives unpopular among a large section of the Indian population; J. H. Hutton would later make a similar argument in his Census Report of 1931. The Age of Consent Report asserted that introduction of birth control in India was an impractical suggestion because it had not been accepted even in the "most advanced" countries. It was believed that an average Indian citizen could not be trusted with understanding and using the available contraceptive technologies. The report also stated a lack of confidence in reform through propaganda, which, it argued, would be a very slow process. Moreover, because birth control could not be legislated, the committee in its final report did not give much weight to the idea of employing contraceptive technologies to negate the impact of early consummation of Indian marriages.

The Age of Consent Report and the evidence it compiled was an important moment when colonial representatives encountered and identified birth control as a topic of public interest and debate. The evidence that the members of this committee gathered and their final report identified marriage and sex as legitimate subjects for state interrogation, and also identified birth control as a potential way to address problems related to early marital sex. While the Age of Consent Report is one of the earliest recordings of official engagement with the subject of birth control, colonial and nationalist archives are silent about policy initiatives or coherent actions that can be traced back directly to this interrogation. For the history of birth control, the Age of Consent marked one of the earliest archival traces of colonial encounter with the subject. Interestingly, though, this early encounter also seems to have marked the nature of future official responses to the topic of birth control in the next decade of colonial presence in India. As will be evident from the discussion below, colonial officials at times appropriated the subject of birth control within their larger discourse of development and progress, yet systematically allocated no resources to promote contraceptive research or usage. An interesting tension existed between discourse and practice, but this was not the first instance of such discrepancies in words and deeds. The colonial state had made quite a successful strategy of not delivering on its own self-constructed modernist projects![15]

Colonial Census: Technology of Biopolitics

The Census of India began in 1871 as a means of colonial management that aimed at generating knowledge about the colonized population. The institutionalization of the decennial colonial census from 1871 represented a "statistical colonial gaze" that constructed the native population as an object of political calculation.[16] Secondary literature on the colonial census highlights the nature of state power exercised through this technique of colonial management. According to Bernard Cohn, the census became a powerful tool that was effectively deployed to codify all aspects of the colonized culture.[17] Gerald Barrier, in the introduction to his edited volume on the study of the census in British India, writes that "for the sheer volume and a range of narratives reflecting the 'official mind,' there is no better source."[18]

The colonial census shaped the statistical knowledge of the national body. This statistical knowledge was deployed to frame the "population question" in colonial India as predominantly the "problem of over-population." David Arnold has argued that the "critical discursive tone of the colonial censuses" was "absorbed and internalized by Indians."[19] Officials and nonofficials used statistical information provided in the colonial censuses to argue that a Malthusian dread was hovering over India because of its dangerously high rate of demographic increase. A concern with rising population was made apparent for the first time in the census data of 1911. From 1872 until 1911, new areas were incorporated into the census coverage; subsequently, the census reported an increase. The 1911 census was the first to register population growth and explained the cause as a direct result of a high birthrate that was higher than in any European country. According to this census report, the overall increase in India was kept under control only by "heavy mortality, especially among the infants." It warned that if the increase in India's population since 1872 was to continue, "it would double itself in about a century and a half."[20] However, the increase recorded in 1911 did not set the trend of an ever-increasing population. The 1921 census actually showed a net decline in the Indian population as a result of the 1918 influenza epidemic. It was only in 1931 that the census figures first demonstrated a substantial demographic increase of 10.6 percent.[21]

The census report for 1931 first articulated the issue of demographic change in colonial India as constituting a "Population Problem," claiming that the increase in India's population by a "little under thirty-four million" was a "cause for alarm rather than for satisfaction."[22] J. H. Hutton, the census commissioner in 1931, deployed the works of Indian men—in particular, P. K. Wattal and B. T. Ranadive—to make a case about the dangers inherent in the increasing size of the Indian population. Hutton warned against India's ability to feed its rising population, although he also asserted that "the point has not yet been reached at which the ability of the country to feed its occupants is seriously taxed."[23] The mechanization of Indian agriculture to increase food production was not a workable option, he argued, because it would only further shorten labor demands for a peasantry whose work took up only part of the year. Nor was industrialization really a solution for providing employment to a rising population, according to Hutton, because industry had a limit beyond which it could not accommodate surplus population, and that saturation point of demand for industrial labor had been reached in India.[24] Although the commissioner agreed that there was pressure on land, he argued that given the "natural environment of a tropical climate," the material wants of the population were lower in comparison with those of people in European countries.

In his discussion of possible "remedies" for the "population problem," Hutton once again drew upon the suggestions of Indian economists who argued that the "only practical method of limiting the population is by the introduction of artificial methods of birth control." Although recognizing artificial birth control as a possible "remedy," Hutton was quick to point out the particularities of Indian culture and society that would make it difficult to get people to accept the use of contraceptives. Hutton presented a list of social prejudices and practices as cultural markers of Indian life that in his estimation would make birth control unacceptable to Indians. For example, according to Hutton, the "vast majority of the population regard the propagation of male offspring as religious duty and the reproach of barrenness as a terrible punishment for crimes committed in a former incarnation."[25] Despite the possible problems in introducing birth control in colonial India, the census commissioner did, as Arnold has argued, see encouraging signs.[26] Hutton pointed out that in the Madras presidency, some men had established a Neo-Malthusian League "with two Maharajas, three High Court judges and four or five men very prominent in public life as its sponsors."[27] According to Hutton, what was needed in India, instead of the "luxury" of baby weeks, were precautions to reduce the birthrate.[28] In his opinion, efforts to reduce infant mortality should, in a country with a "population problem" such as India, have come second to birth control. In critiquing the newly instituted practices of baby weeks, Hutton might have been responding to the fact that India's population increase in the 1920s–1930s was marked by a decline in mortality rather than any increases in fertility rates. It might be useful to point out here that most advocates of birth control failed to take into account this simple fact of Indian demographics: that the population rose not because people were having more children, but because fewer people were dying.[29] The rhetoric of birth control advocates for the most part glossed over this "inconvenient" but rather significant piece of information from their overall analysis and program of action. If the advocates made apparent that increase in India's population was not based on fecund colonial bodies or more people procreating "irresponsibly," then clearly there would be few takers for their thesis of controlling births and policing subaltern sexuality to resolve what they represented as India's impending "population problem."

While calling into question pro-natalist health initiatives such as baby weeks that were intended to lower mortality rates, Hutton's commentary favored the promotion of birth control to "combat" what was represented as the problem of "overpopulation." An argument for the colonial management of reproduction in India was not intended as a modality of empowerment of Indian women, nor for specific health benefits that it would ensure for the people of India, nor indeed for providing spacing between births, or even to help maintain a high standard of living. What was stressed, instead, as the most important reason for introducing and disseminating birth control information in colonial India was to check the menacing increase of India's population. The overriding concern was with numbers, even at the expense of providing better health care for Indian people. This, unfortunately, has been one of the baneful legacies of the discourse on "overpopulation" that different constituencies articulated in the twentieth century. The discourse on "overpopulation" was effective in writing out people and replacing them with a faceless mass of numbers. The other possible "solution" to the problem of population, according to Hutton, and one that he argued had been effectively tested in Europe, was to raise the standard of living, as such an increase would be "*normally* accompanied by a fall in the birth-rate." However, Hutton added, this particular step would not work in India because it seemed "doubtful if a materialistic standpoint would commend itself to Indian culture."[30] Rhetorical strategy of "othering" worked to shift the responsibility from colonial state to the colonized culture. Modernity accompanied with high standards of living, lower fertility, and small families was deemed unrealizable in India given the recalcitrant native cultural tendencies vis-à-vis capitalist materialism.

Although the census of 1931 defended the advocacy and propagation of birth control in colonial India, it did not identify the state as the institutional site for either conducting research on contraceptive technologies or for disseminating contraceptive knowledge and usage. Despite Hutton's support for birth control, it was too early in 1933 for the colonial state to embrace and promote the cause of birth control. It is important to point out that official attitudes toward birth control in the 1930s were anything but crystallized or coherent either in their support or opposition.

Before mapping other important moments of colonial/official presence in the public debates on birth control, it is important to stress the overlaps between Hutton's understanding and those of his Indian and Western contemporaries who defended the cause of birth control. Noting these overlaps and parallels is helpful in reminding ourselves of the messy boundaries between the colonizers/colonized and in allowing us to recognize the complexity of colonial mixtures and interactions. It is equally important in highlighting the dominant transnational discursive histories of birth control and their effective deployment across national boundaries in the early twentieth century. Despite differences in language, especially Hutton's representation of Indians in orientalist stereotypes, his position was not all that different from his Indian contemporaries such as Wattal or Mukherjee.[31] Indian elites and their Western cohorts supportive of birth control framed their demand for wider dissemination of contraceptive information in a manner that was antipeople, even when they claimed to be speaking on their behalf. The census report was just one more instance of the antipeople approach that fed into the dominant discourse that constructed birth control as a "cure" for many of India's ills, in particular—"overpopulation."

Layered Administrative Apparatus and Conflicting Visions: Secretary of States and Viceroys, 1930–46

Interesting fissures appear within the layered colonial administrative apparatus on the issue of birth control, especially when one examines the correspondence exchanged between the secretary of state, the British colonial representative in London, and the British viceroy of India. Marquess of Zetland, who served as the secretary of state in 1935, and Lord Pethick Lawrence, who served in this office during 1946, both wrote to the Indian viceroys, the Earl of Willingdon and Field Marshal Lord Wavell, to inquire into the possibility of introducing birth control knowledge and usage in India.

In a long letter to Willingdon dated June 28, 1935, Zetland suggested a need for a systematic study and "reliable up-to-date information" on the "physical condition of the people of India."[32] In his estimation, any future government of India would have to "grapple with the vast problem of over-population in India."[33] Zetland's letter presented the "vast problem of over-population" as a given and proceeded to outline a plan of action that he hoped the government of India would be willing to undertake. In his plan he stated the need for "simple instruction in biology, with special stress on the realities of life, so that children may learn the necessity for avoiding improvident reproduction and wasteful social customs."[34] Following what was suggested during the Council of State debate on birth control in 1935, Zetland also proposed the use of schools as a site for disseminating certain kinds of information about birth control. Radio broadcasts too were seen as an appropriate platform through which this sort of information could be disseminated, but if the subject was considered unsuitable for broadcasting, he suggested the use of maternal and child welfare centers where training and instruction could be provided.[35]

The viceroy's office in India took nearly six months to respond to the issues raised in Zetland's letter. In his reply, Willingdon stressed the need to proceed on the question of population on "modest lines" of intervention, especially for a colonial state. He stated that both in terms of "initiative and control," the issue was mainly provincial, and at best the government of India could help with suggestion and advice wherever and whenever they consider this advisable.[36] Instead of rushing in to manage the fecund colonial bodies, British officials in India advised caution and restraint. In this instance, it is apparent that boundaries of authority and responsibility were understood differently at different levels of the colonial apparatus. While the secretary of state in London sought greater manageability of Indian bodies as reproductive bodies, Viceroy Willingdon recognized the restricted accessibility colonial authorities had to Indian bodies and was hesitant to extend its hold.

Lord Pethick-Lawrence, in his letter to Viceroy Lord Wavell on February 15, 1946, after his meeting with Marie Stopes in London, also inquired into the possibility of advocating the need for wider dissemination of contraceptive information in India.[37] Marie Stopes was a family friend of the Lawrences and had sought the secretary of state's help in assisting her to broadcast her messages on birth control in India. In her meeting, Stopes impressed upon the secretary of state that birth control was "the only solution for India's economic and social troubles." Lawrence was himself sympathetic to Stopes's evaluation, even though in his own exchanges with Stopes he made no commitment of resources to her for broadcasting her message to India. Lawrence sought the advice of the viceroy on how the government of India should approach the subject of birth control. He wondered if a direct approach on birth control, or even an inquiry into the subject, would be premature. He wanted to know what progress if any was being "made with the investigation of the population problem."[38] By the 1940s, it seems the phrase "population problem" had acquired a naturalized and commonsensical usage in the popular discourse on demography and birth control in India.

In his reply to Lawrence, Wavell unambiguously stated that birth control was not an issue that the government of India needed to address at the time.

He wrote, "I am sure the present Government should do nothing to assist such propaganda, it is a delicate matter on which leaders of Indian opinion themselves are divided, and to which there is probably much hostility particularly if it were initiated by an outsider. It is a matter for the new Government to take up. The Bhore Committee, you will notice hedged very cautiously on the subject in their report."[39] One can draw a number of observations from the brief communication between the secretary of state and British viceroy in India. In making a case against state propaganda of birth control, Viceroy Wavell argued for the need to keep in mind the reception of such interventions in India. He especially warned of a hostile response from Indians who viewed the colonial government as an "outsider!" Clearly, by 1946, with decolonization imminent, even the viceroy's office was willing to submit that the British were viewed as a "foreign" power that lacked support in India to put through measures that were socially or culturally sensitive.

The colonial archives do not provide evidence of a consistent engagement with the subject of birth control from the office of British secretary of states in London. Archival traces also make it difficult to conclude that the viceroy's office in New Delhi was consistently indifferent to the issue. As is evident from the opening quote in this chapter, Linlithgow was willing to accept the epithet of being India's "contraceptive Viceroy"! Drawing upon archival evidence, it would be fair to conclude that individual interests of colonial officials played a part in either obfuscating an issue such as birth control or endorsing it. Official obfuscation or endorsement operated largely at a discursive level, for neither position financially or institutionally impacted the subject of birth control one way or another. Besides the uneven engagement at the upper levels of colonial bureaucracy, there were some individual colonial officials such as Malcolm Darling who were committed to the introduction of birth control in order to improve the economic situation of poor peasants and the general standard of living in India.[40]

The official correspondence also demonstrates that the colonial administrative machinery was internally split, with various levels of the administration taking somewhat of a different position on the issue of birth control. Some of the scholarship on colonial India has emphasized the disciplining nature of colonial knowledge and discourse of power. Scholars have argued for a "coding of India in ways that rendered it increasingly available for colonization."[41] However, the gaps of understanding between the London Office and the Viceroy's office in New Delhi, especially on the subject of birth control, fail to convey a picture of neat "investigative modalities" that sought to collect facts and use this knowledge for efficient administration of India.[42] When seen through the lens of birth control, the colonial project does not appear to be an overwhelmingly coherent system of power. Instead of a panoptical, all-pervasive presence on the Indian political, social, and cultural landscape, the colonial state appears doubtful and nervous about undertaking policy initiatives, opting instead for minimal intervention and, at times, for outright retreat from positions of leadership.

Call for State Action: The Council of State Debates, 1935 and 1940

Two elected Indian representatives in the Council of State at New Delhi introduced resolutions, five years apart, calling upon the British colonial state to disseminate contraceptive information.[43] As part of the colonial administrative structure, the Council of State represented the Upper House with a membership of fifty. This forum allowed Indian representatives to bring issues to the attention of the colonial state. Given the extremely restricted franchise based on property qualifications, Indian male representatives in the Council of State were mainly drawn from a select group of indigenous elites. Even as these elites sought to represent their positions in universal nationalist terms, it is important to keep in mind that for the most part they addressed issues from a specific political, social, and economic vantage point that necessarily reflected their subjective biases.

Mr. Hossain Imam, a Muslim member from Bihar and Orissa, placed the first resolution before the council on March 18, 1935. Mr. P. N. Sapru, a Kashmiri brahman from Allahabad, placed the second resolution on March 18, 1940. Hossain Imam's resolution failed to win a majority vote, although a thin margin of one vote helped secure the adoption of the second resolution in 1940. In 1935, the colonial government representative, M. G. Hallett, home secretary, voted against the resolution, while in 1940 the colonial representative Sir Jagdish Prasad, minister from the Department of Education, Health, and Lands, maintained a neutral position during the voting on the resolution.

The Council of State resolution in 1935 called for recommendations to the "Governor General in Council to take practical steps to check the increase in the population of India." In introducing his resolution, Hossain Iman asserted that the rise in population was "a matter which primarily concerns the masses, *the dumb millions,* whose voices are never heard in the councils of the Government. Representing a fairly large electorate indirectly in this House, I claim, Sir, that it is our duty to place before the Government and the House the evil results of the increase in the population which is going on at the present moment."⁴⁴ Imam pointed out that just as the state had passed the Child Marriage Restraint Act of 1929 out of a sense of duty despite opposition from Muslim members in the council, so too should it act on this measure out of a sense of duty toward its people. Imam laid down that the state could introduce chapters in the curricula of secondary education on the disadvantages of a rapid increase of population and provide a few hints on contraceptive methods.⁴⁵ He also suggested that the government use traveling clinics to spread the message of birth control. According to Imam, demographic increases warranted state intervention.

Dr. Sir Nasarvanji Choksy, a nominated nonofficial from Bombay in the council, declared that even in Britain the movement for birth control had been very slow and there was much foot dragging before it was accepted. He warned that the situation in India was different because little propaganda work had been done to promote the issue among people. Choksy suggested that voluntary agencies should take the lead in this issue rather than the state whose intentions would be regarded with suspicion. He pointed out that in order to promote birth control, centers were required all over the country "not only to give advice to women, but to the husbands as well, because unless they are made to realise the gravity of the subject, there is not much likelihood of improvement in the present situation."⁴⁶ As a nominated nonofficial, Choksy tried to articulate a nonpartisan position, assigning social welfare and medical responsibilities to voluntary agencies rather than the state. Ironically, even while safeguarding state interests, Choksy's statement makes apparent the cracks in colonial legitimacy at the popular levels. However, Choksy did add an important though rare argument in the debates on birth control during this period; he called for the need to draw men into family planning and fertility control programs rather than burden women with the sole responsibility of child bearing and family planning.

Those opposed to birth control in the council pointed out that it was largely a product of Western society and had little room in Indian culture. The opponents of birth control represented Indian culture and Indians as "mostly conservative in their temperament."⁴⁷ Jagdish Chandra Banerjee reminded those who supported the cause for birth control in the council to "always remember that east is east and will always remain east, and it is beyond the power of my friend or any body of his way of thinking to convert east into west as the two can never meet."⁴⁸ Both Europeans and Indian elites selectively and strategically deployed essentialist "othering" to advance their arguments; as happens with most essentialisms, Banerjee's argument conveyed a rather mistaken impression that birth control was a popular movement in the West. There was very little in Banerjee's comments that would have allowed his audiences to recognize that birth control was a highly controversial and deeply conflictual issue even within the Western world. Opposition to birth control in places like the United States, Canada, and France was even more pronounced than in countries such as India.

P. N. Sapru, defending the resolution in 1935, called for the state to support voluntary organizations working on birth control through financial assistance. He mentioned that women's organizations were also supporting the cause of birth control, and the state should provide these organizations with financial contributions to expand their propaganda work. Sapru asserted that the state could help in the propaganda work through using cinema and magic lantern shows in rural areas. The state should "declare itself on the side of the reformers in this matter," Sapru said, pointing out that the "ordinary villager in this country is fairly intelligent and shrewd," although he also warned that the levels of illiteracy and superstition would make propaganda work hard and progress would be very slow.[49]

M. G. Hallett, the government spokesperson, inquired if birth control fell under the jurisdiction of the secretary of industries and labor or the director general of the Indian Medical Services. He argued that his department was responsible for maintaining internal order and had become unpopular because many held it responsible for introducing repressive political policies. Hallett was concerned that state support for birth control would merely reinforce that coercive image of the Home Department. In arguing against the need for birth control, Hallett pointed out that the incidence of epidemics and famines, though under control, still claimed many lives. He challenged the idea that India was "overpopulated" and mentioned complaints from big landholders about labor shortages in rural areas. Recognizing birth control as an issue fraught with possibilities of conflict, he argued that if the colonial government took up vigorous propaganda on behalf of birth control, it would be accused of attempting to reduce India to a "third-rate nation." Moreover, Hallett suggested that if birth control was really a measure for the good of the country, then the Indian National Congress should take it up. Hallett called for the motion to be opposed.[50] The colonial state representative unambiguously acknowledged the lack of confidence colonial subjects had in the actions of the state. Far from representing the colonial state as all-powerful, Hallett's statements allow us once again to recognize the state's vulnerability, even by the mid-1930s, to pressure from its colonized subjects. It is also interesting to note how it became convenient for Hallett to suggest that the Congress party was the true representative of the will of the Indian people, and to devolve upon them the responsibility for undertaking propaganda and promotional work on social issues such as birth control that were deemed beneficial for Indians.

Five years later, P. N. Sapru placed a second resolution in the Council of State in 1940. In his resolution, Sapru clearly laid down the role of the state in supporting propagation of birth control. Presenting demographic increase as a given, Sapru's resolution stated, "This Council recommends to the Governor General in Council that in view of the *alarming growth of population in India,* steps be taken to popularise methods of birth control and to establish birth control clinics in centrally administered areas."[51] State representative Sir Jagdish Prasad, minister of education, health, and lands, challenged Sapru's representation of India's demographic situation. He argued that India's population had not increased at an alarming pace, pointing out that the population density in Baluchistan, a centrally administered area, was only nine people to the square mile. Prasad argued against framing a resolution on birth control as a solution to the problem of overpopulation. According to Prasad, framing the issue in this manner would lead to community tensions because the Sikhs would not agree with the assessment that there was an alarming rise in their numbers. He stressed that population was regarded as an object of political calculation,[52] and even a popular government would come under criticism for its support of birth control on the grounds of overpopulation and the state would be blamed for "deliberately trying to keep down the numbers of a certain community or class."[53] Prasad laid down a position of state retrenchment on the issue. In response to a comparison with England, Prasad emphasized strict medical grounds on which the British state supported birth control. Another practical limitation in introducing birth control in India, Prasad emphasized, was the very small number of women doctors. There were around 700 biomedically trained women doctors in India in the 1940s. Having outlined the problems he anticipated if the state extended its support to this resolution, Prasad adopted a neutral position when voting on this subject as a state representative. Here again is a good illustration of the lack of internal coherence within the colonial discourse. Colonial authorities spoke in more than one voice to adopt conflicting positions—Hallett and Prasad as colonial spokesmen in the council in 1935 and 1940, respectively, challenged the very notion of India being overpopulated, a position that the colonial census commissioner Hutton unambivalently affirmed in the early 1930s, and one that Secretary of State Zetland in 1935 and Viceroy Linlithgow in 1936 reaffirmed as a given reality of Indian demographics.

The neutrality of the state representative in the Council of State in 1940 did not go unchallenged. Members supporting the resolution pointed out that although the state had actively intervened in raising the age of marriage in the Sarda Act, which was undoubtedly a religious issue, the state should not remain neutral on the issue of birth control, especially because this issue was "already finding favour with women who have received education."[54] Sapru, in his comparisons between the Sarda Act and the resolution on birth control, stated that, unlike the Sarda Act, he was not calling for legislation that would make birth control compulsory. He emphasized its voluntary nature and the element of choice whereby the individuals would decide for themselves if they wanted to use birth control to space their children or limit their family to maintain economic standards. Sapru argued for the introduction of birth control in order to promote better health for Indian women. He pointed out that too often child bearing was a tremendous mental and physical drain on woman's health. Extending an argument based on gender equality, Sapru argued that women had the right to determine their fertility. According to him, "Sir, as men who claim to determine our own destiny we cannot surely deny our mothers and sisters and daughters and wives the right to determine their own destiny."[55] In terms of state intervention in contraceptive propaganda, Sapru laid down that the government should help by providing facilities in existing hospitals for teaching these methods under proper safeguards. He emphasized that the state should place itself at the head of the birth control movement, especially because "people are accustomed to look to Government for leadership in these matters."[56]

In constructing the state as an instrument of public benefit, Sapru mentioned the example of the government of the princely state of Mysore, which provided birth control information in the four principal state hospitals. Sapru also cited examples of Western governments supporting the cause of birth control, mentioning, for instance, that in England the Order of Council had laid down that a woman should be given birth control advice on health grounds, and in 1934 there were 1,200 centers that were providing birth control information. Finally Sapru deployed the eugenic argument about improving the future race of India, claiming that "we want a race of useful citizens. We want a race of healthy, normal, strong citizens, citizens who will be able to supply us with material for building up a mighty future, and we ought to approach this question not from the point of view of sentiment but from the point of view of reason."[57]

Sapru made a case for state intervention and support for promoting women's health and the overall well-being of Indians. In this particular instance, Sapru appeared to be calling upon the colonial state to deliver on its "civilizing mission" and to institute its much promised colonial modernity, particularly in the realm of public health and women's rights. Sapru's expectations from the state appear to be akin to that of citizen of a welfare state rather than one of a colonial subject. However, my own reading of Sapru's naïveté could well be a limitation of a historian's gaze seeking to construct an inherent distinction between the colonized and colonizers. The irony, in this instance, could well be one of my own making rather than one that was lost on historical subjects who occupied complex locations, which escape neat archival coding. Supporting Sapru's resolution in 1940, Imam reminded the council that he had placed a similar resolution five years ago. Using an eugenic plea similar to Sapru's, he stated that "I want that there should be healthy, normal, intelligent and vigorous children born in India. It is not only quantity which is required but quality also must count, and in order to have quality you must have restrictions, because that is the natural law of selection."[58] The resolution was adopted by a narrow margin of one vote.[59]

Other than these two times when the issue of birth control was debated at some length within the Council of State, there were a few questions that were raised on the subject within the legislative assembly debates. For the most part, state representatives summarily dismissed the questions as nonissues. Indian representatives primarily raised these questions while inquiring about colonial state policy in the matter. Indian representatives were anxious to know if the state was willing to address the issue and provide support to the cause of disseminating contraceptive technology in India. For instance, on February 7, 1936, Mr. Akhil Chandra Datta asked a question about the food problem in India and its relationship to the rapid growth of population. He wanted to know if the government of India was thinking of adopting birth control as a means to solve the issue. In his response, Sir Girija Shankar Bajpai, the colonial representative, presented an argument that Viceroy Willingdon repeated in his response to the India office. In the legislative assembly, Sir Bajpai stated, "As regards birth control the Government of India feels that the matter is primarily for local governments to deal with, with due regards to public opinion."[60] In the legislative assembly, the state representative mentioned that colonial authorities were not willing to undertake any propaganda work on behalf of an issue they regarded as overly sensitive and thought it best to be dealt with at the local level. Far from being an all-present, all-controlling Foucauldian state, the colonial authorities avoided addressing issues considered controversial. Colonial authorities and representatives appear to have shared a keen awareness of their limited power within the Indian political, social, and cultural landscape.

The two debates in the Council of State and the occasional questions that Indian representatives raised within the legislative assembly between 1930 and the 1940s were important moments when the British colonial state was being called upon to take on leadership responsibilities and provide institutional support for birth control. This was not a novel modality for seeking legitimacy for socially controversial issues. Indian reformers, nationalist leaders, and organized feminists had campaigned effectively for state support to enact family and gender reforms from the early nineteenth century.[61] The colonial state was disinclined to concede resources to promote a potentially divisive issue, especially one on which there was no consensus either among Indian leaders or colonial officials. A lack of consensus among colonial authorities similarly plagued two other important official investigations into the questions of development, demography, and birth control in the last leg of colonial rule.

Colonial Polyvocality: Politics of Development and Health, 1943–46

During its last few years of presence in India, the colonial state continued to deploy an internally split discourse as an effective political strategy to speak in multiple and competing voices on the controversial subject of birth control. An internally fractured and multivocal discourse enabled the state to claim fair representation of competing perspectives while maintaining a minimalist regulatory presence on issues related to national health, development, and contraceptive usage. Two nationwide colonial surveys, the Famine Inquiry Commission in 1945 and the Report of the Health Survey and Development Committee in 1946, epitomize the state's Janus-faced position on birth control. Colonial officials and representatives at various levels of the colonial bureaucracy simultaneously made a plea for state action and inaction on making contraceptive technology and knowledge available to Indians. Colonial reports and commissions cancelled out each other's assessment to inconclusively project Indian demography both as plagued by an impending Malthusian dread and as hovering below the mark of national demographic catastrophe.

Sir John Woodhead chaired the Famine Inquiry Commission to examine the cause of the devastating Bengal famine of 1943. In its 1945 report, the Famine Commission discussed the issue of "population increase" to determine the causes of and remedies to prevent future famines in India. The report asserted that despite its large population, India was not "overpopulated." Instead, the *primary* problem in India was "of underdevelopment of resources, both agricultural and industrial, in a wide sense of the term."[62] In its section titled "Is India Over-Populated?" the report asserted that India's food production had kept pace with the increase in the size of its population and concluded that at present there was no danger of "overpopulation." However, the report asserted that if the present rate of growth was to be continued, there might arise a problem in the future. It suggested family limitation as one of the ways for "checking the growth of population."⁶³

In the questionnaire that the Famine Commission circulated to provincial governments and private individuals, the following question was included: "Having regard to the present size of the population of your province and its potential growth, and having regard also to the present and potential resources of your province, are you convinced that measures should now be taken for securing a limitation of the rate of increase of the population? If so, state and discuss the measures you would recommend for this purpose."⁶⁴ Respondents to the questionnaire recognized the value of family limitation, but they emphasized the problems of introducing birth control on a more popular scale. Many respondents argued that there would be difficulties in encouraging the practice of birth control "both for religious reasons and because of the low economic condition of the people."⁶⁵ Respondents from provinces also suggested the need to raise the age of marriage and argued that a rise in living standard was an essential preliminary to family limitation. It would be reasonable to conclude that there was a wide spectrum of competing opinions on the appropriate role of the colonial state to promote the knowledge and use of contraceptives.

Even though in its own commentary the Famine Report gave the use of birth control cautious support, some respondents to its questionnaire called for a more aggressive and active role of the state to promote the use of birth control. The deputy commissioner of Assam, for instance, stated, "It is obvious that correct birth control should be taught and appliances made cheaply available." He believed it was the "inefficiency" of public health measures that was keeping the death rates high and therefore checking the overall growth, and that once these measures improved, "the need for birth control would become even more pressing."⁶⁶ The government of Bihar pointed out the public prejudice that any policy of birth control might have to encounter. The "solution," it suggested, was to organize public opinion on the topic and follow a persuasive and voluntary policy toward birth control. In their response, the Bihar representatives mentioned that the state should be "prepared in course of time to open birth control clinics in suitable places in all districts and Government hospitals and dispensaries." Other measures suggested to control population increase were "compulsory sterilization of the unfit, raising the age of marriage, education of women, with the view to secure their economic independence and abolition of polygamy." The colonial state was to initiate these measures, the Bihar representative specified, only once public opinion favored them.⁶⁷ The representative of the Madras government called for birth control, which was argued as being a "really effective method of preventing the growth of population."[68]

The government of the United Provinces stated clearly that "matters cannot be left to Nature's ruthless method of establishing an equilibrium by bringing in pestilence, famine, and war. The theory that planned parenthood is what is actually required will be widely accepted but the methods to be employed to attain it admit of no easy solution." The suggestion was for the state to set up "free birth control clinics through Public Health and Maternity Services and cheap or even free supplies of contraceptives should be provided."[69] United Province representatives argued against an imposition of a tax on large families and warned that families were already poor and could not be further economically burdened. Moreover, taxation would interfere with the liberty of the individual in the exercise of primary instincts and would lead to criminal abortion and infanticide.[70]

As pointed out above, the provincial opinions were far from unified on the issue. For instance, the governments of Bombay and of the Central Provinces and Berar noted that birth control would not be a practical method for limiting population. The costs of contraceptives would make them inaccessible and unavailable to the poorer classes. The state representative from Bombay suggested the spread of education, whereas those from Central Provinces and Berar claimed that birth control could only be given to people on medical grounds.

Though the report did not outrightly endorse Malthusian positions on population, the official response was divided and conflicted about the role the state apparatus should play in controlling fertility patterns among Indians. As is evident from the above discussion, the state position on regulating reproduction of its colonized subjects ranged from outright interference via sterilization to minimal intervention through education and finally to a complete hands-off noninterference in a subject deemed private and sensitive. Birth control as a topic of public discussion did elicit strong responses from colonial officials. However, these responses were locked in a rhetorical imperative that short-circuited any policy initiatives.

In October 1943, the government of India appointed the Health Survey and Development Committee, which issued its report in 1946. The report was popularly known as the Bhore Committee Report, after its chairman, Sir Joseph Bhore. This committee was assigned to conduct a broad survey of the prevailing health conditions and health organizations in British India and to make future recommendations. In its report, the committee highlighted the "population problem," remarking that "the steady growth of population, which has taken place [in India] during the past few decades, has had its repercussions on all such matters as housing, clothing and feeding of an additional numbers.... No programme of social reconstruction can therefore afford to ignore the implications of the population problem."[71] The Indian demographic situation was once again represented as marking an unambiguous "population problem," with far-reaching implications for progress and development.

The chapter on "The Population Problem" in the Bhore Committee report drew upon census data to highlight the increase in India's population, even though the Famine Commission and other state representatives had challenged the demographic assessment of the 1931 census. The Bhore Committee attributed the increase in India's population to its lack of urbanization and modernization. Economic backwardness and lack of development led to high fertility among Indian subalterns—the working classes, agricultural workers, and the peasantry, according to this report. The lowering of fertility among the subaltern section of the population, it was argued, would depend on improving their economic condition because among them, children as workers were considered important to ensure a reasonable standard of living. Correlating fertility patterns to national development left a lasting legacy well into the postcolonial period.

The committee delineated instances in which the use of birth control required no justification, such as the spacing of births to safeguard the health of the mother and child.[72] Where the use of birth control was related to reasons of health, it was argued that the state should make contraceptives available free of cost to women. Recognizing certain "valid" grounds for the use of birth control, the committee's report warned of possible misuse whereby "upper and middle class Indian women were likely to attain a considerable degree of social emancipation, ... and would refuse to adopt the drudgery of continuous child-bearing."[73] The Bhore Committee represented dysgenic use and feminine emancipation as two potentially evil outcomes of contraceptive usage among middle-class women.

In its list of disadvantages associated with promotion of contraceptives, the committee's report gave voice to its middle-class bias. It argued that the use of birth control would lead to social promiscuity with a rise in venereal diseases, and as such would threaten the sanctity of home life. If the use of birth control was driven by economic desires to maintain a certain standard of life, it would encourage a materialistic attitude, leading to "people preferring a baby Austin [car] to a baby."[74] Moreover, it argued that the use of birth control would not be without its own problems; for instance, it was doubtful "whether a contraceptive which is both efficient and safe" had yet been discovered. The report warned that before promoting the use of birth control, it was essential to ensure that contraceptive technologies were harmless. The report feared a dysgenic spread of birth control knowledge and use among the "more energetic, intelligent and ambitious sections of the population, which make the largest contribution to the prosperity of the country."[75] It warned that if this class of people were to adopt birth control, it would have serious consequences on national welfare.

The committee was unanimous in favor of control over the manufacture and sale of contraceptives. To secure the economic well-being of India (which was of course linked to the well-being of the middle class and low fertility among the working subalterns), the state could provide facilities for imparting knowledge of birth control, but "only if there is substantial support from public opinion."[76] There would be some practical difficulties in any large-scale extension of birth control, which included a lack of education among women, that would make it hard for them to follow contraceptive practice satisfactorily. Moreover, given people's economic situation, it would be enormously expensive for the state to place safe and effective contraceptives within their reach. The report also noted the shortage of women biomedical personnel who were required to impart contraceptive information to women in India. Finally, it claimed that some Indians would have religious objections to the use of birth control. Despite pointing out the relevance of birth control in improving maternal and infant health care, this report mentioned that a "rapid extension of the practice of contraception among the people is unlikely in the immediate future."[77] It did not call for official advocacy and support to the cause of birth control, but merely identified it as one of the factors responsible for improving national health—in particular, women's health.

The two reports analyzed in this section are interesting documents that highlight internal differences among colonial officials on birth control. However, neither of these two reports, very much in keeping with other official utterances, outlined any definite guidelines for state action. At the state level, there were different competing positions with few supporting policies for implementing change and reform.

Colonial Nonresolution of the Population Question

It is only logical to wonder why there was such a glaring lack of coherence on the issue. How was it that the colonial representatives recoiled from stating any clear objectives about birth control or outlining a policy on the subject for over two decades? Given that one is limited by the evidence one has, at best one can peril speculation. Among many possible explanations, one could well be chronological, given that the specific historical period when the issue of birth control became a matter of serious public debate in India was in the late 1920s and early 1930s. This period is not considered the high point of British empire in India; many scholars refer to the 1930s up to 1947 as a period of colonial decline.[78] The British colonial government in India, at the end of World War I and during the emergence of strong nationalist challenges following the Gandhian Non-Cooperation and Khilafat movements, lost its earlier political confidence and hold over India.[79] The government was reluctant to introduce reforms or policies that it feared might alienate its support base among the more conservative elements within Indian society. Therefore, the colonial state was reluctant to address any controversial subject, and birth control certainly seemed dispensable given its potential for causing opposition from both within the colonial ranks and from certain sections of the Indian population. In India, prominent political figures, most notably Mahatma Gandhi, had opposed the use of chemical and mechanical contraceptives.[80] Lack of Gandhi's support to the cause must have made the imperial authorities even less willing and more nervous about broaching the topic, given that by the 1920s they had increasingly come to recognize Gandhi as the true leader and representative of Indians.

Many colonial officials argued that health came under provincial jurisdiction and preferred to leave controversial topics such as birth control to be handled by Indian representative bodies at the local levels to avoid further alienation and public uproar. What is apparent in colonial India around the subject of birth control is an absence of state persuasion or coercion to control the intimacies of the reproductive and sexual lives of their subjects. Furthermore, the cost of introducing systematic access to birth control made it that much more unappealing to imperial authorities who were strapped for funds during the 1930s and early 1940s because of worldwide depression and the increased demands of World War II.

Another possible explanation for the absence of official coherence and resolution on the subject of birth control should be located within the interlocking global discourse on demography and birth control. Until the 1930s, the subject of birth control was far from being unconditionally endorsed within India—or, for that matter, in most parts of the world about which we have information. In the United States, the draconian Comstock Laws passed in 1873 prohibited the sale and postal exchange of information on contraceptive devices.[81] Margaret Sanger was imprisoned in 1917 for admitting that she had given out birth control information.[82] The metropolitan government in Britain had very reluctantly accepted the demand for wider dissemination of contraceptive information at home. In 1930, the British Health Ministry passed a memorandum allowing maternal and child welfare centers to provide birth control information to married women strictly on medical grounds.[83] In both these countries, the domestic opinion was greatly divided about the moral implications of introducing contraceptive information and usage.

In 1920, the French government passed legislation banning birth control because of the "fear that declining rates would translate into military and economic weakness."[84] Also, the gender politics in post–World War I France created tremendous social anxiety about the decline in national fertility. French pro-natal policies in the early twentieth century regarded a larger population as a source of national assent rather than a liability, especially in the context of its rivalry with Britain, which at this point had a much larger population. The French government did not repeal the ban on birth control until 1967. French colonial settlements in India prohibited the practice of birth control and various methods of preventing conception during the 1930s. French colonial authorities also banned the transport of literature on this subject into French territory in India.[85] In its colonies, the French deemed a higher population to be an important resource for cheap labor. The Belgian colonial state in Congo in the early part of the twentieth century likewise adopted policies to discourage traditional spacing and birth control methods that women adopted to control their fertility with the objective to raise birthrates of the African labor force.[86] The British colonial demographic anxiety in Kenya in the early twentieth century too was linked to a decrease in population. According to Lynn Thomas, the colonial authority in Kenya rested upon attending to matters of the womb, which in this case translated to policies that would raise rather than curb fertility rates among Kenyans.[87] Given the hesitant and at times unfriendly political reception worldwide to the cause of birth control, it is not surprising that there was a lack of official enthusiasm toward birth control in India. Here it is useful to remind ourselves that the British colonial government did not operate in a political vacuum; instead, quite like the colonial state in Kenya, it "operated at the nexus of forces from below, above, inside and outside the colony and nation."[88] To best understand the history of birth control in India, as elsewhere, it is important to break down the reified polarities of the metropole and nonmetropole worlds and locate the unfolding of its trajectory at the complex intersection of local, national, and global politics.

Having asserted above that birth control lacked official state support in many parts of the world in the early half of the twentieth century, it is also important to remind ourselves that there was an equally strong opinion shared among elites in the Western and non-Western worlds, one that called for the need to control the fecundity of subaltern sociocultural groups. There was a dominant discourse of "race suicide" that was beginning to appear on the global scene, with organizations such as the eugenic societies and neo-Malthusian leagues opening local chapters in many parts of the globe. British colonial authorities in parts of the West Indies, South Africa, and Southeast Asia and American colonial authorities in Puerto Rico were growing increasingly alarmed at the high rate of fertility among its nonwhite colonized subjects.[89] In response to what was represented as an impending racial demographic crisis, the British and American colonial authorities began providing funds to support birth control clinics in some of their colonies, such as South Africa and Puerto Rico, in the 1930s.

As is evident from the brief description of the global discourse and politics on demography and birth control, one can better appreciate the lack of coherence among British colonial officials in India on the subject. British colonial administration, like most administrative machinery, spoke with many different voices on this subject, encompassing a range of opinions from those who called for sterilization, free distribution of contraceptives to the poor dysgenic populations in India, to officials who opposed state support in any shape or form.

Conclusion

An examination of the various colonial reports, committees, commissions, and debates on the issues of population and birth control in this chapter point toward the discontinuities within colonial/official understanding of the issue, allowing us to recognize the heterogeneity that shaped colonial administrative structure and its discourse. Many different perspectives jostled, making it impossible to frame policies, set guidelines on the role of the state in extending contraceptive information to the people, or even formulate an official position on the "population question." The state was not administratively homogenous; different colonial authorities articulated competing visions of the role assigned to the state in furthering and supporting the spread of contraceptive information. In their hesitation to support the cause of birth control, a set of colonial representatives argued that they feared the colonial state would be acting against the sensibilities of Indians if it officially endorsed and supported wider dissemination of contraceptive information. The colonial representatives were even divided on the question of whether India qualified as an "overpopulated" country. Many saw the demographic problem not so much as one of sheer numbers but one of eugenics, where the birthrates of the "desirable" social, economic, and cultural elites were lower than those of the prolific subaltern orders.

The colonial apparatus lacked internal coherence to deal with the controversial subject of birth control. Colonial project of knowledge production was certainly not an all-embracing, all-encompassing social and political force. Antoinette Burton, along with many others, has cautioned well against a perspective that constructs the colonial state as "the proverbial juggernaut, razing opposition . . . fixing with absolute authority the social and cultural conditions out of which citizens and subjects could make and remake their relationships to the state and civil society."[90] Colonial attitudes were infused with tension and conflict on the subject of birth control. The colonial state aggressively represented itself as an agent of modernity in India, particularly as this related to "improving" Indian women's health. Yet when birth control was related to Indian women's maternal health, it became an embattled issue within the inflated colonial narrative of modernity. Despite claiming to champion the cause of Indian women, seeking to save the "brown woman from the brown man," the colonial state during the 1920s, 1930s, and 1940s was reluctant to advocate reform policies that it feared might alienate the more conservative elements within Indian society. The Age of Consent Committee in 1929 received greater support from Indian women's organizations than from the colonial state, which was very reluctant to raise either the age of marriage or the age of sexual consent within marriages for Indian women, given the strong opposition to the 1891 Age of Consent Act. In the Council of State debates, the government representatives were unwilling to defend the demand for state support of birth control, even when it was framed as a health issue.

The mapping of the densely conflicted and contradictory utterances within the colonial camp on the issue of birth control amply demonstrates the futility of trying to sustain a neat linear narrative on the cultural or political idiom of colonial domination in India. Far from a united conquering colonizing elite, what we see is the colonial state and its representatives hesitantly acting and being acted upon by pressures from different colonized groups. The debates around birth control in India amply demonstrate that discursive power was far from being possessed entirely by the colonizer.[91] The state lacked a coherent policy to manage the reproductive practices of its subjects, even when Indian representatives called for intervention and warned against the consequences of state inaction. A close examination of the moments of colonial presence in the public debates on birth control calls for a more nuanced and layered insertion of colonialism into the story of the making of modern India. We need to recognize the complex character of colonial presence, one that was fraught with internal uncertainties and pressures as much as resistance and challenge from its colonized subjects.

In the final analysis, birth control in and of itself is neither inherently progressive or pro-people, nor is it reactionary and antipeople. Instead, it is the discursive and epistemic construct that determines the outcome of promoting contraceptive technologies within a given historical context. Nothing demonstrates this better than examining the role of health professionals. It was to them that so many advocates and opponents of birth control in India looked to for providing the scientific, technological, and objective point of view on the issue of birth control. Many of the people in the business of health care were strongly of the opinion that this was a subject that should be the province of trained medical professionals. Yet, as the next chapter reveals, they too were not only hopelessly divided among themselves based on cultural preferences, but also their own dialogues were circumscribed by the same sort of discursive and epistemic limits that shaped the role of other actors in such discussions.

5 Untrained "Professionals": Medical Practitioners and the Politics of Birth Control in Colonial India, 1920–47

> The average doctor has a very hazy notion of birth control; he has not taken the trouble to acquire whatever knowledge is available on the subject, nor is birth control included in the curriculum of any medical college.
> —Dr. J. N. Ghosh, 1936

Contending traditions of biomedicine, *Ayurveda* and *Unani,* shaped the medical landscape in colonial India in the early twentieth century. These different medical traditions and practitioners jostled with each other to gain hegemonic control over the Indian body, for none of them enjoyed universal acceptance or unquestioned authority among Indians in the early twentieth century. When we examine the medical landscape through the birth control lens, it becomes evident that neither biomedical nor indigenous practitioners had come to a consensus among themselves on this subject. In terms of their knowledge, experience, or professional training, the different practitioners of medicine were far from ready to shoulder the responsibility of disseminating contraceptive information to their clients/patients. In their lack of expertise and enthusiasm for the subject, medical practitioners belied the hopes of the early advocates to medicalize and professionalize birth control in colonial India. This chapter focuses on the ideas and writings of biomedical and alternative medical practitioners, as historical actors, to understand their contributions in shaping the intellectual and political trajectory of birth control in colonial India.

As is evident from the preceding chapters, the debates on birth control in colonial India appear to be locked in an oppressive trajectory, and as such provide a rich site for understanding elite agenda and exercise of power. The entrance of medical professionals did not substantially alter the terms of the debate, for they were not radical advocates of social justice or of women's empowerment. In the sections below, I examine the writings of biomedical male and female practitioners and the writings of indigenous practitioners on the topic. The gendered nature of the medical establishment in colonial India warrants a separate section on the responses of male and female physicians on the subject. In colonial India, as elsewhere, gynecology and obstetric care was primarily a female preserve because women patients and their families, for the most part, were reluctant to have a male physician physically examine women or be in attendance during birthing. The early recognition of a cultural preference for women physicians among Indians led to the establishment of the Dufferin Fund and the Victorian Memorial Scholarship Fund.[1] Interestingly, despite the gendered structure of the biomedical establishment, judging from the articles in medical journals, some male physicians participated in the discussions on birth control. What follows below is a close reading of medical journal articles to outline the terms of the debates and the concerns of some male physicians on the controversial topic.

Western-Trained Biomedical Men

Although a group of Western-trained biomedical men saw birth control as an appropriate subject of discussion, others considered the subject vulgar, beyond the pale of decency, and as such unworthy of any serious consideration. Those opposed to birth control argued that if doctors extended their support to the use of contraceptives, they would seriously jeopardize their professional standing, which a section of the Indian population already viewed with suspicion.[2] At the same time, some selected Indian biomedical journals carried articles in which doctors debated the topic. There were some medical college magazines that devoted their entire issue to the subject, soliciting articles from Western advocates, college faculty, and medical students in order to encourage debate on and understanding of birth control. Many of the biomedical journals carried illustrated advertisements of the various contraceptives; a close review of these advertisements demonstrates the nature of contraceptive technology available in the 1930s and 1940s.

During their Indian tours in the 1930s, Margaret Sanger and Edith How-Martyn contacted medical doctors and addressed medical college faculty and students on the topic of contraception. Sanger and How-Martyn distributed sixty gyneplaques (models of female reproductive organs) to doctors in 1936. These models were found to be indispensable in training doctors and in birth control clinics to demonstrate the use of various contraceptives.[3] Their visits to India generated interest in the subject of birth control within the medical community; for instance, the Patna Medical College published a special issue of their college magazine on the subject in 1936.

In her work in the United States, Sanger had emphasized the importance of recruiting the support of the medical community to ensure wider acceptance for birth control. Likewise, in India Sanger also sought the endorsement of the biomedical profession, stressing the need for doctors to be trained in birth control. However, not all birth control advocates favored the biomedical monopoly over birth control. Marie Stopes was suspicious of the medical community, and in Britain she preferred to disseminate information on birth control through her own clinics rather than hospitals.[4]

In India, Sanger, How-Martyn, and Eileen Palmer stressed the need for medically trained personnel to disseminate birth control information. Seeking to convince doctors opposed to the use of contraceptives, How-Martyn sketched a scenario whereby the knowledge falling into the hands of commercial people would result in the propagation of harmful, unscientific methods and, more threateningly, the sale of abortifacients as contraceptives.[5] How-Martyn, in her meetings with Indian doctors, was interested in identifying those who would be willing to train their colleagues on birth control. She wrote to Indian doctors who were regularly providing contraceptive information in their clinics, asking them if they would be willing to train others.[6]

A section of the medical community was eager to appropriate the right to disseminate and control this new knowledge; articulating this eagerness, B. L. Raina wrote that it was "imperative on the part of the medical profession to take up this work in right earnest . . . and give right information and correct guidance, a work which medical profession alone is competent to do in as much as patients come to them for advice and assistance."[7] Although Raina argued that the medical profession alone was competent to give out birth control information, medical schools and colleges in India provided limited training to their students on the subject in the early 1930s. Many doctors and medical students who were exposed to the works of Stopes and Sanger raised the issue about the lack of training in this particular field. In an article in the *Prince of Wales Medical College Magazine,* Dr. J. N. Ghosh, a professor at the Patna Training College, asserted that the "medical profession has signally failed to do its duty in the matter of birth control." Lamenting the lack of medical training on birth control among practitioners he wrote, "The average doctor has a very hazy notion of birth control; he has not taken the trouble to acquire whatever knowledge is available on the subject, nor is birth control included in the curriculum of any medical college."[8] Dr. H. K. Chaudhury, supporting birth control, wrote in the *Indian Medical Journal* in 1937 that "instruction on these subjects [birth control] should form a part of the education of medical students in all medical schools and colleges.

Those who are now in charge of training our future medical practitioners should bear in mind that there is no single health measure so important to the community at large as this."[9] Reiterating a similar sentiment, Dr. C. G. Mahadevia, a medical officer at Una, Junagad, wrote that even though occasionally doctors were called upon to give practical advice on contraception, the subject was not taught in medical schools and colleges. Many of the doctors who had no formal training relied upon books to self-train themselves. Stopes's *Contraception* and Michael Fielding's *Parenthood Artificial by Design* were popular among physicians.[10]

Lack of training made it difficult for the biomedical community to articulate a clear and coherent understanding of birth control from a "scientific" and medical perspective. Many physicians who supported the cause of birth control accepted the Malthusian argument of overpopulation as a problem vis-à-vis national resources. Editorials and articles entitled "The Problem of Population" were published as early as February 1929 in *Indian Medical Gazette*; similarly, an editorial titled "India's Teeming Million" was published in the *Calcutta Medical Journal* in November 1938; and a report, "Rapid Increase in the Population of India," was published in *Indian Medical Record* in August 1938.[11] Dr. Santosh Mukherji, in *Birth Control for the Millions,* stated categorically in his preface and in the chapter "The Problem of Over-Population in India and Control of Conception" that the real need for birth control in India was because of overpopulation. The Indian population was "increasing unchecked with great rapidity without any corresponding increase in the source of income."[12] He maintained that the population in India had exceeded the limit of subsistence and the total quantity of foodstuffs produced in India was not sufficient to maintain a large population, adding that even "if these were divided equally everyone will be under-fed."[13] Mukherji, like many others, framed the issue in Malthusian terms, as one of numbers, whereby resource redistribution would not solve the crisis of overpopulation. He presented the numerical increase in the size of India's population as a grave danger to India's future.

Eugenic arguments also found intellectual favor within the biomedical community. Physicians supporting birth control cited the eugenic argument of "better racial stock," complaining that the middle classes were using birth control devices to create a dysgenic problem. Biomedical supporters of birth control, like some of the other enthusiasts, also represented the working classes as the "ideal consumers" of this technology; however, they complained that this class, unfortunately, had little access to and knowledge about birth control methods. As a result of the class character of contraceptive usage, *Calcutta Medical Journal* argued that the practice of birth control in India was "slowly but surely killing the growth of 'A-grade' population. In other words, birth control in India today is producing quantity in place of quality."[14] In a similar vein, Dr. Mukherji wrote that "control of breeding was more necessary in the case of the poor; but they do not practice it and go on begetting children freely without any check. It means an increase in the number of inferior stock which is undesirable in the interest of the future generation. Birth control clinics should be run by the state to teach this class of people the way of prevention of conception." He added, moreover, that "*birth control should not be practiced by the higher class except in exceptional cases.*"[15] Male biomedical practitioners such as Mukherji saw contraceptive technologies as a means of extending regulation of sexual and reproductive autonomy among subaltern groups. In his support of birth control, he expressed a strong desire to ensure and promote the interests of the middle classes, rather than express concerns for providing women with better knowledge of their bodies or giving them the right to determine their fertility. Male physicians did not espouse a "woman-centered" agenda; in their writings on birth control, they rarely address issues of maternal and infant mortality. For the most part, they were reluctant to frame birth control as an issue that would grant women authority as a "knower" of their own bodies.

In "Population Control," Dr. A. N. Chatterji, a professor of hygiene and public health, articulated a strict agenda to check what he termed the disorderly growth of population.[16] He proposed a "comprehensive scheme" to combat the problem of "over-population" that revealed an underlying desire for social engineering to establish a social order appealing to middle-class values. For instance, he stated that "arrangements should be made for sterilisation of the unfit and of habitual offenders of law particularly of those concerned in rape and outrages against women."[17] However, he left the very category of the "unfit" itself undefined, suggesting that it was a given natural category not requiring definition. Chatterji also demanded an "effective censor against all indecent literature and advertisements."[18] Unlike some of his other colleagues, he suggested that greater facilities should be provided to "public women" for the use of contraceptives. His program called for strict class-based social control programs and an imposition of a strict moral code.

Dr. J. N. Ghosh, also in favor of sterilization of the "unfit," declared in even stronger terms the desirability of state intervention to ascertain who could and could not reproduce. Laying down a strict socially selective reproductive scheme, he noted that "[n]ear morons . . . who congenitally lack all prudence and fore-sight, and are never bothered by any thoughts of improving their social condition" were the types of socially irresponsible folks that needed to be compulsorily sterilized. In his vision of future society, he advocated eugenic sterilization and demanded that parents-to-be "apply to some state department to satisfy it that they are fit people to have children. No one will be allowed to have children without proper license. The interests of the individual will have to be sacrificed to the welfare of the community."[19] A similar concern with protecting the "physical and intellectual quality of the race" led Dr. Mukherji to demand greater state support for providing birth control appliances to poor women.[20] The agenda of these physicians did not seek to democratize the access and usage of techno-scientific contraceptive products. Instead of a democratic imperative, eugenics and Malthusian rationality underlined the physicians' demand for dissemination of contraceptive information. The physicians believed their social engineering schemes legitimized their intrusive interrogation of sexual and procreative practices. Human reproduction was understood to have very significant consequences on national and social well-being, and as such this sociosexual practice could not be allowed free expression.

Gender and class biases that shaped the understanding of Indian male physicians about contraceptives became transparent in their discussion on the impact of birth control on conjugal sex for men and women. Dr. H. K. Chaudhury argued that the propagation of birth control would help "certain nervous women who as a result of very bad time at previous child birth, are afraid of conjugal advances of their husbands and go so far as to refuse all coitus. They are not only the source of discomfort and distress to the husband but also tend to social instability, divorce and fostering prostitution and sex evils. To such people proper instruction of contraceptive methods would re-establish harmony and peace in the home."[21] Use of birth control was represented as an ideal method for management of sexuality within marriage. It was argued that the use of birth control would ensure that married women fulfilled their assigned patriarchal role of providing sexual gratification to their husbands. According to Dr. Chaudhury, when wives failed to provide sexual services to their husbands because of traumatic experiences of childbirth, they became objects of social instability. It was the wife's failure as a sexual provider that led the husband to seek sexual gratification outside of marriage. Chaudhury represented sexual gratification as an inviolable right for men, particularly within matrimony. Naturalizing male sexual desires, especially within matrimony, worked to extend and legitimize male authority. Dr. T. S. Balasubramania Iyer considered contraception as a solution for reducing the incidence of venereal diseases and argued that "it will lessen prostitution by promoting a happy married life in that it allows the husband to have all the sexual life at home without the fear of injuring the health of the wife."[22] The male physicians favoring birth control claimed that conjugal happiness could be ensured only when wives provided sexual services to their husbands. Women as wives were contrasted with the sexually active and corrupting prostitutes. The "affective repertoire" of the couple within marriage was constructed to protect and promote masculine interests and no attempts were made to accommodate or even address issues of sexual satisfaction for women within marriage.[23] Male physicians who addressed the impact of contraceptives on conjugal sexuality seemed to focus primarily on the sexual needs of men, representing women as passive sexual providers, especially in their roles as wives.

The debates on birth control provided a useful entry point to biomedical authorities in the early twentieth century and allowed them to address the role of sex within marriage and to construct appropriate norms of conjugal sexuality. Although some physicians sought to regulate and control sexual expressions within marriage, for the most part, they did not share a uniform position on the vexed subject of human sexuality. For instance, Iyer stated that abstinence as a method of contraceptive, although ensuring complete success, was not ideal because it negatively impacted the health of both men and women who practiced it for too long. Abstinence, he argued, placed too much strain on controlling all "natural" sexual expressions between husbands and wives and if practiced could lead to psychosis and destroy conjugal happiness.[24] Sexual abstinence or self-control was a subject on which the biomedical opinion was at best muddled and confused. Dr. Iyer wrote that although self-control was the "best method, ancient, good for the soul, and good for the body,"[25] he simultaneously asserted that "sexual appetite, next to hunger, is the most dominating and insistent instinct of life, through society. Ignorant of the overwhelming importance of the subject many clamour for its suppression. Self-control implies the repression of a natural and necessary instinct, and it is a psychological truism that repression of such an instinct is more harmful than its expression. Young and normal couples cannot for long carry out this repression without mental, physical and moral deterioration."[26] Physicians and practitioners of biomedicine deployed "science" to make normative arguments about male/female sexuality. They assigned singular normative meaning to sex as akin to hunger. As in the above quotation, doctors represented sex as a "natural" bodily response rather than a cultural construct mediated through specific gender, class, and caste dynamics. Jeffery Weeks has argued that such "natural" constructions of sex, gender, and sexuality lock them together as biological imperatives.[27]

Sex only for procreation was considered a theological dogma, "thoroughly pernicious," because for men it "had assumed a sacramental value,—an outward manifestation of an inner grace."[28] Dr. Mukherji argued that abstinence was medically harmful for married men and suppression of sexual feeling would lead to a state of sexual frustration making the "sexual centers" hyperirritable. Medicalizing gendered sexual differentiation, he added that "should this condition last for a long time without satisfaction there may be a break down of health of the sexual organs resulting in impotence.... [F]orcible suppression of sexual excitement caused by close relation with the wife is injurious to health. Very few men can practice complete self-control under the marital condition."[29] In their critiques of abstinence, some physicians ascribed a scientific-medico neutrality to male sexuality to argue that denial of physical expressions within marriage would have dire physical consequences for the men. The dominant biomedical discourse projected a paradigm of female sexuality that portrayed women as passive sexual providers who ensured the sexual, psychological, physical, and also moral well-being of men. Women as spouses were held responsible for keeping men healthy, safe from sexually transmitted diseases, and away from prostitutes. There was little room in the writings of male biomedical supporters of birth control for women to express themselves as autonomous subjects making procreative decisions based on their physical or economic needs and situations. It would be fair to argue that the male physicians expressed a patriarchal antipathy toward female sexuality, failing to acknowledge sexual pleasure or the sexual needs of women.

Even though some physicians promoted the cause of contraceptives, divorcing sex from procreation, there were others who were greatly suspicious of sex. For instance, Dr. A. N. Chatterji called for rational and disciplined sexual expression for men within matrimony, asserting that "society with the opposite sex is a tonic and a stimulant. Like all tonics and stimulants it should be properly utilised under control. Disaster follows in the absence of required control.... Persons without control over sex can hardly be helped by artificial birth control.... Married life should not mean frequent sex. Men should learn manners and the art of enjoying the society of women without a thought of the desires of flesh. It is a vice to resort to sexual intercourse as a routine even in married life."[30]

In the various articulations on sexuality examined above, it becomes apparent that women were not allowed the freedom to act out their sexuality or express their fantasies or desires even within marriage. Although sexual impulses were identified primarily as masculine, men too were required to ideally reserve their sexual expressions within heterosexual monogamous marriages. Interestingly though, read together, the statements above demonstrate the deep divisions within the medical opinions on the merits of sex. Male physicians did not speak with a uniform voice. In the early twentieth century, there were many differences of opinion and much confusion among them on the subject of human sexuality and birth control. The community of biomedics was split on the issue; those in favor of birth control complained about the lack of training of the medical personnel and, even while extending their support to the cause, doctors were uncertain about the most reliable method of contraceptive that they could recommend to their patients.

Another issue of confusion among "professionals" supportive of birth control had to do with a method of contraception considered most appropriate. Part of this confusion can be explained through the nature of contraceptive technology, which in this period was in its infancy. New technologies were still being researched and engineered to enhance control over reproduction. Medical journals carried reviews of books that supported the "safe period" as the best method of birth control, but with a cautionary note: "[T]he problem is still subject to debate, and the public should be informed that the matter is not settled."[31] Dr. Mukherji, in his discussion of contraceptives, suggested that in reality there was no safe period. He also discredited a popular belief among Indian women that conception would not take place so long as women were lactating.[32]

Mukherji's book carried an appendix with a long list of mechanical and chemical commercial contraceptives available in the market with brief explanations of their properties. He also provided his readers with addresses of chemists who carried the products. Many of the mainstream biomedical journals carried advertisements of contraceptives. These advertisements contained a brief description of the contraceptives, their cost, and addresses of chemists where they could be purchased. Mil-San was one such contraceptive—a spermicidal and antiseptic jelly manufactured in England that had distributors in Lahore, Bombay, Karachi, and Calcutta. The advertisement assured its users that Mil-San "cannot be detected in use, is odourless and does not stain linen."[33] The language in this particular advertisement suggests that women might have used contraceptives secretly and not always with the consent of their husbands.

Other contraceptives advertised in the biomedical journals included Lantex Protectives and Lantex Paragons. These male condoms could either be ordered directly from London or from the company's agents in Bombay.[34] Likewise, Ortho-Gynol could be ordered from London or from retailers in large Indian cities such as Bombay, Calcutta, and Madras.[35] Gynomin and Rendell were other commercial contraceptives that were also advertised in the journals, but with only a London address, suggesting that these contraceptives had to be imported, adding to their cost and thus making them unaffordable for the poor.[36] Although women were the targeted consumers of most of these advertised contraceptives, husbands were also required to shoulder the responsibility of family planning. The announcement of Contrabab, ensuring reliability and safety, declared, "The welfare of a nation depends on the health of its women . . . for if a woman is not perfectly healthy, her sons also will not be constitutionally perfect; and with a nation of weak women, physical degeneration of the race must result. Every husband, therefore, is in duty bound to adopt suitable means to preserve his wife's health ... to see that her constitution is not weakened by the too frequent bearing of children."[37] In this advertisement, women were primarily represented as icons of national maternity, responsible for begetting healthy male progeny for the nation. Use of contraceptives was regarded as necessary for "scientific" management of procreation. Interestingly, here is also one instance of addressing men's shared responsibility in making reproductive decisions, even though women were for the most part the targeted consumers of contraceptive technology in this period.

There were many physicians who were outrightly hostile to the idea of the biomedical community providing contraceptive information and devices to their clients/patients. The contradictory positions, in favor of and hostile to the dissemination of contraceptive information, highlights the internal fissures, factionalism, and inconsistencies within the biomedicinal community. This allows us to recognize the complex and messy tradition of medicine rather than as a closed and uniform system in the early twentieth century.

Those within the biomedical community who were opposed to birth control provided a number of reasons to support their opposition. The opponents, quite like the supporters of birth control, provided both medical and sociocultural reasons to support their claims that birth control was harmful. For instance, in "Birth Control by Self Control," I. Ahmed, a sixth-year medical student at the Patna Medical College, argued that the spread of birth control was having a dysgenic effect on India's population. "People who should transmit the best heredity practice birth control extensively and successfully, the less intelligent, not nearly so generally and successfully." He continued, "It has been found that where birth control is most desirable there it is least acceptable and where most acceptable it is least desirable, so the population increases by the multiplication of the inferior strata and the relative decrease of the superior. A long continuance of such conditions will inevitably end in the decadence of the race."[38] Ahmed presented a class-specific and elitist grievance against contraceptive usage. He understood that the disproportionate success of the middle class in eliminating pregnancy as a sexual consequence constituted a national demographic crisis. Ahmed shared his fear of dysgenic procreative practices establishing a hold on national demography with the supporters of birth control. Those who supported birth control shared Ahmed's bias against the lower classes but, unlike him, they believed that birth control was the solution, not the problem, and that "proper" use of contraceptives would work to reverse class-based fertility patterns in favor of the middle classes.

Although opposing birth control by artificial methods, Ahmed argued that self-control was the only natural and most desirable form of birth control; therefore, it was the "*duty* of medical men to find out the means of self control." Taking a functionalist position on sex, Ahmed linked it to procreation, writing that "biological union is not meant for pleasure but for bringing forth progeny and union is a crime when the desire for progeny is absent. . . . Artificial methods are likely to put premium upon vice. They make a man and woman reckless to indulge in the act."[39] The use of birth control, T. B. Gupta, a fifth-year medical student at Patna Medical College, argued, had a negative impact on women. "Many women became victims of menstrual disorders, hysteria and other nervous diseases. We often come across dissatisfied and neurotic women whose sexual instinct, we have reason to believe, has been unduly stimulated, without there being periods of natural quiescence produced by pregnancy and lactation."[40] Gupta warned that women would experience nervous disorders if the sexual activity was divorced from their "natural" biological function of reproduction and if the use of birth control denied women the physical telos of motherhood. This essay strongly condemned the "modern woman" who readily adopted birth control and enjoyed public activities, finding "life in the home with their children . . . as something cursed. They have therefore taken a fancy for independent life, and in many countries they work side by side with men in workshops and factories." Too much freedom and taste of the outside world had become "the root of their [women's] distaste for motherhood."[41] Gupta stigmatized the modern women in their attempts to avoid motherhood, and warned that women relinquishing their primary duty and function of motherhood would unleash an unacceptable spectacle of social chaos. In his opposition to contraceptives, the author called to confine women to maternity and to the private realm of the home.

An earlier article by M. S. Nawaz, a physician in the *Indian Medical Record,* represented the spread of birth control as a negative manifestation of the advance of "modern civilization" that in America had infused women with such "an unhealthy spirit of emancipation and liberty that they were not prepared to undergo the *hardships of pregnancy, childbirth and lactation, incident to marriage.*"[42] This reluctance among women to fulfill the "grand function of maternity," the doctor argued, would have dire consequences on their health, causing "its *victims* to become physical."[43] Nawaz was not alone in expressing his fears of the potential freedom birth control technology would place in the hands of the "modern" women to enact their sexuality outside of motherhood and marriage; as seen earlier, similar concerns marked the writings of other male physicians and medical students who opposed the spread and use of birth control.

It would be fair to conclude that despite the differences on the importance of birth control among male doctors, they shared a common understanding of "natural" male sexual desires and a corresponding need to enforce female sexual passivity as normative. In their enthusiasm to locate women as mothers strictly within the private sphere, male physicians failed to recognize family and motherhood as potential sites of women's oppression. Within the biomedical discourse examined above, there was no room for expressions of female sexual autonomy. The attempt was to police, control, and discipline middle-class women, constructing them as repositories of national identity and culture.

Western-Trained Biomedical Women and the Politics of Birth Control

As suggested in the introduction, the nature of services and the interactions between physicians and their clients in colonial India during the early twentieth century was gendered. Women clients and their families preferred women physicians. However, despite a rising demand among a section of the Indian middle classes for medical education for women, medical schools in colonial India reluctantly accepted applications from women students in the late nineteenth century.[44] Before Indian women were trained in medicine, there were Western women doctors who found jobs in India, beginning in the late nineteenth century.[45]

In this section I examine the involvement of women physicians, both Western and Indian, in the debates on birth control in colonial India in the early twentieth century. For the most part, advocates of birth control in the early twentieth century constructed and presented contraceptives as a necessary intervention aimed at improving maternal health of Indian women by lowering maternal and infant mortality. However, quite like among male physicians, the subject of birth control was also contentiously debated among women doctors who were equally divided on the issue. They expressed a fragmented understanding of the issue, similar to their male cohorts. Although some women physicians were eager to embrace birth control as an additional knowledge necessary to further their professional careers, there were others who regarded contraceptives as potentially endangering the sociomoral fabric of society. Like male physicians, women discussed the issues of lack of training and appropriate technologies of contraceptives.

The debate among women physicians about the legitimacy of birth control occurred largely within the *Journal of Association of Medical Women in India* (*JAMWI*).[46] Western women physicians practicing in India were the main contributors to this journal; the voices and opinions of Indian women doctors and patients are infrequently heard in this journal. Because this journal was published for private circulation, Indian women doctors who were in private practice and not members of the Association for Medical Women in India (AMWI) had limited access to it. In order to compensate for the absence of Indian women's voices in written sources, I conducted interviews with three Indian women gynecologists who started their practice in the north Indian city of Kanpur (Cawnpore during the British period) during the 1930s and 1940s. Interviews with these three women doctors filled in the silences and gaps in *JAMWI* and provided important information about the training of medical students in birth control methods in the early twentieth century; the demands, if any, their clients made for contraceptive information; and what advice the doctors gave on fertility regulation.

Mrs. Lilias M. Jeffries's article "Prevention," published in May 1921, was the first one on birth control in the *JAMWI*.[47] Commenting upon the lack of medical training in birth control among women physicians, Jeffries feared that their ignorance and "personal opinions" might lead women patients to use harmful methods of prevention; that is, abortion. The article argued that medical women should "take their share of the thinking needed and be ready armed with full scientific information." Abstinence as a method of birth control was considered "unnatural, a violent severance of a normal relationship, which has a crippling if not potently harmful effect on the ordinary human pair, physically, morally and spiritually too. The physiological loss to each is well known and the reaction from such repression of a *natural function* may have far reaching manifestations."[48] While constructing sex as a natural function, she was quick to add a note of caution, stressing that moderation in sexual behavior was always to be upheld, even among married couples. The ideal goals of prevention were "to provide the best possible chance for the offspring to be healthy and to be properly brought up; that is, in a favorable environment with sufficient educational and social opportunities. To protect the mother from too rapid child bearing ... to prevent the transmission of hereditary disease. To maintain normal marital relationships even when pregnancy is undesirable."[49] Pro-natal concern along with the desire to ensure healthy progeny seem to underline Jeffries's advocacy of birth control. For the most part, Indian male doctors rarely expressed any pro-natalist concerns in their demands for wider dissemination of contraceptive information. Although stressing the importance of contraceptives, Jeffries, like some of her male colleagues, constructed marital sex as normative and argued that birth control was an essential instrument for ensuring "normal marital" relationships. However, there was a difference in Jeffries's position from that of male physicians, in that she did not outline an essentially gendered sexual guideline for a "normal" martial relationship.

In her discussion of various contraceptive methods, Jeffries asserted that for contraceptives to be effective, they had to be reliable and inconspicuous so as to retain spontaneity and naturalness. The preferred method should not prevent "absorption from vaginal mucous membrane, of the seminal fluid, or that portion of it that is advantageous to the female metabolism." She discussed contraceptive methods that men and women could use and concluded that the woman "should retain this degree of control of marital intercourse." Jeffries recognized women as active agents in control of sexual knowledge and assigned them the responsibility of making procreative decisions for their families. The article concluded with a strong plea to women doctors to address this "really important and burning subject, in a purely scientific spirit. Let there be no needless air of disreputability about it. Let it be clearly understood as a means towards the improvement of the race; the elimination of the unfit, the maintenance of maternal health, and the production of the largest possible number of the best possible surviving offspring, under the best possible conditions for their up-bringing."[50]

Because it was the first article on birth control in *JAMWI*, it is helpful to analyze the responses among its readers to understand how female physicians framed the topic and their contributions to the debate. Before evaluating the responses to Jeffries's essay, it is useful to briefly highlight the issues she emphasized and some of the underlying tensions within her position. Unlike her male colleagues, Jeffries represented sex within marriage as natural, not only for men but also for women. Women were represented as ideal subjects for receiving, controlling, and executing contraceptive knowledge. This positive representation of women as subjects of knowledge was absent in the debates among male physicians. Moreover, unlike the male physicians, Jeffries constructed women both as sexual subjects and also as mothers and wives. This woman doctor called for an examination of the subject of birth control in a "scientific" spirit, stressing the need for greater attention to the facts of empirical observation over those of moral prejudices. Despite her positive articulation of the topic, a eugenicist bias against the "unfit," with a desire to eliminate them from society, marked Jeffries's understanding. In her conclusion, Jeffries emphasized how birth control would ensure eugenic results, improve the race, and eliminate the "unfit." She valued the rights of certain reproductive subjects over others, selectively bestowing family privileges. The politics of ensuring a desirable citizenry from the appropriate "fit" race and class limited Jeffries's otherwise radical gender understanding.

This issue of *JAMWI* carried an editorial comment opening its pages on the debate about birth control among its readers. Readers were invited to send in "any communications critical or otherwise on the subject." As was to be expected, Jeffries's article evoked both supportive and negative responses on the topic and related issues of medical training for women doctors in contraception, appropriate birth control technology, and the role of sex within marriage. The women physicians opposed to birth control argued that the only suitable and acceptable form of birth control was "abstention from marital intercourse."[51] According to Mary O'Brien Beadon, women who used contraceptives would not be free but rather be debased to the level of the lowest men. "Such measures are truly a negation of the womanhood in woman and the seal of her subordination to man. Prevention is at best an expedient, let it be admitted as such, and not glorified as the charter of women's freedom. Women, by using these means, instead of stimulating their husbands to rise to the highest of which they are capable, capitulate to the lowest."[52] Women were represented as "agents of salvation" for their men, and as such, sexless women were upheld as prescriptive models for middle class women.[53] Signs and expressions of sexual desires among women was read as a negation of their inherent womanhood and their feminine selves.

Dr. Beadon drew up a connection between the lack of willpower to exercise sexual abstention and its effects on degeneracy of the race. She argued that "if we cannot control ourselves how can we control our children? Or how can we hope to *maintain our empire over subordinate races* when once we have lost our moral superiority?"[54] Beadon understood sexuality as an antisocial force, articulating a sensitivity common even in post-Victorian Britain, which considered sexual control as a mark of gentility, reserved for the middle classes. Historians have argued that the middle classes constructed working-class and non-Western sexualities negatively; for instance, "the working classes and native blacks supposedly allowed their sexuality to spill out over their total lives, diverting them from the goal of achievement through work, wasting their energies and draining their vital forces."[55] Beadon deployed a racist and colonial perspective to emphasize the special burden that white women shouldered in the colonies. White women were required to set high standards in sexual and moral behavior, as symbols and markers of Western culture. Although the opponents argued that the use of birth control would lead to racial decline, it is important to emphasize that the supporters of birth control certainly did not intend to dismantle social distinctions based on race and class. On the contrary, as we saw in the earlier section on male biomedical practitioners and also in Jeffries's article, supporters of contraceptives understood this technology as necessary for ensuring racial and social hierarchies. For the most part, advocates of birth control in the early twentieth century wanted to ensure the propagation of a "fitter" race of people, rather than promote democratic access to new technologies.

Jeffries's article elicited mixed responses from other readers of *JAMWI*. O. B. Flak and Jeffries responded to Beadon's objections to birth control, arguing that the use of birth control did not render women defenseless against the sexual demands of husbands. In her response, Jeffries reinforced the importance of sex within marriage, quoting Edward Carpenter at length to support her position. "The bodily intimacy or endearment may not be the object for which they come together: but if it is denied it will bar any real sense of repose and affiance, and make the relation restless, vague, tentative and unsatisfied."[56] As has been argued in earlier chapters, the early twentieth century witnessed a recasting of the ideal of conjugality to include "good sex" as an important component of compatibility and companionship.[57] Extending the case for "good sex" within marriage, Jeffries denied that the use of preventives would cause excessive sexual indulgence or mean the prostitution of the wife in marriage.[58]

Margaret Balfour, an important and well-known woman physician who worked mainly in Punjab from 1892 to 1924, raised objections to birth control on the grounds that its practice had a dysgenic effect.[59] She argued that middle-class women were using birth control because "they did not wish the trouble and suffering of child-bearing and because their husbands (and they also) do not wish the expense of large families." Wondering about the outcome of this, she continued, "[T]he poorest classes who are not in a position to bring up their children satisfactorily, continue to have large families, while better classes who have generations of educated and self-respecting citizens as their forebears, are tending to die. What will be the result in the future?"[60] Class-based fertility patterns, she argued, would have dysgenic effects on the nation's population. She lamented, like some of her male cohorts, that the "ideal" racial stock—the middle classes—were shying away from their national duty of providing "ideal" citizens, whereas the working poor were multiplying at an alarming speed, threatening to demographically outnumber the middle classes.

Still, Balfour lent hesitant support to the cause of birth control, laying down guidelines for this knowledge to be placed strictly under the control of biomedically trained personnel who would selectively make this information available to their clients/patients. Only medical conditions could justify providing this information to women patients, and she stressed that it should certainly not be passed on to married women who wanted to avoid pregnancy. Emphasizing maternalism for women, Balfour asserted that women seeking to exercise control over their bodies were not entitled to receive birth control information from physicians. Medical training was considered a license that granted practitioners the right to intervene in the sexual lives of married people. Balfour was anxious to establish biomedical hegemony over the emerging field of contraceptives within women's health care.[61] Jeffries challenged Balfour's extension of the boundaries of medical practitioner. The "wishes of the patient," Jeffries wrote, had to be considered: "In our modern civilization potential parents must take the responsibility of producing offspring or not, into their own hands," she said.[62] In her letter to the editor, she provided the postal address of Stopes's clinic in London for interested readers.

Dr. Ruth Young, director of the Maternity and Child Welfare Bureau, spent many years practicing biomedicine in India and was one of the few leading women doctors who supported birth control. In "Medical Women and Conception Control," published in *JAMWI* in 1934, she argued for medical women to acquaint themselves with the subject of birth control.[63] She did not think that birth control clinics should replace child welfare clinics, because the child welfare centers stood for better babies rather than for fewer babies. She recognized that there may have been some overlapping principles between child welfare centers and birth control whereby "child welfare might well include conception control to ensure proper spacing of children, so that each gets an adequate start in life and allow the mother to regain her health, and to prevent unduly large families."[64] Young called for women physicians to be proactive and suggested that the onus of providing information on birth control should rest with women doctors. The doctors should "not always wait to be asked for advice"; instead they should "try to prevent women being worn out by repeated pregnancies and further feeble infants being brought into the world." She stressed the need for medical women to be trained in the subject, so they could displace the "quacks or unscrupulous commercial firms" from providing the necessary information.[65]

Medical practitioners were eager to stake the territories of their profession, and this anxiety was much more pronounced in India because the hold of traditional birth attendants, *dais,* constantly frustrated the efforts of biomedics to have access to the birthing bodies of Indian women. Young's article reflects the desire to displace and discredit indigenous midwives as primary caretakers of Indian women. She represented these women as "professional abortionists" without backing this accusation with proof. In her own words, "I am quite sure that the ordinary country *dai* knows a good deal in an empirical way about methods of procuring abortion although it is very difficult to get information on the subject."[66]

Addressing the concern about the efficacy of contraceptive technology, Young cautioned that there was *no* method that could be regarded as absolutely reliable, and that any method that ensured the highest degree of safety involved a "certain amount of trouble and intelligence." She mentioned that a Dutch pessary together with a tube of jelly cost about 7 rupees and was considered one of the more reliable methods. There was a clear disjuncture between the high costs and lack of accessibility of reliable contraceptives for the working poor who were constructed as the "ideal" consumers and target group for the use of birth control. Recognizing this tension, there was an effort on the part of some doctors to offer cheaper though less reliable methods of birth control for the poor. Some of the methods that Young presented as "suitable" for the poor were "plugs soaked in vinegar and water equal parts" and cotton wool dipped in olive oil, suggesting that in India *neem* oil could replace olive oil. Young mentioned that some of her patients objected to both these methods—some women found vinegar too smarting, and neem oil was disliked because of its smell.[67] Among physicians, Young was one of the few who linked the use of birth control with women's rights over their bodies. She argued that women should have the right to decide the number of children they wanted to have and the medical community should provide them information on proper spacing of children.[68]

The Association of Medical Women in India tried to instill interest in the subject of birth control among women doctors. In 1934 it sent out 300 copies of a questionnaire on birth control. The *JAMWI* carried a short report on the response to this questionnaire. A mere thirty-six replies were received, and that, the report complained, reflected the "curious apathy to what is, after all, an important problem of present-day medical life."[69] The survey raised the issue of the need for training medical students on the subject of birth control in order to "prevent the knowledge getting into the hands of dais or other unsuitable persons."[70] Welfare centers and women's clubs were identified as ideal forums for discussing and advertising the subject among women.[71]

Nonmedical proponents of birth control also debated the appropriate sites for disseminating contraceptive information. How-Martyn and Palmer mentioned that in 1936 there were eighteen birth control clinics in different cities in India; this number went up to twenty in 1937, and if private clinics, hospitals, and maternal welfare centers that also gave birth control information were included, the number of clinics was close to sixty in 1937. At times combining birth control work within more general work in a hospital created restrictions; for example, in the Dufferin Hospital in Calcutta it was hard to publicize birth control. Despite the rise in clinics that provided birth control information, there was always a concern of making these known to women and also of bringing women into these clinics. It was suggested that members of the clinic personally escort poor women to help them overcome their natural shyness in such matters.[72]

There were a few Indian women doctors in the Association of Medical Women in India; some of these women contributed to the ongoing discussions on birth control in the *JAMWI*. Dr. Miss Jerbanoo Mistry was one such doctor who lent her support to birth control.[73] A specific class and gender understanding of sexuality informed Mistry's hesitant advocacy of birth control. According to her, working-class men and men from backward classes were "ignorant as to ways and means of restraining their impulses."[74] This class of men lacked higher ideals and their sex instinct predominated over every other consideration. She asserted that if their wives denied these men sex, they might use other means to satisfy their desire—probably prostitution. There were interesting overlaps between Mistry's representations of working-class/subaltern sexuality and Beadon's representations of working-class and non-Western sexualities. Both women projected their own elitist cultural constructs of sexuality as normative and ideal.

Dr. Mistry was, reluctantly, willing to advocate birth control for the "less enlightened communities," upholding the principle of "to do a great right do a little wrong." However, despite accepting birth control as a necessary evil in some cases, Mistry argued that there were no satisfactory methods available that could be recommended. For most doctors in the early twentieth century, not just in India but also in Britain and the United States, birth control was not a simple subject.[75] There were complex issues related to birth control on which the medical profession was seeking more information. Although many practitioners were unambivalently opposed to the practice of birth control, there were a few who tried to make concessions and accommodate the use of birth control under specific conditions.

Mistry was one of those doctors who tried to struggle with the issue of birth control rather than reject it outright. She presented a paper on "Birth Control" at the annual meeting of the Association of Medical Women in India in 1933, and this later appeared as an article in *JAMWI*.[76] By 1933, Dr. Mistry had acquainted herself with the publications of Sanger and Stopes and had visited Stopes's clinic in London. She made a cautious case for allowing the spread and use of birth control, listing available methods and techniques of contraceptives. Dr. Mistry confined her limited support for birth control to "the really poor and over-prolific or diseased mothers," and suggested that these "ideal" candidates should be provided a free supply of appliances through the antenatal clinics, maternity homes, and the infant welfare centers.[77] Dr. Mistry presented these institutions as acceptable sites for giving information and distributing free birth control appliances to the deserving poor, rather than opening special birth control clinics. In 1936, Mistry wrote a brief descriptive account of the debates on birth control for the AIWC conference in Trivandrum, which passed a resolution supporting the need for contraceptive dissemination.[78]

Dr. J. Jhirad, in her reprinted essay "Practical Aspects of Birth Control," argued that given the "Indian temperament, . . . even a woman of several children is too reticent to discuss sex matters with her own doctor." So separate birth control clinics were unnecessary and information on birth control could be provided in maternal and infant care centers. She also warned that the use of contraceptives would lead to a rise in "materialistic" tendencies that would put "back the spiritual progress of mankind." The new emphasis on spacing and small families would have a negative impact on women, causing more harm than good because a "woman's main occupation has been the home and children. Too wide a spacing and limitation may mean little occupation to the woman if she has no other interests and occupations to fall back on." The reference here to leisure was certainly a class-specific condition, one that mostly plagued women of the middle classes! Evidently, experiences of working-class women and their need for child care did not inform this physician's understanding of the subject. The class bias of Western-trained Indian women doctors once again becomes clear in Dr. Jhirad's discussion of the specific class pattern of contraceptive usage. Expressing her fears of working-class fecundity, she asserted that "contraceptive measure will find greatest favour amongst the leisured and other better classes, indeed the methods at present in vogue can only be used effectively by the intelligent classes—the poor and the ignorant will continue to remain untouched for a long time; the result one may imagine, will be an overwhelming population of latter—a C3 nation." Her solution to this middle-class nightmare was to encourage the poor classes to adopt birth control and the "better classes" to "rise to their responsibility to the State and populate it with the '*right stuff.*'"[79] Eugenic considerations underscored Jhirad's advocacy of birth control. She understood parenthood simultaneously as a mark of social privilege and an act of patriotic duty—and as such called for it to be selectively bestowed upon social elites.

Although the *JAMWI* is an important source for reconstructing the debates on birth control among women physicians in colonial India, it does not give much information on the interactions between Western-trained Indian women doctors and their clients. To evaluate this interaction, I draw upon my interviews with three gynecologists who began their private practices in Kanpur during the 1930s and 1940s under British colonial control. Many of the Indian women doctors upon completion of their studies could not always find suitable positions in government hospitals or in hospitals run by the Dufferin fund.[80] The three gynecologists I interviewed, Chandrakanta Rohatgi, Lakshmi Sahgal, and Premila Gokhale, belonged to resourceful middle-class families. These women preferred to set up private practices rather than seek jobs in government hospitals, where they feared they would face discrimination on the grounds of their race and/or religion.[81] Their mode of consultation was clinical visits and home visits, mainly for confinements. In the city of Kanpur, according to these doctors, births for most classes and communities took place at home until the late 1960s, after which there was a visible shift from home to hospitalized births.[82]

As for contraceptive information, the three doctors had somewhat different things to relate about their training and their own familiarity with available contraceptive technologies in the early twentieth century. Dr. Chandrakanta Rohatgi attended lectures on birth control while completing her M.B.B.S. from King Edward's Medical College in Bombay in 1934. A "south Indian male professor" conducted lectures and used women volunteers and clay models to demonstrate the use of contraceptives.[83] Rohatgi carried foam powder and square sponges from Bombay to give to her patients for use as a contraceptive in 1938. Women used oil tampons as a contraceptive during the war in the 1940s. Rohatgi advised her patients to use cap pessaries with jelly, promoting the use of contraceptives among her patients. The demand for birth control came from her women patients, because according to her, childbirth for most women was a near-death experience; therefore, women looked for ways to avoid repeated pregnancies.[84] She had heard of Ortho-Gynol, a jelly marketed by Johnson and Johnson in London. The biomedical journals carried advertisements of this and other contraceptives, but Dr. Rohatgi was able to recall only this one contraceptive brand. Dr. Gokhale and Dr. Sahgal found none of the contraceptives advertised in Indian medical journals familiar.[85] All three doctors complained about the lack of information and availability of contraceptive methods until as late as 1952, which is when the independent Indian state formally adopted a family planning policy.

In the postindependence period, Dr. Rohatgi usually advised the use of Planitab, which was locally manufactured in Kanpur. Hind Chemicals manufactured and marketed Planitab in Kanpur during the 1950s.[86] Her brother, Dr. Surendra Rohatgi, owned the company. Dr. Chandrakanta Rohatgi persuaded her brother to manufacture Planitab despite his initial reluctance to carry out research on contraceptives. It was her assessment of the general need among women for a safe and effective contraceptive and her awareness of governmental intent to assign the research on contraceptives certain priority that convinced her brother to conduct research in this area. Dr. Surendra Rohatgi manufactured the pill and presented it to the Indian government for approval without conducting any clinical tests.[87] This pill was an ovule that needed to be inserted into the vagina before each coitus. Apparently, the pill failed the initial governmental approval because of its toxicity, but this was brushed aside later by the Ministry of Family Planning and Planitab was distributed through family planning clinics that the Indian government set up after 1952. In an interview, Dr. Surendra Rohatgi spoke casually, comparing the toxicity of Planitab with that of cigarette smoking! According to him, if smoking was not banned on grounds of toxicity, how could Planitab be singled out, especially because its toxic limits had not even been clinically proven.[88] The Indian state's complete lack of concern for Indian women's health is apparent in the manner in which Planitab was allowed to be introduced as a "viable" contraceptive through the family planning program. Market forces and profit motives were influential in Dr. Surendra Rohatgi's undertaking to manufacture Planitab. The story of introducing Planitab reflects how contraceptive usage in postcolonial India was largely aimed at controlling population rather than empowering women and granting them reproductive autonomy; in this respect, unfortunately, it was not very different from the politics of birth control in colonial India.

All three doctors mentioned the demand for contraceptives among their women patients. Although they discouraged abortion as a method of contraception, they did provide this "service" to ensure women did not turn to midwives or resorted to "harmful" home remedies to induce miscarriages. Clearly, there were gaps between the medical rhetoric and practices among women physicians, both guided by demands of their "clients" and practical demands of private practice and the fear of losing their potential clients to midwives and local *dais,* who were active in urban centers until the early 1960s.[89]

Correlating data from biomedical journals and my interviews in Kanpur, it becomes clear that even when physicians claimed to be engaged in the modernist project, seeking to enhance control over life itself, their claims were based on flimsy and shaky grounds. On the subject of birth control, the biomedical profession was deeply fissured about its medical importance, moral implications, and its eugenicist potentials. In terms of technology, biomedics had little to offer to the ongoing search for viable reproductive technologies that would promote the elitist programs of discipline and surveillance of subaltern sexual and fertility practices. The interviews with women gynecologists brought out sharply the issues of power, hierarchy, and stratification within the medical profession along axes of gender, race, class, and community. In their interviews, the women doctors communicated the struggles they encountered as Indian women to find suitable jobs within governmental and Dufferin hospitals. As women of the middle classes, their families resented their interaction with lower caste and, in some cases, Muslim clients.[90] Unlike the medical journal articles, the interviews also highlighted the fears among biomedics and the lack of professional confidence even while they deployed the language of science and its emphasis on empiricism and research to make a case for the superiority of biomedicine over other competing traditions of healing. The shrill and persistent critiques of midwives in medical journals are a clear indication of the professional insecurities among women and men physicians. Dr. Gokhale recruited a local *dai* as her assistant, recognizing the important hold she had over local people for whom biomedicine was a relatively new system of healing.[91] The interviews also highlighted more than one instance when physicians worked to accommodate the demands of their clients instead of imposing their professional authority.[92] From the 1930s to the 1950s, the practitioners of biomedicine did not singularly dominate the health care system in India. When examined through the prism of birth control, the story of biomedicine in colonial India was not one of success. Instead of establishing its professional hegemony over Indian bodies, biomedicine was a project fraught with tensions of class, race, and gender politics.

Indigenous Practitioners of Medicine and the Discourse of Birth Control

Besides male and female biomedical practitioners, practicing homeopathic, *ayurvedic, hakims,* and *vaids* also discussed the subject of birth control in the Indian vernacular press. This community, like its Western-trained counterparts, was also divided on the subject. Some individual practitioners placed advertisements in favor of birth control in popular magazines such as *Madhuri* and *Sudha,* claiming to have discovered the most reliable contraceptive. Many of these advertisements tended to conflate birth control with other sexual dysfunctions and claimed to provide quick treatments, ensuring patient privacy and protection in mailing the medicine and in providing consultations. The advertisements themselves gave very little information about the product other than its name and assurance that it would work without harming the health of the user.

Madhuri and *Sudha* were Hindi magazines published from Lucknow in the 1920s and 1930s. These journals were popular among women readers and carried many articles that women wrote on various subjects such as women's suffrage, literacy, and health.[93] Individual practicing *vaids, hakims,* or *kavirajs* placed advertisements for their contraceptive methods in issues of *Sudha* and *Madhuri* during the 1930s and 1940s. Most of these contraceptives could be mail-ordered. Many advertised contraceptive products did not have brand names; for instance, an advertisement in *Sudha* only gave the name of the *vaid,* Pandit Chandrashekar Vaidshastri, who, it claimed, with his thirty years of experience offered a *"chamatkari aaushadhi"* [miracle drug] that would ensure that the woman would never conceive again. This particular advertisement addressed the husband rather than the wife, assuring the readers that the product would in no way harm or affect the health of the woman, nor would she stop menstruating. But it warned that once the medicine was consumed, one would have to forgo pregnancy for life. What was being offered was an irrevocable method of birth control.[94]

Advertisements in *Sudha* reflect notions of an "ideal" contraceptive that was presented to the clients and some of the conditions under which the indigenous practitioners of medicine considered the use of birth control appropriate. Poverty, women's poor health, preservation of beauty, premature death in women as a result of repeated pregnancies, and the desire of poor parents not to increase the numbers of slaves and orphans were some reasons considered valid for adopting birth control.[95] As would be evident from the above list, some of the alternative practitioners identified a series of situations that warranted the use birth control, which included evaluations of people's economic situation, women's health, and also aesthetic considerations, such as preservation of beauty. Contemporary biomedics, especially younger men, would have heaped scorn on this last reason. Although the vernacular women's magazines carried contraceptive advertisements, these magazines sometimes also had advertisements, like the one in *Sudha,* that simultaneously proclaimed to offer treatments for "barren women," for "women who suffered from hysteria," or to "ensure immortal beauty remedies" as well as "birth control" and "breast-tone."[96] Vaidraj Akhil Kishore's full-page advertisement in *Sudha* claimed to have remedies for birth control and for any other "women's illness," such as problems with her monthly menstruation, inability to bear children, miscarriages, premature births, or weak children. Unlike the biomedics, the vernacular practitioners seemed to have treated birth control not as a separate issue for women, but one that was a part of a series of issues that impacted women's reproductive health—fertility control and issues of infertility were addressed together, and practitioners offered remedies for both these conditions. Also, interestingly, most of the practitioners who placed their advertisements in these magazines insisted on adding that they were registered with the government. Being registered with the government might have bestowed legitimacy to the products and also reassured the clients that alternative medicine and practitioners were strictly supervised and professionally structured, rather than being a loose collective of individuals with no "professional" training and qualifications.

Unlike the biomedical community, vernacular practitioners—men and women—seem to have shared a common platform in the print media. Women *vaids* also placed a few advertisements in these magazines. Shrimati Chameli Devi, Shrimati Gangabai, and Chapaladevi advertised treatments specifically for women's problems. Chameli Devi's full-page advertisement mentioned a long list of women's health problems for which she offered treatments but stated categorically that she would not offer any advice on birth control or related *"gande"* (bad) issues because these, she warned, perpetuated sin and immorality.[97] Shrimati Gangabai's announcement mentioned that she was registered with the government and offered treatments for problems related to pregnancy.[98] Chapaladevi ran advertisements in both *Madhuri* and *Sudha* announcing that she was registered with the government.[99] She claimed that she offered cheap medicine that ensured that a woman never became pregnant again. The reasons for seeking birth control advice highlighted in this advertisement were poverty, physical weakness in women who wanted to save themselves from repeated pregnancies, and avoidance of "the great crime of abortion." Women were directly addressed in this announcement, urging them to write and order the medicine themselves. This advertisement was repeatedly carried in *Madhuri* and its later version added that the use of Chapaladevi's medicine, *"Bandhayakarak,"* would in no way interrupt normal sexual happiness.

Besides placing various contraceptive advertisements, a few indigenous practitioners also wrote booklets in Hindi on the subject of birth control. Like the biomedical writings on the subject, they too presented medical and sociocultural arguments either to support the cause or to condemn the widespread use of contraceptives. Yadhuvirsingh, in *Gupt Sandesh* [Secret Message] published in 1937, outlined hesitant support for the cause of birth control. His book opened with the quotation *"desh raksha aur dharam raksha, garbh raksha mee garbhit hai"*;[100] roughly translated: the well-being of the nation and of religion is based on protecting the womb. The book made a strong argument in favor of extending maternal health benefits to women to ensure a strong nation and religiously sound society. According to the author, Indian women were physically weak and therefore to ensure their health and to provide India with brave, strong, and handsome male children, a couple should ideally have two children. The author deployed the latent nationalist patriarchal spirit of the 1930s to call for the need to build and produce strong national bodies.

The most appropriate form of contraception Yadhuvirsingh advocated was abstention. In defense of this position, he quoted John Stuart Mill, who compared sexual indulgence with drunkenness to argue that "little improvement can be expected in morality until the producing of too large families is regarded with the same feeling as drunkenness or any other physical excess."[101] He presented some views against the rhythm method and the popular notions of a safe period, usually considered to be days when a woman was menstruating and while she was breast feeding. Both these periods in a woman's life, he argued, were not a barrier against conception because the period of safe days had not been definitively established. He divided contraceptive technologies in two categories based on who used them, men or women. Male contraceptives, according to Yadhuvirsingh, did not allow for seminal absorption by the woman, and thus denied her extra energy. Therefore, he advised against their use. Female contraceptives that he mentioned were pessaries, which, according to him, ensured sexual pleasure without the attending responsibility of pregnancy, and therefore were better than male contraceptives. But he warned that if women extended usage of contraceptives, it could harm their uterus and he advised that they should only be used very rarely and under special conditions.

Yadhuvirsingh's booklet also presented a "formula" for ensuring the desired sex of the child. Here he relied upon the tool of intellectual hybridity, combining ancient wisdom and the traditionalism of *Manusmriti* with the modern Western biomedical authority of Dr. Packman to argue that people could actively determine the sex of their desired child. The mixing of authorities and evidence from seemingly incompatible sources did not appear contradictory to this indigenous medical practitioner. Here it is helpful to draw upon what Gyan Prakash suggests in his study on science in colonial India, in which he has argued that Indian modernity shaped in the specific historical moment of colonialism was forced to negotiate between "the polarities of secular and religious, community and state, science and culture," and that such hybridizations formed the stuff of India's historical experience.[102]

Kaviraj Vimla Devi Vaidya, an *Ayurvedic* practitioner and a specialist in sex diseases, supported the cause of birth control in her booklet *Garbh Nirodh* [Birth Control].[103] Her writing also presents an eclectic borrowing and medical understanding, drawing selectively from biomedicine and more traditional treatments, to offer readers various options of contraceptive methods. Written in Hindi in 1940, the preface states that although there was an impressive literature on the subject of birth control in English, not much was available in Hindi for women, and, unlike men, fewer women in India could read English.[104] Arguing for birth control in her book, Vimla Devi represented sexuality as a "natural" impulse among men and women. Although she does not represent sexuality negatively, and instead regards it as an acceptable expression of conjugal love, she does, however, stress a strict code of sexual discipline for both men and women within marriage. This code of conduct sought to ensure sexual restraint within marriage, prescribing that the husband and wife should not share the same bedroom. If that were not possible, she advised that the couple should certainly not share the same bed. She advised dietary restrictions to aid in controlling sexual energies. Foods that were popularly considered "hot" and overly spicy were regarded as exciting sexual desires and as stimulus, and therefore she suggested these should be avoided. Similarly, Vimla Devi argued that cinema and reading romance novels were sexually corrupting influences and should also be avoided.

Legitimate sexual expressions within marriage, Vimla Devi suggested, were to be determined on the basis of age. In order to safeguard their own health and to keep their wives healthy, husbands were instructed to have sex only twice a week until thirty-five years of age; after the age of forty, once a week; and after fifty, only once a month. Men were warned against having sex with their wives when they were either menstruating or pregnant. Other sexual restrictions applied to having sex with women after menopause and with older women because sexual relations with these women, it was believed, would cause premature aging in men.[105] Sexual guidelines were laid down primarily for masculine gratification, and the chronology for normative marital sex was also understood in masculine terms, seeking to ensure the physical well-being of men. In the matrimonial sexual guidelines of the author, she made no references to women's sexual desires or to their sexual needs changing chronologically. Despite her myopic gendered imagery, she does embrace a less hostile class perspective on fertility patterns. The author rejected the eugenic argument that favored selective high fertility among the middle classes. According to Vimla Devi, high fertility and more children even among the rich would adversely effect the health of the women. Unlike many other advocates who called for class-based fertility behavior, one that usually favored the middle classes with reproductive liberty and imposed reproductive regulations on subalterns, Vimla Devi was more democratic in her call for restricting fertility to ensure national well-being.

Vimla Devi, unlike some of her biomedical colleagues, did not represent working-class sexuality as excessive. As opposed to the dominant representations of the working classes as hypersexual with unusually high fertility rates, she argued that the working classes often had low fertility rates. Their overworked lifestyles allowed them little leisure time and sapped their physical energy. She asserted that the working classes generally had sex in the morning after which the women usually went out to relieve themselves. Because of the specific toilet habits among this class of women, the semen was flushed out of the women's system, preventing conception.[106] Quite like other advocates, intimate domains and practices of working classes were treated as legitimate sites for elite inspection and evaluation, even by Vimla Devi.

Vimla Devi discussed a number of contraceptives, recommending both biomedical and more traditional methods. While describing how condoms worked, she stated that primarily rich people used them and cautioned that if used on a long-term basis, they would have harmful effects on the health of the couple. Condoms interfered with women experiencing complete sexual satisfaction during coitus and could also cause impotency in men.[107] Pessaries and spermicidal ointments were discussed, and it was mentioned that women in Europe and America used them and found them to be satisfactory.[108] She also suggested some indigenous methods such as neem oil, old jaggary juice, and other concoctions that, if used by women, would ensure protection from unwanted pregnancies and were harmless.[109] Because I was unable to obtain more information on the readership and the response to the book, it is difficult to ascertain if the alternative methods of birth control discussed in this book were used and, if so, with what degree of success. Ruth Young mentioned the use of neem oil as a contraceptive, adding, however, that some women complained about its strong odor and pungency.[110]

Drawing upon the evidence on indigenous practitioners examined in this chapter, one can conclude that they constructed an alternative modernity, mixing "science" and "culture."[111] But this alternative modernity, despite allowing room for recognition of female sexual agency, was not necessarily liberating. The indigenous practitioners such as *vaids* and *hakims,* like their biomedical competitors, were anxious to regulate and discipline conjugal sexuality, strictly confining all expressions of sexuality within marriage. Practitioners such as Yadhuvirsingh and Vimla Devi celebrated healthy masculine bodies as the ideals for national bodies. At this point, it appears fair to conclude that all medical participants in discussions on contraception in colonial India—foreign advocates, Indian middle-class men and women proponents, biomedical practitioners, and practitioners of alternative medicine—articulated the issue of birth control as one of surveillance and restraint. Birth control became a site for regulating and disciplining subaltern bodies, feeding into the elite hegemonic projects of neo-Malthusianism, eugenics, nationalism, and even feminism. In other words, birth control became a site where other debates and agendas are given expressions, in turn configuring, reconfiguring, and shifting power relations among elites.

Conclusion

Even while Western advocates of birth control such as Sanger and How-Martyn emphasized the need for medical doctors to provide their clients with birth control information, leading biomedical journals and practicing gynecologists lamented the lack of training in medical schools and colleges and the unavailability of appropriate and cheap contraceptives in the market. Although the biomedical community sought to hegemonize the health care sector in colonial India, discrediting and displacing other alternative systems of healing in the process, they did not have the necessary training and knowledge to speak with authority on subjects like birth control. In colonial India, biomedical practitioners were one of many contenders in the newly emerging "science" of birth control. Even while some advocates desired them to become vanguards of the movement, biomedics did not have an intellectual monopoly on the subject. More important, they lacked consensus among themselves on the value of embracing reproductive technologies as part of their professional training. It was not until the postcolonial Indian state institutionalized family planning that the knowledge and the dissemination of birth control information was firmly placed within the hold of the biomedical community.

In colonial India, the newly emerging field of biomedicine was seeking to "colonize" the native body, castigating the indigenous practitioners and *dais* as repositories of superstition and ignorance. At this time, the biomedical discourse certainly did not become a part of the commonsense understanding of the human body, and it failed to assume the hegemonic dominance it set out to acquire for itself. It is also important to question the unitary position of Western biomedicine; for example, even while challenging other "medical" paradigms, it ultimately sought to work a compromise with other health care practitioners. Dr. Premila Gokhale, for instance, recruited a local *dai* as her assistant and recognized the importance of massages and of dim light in the birthing room for the mothers.[112] This attempt at co-opting *dais* was recognized as a necessary modality for extending the hold of Western biomedicine over recalcitrant Indian women.

Vaids and *hakims* recognized the professional threat of biomedicine and many of them sought to appropriate certain ideas from Western medicine.

The indigenous practitioners, in their writings, recommended both the new biomedical as well as the more traditional methods of birth control to their clients. Like their Western counterparts, the indigenous medical practitioners also represented the Indian *dai* as a symbol of ignorance. It would be fair to conclude that practitioners of biomedicine and of alternative traditions of medicine in colonial India, despite being divided on the issue of birth control among themselves, shared a common agenda of marginalizing practicing midwives and discrediting their hold on the bodies of Indian women. Those within biomedicine and alternative systems of medicine who were supportive of birth control, saw in it a useful device of extending their elitist agenda of surveillance and exerting power over the lives of the working classes and other subaltern groups. Biomedical physicians and indigenous practitioners who supported birth control embraced ideas of regulation and discipline rather than seeking to empower their patients. However, instead of presenting elite narratives and sources as unitary and homogenous, it is important to recognize that many of these also carry within themselves registration of resistance to their oppressive agendas; for instance, the repeated laments in medical journals about the refusal of Indian women to comply with the biomedical injunctions on birthing and the recalcitrant hold of *dais* over Indian women. The instances of resistance noted within the elite sources are important, but they still do not permit the perspectives of practicing *dais* and subaltern women to challenge the dominant negative representations of these women. It is with their perspectives that I end this book.

Epilogue

> Children are god's blessings, one can try to drop a child (*baccha giraana*), use all kinds of methods, but if god is willing then the child will be born.
> —Padma Devi, Sainji Village

The chapters in this book outline the dominant historical sentiments on birth control that various indigenous and Western elites in colonial India articulated during the early twentieth century. The voices of middle-class Indian male nationalists, Western enthusiasts, middle-class feminists — Indian and Western, members of the biomedical profession, and indigenous medical practitioners, along with colonial officials — British and native, were privileged in the public debates on birth control. To undercut an impression that elite articulations were internally coherent and homogenous, the preceding chapters highlight internal paradoxes that marked the debates on the subject among various proponents and opponents of contraceptive usage. However, despite internal tensions and contradictions among themselves, indigenous and Western elites discursively disenfranchised subaltern experiences and perceptions while severely restraining their reproductive freedoms.

The preceding chapters outline the history of "othering" and silencing of subaltern groups. Members of the Indian working classes, lower castes, Muslims, and rural poor were predominantly represented as embracing irresponsible procreative behaviors. Elite advocates of birth control argued that for the well-being of a fledgling nation aspiring toward self-determination from colonial dominance, prudent sexual and reproductive practices were particularly important. To promote a eugenically fit and viable Malthusian national entity, Begum Hamid Ali went so far as to call for the sterilization of the "unfit."[1] Gandhi was one of the lone voices in the early twentieth century who challenged the Malthusian assertion that underscored elite support for contraceptives, although for the most part Gandhi grounded his opposition on a "doctrine of sexual essentialism," constructing all nonprocreative sex as inherently corrupt and corrupting.[2] The chapters in this book critically examined elite representations, especially as these claimed universal epistemic validity even while presenting partial and situated understandings.

Searching for embodied subjects "coming to voice"[3] and adept at resisting the dominant knowledge practices led me to explore the perspectives and experiences of *dais*—midwives, largely demonized in colonial, nationalist, feminist, and medical texts.[4] Seeking to disrupt the oppressive, transnational discourse and to demonstrate the limits of its universal import, I spoke with practicing midwives and their clients in the tribal block of rural Jaunpur in Tehri Gharwal district of Uttranchal. These conversations were guided by a strong desire to insert cultural complexities and pluralities that would provide potentially alternative perceptions of the body, birth control, and reproduction. This part of my research did not aim to make an argument about local insularity or attempt to make Jaunpur available in some comprehensive knowable terms, terms that seek to capture the pristine "otherness" from the dominant understanding of rational sexed subject. Jaunpuri views are included because they allow for 'more reality,' for direct experience and for first-person testimonies, which challenge and bring into crisis the normative and universal elitist understandings of human bodies, sexualities, and procreative practices.[5] Moreover, Jaunpuri women's voices are consciously included in this study with the hope of generating honest and self-reflective academic conversations that bear testimony to the history and concerns of these marginalized subjects.

The move from the archives to the "field" was made out of frustrations with different archives in the United States, New Delhi, Lucknow, and London. As demonstrated in the earlier chapters, these archives are important for understanding and tracing elite politics and agendas. It has been rightly remarked that even official archives hold "warring discourses."[6] The early writings of Ranajit Guha and the articles in the initial volumes of *Subaltern Studies* are excellent examples of how historians have used elite/colonial sources to narrate subaltern histories.[7] Yet for my subject, I found relatively few, if any, voices in official archives that challenged the dominant narrative on birth control as a tool for regulating, disciplining, and policing subversive and disruptive social/sexual practices, particularly among subaltern groups. Jaunpuri women present counternarratives that challenge popular mythologies associated with birth control technologies as essentially desirable and liberating for women. For the most part, elite recordings as noted in the preceding chapters and even contemporary discussions on television and the Internet, as noted in the introduction, do not make public debates on population, birth control, and national health available to marginalized groups, even as these groups are made targets for new directions and policy initiatives. A shift, therefore, in archival and ethnographic location to Jaunpur not only allows subaltern perspectives a voice, but it also presents a useful vantage point from which to highlight the limits of dominant discourse to enable us to recognize the partiality that shaped and continues to shape dominant views on population, birth control, and women's rights.

The perspectives of Jaunpuri *dais* simultaneously bring into view the relations of domination and challenge the unidimensional elitist representations of subalterns as always already the other. In opposition to the highly charged negative, exclusionary, and stereotypical colonial, nationalist, feminist, and biomedical representations of *dais,* Jaunpuri *dais* occupy a place of honor and recognition within their communities.[8] Younger women in Jaunpur know their local *dais* and hold them in high regard for their skills and the services they provide to women not only during their pregnancies and childbirths, but also with other gynecological problems.[9] While being highly visible and respected members of their local communities, these *dais* are also well-known among nongovernmental organizations, such as the Society for the Integrated Development of the Himalayas (SIDH) and the Society for Health and Rural Education (SHARE) that are active in this region. Any health initiatives that are introduced into this region rely on recruiting the help and support of practicing *dais* for their acceptance and success within these rural communities.

Jaunpuri women allow us to see how rural women, as active subjects, constitute complex selves and identities among themselves. The birthing practices and beliefs circulating among Jaunpuri *dais* and their clients are an ideal archival location for trying to retrieve, in however limited and fractured sense, subaltern voices on reproduction, birthing, and the need for contraceptives. It is their skills as midwives and their experiences in the birthing rooms that Jaunpuri women deploy as tools to narrate their life stories, their historical memories, and experiences, and as such these function as archival repositories on intimate and private affairs of these women and their clients. As archival sites, the conversations with Jaunpuri women capture reproductive experiences and aspirations outside of the dominant discourse to highlight its limits and demonstrate its exclusionary aims.

In using these oral history sources as a "private" archive, I am fully aware of the limitations they pose in terms of memory reconstructions and slippages. The locations of me as a researcher and that of my subjects of research adds additional subjective variables, making these sources that much less transparent.[10] I also realize that "private" archives, unlike the official archival sources, are not accessible for verifications and counter-verifications. The issues of translations and the deliberate constructions of what Jaunpuri women communicated to me, as a researcher and as an "outsider," make these sources less malleable and pliable than they might appear at a cursory glance.[11] The contamination of these "authentic" sources is inherent in their contact with the historian, leading to a "hybridized, mongrelized and miscegenated" discourse, according to Portelli.[12] Despite the limitations of these ethnographic sources, I find them useful insofar as they allow rural midwives to reclaim their work and their lives within elite scholarly research, at many removes from the lives and world these women inhabit. In using these interviews as sources, I agree with Harriet Bradley that "partially determined speech may be better than silence."[13] These "partial" voices from the margins allow us to highlight the limitations of the elite hegemonic project seeking to exercise reproductive restraints on Indian bodies, especially those of subaltern groups whose fertility was believed to threaten national prosperity and well-being. Wherever possible we should consider oral sources as tools that help us craft our narratives and use them with the same cautionary note that we assign to logocentric sources. The recognition that colonial and nationalist sources are contaminated has not led historians to abandon written records. Instead, researchers have adopted a self-reflexive methodology in reading these sources and have come to accept the internal fragmentation that marks various written records. We need to be able to do the same with oral sources and not assign them any more or any less adulteration.

As examined in the earlier chapter on medicine, most biomedical and vernacular medical literature carried endless series of negative, stereotypical representations of the Indian *dais,* constructing them as objects of suspicion and holding them responsible for the poor health of Indian women. For the most part, elite sources either negatively represent the Indian *dai* as the epitome of ignorance or only record the efforts made at transforming this figure of the *dai* into an agent of modernity who would uphold the ideals of antiseptic biomedicine.[14] The perspectives, voices, and ideas of the midwives themselves are never available to historians and researchers in these sources. Because for the most part these women were not formally educated, they have not left any written records for us to reconstruct narratives including their part of the story.[15] In the absence of written records of Indian midwives, I used oral history as a means to fill the gap in our understanding of how these women negotiated with the dominant biomedical discourse that aimed at medicalizing indigenous midwifery practices.

Most elite sources constructed Indian midwives as visible markers of tradition and superstition. In colonial India, *dais* became a highly charged symbol in the evaluations of Indian women's poor health, with particular emphasis on maternal and infant mortality figures.[16] The newly emerging biomedical practitioners saw in the person of the Indian *dai* potential professional competition and threat. As Dr. J. Jhirad declared in 1929, "Their opinion is so highly valued, and many a time, I have noticed that, even if eminent doctors have urged certain treatments, unless the *dai* agrees with it, patients will not follow the doctor's advice!"[17] Many commentators pointed out that the "sweeper-cum-*dai*" had an uncanny hold on mothers and mothers-in-law who managed the confinements of their daughters and daughters-in-law. In their anxiety to displace the *dai*, the biomedical community was quick to cast all rural women negatively as "illiterate, superstitious, and ultra-conservative."[18]

The realization of the stronghold of the indigenous *dais* on the Indian women led some to suggest that they be co-opted in order to ensure the success of the biomedical establishment. Begum Hamid Ali, recognizing the professional threat *dais* posed to the Western trained medical establishment, argued:

> Every effort must be made both in towns and villages to get the local dais to co-operate with the trained worker. It is a good plan to ask the local dais to go around with the worker and employ and train the most influential dais to help in each maternity center that is opened in any town or village so that they may not feel that bread is being taken out of their mouths. Unless that is done, there is a great likelihood of maternity homes being opened but no cases coming in. I remember once a beautifully equipped Home had to be closed for lack of cases.[19]

The latent enthusiasm to train *dais* was an attempt to co-opt them as allies of the biomedical establishment. Begum Hamid Ali suggested that the "*dai* box"[20] was a great attraction for *dais* who could not have been induced otherwise to attend the lectures. The Maternity and Child Welfare Center at Gujranwala in Punjab, gave out *dai* boxes, which were proudly displayed in the front of a group photograph of the trained *dais* taken in 1933.[21]

The Annual Report of the Director of Public Health of the United Provinces of Agra and Oudh for the year 1925 states with regret "that a better class of girls are not coming forward to take up this work." According to this report, out of forty-eight midwives who were under training in 1926, only ten passed, seven failed, eleven left, and twenty were still under training. In 1926, at the Benaras Baby Week, *dais* who had reported more than twenty births at municipal registration offices within six months were called and given *dai* sets, and fifty-one such sets/kits were given away in Benaras in 1926. As is evident from the above examples, the closed discourse among elites regarded the hold of native *dais* over the bodies of Indian birthing mothers as a direct threat to the biomedical establishment, and therefore sought to convert practicing *dais* into professional allies. In most of the elite writings and discussions on *dais,* the Indian midwives were themselves an underrepresented group who were not allowed to be present in these conversations, even while their work was being targeted and reconfigured by new medical technologies and scientific discourses.

In seeking a different narrative, I interviewed midwives, but the local suspicion of strangers made it difficult for me to ask *dais* and their clients questions related to their reproductive behavior. It was, therefore, largely through the support of a nongovernmental organization, SIDH, and more specifically Savitri Tamta's research assistance, that I was able to identify practicing *dais* and conduct interviews with them and their clients in this area.[22] Despite the temporal shift from written sources produced fifty years earlier, the interviews are necessary correctives to these conventional sources. Moreover, conversations with Jaunpuri *dais* were not only about the present, nor would they be because birthing and midwifery practices are handed down through oral traditions from mothers-in-law to daughters-in-law.[23] On the question of time, it is important to point out that linear historical divisions between colonial and postcolonial times are not necessarily universal in organizing people's understanding of the past and the present. Again to borrow from Portelli's argument, the historian's need for mapping change is not always shared by their subjects, in my specific case—Jaunpuri women.[24] Jaunpuri *dais* were eager to recall for me the continuity in their traditional birthing practices and how these practices had descended down the female line from one generation to another. Many *dais* proudly claimed that their practices were rooted in birthing practices that had survived the test of time and as such were part of their mature and collective local knowledge-base. My conversations with practicing *dais* in Jaunpur were very productive and enlightening. In our conversations I heard their very different ideas about motherhood, sexuality, and birth control that were at times in sharp variance from my own liberal humanist conception of choice and agency.

Although reproductive behaviors seem to have altered somewhat over the past two decades, Jaunpuri women continue to practice traditional birthing techniques. Almost all confinements in the villages of Jaunpur take place at home with the help of local *dais.* In this tribal area in the Himalayan foothills, access to hospitals, located mainly in the urban areas, is limited. Most Jaunpuri women prefer the traditional squatting birthing position rather than the horizontal position, which in Jaunpur is pejoratively referred to as the "hospital" position. The horizontal position, according to *dais* and most Jaunpuri women, hinders a woman's ability to actively control her own body and do what is necessary to ensure a normal birth. The local *dais* believe in the least intrusive method of childbirth, whereby the focus is on abdominal massages rather than inserting any "tools." In rare cases they may examine the pregnant woman internally. In the words of Rukhma Devi—a *dai* from Bhatoli village—"we have no machines, we cannot see what is happening inside a woman's stomach. We people work with our hands."[25]

The introduction of midwifery training by Christian missionary organizations who work in Jaunpur, such as SHARE, is challenging traditional birthing practices. As in the colonial period, this contemporary missionary organization has distributed *dai* kits among the practicing *dais*, which include a plastic sheet, a blade, two soap cakes, thread, gloves, and a bottle of antiseptic solution. In many cases, these kits are kept as trophies, proudly displayed to researchers from outside, like myself. The contents of many such boxes I was told, are selectively removed by members of the *dai*'s family as and when the need arises. Bhuri Devi's grandson, for instance, took the bottle of antiseptic solution to his city hostel, failing to understand why his old grandmother needed it.[26] The use of these kits has not become common practice among the *dais*; there appears to be a general lack of enthusiasm in translating the use of these kits into practice.

Jaunpuri women were comfortable talking about their birthing practices and some of the older practicing *dais* generously offered to help me deliver my child! Most women, however, were reluctant to share local knowledge and information on indigenous fertility control methods and abortifacients. Initially, the midwives strongly denied any knowledge about abortions, which according to them, is the biggest sin any woman could possibly commit. They claimed that, as *dais,* they were responsible for bringing life into the world, and abortion, therefore, fell beyond the purview of their vocation.[27] It was only after talking with many of them and seeking to understand how local women dealt with unwanted pregnancies that I found out about some of the local plants and domestic products that Jaunpuri women used as abortifacients. Among the products mentioned were *rakha,* the burned-out wood and cow-dung fuel procured from stoves at home. This substance is made into a hot drink by mixing it in water that women consume, although the women were not willing to comment upon its reliability as a method. This method was also mentioned in Kaviraj Vimla Devi Vaidya's booklet *Garbh Nirodh* [Birth Control],[28] discussed in the previous chapter on medical practitioners. Another abortifacient is a drink made by boiling the bark of the *bhimal* tree, which is indigenous to the region. Although the knowledge of abortifacients is part of women's subcultures in Jaunpur, there is a stronger belief in destiny, especially as it relates to pregnancies. It is largely believed that "children are god's blessings, one can try to drop a child (*baccha giraana*), use all kinds of methods, but if god is willing then the child will be born."[29] Abortions are discouraged because the dominant belief is that if any woman does have an abortion, she will not be able to conceive another child when she desires one.

Jaunpuri women make a clear distinction between abortions and birth control. Even though most of the older *dais* I spoke with scorned the idea of "controlling" or managing fertility, a practice they believe to be common only among "*shahari*" (city) girls, some younger women in Jaunpur are beginning to use certain forms of contraceptive methods available in nearby urban markets and government hospitals. Here, is it important to recognize the multiplicities and contradictions that frame Jaunpuri women's embodied standpoints. Variations in age determine the different subject locations Jaunpuri women occupy within their families and communities, and this in turn shapes their varying reproductive aspirations and responsibilities.

Among younger women in Jaunpur, the most popular contraceptive method is irreversible sterilization of women, referred to in the local lexicon as "operation."[30] Sterilization continues to be the most accessible and thus the contraceptive method of "choice" among Jaunpuri women. However, within the reality of their context, sterilization needs to be recognized more as a "coerced" rather than a free choice. Many Jaunpuri men and women complain bitterly about the many side effects of sterilization, ranging from loss of appetite to physical weakness bordering on physical disability. Adding to the negative health consequences of sterilization, many Jaunpuri women also speak openly about their experiences of humiliation and alienation at the hands of the biomedical establishment. Medical doctors largely perform this procedure in a culturally alien and alienating sites of government hospitals located in urban centers. Doctors in the city hospitals for the most part communicate either in English or Hindi rather than in the local Jaunpuri dialect. Within Jaunpur, English and Hindi are associated with urban elitism and as such these are alien languages for women. Jaunpuri women are, therefore, further intimidated on account of their unfamiliarity with the languages of their attending physicians or gynecologists.[31]

Younger Jaunpuri women usually undergo sterilization, not with the intention of enhancing their sexual autonomy, but more because of a shared fear among men and women that if a man is sterilized he would become weak and his family might lose its principal breadwinner.[32] This belief prevails despite the fact that women's operations are medically more intrusive and complicated. Ironically, this belief also makes invisible women's work in Jaunpur, work that involves heavy physical labor of fetching fuel from the forest, grazing and caring for their cattle, working in the family fields, and, over and above the household chores, child care and other responsibilities.

A shift in younger women's reproductive trajectory in Jaunpur can be better grasped when located within the larger changes that are palpable in this region. In contemporary Jaunpur, market forces are increasingly threatening the "tribal" ways of life. Even in the absence of drinking water, small village shops are stocked with Coke and Pepsi, creating false consumer demands in otherwise economically poor communities. Men are leaving the rural areas to find employment in cities. Villagers have come to assign great respect to those who come home loaded with consumer durables such as televisions and tape recorders. The consumer culture intruding into even remote areas like Jaunpur makes smaller families a desirability. Capitalist consumerism has marked a rise in living costs and in expectations, making it difficult for Jaunpuris to disregard limiting the size of their families. Women are increasingly shouldering the reproductive responsibility of limiting the size of the family by adopting the irreversible method of sterilization as their preferred "choice" over some of the other more expensive and less accessible modern contraceptive technologies.

It is important to point out that, despite some visible shift in the size of families in Jaunpur, traditional reproductive practices have not all been abandoned. Most women still prefer traditional birthing practices and the *dai* continues to assist birthing mothers. The local belief in reproductive destinies continues to be strong, both among older and younger women. Children are cherished in Jaunpuri families as signs of divine blessings.[33] Within this cultural milieu, childlessness is understood to be a curse, and women without children are highly stigmatized within local communities and families. Most women in Jaunpur strongly desire and aspire toward maternal identities. For these women, feminine selfhood is firmly grounded in motherhood, even as Jaunpuri women share maternal responsibilities through collective mothering. Given that most Jaunpuri households continue to be multigenerational rather than nuclear families, the experience of mothering for Jaunpuri women is not a privatized, isolating, alienating, or socially disadvantageous activity—experienced largely as such within modern Western societies.[34] Tied to their familial arrangements and experiences of motherhood, Jaunpuri women embrace a more relational sense of self as opposed to modern autonomous individualism.

Even though some younger married couples in Jaunpur are seeking to control the sizes of their families in keeping with modern articulations of "rational" family sizes, procreation is understood to function largely outside of human control. It would be fair to conclude that Jaunpuri worldviews are in sharp contrast to the confidence in techno-scientific management of reproduction shared among indigenous and Western elites. Given their experiences, it is no mystery that women and men in Jaunpur do not share the elite confidence in reproductive technologies. For them, procreation is not a mere random expression of nature, but instead is understood to be divinely ordained, and as such outside the realm of human control and scientific management. Given their general suspicion of human ability to manage procreation, the modern state dictates of normative sexual/reproductive expressions do not find favor within the local Jaunpuri culture.

It is important here to reiterate the varied cultural and ideological configurations that shape reproductive and sexual expressions at local levels such as Jaunpur. However, the focus on Jaunpuri difference is not intended to imply homogeneity or uniformity of local cultures, but it is used to demonstrate the necessary limits of universalist claims that shape dominant discursive constructs. Jaunpuri women's perspectives themselves are not presented here as universally "better," and hence as preferable replacement of the dominant views, but these are inserted into the discussion to highlight the "kaleidoscope of truths" that are continually shaped and reshaped as more and different women begin to work together.[35] Taking Jaunpur as a vantage point does not automatically lead to some objective truth. However, it does allow for an account that Sandra Harding has termed "less false, less partial, and distorted."[36] It captures how dominant and elite systems of representations, especially those presented in the earlier chapters, sought to transform and impose modern notions of procreation, sexuality, and body. The elite systems are problematic because they rest their claims on false universalisms, and as such are unable and unwilling to make room for differences that have shaped and continue to shape subaltern women's historical and lived experiences. For the purposes of this work, Jaunpur provides a useful reference point from which to challenge the epistemic privilege bestowed upon elite views and as such it allows us to see the partiality that shapes dominant understanding.

Ethnographic research in Jaunpur marked a temporal leap in my search for counternarratives to those of mainstream elitist positions on the use of contraceptives in colonial India. The interviews with women in Jaunpur presented above are not transparent sources and I do not purport to claim innocence and naïveté in presenting these sources as unmediated "subaltern" voices. Their articulations are refracted through my definite research agenda and specifically tailored questions. Despite these obvious limitations and problems with these sources and the necessary temporal shift, I find them helpful to rethink the agenda of birth control as it was framed in colonial India, and that in many ways has been perpetuated in the postcolonial era without taking into account or addressing the needs of those for whom it was intended. Instead of seeing reproduction as a prepolitical natural phenomenon, Jaunpuri women clearly demonstrate how ideas about sexuality and reproduction are always culturally produced and contingent.

Ethnographic research allowed me to recognize the disjuncture between elite programs of social/sexual discipline and subaltern modalities of resistance. For instance, the trendy state slogan on family planning, advertised by the postcolonial government in numerous urban public spaces during the 1990s, "One Is Fun," failed to resonate with Jaunpuri women. According to Bhura Devi, it was just another instance of *sarkari bhasha* (government language) that does not relate to the reproductive lives, desires, and experiences of Jaunpuri women.[37] Jaunpuri women I spoke with expressed ambivalence toward the state objectives as captured by some of the above mentioned family planning slogans. Local perceptions and sensibilities block mindless acceptance of state aspirations, and Jaunpuri women do not by and large read state-led initiatives as efforts to extend democratic enfranchisement. Rural Jaunpuri encounters with state and elite cultures seem quite similar to the experience of rural Egyptians, captured in Lila Abu-Lughod's recent work. Abu-Lughod, writing about modern television politics in Egypt, argues that "state culture positions the rural and uneducated people as people who must be taught the most basic things in the name of national development."[38] State and market interventions in Jaunpur also seek to impose new ideals of responsible citizenry and modern development. These new ideals are an assault on Jaunpuri cultural traditions, and as such are contrary to the local worldview and reproductive goals of these rural communities. Most Jaunpuri women identified a family of three children, with two sons and one daughter, as an ideal family. Local Jaunpuri reproductive objectives and family ideal are in sharp contrast to the postcolonial state's ideal of family size as captured by its slogan of "one is fun," or an earlier slogan from the 1970s–80s *"hum do hamare do,"* translated in English into "we two our two." The limits of hegemonic and dominant discursive regimes are captured well through Jaunpuri recalcitrance of holding on to their ideal of three children as a desired family demographic goal in the face of aggressive state-sponsored campaigns for smaller families. The Jaunpuri ideal of two sons and one daughter, it should be pointed out, is also a local exception to the dominant *"beti-maro* mind-set" in parts of north India where increasingly the middle classes, the lower-middle classes, and, in some instances, the poor peasantry are making use of commercialized reproductive technologies to determine the sex of the unborn fetus to selectively abort females.[39]

In narrativizing the reproduction saga through the history of birth control in India, I have sought to understand not just how the national and global impulses interact but also how local people carefully sieve these ideas through their cultural grid and selectively endorsed some and not others. Capturing Jaunpuri discursive space and local subcultures, however inadequately, allows us to make room on the table for dissent and variations from dominant elite perceptions that claim false universalisms for their agendas. My conversations with Jaunpuri women forced me to rethink my own underlying liberal feminist assumptions of an expressly inviolable control over one's body and self as integral to any feminist project. My conversations with the women in Jaunpur not only brought out a different understanding of body, sexuality, and reproductive "rights," but it also highlighted the distance between my own feminist understanding and those of the women I talked with. These field conversations also helped me better understand the elitist character of the demand for birth control that different proponents in colonial India articulated. The early advocates and the postcolonial Indian state framed the demands for birth control in ways that do not resonate with the needs, experiences, understandings, beliefs, and practices of the subalterns they seek to represent. These conversations also helped me identify the underlying elitism of constructing a necessarily liberatory telos for birth control. By incorporating a wide range of sources to construct the history of birth control in India, *Reproductive Restraints* hopes to disrupt neat recordings of elite utterances claiming to speak for the nation or on behalf of universal sisterhood.

Finally, in presenting a postcolonial feminist critique of the history and politics of birth control in colonial India, this work hopes to un-ghettoize non-Western histories. It does not seek to reinforce yet again the distinctions and exceptionalism of Indian experiences, only to reemphasize some inherent differences between Western and non-Western histories. I strongly want to resist impulses within dominant Western histories and politics that label non-Western histories as "freakish" and nonliberal manifestations of an essentially modern/liberal impulse that goes all wrong in its importation into "traditional" societies.[40] What I hope this work will allow us to do is to reevaluate the foundational assumption about birth control as necessarily empowering for all women across time and space. The global interpretative historical lens of this study reflects on the failure of contraceptive technologies to allow free "choice" in intimate sexual matters or extend democratic empowerment of all women. Moreover, historically, the opening up of the private sphere to public gaze, especially in the instances of interrogating subaltern spaces, was not an instrument of empowerment and emancipation.[41] For subaltern groups, it entailed a loss of privacy and a hostile assessment of their lifestyles by self-appointed elite reformers and birth control advocates. What my work hopes to achieve is to raise questions and productive challenges, especially those that emerge out of the experiences of Jaunpuri women, and see these as shaping our historical narratives of birth control.

This study is energized by the politics of postcolonial intellectual enterprise that attends to the possibilities of rethinking our categories, drawing upon alternative historical experiences, not those necessarily emanating from the French Revolution, Seneca Falls Convention, or Pax-Britannica! Adding Jaunpur to our stories of reproduction not only brings the necessary geographical variation to our traditional locations of historical recounting within both national and global scripts, but, more important, destabilizes and interrupts the grand narratives of modernity and liberal conceptions of subjectivities as well. Jaunpuri women help us recognize that the power to shape and determine intimate reproductive practices has not been unidirectional, and that hegemonic interventions have been incomplete and fractured in the face of local cultures and their resilience. A majority of voices recounted in *Reproductive Restraints* provide credence to Foucauldian notions of power as determining and shaping normative ideas about intimate sexual arrangements. However, it also seeks to leave us with a more enabling script, one that allows us to recognize and celebrate the ability of human cultures to resist monocultural inscriptions and instead embrace diverse and competing ideas about sexuality and procreation.

Notes

Introduction

1. Because I have been asked whether I want to be a feminist or a historian by a number of my male professors, both in India and the United States, I start with this separation. I sincerely hope the rest of this book will demonstrate that it is perfectly possible to be both!

2. NDTV Forums, http://www.ndtv.com/mb/messagethread.asp?TopicId=89& tablename=Youdecide DO WE NEED COMPULSORY BIRTH CONTROL IN INDIA?

3. A brief sampling of responses to the question "Do we need compulsory birth control in India?" from the Web discussion highlights the terms of contemporary debate on the topic. "Yes! Yes! Yes! No doubt about that. This is the only cause for India not progressing at a pace as it should do"; "Gentlemen, paying tax is compulsory. Is it undemocratic or an obligation to the welfare of the Nation?"; "Only thing that lies between India and glory is population explosion"; "Strict enforcement of birth control measures should be adopted and people should be socially isolated for not following norms"; "It is the Muslims who are taking this country for a ride..."; "Yes!! We Indians only understand the language of stick, it should be made compulsory at the earliest"; "Definitely, especially among Muslims"; "Yes, in the absence of self compliance, it has to be imposed. The population explosion has to be contained at any cost."

4. Mohan Rao, "Abiding Appeal of Neo-Malthusianism," 1.

5. Digvijay Singh, "Treason, Not Reason."

6. Taking on "emergency powers," Prime Minister Indira Gandhi, between 1975 and 1977, not only suspended all civil liberties and fundamental rights, but also unleashed an extreme expression of state power in seeking to control the fecund Indian body. It is believed that the Indian state undertook draconian measures to forcibly sterilize more than a million people during this two-year period, all in the name of national development and modernization. For a recent ethnography about memories of the Emergency, see Emma Tarlo, *Unsettling Memories*.

7. Adele E. Clarke, *Disciplining Reproduction*, 235.

8. Jane Flax, "Postmodern and Gender Relations in Feminist Theory," in Linda J. Nicholson, *Feminism/Postmodernism,* 39–62; also see Beatrice Hanssen, "Whatever Happened to Feminist Theory?" in Elizabeth Bronfen, *Feminist Consequences,* 58–100.

9. Linda Gordon, *Woman's Body, Woman's Right.* Gordon's work has been a source of inspiration and has helped shape my project in many ways.

10. Betty Joseph, *Reading the East India Company,* 17.

11. Barbara Ramusack and Antoinette Burton, "Introduction: Special Issue on Femi-

nism, Imperialism, and Race"; Antoinette Burton, *Burdens of History* and "Who Needs the Nation?"; Kumkum Sangari, "Relating Histories," in Svati Joshi, *Rethinking English*, 242–72; Mrinalini Sinha, *Colonial Masculinity*; Nancy Rose Hunt, *Colonial Lexicon*.

12. Eileen Palmer Collection, MSS. EUR D1182/5, Oriental and India Office Collection (henceforth OIOC), British Library (henceforth BL), London.

13. Tanika Sarkar, *Hindu Wife, Hindu Nation;* Barbara Metcalf, *Perfecting Women;* Gail Minault, *Secluded Scholars;* Uma Chakravarty, "Whatever Happened to the Vedic Dasi?" in Kumkum Sangari and Sudesh Vaid, *Recasting Women*, 27–87; Prem Chowdhry, "Popular Perceptions of Widow-Remarriage," in Bharati Ray, *From the Seams of History*, 37–66; Anshu Malhotra, *Gender, Caste, and Religious Identities*; Charu Gupta, *Sexuality, Obscenity, Community*; Partha Chatterjee, "Nationalist Resolution," in Kumkum Sangari and Sudesh Vaid, *Recasting Women*, 233–53; Dipesh Chakrabarty, "The Difference-Deferral"; Faisal Devji, "Gender and Politics of Space"; Mytheli Sreenivas, "Emotion, Identity and the Female Subject."

14. Barbara N. Ramusack, "Embattled Advocates"; Aparna Basu, "The Role of Women," in B. R. Nanda, *Indian Women*; Kumari Jayawardena, *Feminism and Nationalism*; Vina Majumdar, "The Social Reform Movement," in B. R. Nanda, *Indian Women*, 16–40; Gail Minault, *Extended Family*; Gail Omvedt, "Caste, Class and Women's Liberation in India"; Gail Pearson, "Nationalism, Universalization," in Gail Minault, *Extended Family*, 174–92.

15. Geraldine Forbes, "The Indian Women's Movement," in Gail Minault, *Extended Family*, 56.

16. Ibid., 76.

17. Geraldine Forbes, "Women in the Nationalist Movement," in Geraldine Forbes, *New Cambridge History of India*, 155–56.

18. Ibid., 156.

19. Gail Pearson, "Nationalism, Universalization," in Gail Minault, *Extended Family*, 174–92.

20. Gail Omvedt, "Caste, Class and Women's Liberation in India," 47.

21. Kumari Jayawardena, *Feminism and Nationalism*, 108.

22. Deniz Kandiyoti, "Identity and Its Discontents," 433, 440.

23. Anne McClintock, "Family Feuds," 67, 78. In this quote, there is also an assumption about a singular feminist politics, one that is always subservient to nationalism and nationalist politics.

24. Lata Mani, "Contentious Traditions," in Kumkum Sangari and Sudesh Vaid, *Recasting Women*, 88–126.

25. In her article, Beatrice Hanssen makes a distinction between empowerment and Foucauldian reference to power that equals a subjecting regime of force or symbolic violence. I find this distinction instructive while thinking about the history of feminism in colonial India. For details, see Hanssen, "Whatever Happened to Feminist Theory," in Elizabeth Bronfen and Misha Kavka, *Feminist Consequences*, 76–77.

26. Mrinalini Sinha, "The Lineage of the 'Indian' Modern," in Antoinette Burton, *Gender, Sexuality and Colonial Modernity*, 207–21; Sanjay Joshi, "An Uneasy *Sangam*," in Sanjay Joshi, *Fractured Modernity*, 59–95.

27. The literature challenging dominant feminist politics within the Euro-American academia is immense. A sample of the different positions within this scholarship

includes Audre Lorde, *Sister/Outsider;* Gloria Anzaldúa and Cherrie Moraga, eds., *This Bridge Called My Back;* Gloria Anzaldúa and Analouise Keating, *This Bridge We Call Home;* bell hooks, *Feminist Theory from the Margin;* Ellen Carol Dubois, *Woman Suffrage;* Antoinette Burton, *Burdens of History;* Valerie Amos and Pratibha Parmar, "Challenging Imperial Feminism"; Chandra Mohanty, *Feminism without Borders;* Andrea Smith, *Conquest.*

28. See Kumkum Sangari, "Relating Histories," in Svati Joshi, *Rethinking English,* 242–72.

29. Kumkum Sangari and Sudesh Vaid, "Recasting Women: An Introduction," in Kumkum Sangari and Sudesh Vaid, *Recasting Women,* 3. Emphasis in the original.

30. A. P. Pillay, *Birth Control Simplified* and *Ideal Sex Life;* N. S. Phadke, *Sex Problem in India;* P. K. Wattal, *Population Problem in India;* Radhakamal Mukherjee, *Population Problem in India.*

31. Gerda Lerner, "Placing Women in History"; Natalie Zemon Davis, "'Women's History' in Transition"; Gisela Bock, "Women's History and Gender History;" Bridget Brereton, "Gendered Testimonies"; Antoinette Burton, *Dwelling in the Archive;* Betty Joseph, *Reading the East India Company.*

32. The pioneering works of Aparna Basu, Bharati Ray, Geraldine Forbes, Barbara Ramusack, and Gail Minault, to name just a few, have been important in this respect.

33. Durba Ghosh, "Decoding the Nameless," in Kathleen Wilson, *Imperial History,* 297–316. In this essay, Ghosh reflects on the difficulty of writing subaltern Indian women's histories given the paucity of archival information. Similar erasure of subaltern women's voices is also evident within the writings and records of Indian bourgeois women in the early twentieth century.

34. Vimla Devi Vaidya, *Garbh Nirodh* [Birth Control]. Copies of this pamphlet were available for purchase from the author's office in Delhi in 1998.

35. A number of recent historical monographs draw upon theoretical insights of literary criticism while being grounded in empirical research. Some of the works that brilliantly tie together theoretical concerns and empirical research are Tanika Sarkar, *Hindu Wife, Hindu Nation;* Mrinalini Sinha, *Colonial Masculinity;* Kathleen Canning, *Language of Labor and Gender;* and Joan Scott, *Only Paradoxes to Offer.*

36. Kirin Narayan rightly cautions against a simplistic and essentialist understanding of a "native" anthropologist as someone who is necessarily "better" situated to research and study their communities. For details of Narayan's argument, see "How Native Is a 'Native' Anthropologist?" in Reina Lewis and Sara Mills, *Feminist Postcolonial Theory,* 285–305.

37. Antoinette Burton, *Dwelling in the Archive,* 139. Burton provides a very thoughtful reading of elite Indian women's engagement with history and advances many sophisticated arguments in favor of feminist scholars' legitimizing women's voices found in nonconventional and marginal archival sites. However, I cannot enthusiastically embrace her call for abandoning archival research in a "faraway place," which incidentally is also "home" to me.

38. Ibid.

39. Nancy Naples, "Standpoint Epistemology: Explicating Multiple Dimensions," in Nancy Naples, *Feminism and Method,* 67–85.

40. Kalpana Ram, "Maternal Experience and Feminist Body Politics," in Kalpana Ram and Margaret Jolly, *Maternities and Modernities,* 275–98.

41. Ruth Behar, *Translated Woman*. Behar discusses the problems feminist anthropologists have while trying to translate meaningfully the words and lives of women living in non-Western countries.

42. Elizabeth Grosz, "Feminism and Anti-Humanism," in A. Milner and C. Worth, *Discourse and Difference*, 63–76

43. Gayatri Chakravorty Spivak, "Can the Subaltern Speak?" in Patrick Williams and Laura Chrisman, *Colonial Discourse*, 66–111.

44. Gayatri Chakravorty Spivak, "Foreword," in Henry Schwarz and Sangeeta Ray, *Companion to Postcolonial Studies*, xix–xx.

45. Bart Moore-Gilbert, "Gayatri Spivak: The Deconstructive Twist," in *Postcolonial Theory*, 101.

46. For an engaging critique of liberal traditions within feminist thought, see Alison Jaggar, "Liberal Feminism and Human Nature," in Alison Jaggar, *Feminist Politics and Human Nature*, 27–50.

47. Cecilia Van Hollen, *Birth on the Threshold*; Kamran Asdar Ali, *Planning the Family in Egypt*; Nancy Scheper-Hughes, *Death without Weeping*; Ruth Behar, *Translated Woman*.

Chapter 1: Demographic Rhetoric and Sexual Surveillance

1. I use the category *middle class* to define a newly emerging English-educated social group in colonial India. What united this group of people was their commonly shared cultural and political enterprise of empowering themselves within the colonial public sphere through various programs of reforms. They also self-consciously defined themselves in opposition to both the subaltern classes below them and the declining landed aristocracy above them. For more details on the Indian colonial middle classes and their various cultural projects of improvement and empowerment, see Sanjay Joshi, *Fractured Modernity*.

2. In the existing literature, there has been some discussion of the reformist nationalist anxieties in the nineteenth century, with what was perceived to be a decline in Indian physique and masculine prowess. See John Rosselli, "The Self-Image of Effeteness"; Mrinalini Sinha, *Colonial Masculinity*; Uma Chakravarty, "Whatever Happened to the Vedic Dasi?" in Kumkum Sangari and Sudesh Vaid, *Recasting Women*. For discussions of how the politics of the body framed nationalist rhetoric in the twentieth century, see Joseph S. Alter, "Celibacy, Sexuality, and the Transformation of Gender," and his arguments in *Gandhi's Body*. Also see Charu Gupta, *Sexuality, Obscenity, Community*.

3. Robert Malthus, *Essay on Population*.

4. Francis Galton, *Essay in Eugenics*, 35, 38.

5. There is now an enormous literature within Indian historiography that has engaged with the issue of examining the nature of intellectual interaction between India and the West, particularly in the context of Indian nationalism. Some of the contending positions are Sudhir Chandra, *Oppressive Present*; Partha Chatterjee, *Nationalist Thought in a Colonial World*; Tanika Sarkar, *Hindu Wife, Hindu Nation*; Homi K. Bhabha, "Of Mimicry and Man" and *Nation and Narration*.

6. Arjun Appadurai, "Number in the Colonial Imagination," in Carol Breckenridge and Peter van der Veer, *Orientalism and the Post-Colonial Predicament*, 333. Also see David Ludden's discussion on the use of statistics in the construction of Orientalism, "Orientalist Empiricism" in Breckenridge and van der Veer, *Orientalism and the Post-Colonial Predicament*. In this essay, Ludden argues that colonial knowledge was available for native consumption and native elites appropriated it for their political projects of empowerment.

7. Bernard S. Cohn, "Census, Social Structure and Objectification in South Asia," in Bernard S. Cohn, *Anthropologist among the Historians*, 224–54.

8. Jacqueline Urla, "Cultural Politics in an Age of Statistics," 819. In this essay, Urla examines the role of statistics in shaping Basque national politics. There is a growing body of literature examining the significance of statistical data in shaping the historical projects of nationalisms; see also Joshua Cole, *Power of Large Numbers*.

9. Census figures and information are discussed at some length in Leela and Pradip Visaria, "Population," in Dharma Kumar, *Cambridge Economic History of India, Volume II*, 463–532.

10. The Neo-Malthusian League was established in 1877 in Britain. It combined Malthusian ideas about poverty being a result of an ever-increasing population with that of limiting fertility with the use of birth control. For more details on the Neo-Malthusian League in Britain, see Rosanna Ledbetter, *History of the Malthusian League*.

11. Margaret Sanger was a well-known American birth control activist who in the 1930s visited India seeking to promote the cause globally. She is credited with having coined the term "birth control" in 1915. For more biographic details on Sanger and her work on birth control, see Ellen Chesler, *Woman of Valor*, for details on Sanger's work and life as a birth control advocate.

12. Edith How-Martyn, *Brief Survey of the Birth Control Movement in India*. My own reference is taken from a personal copy of the essay in the collection of Professor Barbara N. Ramusack at the University of Cincinnati. Ramusack's unpublished paper, "Maternal Infant Health, Population Control or Eugenics: Reproductive Control in India, 1920–1940," also has a wealth of information on this subject from which I have benefited.

13. B. L. Raina, *Planning Family in India*, 87.

14. See S. Anandhi, "Reproductive Bodies."

15. Brijnath N. Sharga, *Legacy of Rama*. Sharga does not provide the exact date when this was written. However given that Rama Tirtha died in 1903, he obviously wrote this before that date, and certainly before the data of the 1931 census were available, which first recorded a significant increase in the size of India's population.

16. S. Anandhi, "Reproductive Bodies," 141.

17. Eugenic Society Papers in Contemporary Medical Archives Center at the Wellcome Institute for the History of Medicine, London, CMAC: SA/EUG/E.8, Indian Eugenic Society: Lahore and Simla, "Eugenics a Bird's Eyeview." The same leaflet mentioned that in 1921 the society had fifty-eight members with seventy-five others who had promised to become members. Among the numerous sympathizers were Swami Shraddhanand, founder and governor of the Gurukul Kangri; the reformist/revivalist Hindu Arya Samaj, Bijnor United Provinces (henceforth U.P.); and Mahatmaji Hansraj,

cofounder of the D.A.V. College, an Arya Samaj institution, in Lahore. Ahluwalia was a member of the Arya-Samaj himself. The Arya Samaj was a leading Hindu reformist sect started by Dayanand Saraswati in nineteenth-century Punjab. The Arya Samaj and its leaders such as Dayanand stressed the need for physical reforms in order to ensure a strong and healthy people for the nation. For details on Arya Samaj, see Kenneth W. Jones, *Arya Dharm*; Anshu Malhotra, "Arya Samaj Movement and Women."

18. For details on Stopes's work and life, see Ruth Hall, *Passionate Crusader*.
19. Gopaljee Ahluwalia, "Indian Population Problem."
20. For more biographical information on Karve, see S. P. Sen, *Dictionary of National Biography*, 244–46.
21. N. S. Phadke, *Sex Problem in India*.
22. For biographical details on Wattal, see B. L. Raina, *Planning Family in India*, 250.
23. P. K. Wattal, *Population Problem in India*. A second edition under the same title was published in 1934.
24. Radhakamal Mukherjee, *Population Problem in India*.
25. Ibid., 8.
26. Ibid., 2.
27. See Lalita Panicker's article, "Population: No More a Game of Numbers."
28. Gopaljee Ahluwalia, "Indian Population Problem."
29. Ibid., 288.
30. A. P. Pillay, "Is Medicine Fulfilling Its Responsibilities?"
31. Malthus in his essay on population opposed public relief of poverty; he saw the "poor laws" in particular as contributing greatly to population growth. For a further critique of Malthus's position on population, see Amartya Sen, "Population: Delusion and Reality."
32. A. P. Pillay, "Eugenical Birth Control for India," 310.
33. N. S. Phadke, "Eugenics for India," 316–17.
34. N. S. Phadke, *Sex Problem in India*, 8.
35. Ibid., 50.
36. Ibid., 137.
37. Ibid., 17–19.
38. For a discussion of the middle class and its cultural projects of improvement, see Sanjay Joshi, *Fractured Modernity*.
39. P. K. Wattal, *Population Problem in India* (1916), 2.
40. Ibid., 2.
41. P. K. Wattal, *Population Problem in India* (1934), 119.
42. Radhakamal Mukherjee, "Population Capacity and Control in India," in Radhakamal Mukherjee, *Population Problem in India*, 7–17.
43. Debendra Nath Ghoshe, "Social Background of Pauperism," in Radhakamal Mukherjee, *Population Problem in India*, 141–52.
44. Ibid., 152.
45. Dagmar Engels, "Women's Work in Bengal Economy," in Dagmar Engels, *Beyond Purdah?*, 203–14. *Beyond Purdah?* discusses the exploitative conditions in mines' tea gardens. Geraldine Forbes also discusses the working conditions for women in mines and factories in *New Cambridge History of India*, 167–71, 176–79.

46. N. S. Phadke, "Birth Control in India," 106.
47. Ibid.
48. Sumit Sarkar, *Modern India*, 168.
49. Ibid., 171.
50. Judith Brown, *Modern India*, 188.
51. Stanley Wolpert, *New History of India*, 297.
52. Sumit Sarkar, *Modern India*, 177–78.
53. Ibid., 208.
54. Ibid., 202.
55. For details on the Gandhian critique of Western modernity, see Mohandas K. Gandhi's own *Hind Swaraj, or Indian Home Rule*; Bhikhu Parekh, *Gandhi*; and Partha Chatterjee, "The Moment of Manoeuver: Gandhi and the Critique of Civil Society," in his *Nationalist Thought in a Colonial World: A Derivative Discourse?*, 85–130.
56. Sumit Sarkar, *Modern India*, 243. *Manusmriti* was a canonical text compiled from about 200 to 400 C.E. This text is seen as combining legal injunctions and moral prescriptions, placing women firmly within the patriarchal structures of family and marriage. Barbara N. Ramusack and Sharon Sievers, *Women in Asia*, 28. For more details on *Manusmriti*, see Wendy Doniger O'Flaherty and Brian K. Smith, *Laws of Manu*.
57. For more details on *shudhi* and *sangathan*, see Kenneth Jones, *Arya Dharm*; see also K. L. Tuteja and O. P. Grewal, "Emergence of Hindu Communal Ideology."
58. See Francis Robinson, *Separatism among Indian Muslims*, or Peter Hardy, *Muslims of British India*, 208. Thomas Blom Hansen also discusses this in "Organizing the Hindu Nation," in Thomas Blom Hansen, *Saffron Wave*, 93.
59. For a detailed analysis of Dayanand's gender and caste politics, see Anshu Malhotra, "Pativratas and Kupattis," 15–39.
60. Sumit Sarkar, *Modern India*, 216, 235.
61. See Pradip Kumar Datta, *Carving Blocs*. The author examines the communalization of demography in Bengal. For an analysis of how numbers were deployed within U.P. to promote communal tensions, see Charu Gupta, "Hindu Wombs, Muslim Progeny: The Numbers Game and Shifting Debates on Widow Remarriage, U. P. 1890–1930s."
62. Sumit Sarkar, *Modern India*, 167.
63. P. K. Wattal, *Population Problem in India*, 16.
64. Ibid.
65. Ibid., 19.
66. For more on the 1936 conference, see B. L. Raina, *Planning Family in India*, 99.
67. Radhakamal Mukherjee, *Population Problem in India*, 206.
68. Ibid., 139 (emphasis added).
69. Urla, "Cultural Politics," 819.
70. Radhakamal Mukherjee, *Population Problem in India*, 139.
71. Lynn M. Thomas, *Politics of the Womb*.
72. N. S. Phadke, *Sex Problem in India*.
73. For details on middle-class politics of defining its agenda in opposition to the working subalterns and aristocrats, see Sanjay Joshi, *Fractured Modernity*, 33–84.
74. N. S. Phadke, *Sex Problem in India*, 300.

75. Ibid., 302.
76. P. K. Wattal, *Population Problem in India,* 99 (1934 edition).
77. Debendra Nath Ghoshe, "Social Background of Pauperism," in Radhakamal Mukherjee, *Population Problem in India,* 152.
78. Mukherjee's introduction to Jai Krishan Mathur, *The Pressure of Population: Its Effects on Rural Economy in Gorakhpur District.*
79. Roy Porter and Lesley Hall, "Good Sex: The Rhetoric of Conjugal Relations," in Roy Porter and Lesley Hall, *Facts of Life,* 202–23.
80. Partha Chatterjee, "Nationalist Resolution," in Kumkum Sangari and Sudesh Vaid, *Recasting Women,* 233–54.
81. Antoinette Burton, *Dwelling in the Archive,* 9.
82. For discussions on nineteenth-century debates on masculinity and nationalism, see Uma Chakravarty, "Whatever Happened to the Vedic Dasi?"; Mrinalini Sinha, *Colonial Masculinity*; John Rosselli, "The Self-Image of Effeteness."
83. N. S. Phadke, *Sex Problem in India,* 169 (emphasis added).
84. Ibid., 295–96 (emphasis added).
85. A. P. Pillay, *Ideal Sex Life,* 221 (emphasis added).
86. Ibid., 208.
87. A. P. Pillay, "Is Medicine Fulfilling Its Responsibilities?"
88. N. S. Phadke, *Sex Problem in India,* 53–54.
89. Ibid. (emphasis added).
90. Ibid., 55.
91. Ibid., 56.
92. Ibid., 97.
93. Ibid., 127.
94. Ibid., 173.
95. Ibid., 190 (emphasis added).
96. A thoughtful critique of anatomy's labeling of the female body is in Lisa Jean Moore and Adele E. Clarke, "Clitoral Conventions and Transgressions."
97. N. S. Phadke, *Sex Problem in India,* 197–98.
98. Ibid., 103–4.
99. In my interviews with Jaunpuri women, the metaphor of seed was used repeatedly for male sperm to explain the process of conception: "*Malik ka beejh*" (Lord/Husband's seed), Bhura Devi, interview by author, Jaunpur U.P, February 13, 1998.
100. N. S. Phadke, "Eugenics for India," 316.
101. N. S. Phadke, *Sex Problem in India,* 210 (emphasis added).
102. Ibid., 211.
103. Ibid., 186 (emphasis added).
104. Ibid., 262.
105. Ibid., 226.
106. The male dominance of contraceptive knowledge seems to have been common in parts of Britain too; for details, see Kate Fisher, "'She Was Quite Happy with the Arrangements I Made...'"
107. N. S. Phadke, *Sex Problem in India,* 236 (emphasis added).
108. *Birth Control News* (August 1924).

109. A. P. Pillay, *Welfare Problems in Rural India*, 115. Because only a thousand copies of this book were published, the readership of such works was limited.

110. Ibid., 117.

111. For a discussion of the gender politics of the reform agenda in the nineteenth century, see Sumit Sarkar, *Critique of Colonial India*, 1–17.

112. A. P. Pillay, *Birth Control Simplified*; A. P. Pillay, *Ideal Sex Life*.

113. A. P. Pillay, *Ideal Sex Life*, 210.

114. Ibid., 208–12.

115. Ibid., 202.

116. Ibid., 226.

117. Ibid., 177.

118. Ibid.

119. Ibid., 200.

120. Ibid., 250.

121. Ibid., 73.

122. Ibid., 77.

123. Ibid., 50.

124. Ibid., 58.

125. Ibid., 137.

Chapter 2: Global Agenda and Local Politics

1. Deborah Cohen, "Private Lives." For more details on Stopes's life and work, see June Rose, *Marie Stopes*; Ruth Hall, *Passionate Crusader*.

2. For biographical details on Sanger's work and life, see Ellen Chesler, *Woman of Valor*. For a critical evaluation of Sanger's political and ideological moves within the American birth control movement, see Linda Gordon, *Woman's Body, Woman's Right*. For a more sympathetic perspective on Sanger's work on birth control in the United States, see Carole McCann, *Birth Control Politics*.

3. There are no biographies of either How-Martyn or Palmer. The Eileen Palmer Collections in the London School of Economics Archives (LSEA) and the Oriental and India Office Collection (OIOC) at the British Library gives information on How-Martyn and Palmer's various tours to India from 1934 to 1939.

4. For details on state intervention on the birth control debates, see chapter 4, "A Fractured Discourse: Colonial Attitudes on Birth Control in the Twentieth Century."

5. Antoinette Burton, *Burdens of History*. Although Burton does not examine the presence and the role of Stopes in Indian politics, her impressive study on early British feminists highlights their complicity with the politics of empire and colonialism.

6. Kumkum Sangari, "Relating Histories," in Svati Joshi, *Rethinking English*, 242–72.

7. Adele E. Clarke, *Disciplining Reproduction*, 29.

8. Fernando Coronil, *Magical State*, 13. Frederick Cooper and Ann Stoler have made a similar argument about interrelational histories, locating the "metropole and the colony in a single analytical field." See the introduction to their *Tensions of Empire*, 4.

9. Sumit Sarkar, *Modern India*, 5–6.

10. Ibid.

11. For instance, neither Linda Gordon nor Carole McCann examine Sanger's interest in promoting birth control in countries such as India or China; see Gordon, *Woman's Body, Woman's Right*; McCann, *Birth Control Politics*. There are a few references to Sanger's work in India; see Ellen Chesler, *Woman of Valor,* 356–64. Studies that examine Stopes's work tend to overlook the importance of India or other non-Western nations to her project of disseminating contraceptive information; see Deborah Cohen, "Private Lives." Biographies on Stopes have very little information on her involvement in promoting birth control in other parts of the world; see June Rose, *Marie Stopes*; Ruth Hall, *Passionate Crusader*.

12. Richard Soloway, *Birth Control and the Population Question*, Peter Neushul, "Marie C. Stopes and the Popularization of Birth Control Technology."

13. Indira Choudhury, "Instructions for the Unconverted"; Susanne Klausen, "Imperial Mother of Birth Control."

14. Here I refer to the works of Barbara Ramusack, "Cultural Missionaries, Maternal Imperialists, Feminist Allies"; Mrinalini Sinha, *Colonial Masculinity*; Antoinette Burton, *At the Heart of the Empire*; Benjamin Zachariah, "British and Indian Ideas of 'Development.'"

15. Fernando Coronil, *Magical State,* 2–18; Caren Kaplan, Norma Alarcon, and Minoo Moallem, *Between Women and Nation*, 1–16.

16. Kaplan et al., *Between Women and Nation*, 12–16.

17. See Richard Soloway, *Birth Control and the Population Question*; June Rose, *Marie Stopes*; Ruth Hall, *Passionate Crusader*.

18. Richard Soloway, *Birth Control and the Population Question,* 307.

19. Ibid.

20. Ibid., 315.

21. Ibid., 310–11.

22. Susanne Klausen, "Imperial Mother of Birth Control."

23. As cited in Ellen Chesler, *Woman of Valor,* 340–42.

24. Ibid., 15.

25. Ibid., 352.

26. Ibid., 364.

27. Ibid., 363.

28. Ibid., 364.

29. Margaret Sanger to Noah Slee, December 23, 1935, Margaret Sanger Paper Project, (henceforth MSPP), reel 10.

30. Margaret Sanger to Noah Slee, December 16, 1935, MSPP, reel 10.

31. Margaret Sanger to Noah Slee, January 12, 1936, MSPP, reel 10.

32. Florence Rose to Bhangwan Gyanee from India, January 28, 1936, MSPP, reel 10.

33. June Rose, *Marie Stopes,* 50.

34. B. L. Raina, *Planning Family in India,* 89.

35. Gopalji Ahluwalia, "Indian Population Problem."

36. N. S. Phadke first published his views on "appropriate" technology in a short pamphlet published by the Bombay Birth Control League in early 1924 and Stopes

responded to this pamphlet. Phadke later reiterated his position in *Sex Problem in India,* 232–38.

37. Marie Stopes to Rabindranath Tagore, March 1, 1926, PP/MCS/A.313, India Various Correspondence c. 1920–c. 1950, Wellcome Institute for the History of Medicine, London.

38. Rabindranath Tagore to Margaret Sanger, September 30, 1925, MSPP, subseries 1, microfilm volumes 3 and 10.

39. Rabindranath Tagore to Margaret Sanger, September 30, 1925, MSPP.

40. Indira Choudhary examines how race and class variables shaped Stopes's work in India and Britain, respectively, in her "Instructions for the Unconverted."

41. Bose was a member of the Swarajist wing of the Indian National Congress. In October 1924, he was detained without trial by colonial authorities for being suspected of terrorist links. He broke up with Gandhi on the issue of his reelection as the president of the Congress in 1939. In 1943 Bose formed the Azad Hind Government and the Indian National Army (INA). The above references to Bose's political activities in colonial India are taken from Sumit Sarkar, *Modern India,* 281, 283, 372, and 411.

42. Subhas Chandra Bose, "Some Problems of Nation Building." Thanks to David Arnold for this reference.

43. Under the leadership of Ambedkar, the untouchable Mahars developed an autonomous movement from the 1920s. The demands of this movement included separate representation, the right to use tanks and enter temples, and abolition of the *Mahar watan* (traditional services to village chiefs). Sumit Sarkar, *Modern India,* 243.

44. See M. P. Mangudkar, *Dr. Ambedkar and Family Planning.*

45. Ibid., 9.

46. Margaret Sanger's secretary to B. R. Ambedkar, October 31, 1935, Box 115, Folder 1144, Sanger Collection. Thanks to Barbara Ramusack for making this reference available to me.

47. Havelock Ellis to Edward Griffith, September 18, 1936, PP/EFG/A.4.

48. A. P. Pillay to Edward Griffith, November 8, 1935, PP/EFG/A.4.

49. Norman Himes to Edward Griffith, March 1, 1936, PP/EFG/A.4.

50. Ibid.

51. C. P. Blacker to Edward Griffith, September 21, 1937, PP/EFG/A.4.

52. C. P. Blacker to Edward Griffith, April 6, 1947, PP/EFG/A.4.

53. For an engaging discussion on contraceptive technologies and the tensions that these created between Sanger and Stopes, see Peter Neushul, "Marie C. Stopes."

54. More recently, women's organizations in India such as Saheli, Stree Shakti Sanghatan, and the All India Women's Association opposed the introduction of Depo-Provera and Net-en. Both these contraceptives are synthetic derivatives of progesterone. SAMA, a resource group for women and health, undertook a study to evaluate the impact of Depo-Provera on women. For details, see SAMA, "India." These contraceptives suppress ovulation to make cervical mucous inhospitable to sperm and to make the lining of the uterus unsuitable for implantation. Depo-Provera is a three-month injectable developed by Upjohn of the United States, and Net-en is a product of Schering AG of Germany. For details on the opposition to these contraceptives, see

"Women Campaign Against Birth Control Injections," *The Hindu* (October 17, 2000), cited in "India Population News Archives July 10, 2005" at http://www.overpopulation.org/IndiaNews.html (accessed May 12, 2007); and T. K. Rajalakshmi, "Cautions on Two Contraceptives," *Frontline* (November 25–December 8, 2000), http://www.frontlineonnet.com/fl1724/17240820.htm.

55. Marie Stopes to P. S. Sharma, editor of *Madras Birth Control Bulletin,* May 10, 1935, PP/MCS/A.314.

56. Ibid.

57. Stopes's secretary Mrs. M. Butler, CBC, to Manager Messrs. C. Ringer and Co., Calcutta, March 12, 1953, PP/MCS/A.315.

58. Mohandas K. Gandhi, *Self-Restraint versus Self-Indulgence*, 208 (emphasis added).

59. Edith How-Martyn, March 1937, OIOC: MSS D.1182/14.

60. Eileen Palmer's interview with Mr. Stevens of Stella and Company at his office in Bombay, December 3, 1937, OIOC: MSS EUR D1182/6.

61. Edith How-Martyn's interview with Mr. Stevens of Stella and Company in Bombay, December 2, 1938, OIOC: MSS D.1182/7.

62. Ibid.

63. Edith How-Martyn's interview with A. P. Pillay in Bombay, December 2, 1938, OIOC: MSS D.1182/7.

64. Edith How-Martyn's interview with Dr. Rose Beals, December 10, 1938, OIOC: MSS D.1182/7.

65. Material dictated by Dr. Pandit to Eileen Palmer, Calcutta, January 6, 1939, OIOC: MSS D.1182/7.

66. Letter from Margaret Sanger to Intimate Friends and Family, December 6, 1935, Box 88, folder 894, Sanger Collection.

67. Confidential excerpt from Helen Countrymen to Margaret Sanger, November 22, 1936, MSPP.

68. Eileen Palmer's discussion with Lady Cowasji Jehangir, December 6, 1937, OIOC: MSS: EUR D1182/6.

69. Margaret Sanger's letter to Lady Cowasji Jehangir, September 15, 1938, reel 15, MSPP.

70. Marie Stopes, "On Some Aspects of Contraception."

71. Ibid., 144 (emphasis added).

72. Marie Stopes to S. N. Datar, April 11, 1929, PP/MCS/A.313.

73. Margaret Sanger to C. P. Blacker, November 14, 1935, SA/EUG/D.21, Box 26 (emphasis added). One could perhaps argue that Sanger deliberately and strategically shaped her appeal to the racism of the Eugenic Society.

74. Edith How-Martyn to Margaret Sanger, box 56, folder 530, Sophia Smith Collection, MSPP (emphasis added).

75. Margaret Sanger to Mrs. Elmhirst, January 7, 1936, box 56, folder 530, Sophia Smith Collection, MSPP.

76. Mohandas K. Gandhi, *Self-Restraint versus Self-Indulgence,* 117.

77. Ibid., 188.

78. Ibid., 45.

79. Anand Hingorani, *To the Women,* 44–45.

80. Mohandas K. Gandhi, *Self-Restraint versus Self-Indulgence,* 91.

81. Ibid., 64.
82. Ibid., 104.
83. Ibid., 153.
84. Marie C. Stopes, "Review of *Self-Restraint versus Self-Indulgence.*"
85. Marie C. Stopes, "India and Gandhi," 3.
86. Ibid.
87. June Rose, *Marie Stopes,* 111.
88. Ibid., 237.
89. A. R. Bustani to Marie Stopes, February 8, 1921, PP/MCS/A.313.
90. T. V. Venkateswara Aiyar to Marie Stopes, November 10, 1921, PP/MCS/A.313.
91. C. P. R. Ayyar to Marie Stopes, 1931, PP/MCS/A.313.
92. The letters are taken from Stopes's papers at Wellcome, PP/MSC/A.313.
93. For more details on changing ideas on sexuality in Britain, see Roy Porter and Lesley Hall, "'Good Sex': The New Rhetoric of Conjugal Relations," in Roy Porter and Lesley Hall, *Facts of Life,* 202–23.
94. Ibid.
95. Adele Clarke, *Disciplining Reproduction,* 30.
96. Marie C. Stopes, "Review of *Self-Restraint versus Self-Indulgence,*" 45.
97. Ibid., 44.
98. Margaret Sanger, "Does Gandhi Know Women?" Subsequent quotes are also from this article.
99. Ibid.
100. Ibid. Postcolonial feminist scholarship has warned against the tendency within dominant mainstream Western feminism to argue for the cult of transparent "experience" as universal. What shapes these universal claims, it has been argued, "are the dominant versions of feminism in Western Europe and North America as the paradigmatic form of feminism per se"; Mrinalini Sinha, Donna J. Guy, and Angela Woollacott, "Introduction: Why Feminisms and Internationalism?" in Mrinalini Sinha et al., *Feminisms and Internationalism,* 1; Chandra Talpade Mohanty, "Feminist Encounters."
101. Carole McCann, *Birth Control Politics,* 31.
102. See Richard Fox, *Gandhian Utopia.*
103. Anand Hingorani, *To the Women,* 174.
104. Ibid., 168.
105. Madhu Kishwar, "Women and Gandhi"; Sujata Patel, "Construction and Reconstruction of Woman"; Geraldine Forbes, "Women in the Nationalist Movement," in *New Cambridge History of India.* Forbes's chapter discusses Gandhi's role in bringing Indian women into public-sphere nationalist politics in large numbers. Tanika Sarkar, in "Nationalist Iconography," argues that it was Gandhi's personality and his emphasis on nonviolence that made it possible for middle-class Indian women to participate in nationalist politics with few objections from their families. David Hardiman, in "Father of the Nation," in *Gandhi in His Times and Ours,* 94–122, outlines very well the contradictory impulses within Gandhian politics and the love-hate relationship of Indian feminism with Gandhian thought and politics.
106. Mohandas K. Gandhi, *Self-Restraint versus Self-Indulgence,* 145.
107. Ibid., 103.
108. Mohandas K. Gandhi, *Hind Swaraj,* 32–33.

109. Ibid., 54.
110. Ibid., 73.
111. Ibid., 74–75.
112. Mohandas K. Gandhi, *Self-Restraint versus Self-Indulgence*, 50.
113. Ibid., 54.
114. Ibid., 111.
115. Anand Hingorani, *To the Women*, 23.
116. Mohandas K. Gandhi, *Self-Restraint versus Self-Indulgence*, 207.
117. For a critical commentary on the "Laws of Manu," particularly as these affected the status of women, see Barbara N. Ramusack and Sharon Sievers, *Women in Asia*, 27–29.
118. Mohandas K. Gandhi, *Self-Restraint versus Self-Indulgence*, 108.
119. Ibid., 95.
120. June Rose, *Marie Stopes*, 198.
121. Mohandas K. Gandhi, *Self-Restraint versus Self-Indulgence*, 57.
122. Ibid., 44.
123. Ibid., 71–72.
124. Ibid., 175.
125. See Carol Smart, "Disruptive Bodies and Unruly Sex: The Regulation of Reproduction and Sexuality in the Nineteenth Century," in her *Regulating Womanhood*, 7–32.
126. Joan B. Landes, "Introduction," in Joan B. Landes, *Feminism: The Public and the Private*, 7.

Chapter 3: Polyvocality, Ambivalence, and Negotiations

1. Mrinalini Sinha has argued convincingly that in the case of the Sarda Act in 1929, organized Indian women's movements claimed "modernity" for themselves and that the "rhetorical agency of organized women played midwife to the birth of the 'Indian' modern in late colonial India." In the case of the debates and discussions on birth control, the position of Indian feminists was internally split and their commitment to modernity in this instance seemed more fragile and doubtful. For details on Sinha's argument, see "Lineage of the 'Indian' Modern."
2. Kumari Jayawardena, *Feminism and Nationalism in the Third World*, 73–108.
3. Deniz Kandiyoti, "Identity and Its Discontents," 429–44.
4. Anne McClintock, "Family Feuds," 78 (emphasis added).
5. I refer to the Women's India Association (WIA) and All India Women's Conference (AIWC) as representing the first wave of organized feminist politics in colonial India because these two organizations, along with the National Council of Women in India (NCWI), had a national focus and presence. I was unable to locate the records of NCWI, forcing me to leave it out of my review of women's politics in this chapter. Although it needs to be pointed out that the focus on the two organizations here does not preclude or write out the history of individual feminist critiques, women such as Tarabai Shinde and Pandita Ramabai presented from the larger history of women in colonial India. Individual women writers in the late nineteenth and early twentieth centuries in India made an important contribution to Indian women's cause

by making public their critiques of upper-caste Brahmanical institutions of sexual oppression. But these critiques were made at an individual level and did not aim to organize women as a distinct group to articulate a political agenda addressing their specific concerns and problems. Moreover, prior to the emergence of the three large national women's groups in colonial India, there were some smaller groups, such as Bharat Stree Mahamandal (Association/Gathering of Indian Women), which can be regarded as a precursor to the later national organizations. I have not looked at this early group because there are no records documenting that they addressed the subject of birth control. For more details on early women's organizations, see Geraldine Forbes, *New Cambridge History of India*, 64–72.

6. Margaret Jolly, "Motherlands?"

7. Ellen L. Fleischmann, *Nation and Its "New" Women*, 10. Fleischmann quotes Frances Hasso to call for a careful assessment of feminism's relationship with nationalist politics.

8. Mrinalini Sinha presents an excellent analysis of current literature on politics of gender and nationalism in her recent publication, *Gender and Nation*. I am grateful to the author for a copy of this publication.

9. The names of these women appear with different spellings in some primary and secondary literature; in this chapter I will refer to each woman by this spelling, disregarding other variants to avoid confusion.

10. In 1891, the colonial state had introduced the Age of Consent Bill that raised the age of consent for sexual intercourse for Indian girls from ten to twelve years. According to Mrinalini Sinha, this bill did not seek to alter the practice of child marriage, but sought to alter the practice of premature consummation of child marriage. For more details on this bill, see Sinha, "Potent Protest: The Age of Consent Controversy, 1891," in her *Colonial Masculinity*, 138–80. A second bill was passed at the beginning of October 1929, which laid down the minimum age of marriage for females as fourteen and for males as eighteen, but it did not mention the age of consent. For details, see Forbes, *New Cambridge History of India*, 83–90.

11. See Ritu Menon and Kamala Bhasin, "Borders and Bodies: Recovering Women in the Interest of the Nation," in Menon and Bhasin, *Borders and Boundaries: Women in India's Partition*, 65–130, for a discussion about displacement of women during partition in 1947 and the steps taken by the Indian and Pakistani governments to reclaim these women.

12. For more biographical information on Rameshwari Nehru, see *Roshni*, "A Special Issue on Smt. Rameshwari Nehru" (October–December 1987), and Om Prakash Paliwal, *Rameshwari Nehru, Patriot and Internationalist*. I am grateful to Ravikant for a copy of this book.

13. For more biographical details, see Muthulakshmi Reddi, *Autobiography of Dr. (Mrs.) Muthulakshmi Reddy*; Muthulakshmi Reddi, *My Experiences as a Legislator*; and S. P. Sen, *Dictionary of National Biography, Volume 3*, 522–25.

14. For more details on Cousins, see Catherine Candy, "Relating Feminisms, Nationalism and Imperialisms"; Barbara N. Ramusack, "Cultural Missionaries, Maternal Imperialists, Feminist Allies."

15. Sen, *Dictionary of National Biography, Volume 3*, 96–97.

16. For more biographical details on Chattopadhyaya, see Radha Kumar, *History of Doing*, 55. Also see Kamaladevi Chattopadhyaya, *Inner Recesses, Outer Spaces*; Sen, *Dictionary of National Biography, Volume 1*, 277–78.

17. I am using the spelling of Laxmibai Rajwade's name as it appears in her article, "Indian Mother," in Shyam Kumari Nehru, *Our Cause*, 73–92. In print, her name was sometimes spelled as Lakshmibai Rajwade.

18. For a good in-depth analysis of issues related to representing marginal groups and claiming to speak on their behalf, see Linda Alcoff, "Problem of Speaking for Others."

19. See Richard Soloway, *Birth Control and the Population Question*, 49.

20. Annie Besant, "Social Aspects of Malthusianism."

21. For details on Gandhi's position on male sexuality, see chapter 2 in this book, "Global Agenda and Local Politics."

22. Annie Besant, "Theosophy and the Law of Population," in S. Chandrasekhar, *A Dirty Filthy Book*, 205–12.

23. The rhythm method is based on the knowledge that ovulation can be expected about two weeks after menstruation. Therefore, it was understood to be safe to have sexual intercourse for the first ten days from the start of the period, and again for the last ten days. During the ten days in the middle, sexual intercourse was to be avoided. The effectiveness of this method has been questioned because it is based on the presumption that all women have regular twenty-eight- to thirty-day menstrual cycles; sometimes ovulation can change with every cycle for a woman. I borrow this explanation of the rhythm method from Saheli Collective, *Womantalk*, 16.

24. *AIWC Annual Reports and Conferences, 1932–1933*, 93, Margaret Cousins Library at AIWC, New Delhi.

25. B. F. Musallam, *Sex and Society in Islam*. In this work, Musallam examines numerous Muslim sources to argue that Islam was not opposed to the use of contraceptives. I am grateful to Barbara N. Ramusack for this reference.

26. Louise Ouwerkerk, *No Elephants for the Maharaja*, 5–13.

27. *AIWC Annual Reports and Conferences, 1936*, 88.

28. Ibid.

29. Ibid., 90.

30. Ibid.

31. Ibid.

32. For details on the emergence of the Hindu community and the increasing enumeration of religious communities in India, see Romila Thapar, "Imagined Religious Communities?"; Pradip Kumar Datta, *Carving Blocs*.

33. Mrinalini Sinha has argued that the Indian women's movement in the early twentieth century embraced a more liberal ideal of unity of "women" in their espousal of nationalist sentiment. For details, see "Suffragism and Internationalism: The Enfranchisement of British and Indian Women Under an Imperial State," in Ian Christopher Fletcher, Laura E. Nym Mayhall, and Philippa Levine, *Women's Suffrage in the British Empire*, 224–39. Jana Everett makes a similar argument about the lack of communalism within the women's movement in a recent conference paper, "The Indian Women's Movement during the Interwar Years." I am grateful to the author for a copy of the article.

34. According to Geraldine Forbes, Hamid Ali, as a member of the Sub-Committee on Women in the National Planning Committee in 1939, in her memoranda urged the committee to consult an authority on Muslim law. She found, when she explained Muslim law to her coworkers, they either did not listen or could not understand her point of view. She protested against the report that was drafted by the subcommittee and finally signed only after Jawaharlal Nehru intervened. Hamid Ali's objections were read as an attempt to communalize the issue by Rajwade. See Forbes, "A Time of Transition," in *New Cambridge History of India*, 199–200.

35. For details on Margaret Sanger's and Marie Stopes's critiques of Gandhi, see chapter 2 in this book, "Global Agenda and Local Politics."

36. Margaret Cousin's letter to Margaret Sanger, May 15, 1936, reel 11, MSPP. Barbara Ramusack also discusses this issue in "Embattled Advocates," 54–55.

37. Reddi, *AIWC Annual Reports and Conference 1932–33*, 90–93 (emphasis added).

38. Ibid., 90.

39. Ibid.

40. Laxmibai Rajwade, "Indian Mother," in Shyam Kumari Nehru, *Our Cause*, 88.

41. Ibid., 88.

42. My references are from a file on Begum Hamid Ali housed in the AIWC archives in New Delhi. There is no file number for this. The paper is titled "Section III: Marriage, Maternity and Succession," 20/2/1940.

43. Ibid.

44. Ibid.

45. Kamaladevi Chattopadhyaya, "Future of Indian Women's Movement," in Shyam Kumari Nehru, *Our Cause*, 401.

46. Ibid., 401.

47. Barbara Ramusack, "Embattled Advocates."

48. Kamaladevi Chattopadhyaya, Private Papers, NMML, "Family Planning," serial no. 138, 4. This is not dated.

49. I find Antoinette Burton's study of British feminist politics useful in trying to understand how feminism as a historical movement was constrained by the political discourses of its time. See Burton, *Burdens of History*.

50. Rameshwari Nehru, as quoted in Om Prakash Paliwal, *Rameshwari Nehru*, 19.

51. Rameshwari Nehru, "Presidential Address at the 15th Session of the All India Women's Conference, Bangalore, 1940," in Rameshwari Nehru, *Gandhi Is My Star*, 192 (emphasis added).

52. Kamaladevi Chattopadhyaya, *Indian Women's Battles for Freedom*, 5.

53. See Antoinette Burton, *Burdens of History*, 171–206, where she argues that middle-class women leaders in Britain during the late nineteenth and early twentieth centuries made a case for female suffrage by projecting themselves as responsible imperial subjects who would ensure and extend colonial interests by civilizing their Indian sisters. These women deployed the dominant colonial ideology of the "white man's civilizing burden," adding that they as women had a similar corresponding burden and responsibility toward their "down-trodden" brown sisters. Ellen Carol Dubois has demonstrated how white women argued that they deserved the right to vote because, as women, they had a distinct "mother instinct for government." The women's suffrage demand in the United States adopted a distinctly racist tone after the passing of the Nineteenth

Amendment in 1878, which gave free black men the right to vote. Reacting negatively, some women leaders responded against the black men's voting rights on grounds that blacks were "their natural inferiors"; see Dubois, *Woman Suffrage and Women's Rights,* 107, 11. Elizabeth Thompson has shown how women leaders in colonial French Syria and Lebanon emphasized women's right to vote on the basis of their "role as defenders of the community." Thompson says that Lebanese feminist Mary Ájamy pointed out, in her 1924 speech in Beirut, that "many men feared women's progress would come at their own expense. She reminded them that Marie Curie and George Eliot had not abandoned their husbands, but rather cooperated with them." See Thompson, *Colonial Citizens,* 124–25. Joan Scott has argued that French feminists deployed the trope of motherhood to argue for women's claims to citizenship: "They based their claims for citizenship on that exemplary figure of duty and devotion, the one being worshiped in Catholic teaching and deified in Romantic eulogies: the mother." *Only Paradoxes to Offer,* 70.

54. Begum Sultan Mir Amiruddin, "Women's Movement and Its Implications," 47–48.

55. Ibid., 49.

56. Kamaladevi Chattopadhyaya, "Gandhiji and Women's Emancipation," serial no. 107, Private Papers, in NMML, New Delhi.

57. Ibid.

58. Mrinalini Sinha, "Suffragism and Internationalism," in Ian Christopher Fletcher et al., *Women's Suffrage in the British Empire,* 224–40.

59. Roland Barthes, "Novels and Children," in his *Mythologies,* 50–52. He has argued how patriarchal societies at best allow for only a limited change. The women too defend their demands on the grounds that all they desire are certain concessions and reforms within the existing order and do not seek to overthrow the system.

60. See John Rosselli, "Self-Image of Effeteness."

61. Laxmibai Rajwade, "Indian Mother," in Shyam Kumari Nehru, *Our Cause,* 73 (emphasis added).

62. Feminist historians have examined how women experienced pregnancy and child birth as a near-death encounter. See Judith Leavitt Walzer, "Under the Shadow of Maternity: American Responses to Death and Debility Fears in Nineteenth Century Childbirth." A more recent anthology by Rima D. Apple and Janet Golden, *Mothers and Motherhood,* is helpful in understanding how feminist literature is critically reexamining and reevaluating dominant cultural and political constructions of maternity and motherhood.

63. Rameshwari Nehru, "Indian Home," in Nehru, *Gandhi Is My Star,* 53.

64. Patricia Y. Miller and Martha R. Fowlker, "Social and Behavioral Constructions of Female Sexuality," in Sandra Harding and Jean F. O'Barr, *Sex and Scientific Inquiry,* 147–64. Miller and Fowlker discuss how women were allowed no sexual autonomy within the "affective repertoire" that male sexologists in the West defined in the late nineteenth and early twentieth centuries.

65. Rameshwari Nehru, *Gandhi Is My Star,* 67.

66. Reddi, *AIWC Annual Reports and Conference 1932,* 92.

67. Ibid., 91.

68. See Mrs. A. Mathews, "Birth-Control and Child Mortality."

69. Shyam Kumari Nehru, *Our Cause*, 400.

70. Ibid.

71. Later, she too revised her position on the subject, almost totally neglecting to write about it in her autobiography; Kamaladevi Chattopadhayaya, *Inner Recesses, Outer Spaces.*

72. Kamaladevi Chattopadhayaya, *Awakening of Indian Women*. The author's name has been spelled differently in this book. I am using the spelling here as it appears in this book, but have not used it in the chapter.

73. Kamaladevi Chattopadhayaya, "Future of Indian Women's Movement," in Shyam Kumari Nehru, *Our Cause*, 385–402.

74. Ibid., 399–400.

75. Ibid., 400.

76. Kamaladevi Chattopadhayaya, *Awakening of Indian Women* (emphasis added).

77. Raka Ray argues that we can comprehend the differences in the Indian women's movement in different parts of the country if we examine the larger political field within which these movements operate. Ray's argument about the latent effects of political fields on women's politics is also helpful in trying to understand the relationship between feminism and nationalism in colonial India; see Raka Ray, *Fields of Protest.*

78. James H. Cousins and Margaret E. Cousins, *We Two Together*, 611.

79. Cousins in her AIWC Presidential address, 1936, *AIWC Annual Report*, 11th session, 19–20.

80. *AIWC Annual Conference and Report, 1932–33*, 95–96.

81. Ibid., 96.

82. Gisela Bock, "Poverty and Mother's Rights," in George Duby and Michelle Perrot, *History of Women in the West*. In this article, Bock discusses the ideology of motherhood and its importance in shaping the welfare states in Europe. For more discussion on the role of motherhood within European feminism, see Karen Offen, *European Feminisms.*

83. *AIWC Annual Conference and Report, 1937*, 80.

84. Mrs. Premelabai Bhandarkar from Indore mentioned the free distribution of appliances; *AIWC Annual Conference and Report, 1937*, 81.

85. Laxmibai Rajwade, "Indian Mother," in Shyam Kumari Nehru, *Our Cause.*

86. Ibid., 84–85 (emphasis added).

87. Ibid., 89 (emphasis added).

88. Lakshmi Menon, *Position of Women*, 1944.

89. Lakshmi Menon, "Woman's Burden."

90. For details on Pillay's and Phadke's position, see chapter 1 in this book, "Demographic Rhetoric and Sexual Surveillance."

91. Begum Hamid Ali, "Section III: Marriage, Maternity and Succession."

92. Ibid.

93. Rameshwari Nehru, "Family Planning and Gandhiji," in her Private Papers, serial no. 84, Nehru Memorial and Museum Library (NMML), Delhi.

94. Ibid.

95. Richard Chinnathamby, "Indian Woman's Movement for Emancipation."

96. Dharam Bir Vohra, "Woman's Revolt against Man."

97. Lila Abu-Lughod, "Marriage of Feminism and Islamism," in Lila Abu-Lughod, *Remaking Women*, 243.

98. Dharam Bir Vohra, "Woman's Revolt against Man," 210 (emphasis added).

99. For the opposition to the birth control movement in the United States, see Linda Gordon, *Woman's Body, Woman's Right*.

100. Linda Alcoff, "Problem of Speaking for Others," 23.

101. Lila Abu-Lughod presents a complex and critical reading of modern Egyptian feminism through a close analysis of television melodramas. She argues that modern Egyptian feminists, in embracing the dominant ideology of developmentalism, compromise the very interests of those whom they claim to represent—the poor and uneducated women. For more details, see the chapter, "Development Realism: 'Real Melodrama' and the Problem of Feminism," in her *Dramas of Nationhood*, 81–110.

Chapter 4: A Fractured Discourse

1. Partha Chatterjee, *Nation and Its Fragments*, 18.

2. Thomas. R. Metcalf, *Aftermath of Revolt*, 96. Also cited in Partha Chatterjee, *Nation and Its Fragments*, 18.

3. For a discussion on the introduction of vaccination in colonial India, see David Arnold, *Colonizing the Body*. Also see the essays in Biswamoy Pati and Mark Harrison, *Health, Medicine, and Empire*.

4. Malavika Kasturi, "Law and Crime in India."

5. Anshu Malhotra examines this aspect of colonial intervention into the lives of Indian women in colonial Punjab; Malhotra, *Gender, Caste, and Religious Identities*.

6. Comstock Laws were passed in 1873 in the United States and were named after one of its chief architects, Anthony Comstock. Under pressure from him, the law criminalized reproductive control under federal and state antiobscenity laws. In Canada, conception prevention was added as an "offense against morality" under the 1892 Criminal Code. For more details on these legislative bans on birth control in the United States and Canada, see entries in Vern L. Bullough, *Encyclopedia of Birth Control*, 78, 41–42.

7. Benjamin Zachariah, "British and Indian Ideas of 'Development.'" This article includes a short discussion on population and birth control in its analysis of the development discourse among Indian nationalists and colonial British authorities.

8. Nicholas Thomas, *Colonialism's Culture*, xi.

9. Child Marriage Restraint Act of 1929, or the Sarda Act, raised the minimum age of marriage for girls from ten to twelve years. See Radha Kumar, "Organization and Struggle," in Kumar, *History of Doing*, 70–72.

10. The 1891 Age of Consent Act raised the age of consent to sexual relations from married and unmarried girls from ten to twelve and thereby provided a statutory foundation for later marriages. See Barbara Ramusack, "Reform Movements and Indian Women," in Barbara Ramusack and Sharon Sievers, *Women in Asia*, 46–47; Mrinalini Sinha, "Potent Protests: The Age of Consent Controversy, 1891," in Sinha, *Colonial Masculinity*, 138–80. In this chapter, Sinha examines the Bengali nationalist resistance and opposition to this particular colonial legislative initiative.

11. For details on the history of this controversial colonial legislation, see Barbara N. Ramusack, "Women's Organizations and Social Change" in Naomi Black and Ann

Baker Cottrell, *Women and World Change*, 198–216; Geraldine Forbes, "Women in Modern India," in *New Cambridge History of India*, 87–90; Judy Whitehead, "Modernising the Motherhood Archetype"; Sinha, "Lineage of the 'Indian' Modern," in Antoinette Burton, *Gender, Sexuality and Colonial Modernity*, 207–21.

12. *Age of Consent Committee, Evidence 1928–29, Volume 1: Oral Evidence and Written Statements of Witnesses from the Punjab, North West Frontier Provence, and Delhi* (Calcutta: Government Publications, 1929). Written Statement of Miss Khadijah Begum Ferozuddin (B.A.), (Hons) M.A., Professor of History and Oriental Languages, College for Women, Lahore, 61.

13. Ibid., 152.

14. Ibid.

15. Historical examples of colonial failures in India abound, especially in the field of women's rights. See Kumkum Sangari and Sudesh Vaid, *Recasting Women*, and Bharati Ray, *From the Seams of History*, among others, for instances of such failures. Also see Sudhir Chandra, *Enslaved Daughters*. Though some may argue it is rather naive to assume that colonialism would necessarily deliver on its promise of "modernity" and "civilization"; however, at the same time, it is important to highlight the gaps between discourse and practice that shaped colonial presence in India.

16. Gyan Prakash discusses the use of census data by the colonial state to produce knowledge about India and its population; Prakash, *Another Reason*, 135.

17. Bernard Cohn, "Census, Social Structure and Objectification," in *Anthropologist Among the Historians*, 224–54.

18. N. Gerald Barrier, *Census in British India*, xii.

19. David Arnold, "Official Attitudes to Population."

20. *Census of India 1911*, chapter 11, "Movement of Population," 35–36.

21. Census figures and information are discussed in Leela and Pradip Visaria, "Population," in Dharma Kumar, *Cambridge Economic History of India*, 463–532.

22. *Census of India, 1931, Volume 1—India: Part 1—Report*, (Delhi: Government of India, 1933), 29.

23. Ibid.

24. Ibid., 31.

25. Ibid.

26. David Arnold, "Official Attitudes to Population."

27. *Census of India, 1931, Volume 1*, 33.

28. See Barbara N. Ramusack, "Motherhood and Medical Intervention." In this paper, Ramusack discusses the emergence of the phenomena of baby weeks as part of a wider program to improve maternal and infant health care in colonial India.

29. Sumit Guha, *Health and Population*.

30. *Census of India, 1931, Volume 1*, 33.

31. Chapter 1 in this book, "Demographic Rhetoric and Sexual Surveillance," discusses the writings of Wattal and Mukherjee on the population question. Chapter 2, "Global Agenda and Local Politics," examines the politics of Western advocates in seeking to promote contraceptive usage across the world.

32. Marques of Zetland to the Earl of Willingdon, June 28, 1935, PP 50–52, Oriental and India Office Collection (henceforth OIOC), D/609/6.

33. Ibid.

34. Ibid.

35. Ibid.

36. All references to the Earl of Willingdon's response are from his letter to the Marques of Zetland, January 6, 1936, pp. 385–387, OIOC D 609/6.

37. Lord Pethick-Lawrence to Lord Wavell, February 15, 1946, pp. 62–68, OIOC, L/PO/10/23.

38. Ibid.

39. Lord Wavell to Lord Pethick-Lawrence, March 5, 1946, PP 76–83, OIOC, L/PO/10/23.

40. Malcolm Darling was a British official posted in Punjab. Darling wrote extensively on the conditions of peasants in Punjab in the early twentieth century. In his work, Darling discussed the importance of introducing birth control to improve the economic standards of rural folks; for details, see Darling, *Punjab Peasant in Prosperity and Debt*. Also see Benjamin Zachariah, "British and Indian Ideas of 'Development,'" for a discussion about Darling's position on birth control and rural development.

41. Nicholas Dirks, "Foreword," in Bernard Cohn, *Colonialism and Its Forms of Knowledge*, xv.

42. Bernard Cohn identifies six different forms of what he calls "investigative modalities," the British colonial state deployed to collect facts about India and Indians. For a discussion of the different modalities, see the introduction to his book, *Colonialism and Its Forms of Knowledge*, 5–15.

43. Under the Reform Act of 1919, the legislative council was enlarged to include a new chamber called the Council of State. This was framed as an Upper House with fifty members. Franchise to this body was extremely restricted on the basis of property qualifications. Membership was based not only on property qualifications but also on previous administrative experience in a central or provincial legislature, service in the chair of a municipal council, or membership of a university senate. Women were not entitled to vote at elections to the council or stand for these elections. There were twenty-one elected members, twenty-five officials, and four non-official nominated members. For more details on this colonial legislative body, see H. H. Dodwell, *Cambridge History of the British Empire*, 599–603.

44. "Extract from the Council of State Debates, Vol. I, No.15," 1, Government of India. Department of Education, Health and Lands, File no. 53–4/40–H, 1940, National Archive of India (henceforth NAI), New Delhi (emphasis added).

45. Ibid., 4.

46. Ibid., 8.

47. Ibid., Jagdish Chandra Banerjee, East Bengal, 9.

48. Ibid., 10.

49. Ibid., 11.

50. Ibid., 18.

51. "Extracts from the Council of State Debates, Vol. I, No. 9, March 18, 1940," 1, Government of India, Department of Education, Health and Lands (Health Branch), File no. 53–4/40–H, 1940, Subject: Resolutions-Council of State, Birth Control and Establishment of Birth Control Clinics, NAI, Delhi (emphasis added).

52. Prasad's fears about demographic politics were well placed. More recently, historians have examined how demographic issues were communalized. See Pradip Kumar

Datta, *Carving Blocs*; Charu Gupta, "Hindu Women, Muslim Men," in her *Sexuality, Obscenity, Community,* 268–320.

53. Extract from the Council of State Debates, 1940, 7.
54. Ibid., 11.
55. Ibid., 2.
56. Ibid., 3.
57. Ibid., 4.
58. Ibid., 5.
59. Unfortunately, there are no files or information available on the implementation of this resolution or steps taken to forward its adoption.
60. Legislative Assembly Debates (Question and Answers). Question 158, "Food Problem in India and Adoption of Birth Control Methods," February 7, 1936, pp. 363, Oriental and India Office Collection, V/9/130. Birth control was raised as a question in the legislative assembly debates a couple of times; see, for instance, Question 432, "Increase in the Population of India," February 14, 1936, pp. 807, V/9/130; Question 920, "Birth Control Propaganda in India," March 3, 1936, pp. 1809, V/9/130; Question 713, "Birth Control Propaganda in India," September 26, 1935, pp. 1868, V/9/129.
61. Prohibition of Sati 1829, Age of Consent Bill 1881, Widow Re-marriage Act, Restitution of Conjugal Rights, Sarda Act. In all these instances, the colonial state did not institute reforms on its own; Indians worked hard to bring about these legislative initiatives.
62. *The Famine Inquiry Commission, Final Report 1945* (Delhi: Manager Publications, 1945), Part II, "Population, Nutrition and Food Policy," chapter 1—Population, 73.
63. Ibid., 94.
64. Ibid., 97.
65. Ibid., 98.
66. Appendix 1, "Population," 427.
67. Ibid., 428.
68. Ibid., 431.
69. Ibid.
70. Ibid., 432–33.
71. "The Population Problem," chapter 28, in *Report of the Health Survey and Development Committee, Volume II* (Delhi: Manager of Publications, 1946), 477–89.
72. Ibid., 479.
73. Ibid., 480.
74. Ibid., 481.
75. Ibid., 482.
76. Ibid., 485.
77. "Summary," in *Report of the Health Survey and Development Committee, Volume IV* (Delhi: Manager of Publications, 1946), 82.
78. Clive Dewey in his biographical and intellectual history of Indian civil service in colonial India discusses the difficulties faced by British officials in the 1930s. He refers to the period of 1930–40 as one marked by the decline of the empire. For details, see Dewey, *Anglo-Indian Attitudes.*
79. For details on the Non-Cooperation and Khilafat movements from 1919 to 1922, see Sumit Sarkar, *Modern India.* Judith Brown, in *Modern India,* 187–223, argues that

the exposure of the subcontinent to World War I created "momentous adjustments" in the political relationships between Indians and the British.

80. For a detailed analysis of Gandhi's position on birth control, see chapter 2 in this book, "Global Agenda and Local Politics."

81. Linda Gordon, *Woman's Body, Woman's Right*, 24.

82. For details on Sanger's trial, see Ellen Chesler, *Woman of Valor*, 150–60.

83. For details on state policy and attitudes toward birth control in Britain, see Richard Soloway, *Birth Control and the Population Question*, 304–18.

84. For more information on the French government's policies on birth control, see Elinor A. Accampo, "Rhetoric of Reproduction." See also Mary Louise Roberts, *Civilizations without Sexes*.

85. *Indian Social Reformer* 43, no. 35 (September 1932–August 1933): 738–39.

86. Nancy Rose Hunt examines the policies of the Belgian state in Congo to raise the birth rate among Congo women; see Hunt, "'Le bebe en brousse.'"

87. Lynn M. Thomas, *Politics of the Womb*.

88. Ibid., 6.

89. Annette B. Ramirez de Arellano and Conrad Seipp, *Colonialism, Catholicism, and Contraception*. This book presents a good historical narrative on the history of U.S. colonial interventions in shaping reproductive practices among Puerto Rico from the 1930s onward. Karl Ittmann, "Colonial Office and the Population Question," provides a good summary of the British colonial attitudes and policies on population and its impact on promoting birth control, especially in Caribbean, Southeast Asian, and African British colonies.

90. Antoinette Burton, "Introduction: The Unfinished Business of Colonial Modernities," in Burton, *Gender, Sexuality and Colonial Modernity*, 1–16.

91. Nicholas Thomas, *Colonialism's Culture*, 46.

Chapter 5: Untrained "Professionals"

1. Historians have demonstrated how the argument of cultural preference was deployed to legitimize the opening up of colonies such as India as sites for professional opportunities and advancement for qualified white women, who had few job openings in the metropolis. For a detailed analysis of the gender and racial impact of the Dufferin Fund and the Victoria Memorial Scholarship Fund, see Cecilian Van Hollen, *Birth on the Threshold*; Maneesha Lal, "Politics of Gender and Medicine"; David Arnold, "Women, Mission, and Medicine," in Arnold, *New Cambridge History of India*; Antoinette Burton, "Contesting the Zenana."

2. There was wide-ranging hostility toward hospitals and the biomedical profession among the masses; this related particularly to the treatment meted out to Indians during epidemics. For more details on this issue, see David Arnold, "Touching the Body," in Ranajit Guha, *Subaltern Studies*, 55–90.

3. Eileen Palmer, "Birth Control in India Third Tour, 1936–37," Eileen Palmer Collection, 3/18, London School of Economics Archives (henceforth LSEA), London.

4. Historians regard Sanger's attempts to involve the medical community in propagating the use of contraceptives in the United States as marking a more conservative move in her feminist political position. See Linda Gordon, *Woman's Body, Woman's*

Right, 245–96. Carole McCann sees this shift in her position as a more pragmatic move aimed at getting wider support and respectability for the controversial issue; McCann, *Birth Control Politics,* 59–98. Stopes was hostile toward the medical profession and regarded herself as better qualified than physicians to give people advice on the use of contraceptives. Richard Soloway examines the tense relationship between Stopes and the medical community in Britain; Soloway, *Birth Control and the Population Question,* 256–79.

5. "Eileen Palmer Travel Book-Press Cuttings, Interviews, etc.," Edith How-Martyn's First Tour to India, 1934–35. Eileen Palmer Papers at the Oriental and India Office Collection (henceforth OIOC), British Library (henceforth BL), London, MSS EUR D1182/1.

6. Ibid.

7. B. L. Raina, "Contraception and Medical Profession," 194. Raina (1911–97) served in the Army Medical Corps. The first director of family planning in the Ministry of Health from 1956–69, he was awarded the Padma Shri in 1969.

8. J. N. Ghosh, "Ethics of Birth Control," 23.

9. H. K. Chaudhury, "Birth Control," 371.

10. C. G. Mahadevia, "Contraception."

11. "The Problem of Population," *Indian Medical Gazette* 64 (February 1929): 91–92; "India's Teeming Million," *Calcutta Medical Journal* 34, no. 5 (November 1938): 440–42; "Rapid Increase in the Population of India," *Indian Medical Record* 58 (August 1938): 243–45.

12. Santosh Kumar Mukherji, *Birth Control for the Millions,* 10.

13. Ibid., 12.

14. "Current Comments," *Calcutta Medical Journal* 35 (January 1939): 38–39.

15. Santosh Kumar Mukherji, *Birth Control for the Millions,* 57 (emphasis in the original).

16. A. N. Chatterji, "Population Control."

17. Ibid., 31.

18. Ibid.

19. J. N. Ghosh, "Ethics of Birth Control," 21–22.

20. Santosh Kumar Mukherji, *Birth Control for the Millions,* 137.

21. H. K. Chaudhury, "Birth Control," 370.

22. T. S. Balasubramania Iyer, "Problem of Birth Control," 273.

23. Patricia Y. Miller and Martha R. Fowlker, "Social and Behavioral Constructions of Female Sexuality," in Sandra Harding and Jean F. O'Barr, *Sex and Scientific Inquiry,* 154.

24. T. S. Balasubramania Iyer, "Problem of Birth Control," 271.

25. Ibid. There were similar debates within the biomedical profession on sexual abstinence in other parts of the world; see Andreas Hill, "'May the Doctor Advise Extramarital Intercourse?'" in Roy Porter and Mikulas Teich, *Sexual Knowledge, Sexual Science.*

26. T. S. Balasubramania Iyer, "Problem of Birth Control," 271.

27. Jeffery Weeks, *Sexuality and Its Discontents,* 69.

28. J. N. Ghosh, "Ethics of Birth Control," 19.

29. Santosh Kumar Mukherji, *Birth Control for the Millions,* 66.

30. A. N. Chatterji, "Population Control," 30.

31. An unsigned review of L. A. Emge's pamphlet, "Safe Period," 111.

32. Santosh Kumar Mukherji, *Birth Control for the Millions*, 67–72; Nancy Rose Hunt, "'*Le bebe en brousse.*'" Hunt argues that the colonial state advertised against the practice of prolonged lactation among working-class Congo women in an attempt to raise their fertility rates. Clearly, the impact of lactation on fertility was not conclusively determined in the early twentieth century.

33. *Indian Medical Gazette Advertiser* 72 (February 1937): lxvi.

34. *Indian Medical Gazette Advertiser* 76 (May 1941): liii.

35. There was an advertisement for this contraceptive in two consecutive years of the journal *Indian Medical Gazette*: *Indian Medical Gazette Advertiser* 71 (August 1936): ixv; and *Indian Medical Gazette Advertiser* 72 (December 1937): lxii.

36. The Gynomin advertisement appeared in the *Indian Medical Gazette Advertiser* 80 (July 1945): xv; *Marriage Hygiene*, a magazine published from Bombay by A. P. Pillay, carried an advertisement for Rendell in 1935.

37. *Indian Medical Gazette Advertiser* 69 (August 1934): xii.

38. I. Ahmed, "Birth Control by Self Control," 52.

39. Ibid., 51 (emphasis added).

40. T. B. Gupta, "Modern Civilization and Birth Control," 39–40.

41. Ibid.

42. M. S. Nawaz, "Indications for Birth Control," 205–6.

43. Ibid (emphasis added).

44. Chandrika Paul's "The Uneasy Alliance: The Work of British and Bengali Women Medical Professionals in Bengal, 1870–1935" examines the difficulties Indian women faced in seeking entry into medicine. Geraldine Forbes's article "Colonial Imperatives and Women's Emancipation" investigates how Indian women gained entry into the field of medicine through support from Indian male reformers and from some colonial officials.

45. For details on how India became a site of professional opportunities for medically trained British women, see Lal, "Politics of Gender and Medicine," and Antoinette Burton, "Contesting the Zenana."

46. This was a quarterly journal of the Association of Medical Women in India (AMWI), which was established in 1909. A forum for its members to keep in touch, the journal offered opportunities to promote professional interests and to gain knowledge. For details on the AMWI, see Jerbanoo E. Mistry, "Association of Medical Women in India."

47. Lilias M. Jeffries, "Prevention"; Barbara N. Ramusack, "What Did They Know and When: Medical Women in India and the Practice of Birth Control, 1920–40," examines some of the debates and writing on birth control among women physicians.

48. Lilias M. Jeffries, "Prevention" (emphasis added).

49. Ibid.

50. Ibid.

51. Mary O'Brien Beadon, "Birth Control."

52. Ibid., 12.

53. For an insightful discussion on the notions of middle-class sexuality in Victorian

England, see Leonore Davidoff, "Class and Gender in Victorian England," in Judith L. Newton, Mary P. Ryan, and Judith R. Walkowitz, *Sex and Class in Women's History*, 21.

54. Mary O'Brien Beadon, "Birth Control," 12 (emphasis added).

55. Leonore Davidoff, "Class and Gender in Victorian England," in Judith L. Newton et al., *Sex and Class in Women's History*, 21.

56. Jeffries, "Note by Jeffries," *Journal of Association of Medical Women in India* 10, no. 2 (August, 1921), 17.

57. Roy Porter and Lesley Hall, *Facts of Life*, 202–23, examines Stopes's new celebrated ideal of "Good-Sex" as an important component of marriage.

58. Lilias M. Jeffries, "Note by Jeffries," 17.

59. Dr. Margaret Balfour worked in the Women's Hospital in Ludhiana and at Nahan from 1892 to 1902. She served in the Lady Dufferin Hospital at Patiala from 1903 to 1914. When she left India in 1924, she was the joint secretary, Countess of Dufferin Fund, and chief medical officer, Women's Medical Service. My information on her career in India is from *Journal of Association of Medical Women in India* 12 (August 1924): 5.

60. Margaret Balfour, "Control of Conception," 17.

61. Ibid.

62. Lilias B. Jeffries, "Letter to the Editor," 30–31.

63. Ruth Young, "Medical Women and Conception Control."

64. Ibid., 6.

65. Ibid., 7.

66. Ibid., 6.

67. Ibid., 10.

68. Ibid., 6.

69. N. Proctor Sims, "Analysis of Replies."

70. Ibid., 30.

71. Ibid.

72. "Eileen Palmer Travel Book-Press Cuttings, Interviews, etc.," Reports, Third Tour to India, 1938–39, Eileen Palmer Papers, OIOC: MSS EUR D1182/7.

73. Jerbanoo Mistry, "Birth Control."

74. Ibid., 18.

75. Adele Clarke has argued that in the early twentieth century, reproductive sciences was highly stigmatized among the Anglo-American medical community. According to her, there was very little research done in this subfield of medicine, and as a result, contraceptive technologies were also very rudimentary until the Pill was discovered in the 1960s. See Clarke, "Maverick Reproductive Scientists," in Ann Rudinow Saetnan, Nelly Oudshoorn, and Marta Kirejczyk, *Bodies of Technology*, 37–89.

76. Jerbanoo Mistry, "Birth Control."

77. Ibid., 21.

78. Jerbanoo Mistry, "Extracts from 'My Impressions of the Tenth All-India Women's Conference.'"

79. All quotations of Jhirad by this doctor are taken from J. Jhirad, "Practical Aspects of Birth Control" (emphasis added).

80. Geraldine Forbes's article "Colonial Imperatives and Women's Emancipation" discusses some of the complaints by Indian women physicians against racial discriminations by the Dufferin hospitals and dispensaries.

81. Chandrakanta Rohatgi is one of the oldest woman gynecologists who was practicing in Kanpur at the time I interviewed her and the two other women gynecologists in February 1998. Rohatgi's family was very active in the Gandhian nationalist movement in Kanpur during the twentieth century. She completed her degree in medicine with a specialization in gynecology and midwifery in 1936 from the King Edward's Medical College in Bombay. Premila Gokhale was Maharashtrian and moved to Kanpur in the early twentieth century, after her marriage. She started a private practice that her daughter-in-law, also a gynecologist, has continued. Dr. Gokhale passed away in 1999. An autobiography of Lakshmi Sahgal published in 1997 gives details of her life as a member of the only all-women regiment, the Rani of Jhansi Regiment, of the Indian National Army. Dr. Sahgal qualified as a doctor from Madras Medical College in 1938. She met Margaret Sanger in 1936 through her mother, Ammukutty Menon, who was an active member of the AIWC and voted in favor of the resolution passed on birth control by the AIWC in 1936. However, she only briefly mentions her medical work in Kanpur in her autobiography; Lakshmi Sahgal, *Revolutionary Life*.

82. Premila Gokhale and Surendra Rohatgi, interview by author, tape recording, Kanpur, Uttar Pradesh (U.P.), February 2–7, 1998.

83. This might have been A. P. Pillay, who gave lectures on birth control in Bombay during the time that Rohatgi was a student in King Edward's Medical College. Chandrakanta Rohatgi, interview by author, tape recording, Kanpur, U.P., February 2, 1998.

84. Judith Walzer Leavitt has examined the fear of pregnancy among American women in her book *Brought to Bed*.

85. Surendra Rohatgi, interview by author, tape recording, Kanpur, U.P., February 3, 1998.

86. Ibid.

87. Surendra Rohatgi, interview by author, Kanpur, U.P., February 6, 1998.

88. Ibid.

89. Lakshmi Sahgal, Surendra Rohatgi, and Premila Gokhale, interviews with author, tape recording, Kanpur, U.P., February 2–7, 1998.

90. Dr. Chandrakant Rohatgi recounted times when her mother disapproved of her visits to the Muslim neighborhood for confinements. During one of her late-night visits, her father accompanied her to her client's house, waiting patiently in the car while she delivered the baby. Likewise, Dr. Gokhale also mentioned the disapproval of her in-laws and husband when she conducted home births for her poor working-class women clients. Surendra Rohatgi and Premila Gokhale, interview with author, tape recording, Kanpur, U.P., February 2–4, 1998.

91. Premila Gokhale, interview, Kanpur, U.P., February 4, 1998.

92. Premila Gokhale spoke about working around some of the popular notions associated with birthing. Despite all her attempts at trying to "reform" practices, she was required to deliver babies in physical settings determined and considered appropriate by the birthing mother and her family. Premila Gokhale, interview, Kanpur, U.P., February 7, 1998.

93. A discussion of Hindi journals and their coverage of gender issues is in Vir Bharat

Talwar, "Feminist Consciousness in Women's Journals," in Kumkum Sangari and Sudesh Vaid, *Recasting Women,* 204–32.

94. *Sudha* 13, 1 (August 1939): 71.

95. This was an advertisement for "Contax," carried both in *Sudha* 10 (August 1936): 149 and *Madhuri* 14, no. 1 (February 1936): 57. This was the only contraceptive that was sold under a brand name without carrying the name of a *hakim* or *vaid.*

96. "*Safal Jivan Ka Mahamantra*" [Big Secret to Successful Living], *Sudha* 14 (May 1940): 687.

97. *Madhuri* 20, no. 1 (February 1942).

98. *Madhuri* 10 (September, 1931).

99. *Madhuri* 19, no. 1 (August, 1940); *Madhuri* 20, no. 1 (February 1942); *Sudha* 14 (May 1940): 687.

100. Dr. Yadhuvirsingh, *Gupt Sandesh* [Secret Message].

101. Ibid., 31.

102. Gyan Prakash, *Another Reason,* 237.

103. Kaviraj Vimla Devi Vaidya, *Garbh Nirodh* [Birth Control].

104. Vimla Devi, meeting with author, New Delhi, April 20–21, 1998. Unfortunately, I have been unable to collect data on either the number of copies this book sold or even on the number of editions issued. In my interview with Vimla Devi, she was unwilling to discuss her practice or provide any other additional information on her writings or attitudes toward contraception.

105. Vimla Devi Vaidya, *Garbh Nirodh* [Birth Control], 26.

106. Ibid., 28.

107. Ibid., 39.

108. Ibid., 39–45.

109. Ibid., 47–48.

110. Ruth Young, "Medical Women and Conception Control," 10.

111. Gyan Prakash, *Another Reason,* 237.

112. Premila Gokhale, interview with author, Kanpur, U.P., February 3, 1998.

Epilogue

1. For details on Hamid Ali's position and of other middle-class Indian feminists, see chapter 3 in this book, "Polyvocality, Ambivalence, and Negotiations: Indian Middle-Class Feminism and Debates on Birth Control in Nationalist India, 1920s–40s."

2. Gayle Rubin, "Thinking Sex," in Carole Vance, *Pleasure and Danger,* 267–391. In this article, Rubin discusses the dominant cultural understanding of sex, one that warranted social repression of this natural human instinct. Rosemarie Tong carefully reviews Rubin's argument in her chapter on "Radical Feminism" in *Feminist Thought,* 45–93. Rubin presents an analysis of sexuality that can be productively used for understanding some of Gandhi's views on the subject. Gandhi understood sex as a natural body instinct but an instinct that he predominantly associated with disorder, discord, and disharmony. Given his distrust of sex, Gandhi advised men to be constantly vigilant to avoid falling prey to sexual desires.

3. Moore-Gilbert, "Gayatri Spivak," 106.

4. See Supriya Guha, "From Dais to Doctors."

5. Alessandro Portelli, *Death of Luigi Trastulli*, vii.

6. Gonzales Echevarria, cited in Harriet Bradley, "The Seductions of the Archive," 111.

7. Ranajit Guha has largely examined colonial records to write his pathbreaking work on peasant insurgency in colonial India. See Ranajit Guha, *Elementary Aspects of Peasant Insurgency in Colonial India*; also see the essays in Guha's *Subaltern Studies I: Writings on South Asian History and Society*. More recently, feminist historians have argued for the need to recognize the untold stories of women's experiences that can be culled from colonial archives in some instances, despite the intended purposes of the records and documents. For details on how to detect women's histories and experiences in the past from colonial records that either completely leave out or at times even misrecord women's names, see Durba Ghosh, "Decoding the Nameless."

8. *Matrika,* project report from the Society for the Integrated Development of the Himalayas (Landour: December 16, 1994).

9. Glenn Jordon and Chris Weedon emphasize the importance of restoring underrepresented voices to challenge hegemonic narratives. In bringing voices from contemporary tribal block into my own research, this study highlights the distance between the narratives from above and the narratives from within subaltern communities. Despite the cautionary warnings against naive illusions and academic arrogance in "bringing in" subaltern voices, Jaunpuri *dais* did highlight their distance from hegemonic understandings and agendas. For more details on the importance of bridging the gap between dominant and marginal representational politics and in making a case for recording subaltern perspectives, see Jordon and Weedon, "When the Subalterns Speak, What Do They Say?"

10. Many recent feminist ethnographers have warned about the dangers of researchers trying to represent the lives of subaltern women. For an analysis of some of the issues involved in academic representations of subaltern women, see Ruth Behar, *Translated Woman*.

11. Historians no longer believe that truth lies "buried in the archives, a sleeping princess awaiting their awakening kiss." The issue of transparency of the archives is as much an issue as that of ethnographic sources. See Harriet Bradley, "Seductions of the Archive," 117. Thanks to Antoinette Burton for this reference. Alessandro Portelli has also warned that just like oral sources, written documents also lack "objectivity," but it is the "holiness" assigned to writing that leads us to forget the limitations and biases that mark written sources; Portelli, *Death of Luigi Trastulli,* 53.

12. Alessandro Portelli, *Death of Luigi Trastulli,* 76.

13. Harriet Bradley, "Seductions of the Archive," 114.

14. Supriya Guha, "From Dais to Doctors," in Lakshmi Lingam, *Understanding Women's Health Issues,* 145–61. See also Anshu Malhotra, "Of Dais and Midwives."

15. For instance, in U.S. history, scholars have used diaries left behind by midwives to reconstruct medical histories that have allowed the voices and perspectives of midwives to disrupt and challenge the dominant biomedical representations of these traditional birth attendants. One of the best works in this field is that of Laurel Thatcher Ulrich, *Midwife's Tale*.

16. Katherine Mayo's scathing critique of Indian culture drew upon the figure of the Indian *dai* and Indian childbirth practices to make an argument for the necessity of British imperialism. See Sanjam Ahluwalia, "Indian Women."

17. J. Jhirad, "Some Aspects of Medico-Social Work, 134.

18. M. B. Kagal, "Maternity and Child Welfare Work," 21.

19. Begum Hamid Ali, "Maternity and Welfare in India," in Evelyn C. Gedge, *Women in Modern India,* 140–41.

20. Ibid., 141.

21. The issue of the *Indian Red Cross Society Journal* 7 (October 1933): 3 and 12 carried photographs of Maternity and Child Welfare Centers, and one of the pictures has *dais* who proudly displayed their *dai* boxes for the camera.

22. I conducted research in four villages in Jaunpur—Bhatoli, Bhediyan, Kandikhal, and Sainji—during the early part of January 1998. These villages generally include ten to twenty families and are demographically typical of villages in the Himalayan foothills because the step agricultural patterns common in this region cannot sustain larger populations. The four villages are located within walking distance of each other. Savitri and I usually conducted interviews in the afternoon after most of the women had completed their domestic chores. During this time women usually socialized, sitting around in small groups, and were therefore willing to spend time talking with us. Savitri, Kamala, and Rekha from SIDH in Bhatoli and Kandikhal helped out with research. I also read *Matrika,* a project report that SIDH compiled after its own workshop with local Jaunpuri *dais. Matrika* (Landour: December 16, 1994). I am grateful to Anuradha Joshi and Pawan Gupta for allowing me access to unpublished SIDH reports and for their help in making it possible for me to conduct research in Jaunpur.

23. Padma Devi recounted how she had trained as a midwife under her mother-in-law. Padma Devi's daughter Leela Devi was now being similarly trained by her mother-in-law. Padma Devi and Leela Devi, interview with author, Sainji Village, January 4, 1998.

24. Alessandro Portelli, *Death of Luigi Trastulli,* 68–69. He questions the partition of historical time within Italian history into pre-Fascism, Fascism, and post-Fascism. He argues that his subjects did not register these changes in the same way that this temporal universality has been encoded within the dominant historical narrative.

25. Rukhma Devi, interview with author, tape recording, Bhatoli Village, January 10, 1998.

26. Bhura Devi, interview with author, tape recording, Bhediyan Village, Jaunpur, January 13, 1998.

27. Rukhma Devi, interview with author, Bhatoli Village, January 10, 1998.

28. Vimla Devi Vaidya, *Garbh Nirodh* [Birth Control].

29. Padma Devi, interview with author, Sainji Village, January 4, 1998.

30. Most midwives mentioned the preference for female sterilization, as did some village women who would sit around while I conducted my recorded interviews. Bhura Devi, interview with author, Bhediyan village, January 6, 1998. "Operation" as the most popular form of contraceptive also came up in the SIDH "Interim Report: Knowledge and Perception of Family Planning Methods in Men and Women," April 1996–March 1997 (Landour: n.p.).

31. Many studies have noted the alienation that rural and subaltern urban women face when confronted with the biomedical establishment through their visits to hospitals. For details, see Cecilia Van Hollen, *Birth on the Threshold.*

32. SIDH, "Interim Report."

33. Ibid.

34. Jaunpuri women's experiences of collective mothering seem somewhat similar to the experiences of rural Egyptian women as accounted in Ali's *Planning the Family in Egypt.*

35. Rosemarie Tong, *Feminist Thought,* 128–29.

36. Sandra Harding, *Whose Science? Whose Knowledge?,* 185.

37. This was the slogan posted in most public spaces, on billboards, buses, and also in hospitals in Delhi, personal observation. It was adopted by the Health Ministry in 1997–98, when Renuka Choudhary was the union health minister in the United Front Government. In my conversations in Jaunpur, I casually asked women if they had heard about it; no one had heard the slogan, and Bhura Devi brushed it aside as an instance of *"sarkari bhasha."* Bhediyan, January 6, 1998.

38. Lila Abu-Lughod, *Dramas of Nationhood,* 61.

39. Indian feminists have campaigned for legal reforms to restrict the abuse of the amniocentesis test. This test has been used since the late 1970s to determine the sex of the fetus, leading to an increase in the abortions of female fetuses. For a journalistic assessment of this practice, see Pamela Philipose, "The *beti-maru* Mind-Set." See also Nivedita Menon's incisive analysis of the peculiar limitations that mark liberal feminist discourse and political interventions on this subject, "Abortion: When Pro-Choice Is Anti-Women," in *Recovering Subversion.*

40. Feminist scholars have highlighted the negative experiences of Native American women and African American women with contraceptive technologies. Instead of expanding or enhancing their fertility and reproductive choices, for the most part, women from the minority community in the United States have found their bodies under assault by new reproductive technologies. For details, see Andrea Smith, "Better Dead Than Pregnant" in Jael Silliman and Anannya Bhattacharjee, *Policing the National Body,* 123–44. Angela Davis writes about the blatant racism that has marked the birth control movement in the United States in her book *Women, Race, and Class.* See also Susan Davis's book *Women under Attack.* A recently published edited volume examines the experiences of minority women in the United States, especially as it relates to issues of reproduction; Silliman and Marlene Gerber Fried, Loretta Ross, and Elena R. Gutierrez, *Undivided Rights.*

41. Feminist historians have examined the work of early middle-class women reformers to comment on the cultural and political bias that informed their opinions about working-class cultures, especially as these related to practices of child rearing. For details, see Christine Stansell, "Women, Children, and Uses of the Streets."

Bibliography

Government Archival Sources

British Library, Oriental and India Office Collection, London
   V series: India Office Records Official Publications Series, 1920–1947
National Archives of India, New Delhi
   Government of India, Files and Proceedings
      Education, Health, and Land Department (Health Branch), 1930–1941
      Home Department, 1885–1944
Uttar Pradesh State Archives, Lucknow
   Government of the United Provinces
      Files, Medical Department, 1913–1932
      General Administrative Department, 1905
      Home Police, 1912
      Proceedings, Medical and Sanitation Department, 1884–1927

Published Government Records

Age of Consent Committee Evidence, Volumes 1–9. Calcutta: Government Publications, 1929.
Annual Report of Civil Hospitals and Dispensaries of U. P., 1878–1930. Allahabad: Superintendent Government Press, relevant years.
Annual Report of the Director of Public Health of the United Provinces of Agra and Oudh, 1921–1931. Allahabad: Superintendent Government Press, relevant years.
Annual Report of the Sanitary Commissioner of the Northwest Provinces and Oudh, 1886–1920. Allahabad: Superintendent Government Press, relevant years.
The Famine Inquiry Commission, Final Report 1945. Delhi: Manager Publications, 1945.
Report of the Age of Consent Committee, 1928–1929. Calcutta: Government Publications, 1929.
Report of the Health Survey and Development Committee, Volumes I-IV. Delhi: Manager of Publications, 1946.
Report on the Administration of the United Provinces of Agra and Oudh, 1912–1921. Allahabad: Superintendent Government Press, relevant years.

Newspapers and Periodicals Consulted

Birth Control News
Birth Control Review
Indian Medical Journal

Indian Medical Record
Indian Red Cross Society Journal
Indian Social Reformer
Journal of Association of Medical Women in India
Madhuri
Marriage Hygiene
Roshni
Science and Culture
Stri-Darpan
Stri-Dharma
Sudha
Prince of Wales Medical College Magazine
Twentieth Century

Private Papers

    Nehru Memorial Museum and Library, New Delhi
        Kamaladevi Chattopadhyaya Papers
        Rameshwari Nehru Papers
        Muthulakshmi Reddi Papers
    Contemporary Medical Archives Center, Wellcome Institute, London
        C. P. Blacker Papers
        Eugenic Society Papers
        E. F. Griffith Papers
        Marie Stopes Papers
    London School of Economics Archives
        Eileen Palmer Collection
    British Library, Oriental and India Office Collection
        Baron Brabourne
        J. H. Hutton
        Paul Marcus Jayarajan
        Eileen Palmer Collection
        Marie Stopes Papers
        Dr. Clare Thomson
        Lord Wavell
    Margaret Sanger Papers Project, New York
        Margaret Sanger Papers (microfilm)

Interviews

Bhura Devi, interview by author, Bhedian Village, Jaunpur Block, Tehri Garhwal District, U.P., January 6 & 13, 1998.

Leela Devi, interview by author, Sainji Village, Jaunpur Block, Tehri Garhwal District, U.P., January 4, 1998.

Padma Devi, interview by author, Sainji Village, Jaunpur Block, Tehri Garhwal District, U.P., January 4, 1998.

Rukhma Devi, interview by author, Bhatoli Village, Jaunpur Block, Tehri Garhwal District, U.P., January 10, 1998.
Vimla Devi, meeting with author, New Delhi, April 20–21, 1998.
Premila Gokhale, interview by author, Kanpur, U.P., February 2–7, 1998.
Chandrakanta Rohatgi, interview by author, Kanpur, U.P., February 2, 1998.
Surendra Rohatgi, interview by author, Kanpur, U.P., February 3–6, 1998.
Lakshmi Sehgal, interview by author, Kanpur, U.P., February 2–7, 1998.
Shantijee, interview by author, Bhatoli Village, Jaunpur Block, Tehri Garhwal District, U.P., January 8, 1998.

Dissertations, Conference Papers, and Unpublished Manuscripts

Ahluwalia, Sanjam. "Indian Women: A History of Representations and Political Agency in the Early Twentieth Century." (Unpublished manuscript).
Arnold, David. "Official Attitudes to Population, Birth Control, and Reproductive Health, 1926–1946." Paper presented at the conference, "Population, Birth Control and Reproductive Health in Late Colonial India," School of Oriental and African Studies, London, November, 18–19, 1999.
Choudhury, Indira. "Instructions for the Unconverted: Birth Control, Marie Stopes and Indian Women." Paper presented at Conference on Population, Birth Control and Reproductive Health in Late Colonial India, School of Oriental and African Studies, London, November 18–19, 1999.
Everett, Jana. "The Indian Women's Movement during the Interwar Years: An Alternative Feminism, an All India Consciousness and/or a Majority Community Perspective." Paper presented at the Thirteenth Berkshire Conference on the History of Women, Scripps College, California, June 2–5, 2005.
Fisher, Kate. "'She Was Quite Satisfied with the Arrangements I Made . . .': Gender and the Conjugal Dynamics of Contraceptive Use: An Oral History Study of South Wales and Oxford Between the Wars." Paper presented at the History of Twentieth Century Medicine Group, Wellcome Trust, London, October 13, 1998.
Guha, Supriya. "A History of the Medicalization of Childbirth in Bengal in the Late Nineteenth and Early Twentieth Centuries" (Ph.D. diss., University of Calcutta, 1996).
Gupta, Charu. "Hindu Wombs, Muslim Progeny: The Numbers Game and Shifting Debates on Widow Remarriage, U.P. 1890–1930s." Paper presented at the Population, Birth Control and Reproductive Health in Late Colonial India, School for Oriental and African Studies, London, November 18–19, 1999.
Hodges, Sarah. "Conjugality, Progeny and Progress: Family and Modernity in Twentieth Century India" (Ph.D. diss., University of Chicago, 1999).
Joshi, Sanjay. "Empowerment and Identity: The Middle Class and Hindu Communalism in Colonial Lucknow, 1880–1930" (Ph.D. diss., University of Pennsylvania, 1995).
Klausen, Susanne. "Imperial Mother and Her Problem Child: Marie Stopes and the South African Birth Control Movement, 1930–1950" (Unpublished paper).
Lal, Maneesha. "Purdah as Pathology: Medical Research and Reproductive Health in 20th Century India." Paper presented at Conference on Population, Birth Control

and Reproductive Health in Late Colonial India, School of Oriental and African Studies, London, November 18–19, 1999.

Malhotra, Anshu. "The Arya Samaj Movement and Women in Punjab c. 1875–1928: Women and the Project of Nation" (M.Phil. thesis, University of Delhi, 1991).

———. "Of Dais and Midwives: Middle-Class Interventions in the Management of Women's Reproductive Health: A Study from Colonial Punjab." Paper presented at Population, Birth Control and Reproductive Health in Late Colonial India conference in School for Oriental and African Studies, London, November 18–19, 1999.

———. "Pativratas and Kupattis: Gender, Caste and Identity in Punjab, 1870s–1920s" (Ph.D. diss., University of London, 1998).

Matrika, Report on *Dai* workshop, SIDH. Landour: December 16, 1994.

Paul, Chandrika. "The Uneasy Alliance: The Work of British and Bengali Women Medical Professionals in Bengal, 1870–1935" (Ph.D. diss., University of Cincinnati, 1997).

Ramusack, Barbara N. "Maternal Infant Health, Population Control or Eugenics: Reproductive Control in India, 1920–1940" (Unpublished paper).

———. "Motherhood and Medical Intervention: Women's Bodies and Professionalism in India after World War I." Paper presented at the Wisconsin Conference on South Asia, Madison, Wisconsin, October 19, 1996.

SIDH. "Interim Report: Knowledge and Perception of Family Planning Methods in Men and Women." April 1996–March 1997, Landour: n. p.

Published Literature

Abugideiri, Hibba. "The Scientisation of Culture: Colonial Medicine's Construction of Egyptian Womanhood, 1893–1929." *Gender and History* 16, no. 1 (April 2004): 83–98.

Abu-Lughod, Lila. *Dramas of Nationhood: The Politics of Television in Egypt.* Chicago: University of Chicago Press, 2005.

———, ed. *Remaking Women: Feminism and Modernity in the Middle East.* Princeton, N.J.: Princeton University Press, 1998.

———. *Writing Women's Worlds: Bedouin Stories.* Berkeley: University of California Press, 1993.

Accampo, Elinor A. "The Rhetoric of Reproduction and the Reconfiguration of Womanhood in the French Birth Control Movement, 1890–1920." *Journal of Family History* 21, no. 3 (July 1996): 351–71.

Ahluwalia, Gopaljee. "The Indian Population Problem: Selective Lower Birth Rate, a Sure Remedy of Extreme Indian Poverty." *Birth Control Review* 7 (November 1923): 288–91.

Ahluwalia, Sanjam. "Demographic Rhetoric and Sexual Surveillance: Indian Middle-Class Advocates of Birth Control, 1902–1940s." In *Confronting the Body: The Politics of Physicality in Colonial and Post-Colonial India,* edited by James H. Mills and Satadru Sen, 183–200. London: Anthem Press, 2004.

Ahmed, I. "Birth Control by Self Control." *Prince of Wales Medical College Magazine* (January 1936): 51–52.

Alcoff, Linda. "The Problem of Speaking for Others." *Cultural Critique* 2 (Winter 1991–92): 5–32.

Ali, (Begum) Hamid. "Maternity and Welfare in India." In *Women in Modern India*, edited by Evelyn C. Gedge, 140–41. Bombay: D. B. Taraporevala Sons, 1929.

Ali, Kamran Asdar. *Planning the Family in Egypt: New Bodies, New Selves.* Austin: University of Texas Press, 2002.

Alter, Joseph S. "Celibacy, Sexuality, and the Transformation of Gender into Nationalism in Northern India." *Journal of Asian Studies* 53 (February 1994): 45–66.

———. *Gandhi's Body: Sex, Diet, and the Politics of Nationalism.* Philadelphia: University of Pennsylvania Press, 2000.

Amiruddin, Begum Sultan Mir. "The Women's Movement and Its Implications." *Roshni* 11 (December 1941): 47–48.

Amos, Valerie, and Pratibha Parmar. "Challenging Imperial Feminism." *Feminist Review* 17 (1984): 3–19.

Anandhi, S., "Reproductive Bodies and Regulated Sexuality." In *A Question of Silence? The Sexual Economies of Modern India*, edited by Mary E. John and Janaki Nair, 139–66. New Delhi: Kali for Women, 1998.

Anzaldúa, Gloria, and Analouise Keating, eds. *This Bridge We Call Home: Radical Visions for Transformations.* New York: Routledge, 2002.

Anzaldúa, Gloria, and Cherrie Moraga, eds. *This Bridge Called My Back: Writings by Radical Women of Color.* New York: Kitchen Table Women of Color Press, 1981.

Appadurai, Arjun. "Number in the Colonial Imagination." In *Orientalism and the Post-Colonial Predicament: Perspectives on South Asia*, edited by Carol Breckenridge and Peter van der Veer, 314–40. Philadelphia: University of Pennsylvania Press, 1993.

Apple, Rima D., and Janet Golden, eds. *Mothers and Motherhood: Readings in American History.* Columbus: Ohio State University Press, 1997.

Arnold, David. *Colonizing the Body: State Medicine and Epidemic Disease in Nineteenth Century India.* Delhi: Oxford University Press, 1993.

———. *The New Cambridge History of India: Science, Technology and Medicine in Colonial India.* Cambridge: Cambridge University Press, 2000.

———. "Touching the Body: Perspectives on the Indian Plague, 1896–1900." In *Subaltern Studies V: Writings on South Asian History and Society*, edited by Ranajit Guha, 55–90. Delhi: Oxford University Press, 1987.

Bala, Poonam. *Imperialism and Medicine in Bengal: A Socio-Historical Perspective.* New Delhi: Sage Publications, 1991.

Balfour, Margaret. "Control of Conception." *Journal of Association of Medical Women in India* 9, no. 2 (November 1921).

Balfour, Margaret, and Ruth Young. *The Work of Medical Women in India.* London: Oxford University Press, 1929.

Banerjee, Sumanta. "Marginalization of Women's Popular Culture in Nineteenth Century Bengal." In *Recasting Women: Essays in Colonial History*, edited by Kumkum Sangari and Sudesh Vaid, 127–79. New Delhi: Kali for Women, 1989.

Barrier, N. Gerald. *The Census in British India.* New Delhi: Manohar, 1981.

Barthes, Roland. *Mythologies.* New York: Granada, 1981.

Bashford, Alison. *Imperial Hygiene: A Critical History of Colonialism, Nationalism, and Public Health.* Basingstoke: Palgrave, 2004.

Basu, Aparna. "The Role of Women in the Indian Struggle for Freedom." In *Indian Women: From Purdah to Modernity,* edited by B. R. Nanda, 16–40. New Delhi: Vikas, 1976.

Beadon, Mary O'Brien. "Birth Control." *Journal of Association of Medical Women in India* 10, no. 2 (August 1921): 11–13.

Behar, Ruth. *Translated Woman: Crossing the Border with Esperanza's Story.* Boston: Beacon Press, 1993.

Beier, Lucinda McCray. "Expertise and Control: Childbearing in the Three Twentieth-Century Working-Class Lancashire Communities." *Bulletin of History of Medicine* 78 (2004): 379–409.

Besant, Annie. "The Social Aspects of Malthusianism." *Malthusian Tracts* 10 (1879): 1–7.

———. "Theosophy and the Law of Population." Reprinted in *A Dirty Filthy Book: The Writings of Charles Knowlton and Annie Besant on Reproductive Physiology and Birth Control and an Account of the Bradlaugh-Besant Trial,* edited by S. Chandrasekhar, 205–12. Madras: Theosophical Publishing Society, 1896.

Bhabha, Homi K. *Nation and Narration.* London: Routledge, 1990.

———. "Of Mimicry and Man." In *Location of Culture,* 85–82. New York: Routledge, 1994.

Blom, Ida, Karen Hagemann, and Catherine Hall, eds. *Gendered Nations: Nationalisms and Gender Order in the Long Nineteenth Century.* Oxford: Berg, 2000.

Bock, Gisela. "Poverty and Mother's Rights in the Emerging Welfare States." In *A History of Women in the West: Towards a Cultural Identity in the Twentieth Century,* edited by Francois Thehard, 402–32. Cambridge, Mass.: Harvard University Press, 1992.

———. "Women's History and Gender History: Aspects of International Debate." *Gender and History* 1, no. 1 (1989): 7–30.

Bose, Subhas Chandra. "Some Problems of Nation Building." *Science and Culture* 1 (October 1935): 258–59.

Bradley, Harriet. "The Seductions of the Archive: Voices Lost and Found." *History of the Human Sciences* 12, no. 2 (1999): 107–22.

Brereton, Bridget. "Gendered Testimonies: Autobiographies, Diaries, and Letters by Women as sources of Caribbean History." *Feminist Review* 59, no. 1 (June 1998): 143–63.

Brown, Judith. *Modern India: The Emergence of an Asian Democracy.* New York: Oxford University Press, 1991.

Bucar, Maria. *Eugenics and Modernization in Interwar Romania.* Pittsburgh: University of Pittsburgh Press, 2002.

Bullough, Vern L. *Encyclopedia of Birth Control.* Santa Barbara: ABC-CLIO, 2001.

Burton, Antoinette. *Archive Stories: Facts, Fictions, and the Writing of History.* Durham, N.C.: Duke University Press, 2006.

———. *At the Heart of the Empire: Indians and the Colonial Encounter in Late-Victorian Britain.* Berkeley: University of California Press, 1998.

———. *Burdens of History: British Feminists, Indian Women and Imperial Culture, 1865–1915.* Chapel Hill: University of North Carolina Press, 1994.

———. "Contesting the Zenana: The Mission to Make 'Lady Doctors for India,' 1874–1885." *Journal of British Studies* (July 1996): 368–97.

———. *Dwelling in the Archive: Women Writing Home and History in Late Colonial India.* New York: Oxford University Press, 2003.

———, ed. *Gender, Sexuality, and Colonial Modernity.* London: Routledge, 2000.

———. "Who Needs the Nation? Interrogating 'British' History." *Journal of Historical Sociology* 10, no. 3 (1997): 227–48.

Candy, Catherine. "Relating Feminisms, Nationalism and Imperialisms: Ireland, India and Margaret Cousins's Sexual Politics." *Women's History Review* 3, no. 4 (1994): 581–94.

Canning, Kathleen. "The Body as Method? Reflections on the Place of Body in Gender History." *Gender & History* 11, no. 3 (November 1999): 499–513.

———. "Feminist History after the Linguistic Turn: Historicizing Discourse and Experience." *Signs* 19 (Winter 1994): 368–404.

———. *Language of Labor and Gender: Female Factory Workers in Germany, 1850–1914.* Ithaca, N.Y.: Cornell University Press, 1996.

Canning, Kathleen, and Sonya O. Rose, eds. *Gender, Citizenships and Subjectivities.* Oxford: Blackwell, 2002.

Chakrabarty, Dipesh. "The Difference-Deferral of (A) Colonial Modernity: Public Debates on Domesticity in British Bengal." *History Workshop Journal* 36 (1993): 1–33.

———. *Provincializing Europe: Postcolonial Thought and Historical Difference.* Princeton: Princeton University Press, 2000.

Chakravarty, Uma. "Whatever Happened to the Vedic Dasi? Orientalism, Nationalism and a Script for the Past." In *Recasting Women,* edited by Kumkum Sangari and Sudesh Vaid, 27–87. New Delhi: Kali for Women, 1989.

Chandra, Sudhir. *Enslaved Daughters: Colonialism, Law and Women's Rights.* New Delhi: Oxford University Press, 1998.

———. *The Oppressive Present: Literature and Social Consciousness in Colonial India.* Delhi: Oxford University Press, 1992.

Chandrasekhar, S. *A Dirty Filthy Book: The Writings of Charles Knowlton and Annie Besant on Reproductive Physiology and Birth Control and an Account of Bradlaugh-Besant Trial.* Berkeley: University of California, 1981.

Chatterjee, Partha. *The Nation and Its Fragments: Colonial and Post Colonial Histories.* Princeton: Princeton University Press, 1993.

———. "The Nationalist Resolution of the Woman's Question." In *Recasting Women,* edited by Kumkum Sangari and Sudesh Vaid, 233–53. New Delhi: Kali for Women, 1989.

———. *Nationalist Thought in a Colonial World: A Derivative Discourse?* Delhi: Oxford University Press, 1986.

Chatterjee, Piya. *A Time for Tea: Women, Labor, and Post-colonial Politics on an Indian Plantation.* Durham, N.C.: Duke University Press, 2001.

Chatterji, A. N. "Population Control." *Prince of Wales Medical College Magazine* (January 1936): 27–31.

Chattopadhyaya, Kamaladevi. *The Awakening of Indian Women.* Madras: Everymans Press, 1939.

———. "Future of Indian Women's Movement." In *Our Cause: A Symposium by Indian Women,* edited by Shyam Kumari Nehru, 358–402. Allahabad: Kitabistan, n.d.

———. *Indian Women's Battles for Freedom*. New Delhi: Abhinav, 1983.
———. *Inner Recesses, Outer Spaces: Memoirs*. New Delhi: Navrang, 1986.
Chaudhury, H. K. "Birth Control." *Indian Medical Journal* 31 (August 1937): 369–71.
Chesler, Ellen. *Woman of Valor: Margaret Sanger and the Birth Control Movement in America*. New York: Anchor Books, 1992.
Chinnathamby, Richard. "The Indian Woman's Movement for Emancipation." *Twentieth Century* 2 (March 1936): 616–23.
Chowdhry, Prem. "Popular Perceptions of Widow-Remarriage in Haryana: Past and Present." In *From the Seams of History: Essays on Indian Women*, edited by Bharati Ray, 37–66. Delhi: Oxford University Press, 1997.
Clarke, Adele E. *Disciplining Reproduction: Modernity, American Life Sciences, and "the Problems of Sex."* Berkeley: University of California Press, 1998.
———. "Maverick Reproductive Scientists and the Production of Contraceptives, 1915–2000+." In *Bodies of Technology: Women's Involvement with Reproductive Medicine*, edited by Ann Rudinow Saetnan, Nelly Oudshoorn, and Marta Kirejczyk, 37–89. Columbus: Ohio State University Press, 2000.
Cohen, Deborah A. "Private Lives in Public Spaces: Marie Stopes, the Mothers' Clinics and the Practice of Contraception." *History Workshop Journal* 35 (1993): 95–116.
Cohn, Bernard S. "The Census, Social Structure and Objectification in South Asia." In *An Anthropologist among the Historians and Other Essays*, edited by Bernard S. Cohn, 224–54. Delhi: Oxford University Press, 1987.
———. *Colonialism and Its Forms of Knowledge: The British in India*. Princeton, N.J.: Princeton University Press, 1996.
Cole, Joshua. *The Power of Large Numbers: Populations, Politics, and Gender in Nineteenth-Century France*. Ithaca, N.Y.: Cornell University Press, 2000.
Comaroff, John. "Governmentality, Materiality, Legality, Modernity: On the Colonial State in Africa." In *African Modernities: Entangled Meanings in Current Debates*, edited by Jan-Geory Deutsch, Peter Probst, and Heike Schmidt, 107–34. Portsmouth: Heinemann, 2002.
Connelly, Matthew. "Population Control in History: New Perspectives on the International Campaign to Limit Population Growth." *Society for Comparative Study of Society and History* (2003): 122–47.
Cooper, Frederick, and Ann Stoler, eds. *Tensions of Empire: Colonial Cultures in a Bourgeois World*. Berkeley: University of California Press, 1997.
Coronil, Fernando. *The Magical State: Nature, Money and Modernity in Venezuela*. Chicago: University of Chicago Press, 1997.
Cousins, James H., and Margaret E. Cousins. *We Two Together*. Madras: Ganesh, 1950.
Darling, Malcolm L. *The Punjab Peasant in Prosperity and Debt*. London: Oxford University Press, 1925.
Darling, Marsha J. Tyson. "The State: Friend or Foe? Distributive Justice Issues and African American Women." In *Dangerous Intersections: Feminist Intersections: Feminist Perspectives on Population, Environment, and Development*, edited by Jael Silliman and Ynestra King, 214–41. Cambridge: South End Press, 1999.
Datta, Pradip Kumar. *Carving Blocs: Communal Ideology in Early Twentieth Century Bengal*. Delhi: Oxford University Press, 1999.

Davidoff, Leonore. "Class and Gender in Victorian England." In *Sex and Class in Women's History,* edited by Judith L. Newton, Mary P. Ryan, and Judith R. Walkowitz, 17–71. London: Routledge and Kegan Paul, 1983.
Davis, Angela. *Women, Race, and Class.* New York: Vintage Books, 1983.
Davis, Natalie Zemon. "'Women's History' in Transition: The European Case." *Feminist Studies* 3, nos. 3/4 (Fall 1976): 83–103.
Davis, Susan. *Women under Attack: Victories, Backlash and the Fight for Reproductive Freedom.* Boston: South End Press, 1988.
Devji, Faisal Fatehali. "Gender and Politics of Space: The Movement for Women's Reform 1857–1900." *South Asia* 14, no. 1 (June 1991): 141–54.
Dewey, Clive. *Anglo-Indian Attitudes: The Mind of the Indian Civil Service.* London: Hambledon Press, 1993.
Dirks, Nicholas B. "Introduction: Colonialism and Culture." In *Colonialism and Culture,* edited by Nicholas Dirks, 1–26. Ann Arbor: University of Michigan Press, 1995.
Ditz, Toby. "The New Men's History and the Peculiar Absence of Gendered Power: Some Remedies from Early American Gender History." *Gender and History* 16, no. 1 (April 2004): 1–35.
Dodwell, H. H., ed. *The Cambridge History of the British Empire: Volume V, the Indian Empire 1858–1918,* 599–603. Cambridge: Cambridge University Press, 1929.
Dubois, Ellen Carol. *Woman Suffrage and Women's Rights.* New York: New York University Press, 1998.
Emge, L. A. "The Safe Period." *Calcutta Medical Journal* 31 (August 1936): 111.
Engels, Dagmar. *Beyond Purdah? Women in Bengal 1890–1939.* Delhi: Oxford University Press, 1996.
Engels, Dagmar, and Shula Marks, eds. *Contesting Colonial Hegemony: State and Society in Africa and India.* London: I. B. Tauris, 1994.
Doolittle, Megan. "Close Relations? Bringing Together Gender and Family in English History." In *Gender and History: Retrospect and Prospect,* edited by Leonore Davidoff, Keith McClelland, and Eleni Varikas, 124–36. Oxford: Blackwell, 2000.
Fisher, Kate. "'She Was Quite Happy with the Arrangements I Made': Gender and Birth Control in Britain, 1925–50." *Past & Present* 169 (2000): 161–93.
———. "Contrasting Cultures of Contraception: Birth Control Clinics and the Working-Classes in Britain Between the Wars." *Clio Medica-Amsterdam* 66 (2002): 141–58.
Flax, Jane. "Postmodern and Gender Relations in Feminist Theory." In *Feminism/Postmodernism,* edited by Linda J. Nicholson, 39–62. New York: Routledge, 1990.
Fleischmann, Ellen L. *The Nation and Its "New" Women: The Palestinian Women's Movement, 1920–1948.* Berkeley: California University Press, 2003.
Forbes, Geraldine. "Colonial Imperatives and Women's Emancipation: Western Medical Education for Indian Women in Nineteenth-Century Bengal." *Modern Historical Studies* 2 (2001): 83–102.
———. "The Indian Women's Movement: A Struggle for Women's Rights or National Liberation." In *The Extended Family: Women and Political Participation in India and Pakistan,* edited by Gail Minault, 49–82. Delhi: Chanakya Publication, 1981.
———. "Managing Midwifery in India." In *Contesting Colonial Hegemony: State and Society in Africa and India,* edited by Dagmar Engels and Shula Marks, 152–72. London: I. B. Tauris, 1994.

———. "Women in Modern India." In *The New Cambridge History of India: Women in Modern India,* edited by Geraldine Forbes, 87–90. Cambridge: Cambridge University Press, 1996.

———. "Women in the Nationalist Movement." In *The New Cambridge History of India: Women in Modern India,* edited by Geraldine Forbes, 155–56. Cambridge: Cambridge University Press, 1996.

Foucault, Michel. *The History of Sexuality: An Introduction.* New York: Vintage Books, 1990.

Fox, Richard. *Gandhian Utopia: Experiments with Culture.* Boston: Beacon Press, 1989.

Friedman, Lester, ed. *Cultural Sutures: Medicine and Media.* Durham: Duke University Press, 2004.

Galton, Francis. *Essay in Eugenics.* London: Eugenics Education Society, 1909.

Gandhi, Mohandas K. *Hind Swaraj or Indian Home Rule.* Ahmedabad: Navajivan, 1938.

———. *Self-Restraint versus Self-Indulgence.* Ahmedabad: Navajivan, 1947.

Gedge, Evelyn C., ed. *Women in Modern India.* Bombay: D. B. Taraporevala Sons, 1929.

Ghosh, Durba. "Decoding the Nameless: Gender, Subjectivity, and Historical Methodologies in Reading the Archive in Colonial India." In *The Imperial History: Culture, Identity, and Modernity in Britain and the Empire: 1660–1840,* edited by Kathleen Wilson, 297–316. New York: Cambridge University Press, 2004.

Ghosh, J. N. "Ethics of Birth Control." *Prince of Wales Medical College Magazine: Birth Control* 4, no. 1 (January 1936): 14–26.

Ghoshe, Debendra Nath. "The Social Background of Pauperism in India." In *Population Problem in India,* edited by Radhakamal Mukherjee, 141–52. Mylapore: Madras Law Journal Office, 1938.

Gluck, Sherna Berger and Daphne Patai, eds. *Women's Words: Feminist Practice of Oral History.* New York: Routledge, 1991.

Goetz, Anne Marie. *Getting Institutional Right for Women in Development.* New York: Zed Books, 1997.

Gordon, Linda. *Woman's Body, Woman's Right: Birth Control in America.* New York: Penguin Books, 1990.

Goswami, Manu. *Producing India: From Colonial Economy to National Space.* Chicago: University of Chicago Press, 2004.

Grosz, Elizabeth. "Feminism and Anti-Humanism." In *Discourse and Difference,* edited by A. Milner and C. Worth, 63–76. Melbourne: Monash University Press, 1990.

Guha, Ranajit. *Elementary Aspects of Peasant Insurgency in Colonial India.* Delhi: Oxford University Press, 1983.

Guha, Ranajit, ed. *Subaltern Studies I: Writings on South Asian History and Society.* Delhi: Oxford University Press, 1982.

Guha, Sumit. *Health and Population in South Asia: From Earliest Times to the Present.* New Delhi: Permanent Black, 2001.

Guha, Supriya. "From Dais to Doctors: The Medicalisation of Childbirth in Colonial India." In *Understanding Women's Health Issues: A Reader,* edited by Lakshmi Lingam, 145–61. New Delhi: Kali, 1998.

Gupta, Charu. *Sexuality, Obscenity, Community: Women, Muslims, and the Hindu Public in Colonial India.* New Delhi: Permanent Black Press, 2001.

Gupta, T. B. "Modern Civilization and Birth Control." *Prince of Wales Medical College Magazine: Birth Control* 4, no. 1 (January 1936): 39–40.

Hall, Catherine. *Civilising Subjects: Metropole and Colony in the English Imagination 1830–1867.* Chicago: Chicago University Press, 2002.

———. ed. *Cultures of Empire: Colonizers in Britain and the Empire in the Nineteenth and Twentieth Centuries.* New York: Routledge, 2000.

———. *White, Male, and Middle Class: Explorations in Feminism and History.* New York: Routledge, 1992.

Hall, Ruth. *Marie Stopes: A Biography.* London: Andre Deutsche Limited, 1977.

———. *Passionate Crusader: The Life of Marie Stopes.* New York: Harcourt Brace Jovanovich, 1977.

Hansen, Thomas Blom. *The Saffron Wave: Democracy and Hindu Nationalism in Modern India.* Princeton, N.J.: Princeton University Press, 1999.

Hanssen, Beatrice. "Whatever Happened to Feminist Theory?" In *Feminist Consequences: Theory for the New Century,* edited by Elizabeth Bronfen and Misha Kavka, 58–100. New York: Columbia University Press, 2001.

Hardiman, David. *Gandhi in His Time and Ours.* New Delhi: Permanent Black Press, 2003.

Harding, Sandra. *Whose Science? Whose Knowledge? Thinking From Women's Lives.* Ithaca, N.Y.: Cornell University Press, 1991.

Hardy, Peter. *The Muslims of British India.* Cambridge: Cambridge University Press, 1972.

Harrison, Mark. *Public Health in British India: Anglo-Indian Preventive Medicine, 1859–1914.* New York: Cambridge University Press, 1994.

Herr, Ranjoo Seodu. "The Possibility of Nationalist Feminism." *Hypatia* 18 (Fall 2003): 135–60.

Hill, Andreas. "'May the Doctor Advise Extramarital Intercourse?' Medical Debates on Sexual Abstinence in Germany, c. 1900." In *Sexual Knowledge, Sexual Science: The History of Attitudes Towards Sexuality,* edited by Roy Porter and Mikulas Teich, 284–302. Cambridge: Cambridge University Press, 1994.

Hingorani, Anand T., ed. *To the Women: By Mahatma Gandhi.* Karachi: Anand T. Hingorani, 1941.

Hodgson, Dennise, and Susan Cotts Watkins. "Feminists and Neo-Malthusianisms: Past and Present Alliances." *Population and Development Review* 23 (1997): 469–524.

hooks, bell. *Feminist Theory from the Margin to Center.* Boston: South End Press, 1984.

———. *Feminist Theory from the Margin to Center,* 2nd ed. Boston: South End Press, 2000.

———. *Talking Back: Thinking Feminist, Thinking Black.* Boston: South End Press, 1989.

How-Martyn, Edith. "Birth Control as Preventive Medicine." *Prince of Wales Medical College Magazine* (January 1936): 8–10.

———. *The Brief Survey of the Birth Control Movement in India.* n.p.: 1938. From the Eileen Palmer Collection, BC17.

Hunt, Nancy Rose. "'*Le bebe en brousse*': European Women, African Birth Spacing and Colonial Interventions in Breast Feeding in the Belgian Congo." In *Tensions of Empire:*

Colonial Cultures in a Bourgeois World, edited by Frederick Cooper and Ann Stoler, 287–321. Berkeley: University of California Press, 1997.

———. *Colonial Lexicon: Of Birth Ritual, Medicalization and Mobility in the Congo.* Durham, N.C.: Duke University Press, 1999.

Ittmann, Karl. "The Colonial Office and the Population Question in British Empire, 1918–1962." *Journal of Imperial and Commonwealth History* 27, no. 3 (1999): 55–81.

Iyer, T. S. Balasubramania. "The Problem of Birth Control." *Indian Medical Record* (September 1935): 268–73.

Jaggar, Alison. *Feminist Politics and Human Nature.* Totowa, N.J.: Rowman and Allanheld, 1983.

Jayawardena, Kumari. *Feminism and Nationalism in the Third World.* London: Zed Books, 1986.

Jeffery, Patricia, Roger Jeffery, and Andrew Lyon, *Labour Pains and Labour Power: Women and Childbearing in India.* New Delhi: Sage, 1989.

Jeffries, Lilias B. "Letter to the Editor: Control of Conception." *Journal of Association of Medical Women in India* 11 (February 1922): 30–31.

———. "Note by Jeffries." *Journal of Association of Medical Women in India* 10 (February 1922): 80–81.

———. "Prevention." *Journal of Association of Medical Women in India* 10 (May 1921): 6–10.

Jhirad, J. "Practical Aspects of Birth Control." *Journal of Association of Medical Women in India* 26 (May 1936): 116–23.

———. "Some Aspects of Medico-Social Work in India." in *Women in Modern India,* edited by Evelyn C. Gedge, 134. Bombay: D. B. Taraporevala Sons, 1929.

Jolly, Margaret. "Motherlands? Some Notes on Women and Nationalism in India and Africa." *Australian Journal of Anthropology* 5 (1994): 41–59.

Jolly, Margaret, and Kalpana Ram, eds. *Borders of Being: Citizenship, Fertility, and Sexuality in Asia and the Pacific.* Ann Arbor: University of Michigan Press, 2001.

Jones, Kenneth W. *Arya Dharm: Hindu Consciousness in the Nineteenth Century.* New Delhi: Manohar, 1989.

Jordon, Glenn, and Chris Weedon. "When the Subalterns Speak, What Do They Say? Radical Cultural Politics in Cardiff Docklands." In *Without Guarantees: In Honour of Stuart Hall,* edited by Paul Gilroy, Lawrence Grossberg, and Angela McRobbie, 165–80. New York: Verso, 2000.

Joseph, Betty. *Reading the East India Company, 1720–1840: Colonial Currencies of Gender.* Chicago: University of Chicago Press, 2004.

Joshi, Sanjay. *Fractured Modernity: The Making of a Middle Class in Colonial North India.* Delhi: Oxford University Press, 2001.

Kagal, M. B. "Maternity and Child Welfare Work in the Rural Areas." *Journal of Association of Medical Women in India* 32, no. 2 (February 1944): 21.

Kalpagam, U. "The Colonial State and Statistical Knowledge." *History of Human Sciences* 13, no. 2 (2000): 37–55.

Kandiyoti, Deniz. "Identity and Its Discontents: Women and the Nation." *Millennium* 20, no. 3 (1991): 429–44.

Kaplan, Caren, Norma Alarcon, and Minoo Moallem, eds. *Between Women and Nation:*

Nationalisms, Transnational Feminisms, and the State. Durham, N.C.: Duke University Press, 1999.
Kapur, Ratna. *Erotic Justice: Law and the New Politics of Postcolonialism.* New Delhi: Permanent Black, 2005.
Kasturi, Malavika. "Law and Crime in India: British Policy and the Female Infanticide Act of 1870." *Indian Journal of Gender Studies* 1, no. 2 (1994): 169–93.
Kishwar, Madhu. "Women and Gandhi." *Economic and Political Weekly* (October 5 and 12, 1985): 1691–1702, 1753–58.
Klausen, Susanne. "Imperial Mother of Birth Control: Marie Stopes and the South African Birth Control Movement, 1930–1950." In *Colonialism and the Modern World: Selected Studies,* edited by Gregory Blue, Martin Bunton and R. Croizier, 182–99. New York: M. E. Sharpe, 2002.
Kumar, Nita. *Women as Subjects: South Asian Histories.* Charlottesville: University Press of Virginia, 1994.
Kumar, Radha. *History of Doing: An Illustrated Account of Movements for Women's Rights and Feminism in India, 1800–1990.* London: Verso, 1993.
Lal, Maneesha. "The Politics of Gender and Medicine in Colonial India: The Countess of Dufferin Fund, 1885–1888." *Bulletin of History of Medicine* 68 (1994): 29–66.
Landes, Joan B., ed. *Feminism: The Public and the Private.* Oxford: Oxford University Press, 1998.
Leavitt Walzer, Judith. *Brought to Bed: Child-Bearing in America, 1750–1950.* New York: Oxford University Press, 1986.
———. "Under the Shadow of Maternity: American Responses to Death and Debility Fears in Nineteenth-Century Childbirth." *Feminist Studies* 12, no. 1 (Spring 1986): 129–54.
Ledbetter, Rosanna. *A History of the Malthusian League, 1877–1927.* Columbus: Ohio University Press, 1976.
Lerner, Gerda. "Placing Women in History: Definitions and Challenges." *Feminist Studies* 3, nos. 1–2 (Fall 1975): 5–15.
Levine, Philippa, ed. *Gender and Empire: The Oxford History of the British Empire.* Oxford: Oxford University Press, 2004.
Lingam, Lakshmi, ed. *Understanding Women's Health Issues: A Reader.* New Delhi: Kali. 1998.
Lonsdale, John and Bruce Berman. "Coping with Contradictions: The Development of the Colonial State in Kenya." *Journal of African History,* 20: (1979): 487–506.
Lorde, Audre. *Sister/Outsider: Essays and Speeches.* New York: Crossing Press, 1984.
Ludden, David. "India's Development Regime" in *Colonialism and Culture,* edited by Nicholas Dirks, 247–288. Ann Arbor: University of Michigan Press, 1995.
———. "Orientalist Empiricism: Transformations of Colonial Knowledge." In *Orientalism and the Post Colonial Predicament: Perspectives on South Asia,* edited by Carol Breckenridge and Peter van der Veer, 250–278. Philadelphia: University of Pennsylvania Press, 1993.
Lugones, Maria. "Playfulness, 'World'-Traveling, and Loving Perception." In *Women, Knowledge, and Reality: Explorations in Feminist Philosophy,* edited by Ann Garry and Marilyn Pearsall, 419–34. New York: Routledge, 1996.

Mackinnon, Jan and Steve. "Agnes Smedley: A Working Introduction." *Bulletin of Concerned Asian Scholars* 7 (1975): 6–11.

Mahadevia, C. G. "Contraception." *Indian Medical Record* 51 (October 1931): 295–97.

Majumdar, Vina. "The Social Reform Movement in India: From Ranade to Nehru." In *Indian Women: From Purdah to Modernity,* edited by B. R. Nanda, 41–66. New Delhi: Vikas, 1976.

Malhotra, Anshu. *Gender, Caste, and Religious Identities.* Delhi: Oxford University Press, 2002.

Malthus, Thomas Robert. *An Essay on Population, Volume 1.* London: J. M. Dent and Sons, 1914. First published 1789.

Mangudkar, M. P. *Dr. Ambedkar and Family Planning.* Poona: 1976.

Mani, Lata. "Contentious Traditions: The Debate on Sati in Colonial India." In *Recasting Women,* edited by Kumkum Sangari and Sudesh Vaid, 88–126. New Delhi: Kali for Women, 1989.

Manna, Mausumi. "Approach Towards Birth Control: Indian Women in the Early Twentieth Century." *Indian Economic and Social History Review* 35 (1998): 35–51.

Mathews, Mrs. A. "Birth-Control and Child Mortality." *Stri-Dharma* 16, no. 4 (October 1933): 613–15.

Mathur, Jai Krishan. *The Pressure of Population: Its Effects on Rural Economy in Gorakhpur District.* Allahabad, United Provinces: Superintendent Printing and Stationery, 1931.

McCann, Carole R. *Birth Control Politics in the United States, 1916–1945.* Ithaca: Cornell University Press, 1994.

McClintock, Anne. "Family Feuds: Gender, Nationalism and the Family." *Feminist Review* 44 (Summer 1993): 61–80.

———. "No Longer in a Future Heaven: Gender Race and Nationalism." In *Dangerous Liaisons: Gender, Nation and Postcolonial Perspective,* edited by Anne McClintock, Aamir Mufti, and Ella Shohat, 352–89. Minneapolis: University of Minnesota Press, 1997.

McLaren, Angus and Arlene Tigar McLaren. *The Bedroom and the State: The Changing Practices and Politics of Contraception and Abortion in Canada, 1880–1997.* Toronto: Oxford University Press, 1997.

Menon, Lakshmi. *The Position of Women.* London: Oxford University Press, 1944.

———. "The Woman's Burden." *Twentieth Century* 3 (March 1937): 479–85.

Menon, Nivedita. *Recovering Subversion: Feminist Politics beyond the Law.* New Delhi and Urbana: Permanent Black and University of Illinois Press, 2004.

Menon, Ritu. "Do Women have a Nation?" In *From Gender to Nation,* edited by Rada Ivekovic and Julie Mostov, 43–62. New Delhi: Zubaan, 2004.

Menon, Ritu, and Kamala Bhasin. *Borders and Boundaries: Women in India's Partition.* New Delhi: Kali for Women, 1998.

Metcalf, Barbara. *Perfecting Women: Maulana Ashraf Ali Thanawi's Bihishti Zewar.* New Delhi: Oxford University Press,1990.

Metcalf, Thomas. R. *The Aftermath of Revolt.* Princeton, N.J.: Princeton University Press, 1964.

Midgley, Clare, ed. *Gender and Imperialism.* Manchester: Manchester University Press, 1998.

Miller, Patricia Y., and Martha R. Fowlker. "Social and Behavioral Constructions of Female Sexuality." In *Sex and Scientific Inquiry,* edited by Sandra Harding and Jean F. O'Barr, 147–64. Chicago: University of Chicago Press, 1987.

Minault, Gail, ed. *The Extended Family: Women and Political Participation in India and Pakistan.* Delhi: Chanakya Publication, 1981.

———. *Secluded Scholars: Women's Education and Muslim Reform in Colonial India.* New Delhi: Oxford University Press, 1999.

Mistry, Jerbanoo E. "Association of Medical Women in India and Its Fifty Years." *Journal of Association of Medical Women in India* 45 (November 1957): 107–27.

———. "Birth Control." *Journal of Association of Medical Women in India* 24, no. 1 (February 1934): 17–21.

———. "Extracts from 'My Impressions of the Tenth All-India Women's Conference'." *Journal of Association of Medical Women in India* 24, no. 2 (May 1936): 38–41.

Mohanty, Chandra Talpade. *Feminism without Borders: Decolonizing Theory, Practicing Solidarity.* Durham, N.C.: Duke University Press, 2003.

———. "Feminist Encounters: Locating the Politics of Experience." *Copyright* 1 (1987): 30–44.

———. "'Under Western Eyes:' Feminist Scholarship and Colonial Discourses." *Feminist Review,* 30 (1988): 61–88.

Mohanty, Chandra Talpade, Anna Russo, and Lourdes Torres, eds. *Third World Woman and the Politics of Feminism.* Bloomington: Indiana University Press, 1991.

Mohr, James C. *Abortion in America: The Origins and Evolution of National Policy, 1800–1900.* New York: Oxford University Press, 1978.

Moore, Lisa Jean, and Adele E. Clarke. "Clitoral Conventions and Transgressions: Graphic Representations in Anatomy Texts, c. 1900–1991." *Feminist Studies* (Summer 1995): 255–301.

Moore-Gilbert, Bart. "Gayatri Spivak: The Deconstructive Twist." In *Postcolonial Theory: Contexts, Practices and Politics,* 74–113. London: Verso, 1997.

Moser, O. N. Caroline. *Gender Planning and Development: Theory, Practice and Training.* New York: Routledge, 1993.

Mukherjee, Radhakamal, ed. *Population Problem in India.* Mylapore: Madras Law Journal Office, 1938.

Mukherjee, Ramandas. "The Problem of Obstetrics and Gynecology in India." *Calcutta Medical Journal,* 33 (May, 1938): 226–242.

Mukherji, Santosh Kumar. *Birth Control for the Millions,* 2nd ed. Calcutta: Medical Book, 1945.

Musallam, B. F. *Sex and Society in Islam: Birth Control before the Nineteenth Century.* Cambridge: Cambridge University Press, 1983.

Naples, Nancy. *Feminism and Method: Ethnography, Discourse Analysis and Activist Research.* New York: Routledge, 2003.

Narayan, Kirin. "How Native Is a 'Native' Anthropologist?" In *Feminist Postcolonial Theory: A Reader,* edited by Reina Lewis and Sara Mills, 285–305. New York: Routledge, 2003.

Nawaz, M. S. "Indications for Birth Control." *Indian Medical Record* (July 1926): 205–6.

Nehru, Rameshwari. *Gandhi Is My Star.* Patna: Patna Pas Bhandar, 1950.

Nehru, Shyam Kumari, ed. *Our Cause: A Symposium by Indian Women*. Allahabad: Kitabistan, n.d.

Nelson, Jennifer, *Women of Color and the Reproductive Rights Movement*. New York: New York University Press, 2003.

Norden, Martin. "Reproductive Freedom, Revisionist History, Restricted Cinema: The Strange Case of Margaret Sanger and *Birth Control*." In *Cultural Sutures*, edited by Lester Friedman, 263–79. Durham: Duke University Press, 2004.

Neushul, Peter. "Marie C. Stopes and the Popularization of Birth Control Technology." *Journal of History of Technology* (1998): 245–72.

Nye, Robert A., ed. *Sexuality*. New York: Oxford University Press, 1999.

Offen, Karen. *European Feminisms 1700–1950: A Political History*. Stanford, Calif.: Stanford University Press, 2000.

O'Flaherty, Wendy Doniger, and Brian K. Smith. *The Laws of Manu*. New York: Penguin Books, 1991.

Omvedt, Gail. "Caste, Class and Women's Liberation in India." *Bulletin of Concerned Asian Scholars* 7, no. 1 (January–March 1975): 43–48.

Osterhammel, Jurgen. *Colonialism: A Theoretical Overview*. Princeton, N.J.: Markus Wiener, 1999.

Ouwerkerk, Louise. *No Elephants for the Maharaja: Social and Political Change in Princely State of Travancore, 1921–1947* [introduction by Dick Kooiman]. New Delhi: Manohar, 1994.

Paliwal, Om Prakash. *Rameshwari Nehru: Patriot and Internationalist*. New Delhi: National Book Trust, 1986.

Panicker, Lalita. "Population: No More a Game of Numbers." *The Times of India*, January 19, 1999.

Parekh, Bhikhu. *Gandhi*. Oxford: Oxford University Press, 1997.

Patel, Sujata. "Construction and Reconstruction of Woman in Gandhi." *Economic and Political Weekly* 23 (February 20, 1988): 377–87.

Patel, Tulsi. *Fertility Behaviour: Population and Society in a Rajasthan Village*. New Delhi: Oxford University Press, 1994.

Pati, Biswamoy, and Mark Harrison, eds. *Health, Medicine, and Empire: Perspectives on Colonial India*. Hyderabad: Orient Longman, 2001.

Patriarca, Silvana. "Statistical Nation Building and the Consolidation of Regions in Italy." *Social Science History* (Fall 1994): 359–76.

Pearson, Gail. "Nationalism, Universalization, and the Extended Female Space in Bombay." In *The Extended Family: Women and Political Participation in India and Pakistan*, edited by Gail Minault, 174–92. Delhi: Chanakya Publication, 1981.

Phadke, N. S. "Birth Control in India." *Birth Control Review* (April 1924): 105–7.

———. "Eugenics for India." *Birth Control Review* (November 1925): 316–17.

———. *Sex Problem in India*. Bombay: D. B. Taraporevala and Sons, 1927.

Philipose, Pamela. "The *beti-maru* Mind-Set: Are We Ready for a Future without Daughters?" *Indian Express*, September 15, 2004.

Pillay, A. P. *Birth Control Simplified*. Bombay: D. B. Taraporevala Sons, n.d.

———. "Eugenical Birth Control for India." *Birth Control Review* (November 1931): 310–11.

———. *Ideal Sex Life: A Doctor Answers Confidential Personal Questions.* Bombay: D. B. Taraporevala Sons, 1944.
———. "Is Medicine Fulfilling Its Responsibilities to Future Generations?" CMAC: SA/EUG/E.8.
———. *Welfare Problems in Rural India.* Bombay: D. B. Taraporevala Sons, 1931.
Portelli, Alessandro. *The Death of Luigi Trastulli and Other Stories: Form and Meaning in Oral History.* New York: State University of New York Press, 1991.
Porter, Roy, and Lesley Hall. *The Facts of Life: The Creation of Sexual Knowledge in Britain, 1650–1950.* New Haven, Conn.: Yale University Press, 1995.
Prakash, Gyan. *Another Reason: Science and the Imagination of Modern India.* Princeton, N.J.: Princeton University Press, 1999.
———. "Writing Post-Orientalist Histories of the Third World: Indian Historiography Is Good to Think." In *Colonialism and Culture,* edited by Nicholas Dirks, 353–88. Ann Arbor: University of Michigan Press, 1995.
Raina, B. L. "Contraception and Medical Profession." *Indian Medical Journal* 34 (July 1940): 194–96.
———. *Planning Family in India: Prevedic Times to Early 1950.* New Delhi: Commonwealth Publishers, 1990.
Rajwade, Laxmibai. "The Indian Mother and Her Problems." In *Our Cause: A Symposium by Indian Women,* edited by Shyam Kumari Nehru. Allahabad: Kitabistan, n.d.
Ram, Kalpana. "Maternal Experience and Feminist Body Politics: Asian and Pacific Perspectives." In *Maternities and Modernities: Colonial and Postcolonial Experiences in Asia and the Pacific,* edited by Kalpana Ram and Margaret Jolly, 275–98. Cambridge: Cambridge University Press, 1998.
Ramirez de Arellano, Annette B., and Conrad Seipp. *Colonialism, Catholicism, and Contraception: A History of Birth Control in Puerto Rico.* Chapel Hill: University of North Carolina Press, 1983.
Ramusack, Barbara N. "Cultural Missionaries, Maternal Imperialists, Feminist Allies: British Women Activists in India, 1865–1945." *Women's Studies International Forum* 3, no. 4 (1990): 295–308.
———. "Embattled Advocates: The Debates on Birth Control in India, 1920–1940." *Journal of Women's History* 1, no. 2 (Fall 1989): 34–64.
———. "What Did They Know and When: Medical Women in India and the Practice of Birth Control, 1920–40."
———. "Women's Organizations and Social Change: The Age-of-Marriage Issue in India." In *Women and World Change: Equity Issues in Development,* edited by Naomi Black and Ann Baker Cottrell, 198–216. Beverly Hills, Calif.: Sage Publications, 1981.
Ramusack, Barbara N., and Antoinette Burton. "Introduction: Special Issue on Feminism, Imperialism, and Race: A Dialogue Between India and Britain." *Women's History Review* 4 (1994): 469–81.
Ramusack, Barbara N., and Sharon Sievers. *Women in Asia: Restoring Women to History.* Bloomington: Indiana University Press, 1999.
Rao, Mohan. "Abiding Appeal of Neo-Malthusianism: Explaining the Inexplicable." *Economic and Political Weekly,* August 7, 2004, pp. 3599–3604.

———. "An Imagined Reality: Malthusianism, Neo Malthusianism and Population Myth." *e-journals: re/productions,* # 1. (n.d.)

———. *From Population Control to Reproductive Health: Malthusian Arithmetic.* New Delhi, Sage Publications, 2004.

Rau, Dhanvanti Rama. *An Inheritance: The Memoirs of Dhanvanti Rama Rau.* New York: Harper & Row, 1977.

Ray, A. P. "For Those Who Oppose Birth Control." *Prince of Wales Medical College Magazine* (January 1936): 53–54.

Ray, Bharati, ed. *From the Seams of History: Essays on Indian Women.* Delhi: Oxford University Press, 1997.

Ray, Raka. *Fields of Protest: Women's Movements in India.* Minneapolis: University of Minnesota Press, 1999.

Raychaudhuri, Tapan. *Europe Reconsidered: Perceptions of the West in Nineteenth Century Bengal.* Delhi: Oxford University Press, 1988.

Reddi, Muthulakshmi. *Autobiography of Dr. (Mrs.) Muthulakshmi Reddy.* Madras: M. Reddi, 1964.

———. *My Experiences as a Legislator.* Madras: Current Thought Press, 1930.

Reed, James. *From Private Vice to Public Virtue: Birth Control Movement in American Society since 1830.* New York: Basic Books, 1978.

Richards, Thomas. *Colonial Archive.* London: Verso, 1993.

Robinson, Francis. *Separatism among Indian Muslims: The Politics of the United Provinces' Muslims, 1860–1923.* Cambridge: Cambridge University Press, 1975.

Roberts, Mary Louise. *Civilizations without Sexes: Reconstructing Gender in Postwar France, 1917–1927.* Chicago: University of Chicago Press, 1994.

Rose, June. *Marie Stopes and the Sexual Revolution.* London: Faber and Faber, 1992.

Rosselli, John. "The Self-Image of Effeteness: Physical Education and Nationalism in Nineteenth-Century Bengal." *Past and Present* 87 (February 1980): 121–48.

Rozario, Santi, and Geoffrey Samuel, eds. *The Daughters of Hariti: Childbirth and Female Healers in South and Southeast Asia.* London: Routledge, 2002.

Rubin, Gayle. "Thinking Sex: Notes for a Radical Theory of the Politics of Sexuality." In *Pleasure and Danger: Exploring Female Sexuality,* edited by Carole Vance, 267–391. Boston: Routledge & K. Paul, 1984.

Saheli Collective. *Womantalk: Contraception, Safety and Our Health.* New Delhi: Saheli Collective, 1994.

Sahgal, Lakshmi. *A Revolutionary Life: Memoirs of a Political Activist.* New Delhi: Kali for Women, 1997.

Said, Edward. *Orientalism.* London: Routledge & Kegan Paul, 1978.

SAMA. "India: A Study on Women's Experiences with Depo-Provera." *Women's Global Network for Reproductive Rights Newsletter* 17 (October 2002): 77–80.

Sangari, Kumkum. "Relating Histories: Definitions of Literacy, Literature, Gender in Nineteenth Century Calcutta and England." In *Rethinking English: Essays in Literature, Language, History,* edited by Svati Joshi, 242–72. Delhi: Trianka, 1993.

Sangari, Kumkum, and Sudesh Vaid, eds. *Recasting Women: Essays in Colonial History.* New Delhi: Kali For Women, 1989.

Sanger, Margaret. "Does Gandhi Know Women? What He Told Me at Wardha." *Illustrated Weekly of India* (January 19, 1936): 1–15.

Sarkar, Mahua. "Looking for Feminism." *Gender and History* 16 (August 2004): 318–33.
Sarkar, Sumit. *Beyond Nationalist Frames: Relocating Postmodernism, Hindutva, History.* Delhi: Permanent Black, 2002.
———. *A Critique of Colonial India.* Calcutta: Papyrus, 1985.
———. *Modern India: 1885–1947.* Madras: Macmillan India, 1983.
Sarkar, Tanika. *Hindu Wife, Hindu Nation: Community, Religion, and Cultural Nationalism.* New Delhi: Permanent Black Press, 2001.
———. "Nationalist Iconography: Image of Women in Nineteenth-Century Bengali Literature." *Economic and Political Weekly* 22 (1987): 2011–15.
———. "Rhetoric against the Age of Consent: Resisting Colonial Reason and Death of a Child-Wife." *Economic and Political Weekly* 28 (September 4, 1993): 1869–78.
Scheper-Hughes, Nancy. *Death without Weeping: The Violence of Everyday Life in Brazil.* Berkeley: University of California Press, 1992.
Scott, Joan. *Only Paradoxes to Offer: French Feminists and the Rights of Man.* Massachusetts: Harvard University Press, 1996.
Sen, Amartya. "Population: Delusion and Reality." *The New York Review of Books,* September 22, 1994, 62–71.
Sen, S. P., ed. *Dictionary of National Biography, Volume 3.* Calcutta: Institute of Historical Studies, 1972.
Sen, Sumanta. "Tagore on Sex Tops Puja fare." *Times of India,* October 16, 1993.
Sharga, Brijnath. *Legacy of Rama.* Lucknow: Rama Tirtha Pratishtan, 1972.
———. *Life of Swami Rama Tirtha,* 2nd ed. Lucknow: Rama Tirtha Pratishtan, 1968.
Sharma, A. K. "The Gandhian Theory of Population: Relevance and Implications." *Journal of Family Welfare* 37, no. 4 (December 1991): 32–45.
Sharma, S. R. *Swami Rama Tirtha.* Bombay: Bhartiya Vidya Bhavan, 1961.
Silliman, Jael, and Anannya Bhattacharjee, eds. *Policing the National Body: Race, Gender and Criminalization.* Cambridge: South End Press, 2002.
Silliman, Jael, Marlene Gerber Fried, Loretta Ross, and Elena R. Gutierrez, eds. *Undivided Rights: Women of Color Organize for Reproductive Justice.* Cambridge: South End Press, 2004.
Sims, N. Proctor. "Analysis of Replies to the Questionnaire on Birth Control." *Journal of Association of Medical Women in India* 23, no. 4 (November 1935): 24–30.
Singh, Digvijay. "Treason, Not Reason: Six Billion and Still Growing." *The Times of India,* October 12, 1999.
Singh, Puran. *The Story of Swami Rama Tirtha.* Lucknow: Rama Tirtha Pratishtan, revised edition, 1974.
Sinha, Mrinalini. *Colonial Masculinity: The "Manly Englishman" and the "Effeminate Bengali" in the Late Nineteenth Century.* Manchester: Manchester University Press, 1995.
———. *Gender and Nation.* Washington, D.C.: American Historical Association, 2006.
———. "The Lineage of the 'Indian' Modern: Rhetoric, Agency and the Sarda Act in Late Colonial India." In *Gender, Sexuality and Colonial Modernity,* edited by Antoinette Burton, 207–21. London: Routledge, 2000.
———, ed. *Selections from Mother India: Katherine Mayo.* New Delhi: Kali for Women, 1998.
———. "Suffragism and Internationalism: The Enfranchisement of British and Indian

Women Under an Imperial State." In *Women's Suffrage in the British Empire: Citizenship, Nation, and Race,* edited by Ian Christopher Fletcher, Laura E. Nym Mayhall, and Philippa Levine, 224–40. London: Routledge, 2000.

Sinha, Mrinalini, Donna J. Guy, and Angela Woollacott, eds. *Feminisms and Internationalism.* Oxford: Blackwell, 1999.

Smart, Carol. *Regulating Womanhood: Historical Essays on Marriage, Motherhood and Sexuality.* London: Routledge, 1992.

Smith, Andrea. "Better Dead than Pregnant: The Colonization of Native Women's Reproductive Health." In *Policing the National Body: Race, Gender and Criminalization,* edited by Jael Silliman and Anannya Bhattacharjee, 123–44. Cambridge: South End Press, 2002.

———. *Conquest: Sexual Violence and American Indian Genocide.* Cambridge: South End Press, 2005.

Soloway, Richard. *Birth Control and the Population Question in England 1877–1930.* Chapel Hill: University of North Carolina Press, 1982.

———. *Demography and Degeneration: Eugenics and the Declining Birthrate in Twentieth-Century Britain.* Chapel Hill: University of North Carolina Press, 1990.

Spivak, Gayatri Chakravorty. "Can the Subaltern Speak?" Reprinted in *Colonial Discourse and Post Colonial Theory: A Reader,* edited by Patrick Williams and Laura Chrisman, 66–111. New York: Columbia University Press, 1994.

———. "Foreword: Upon Reading the *Companion to Postcolonial Studies.*" In *A Companion to Postcolonial Studies,* edited by Henry Schwarz and Sangeeta Ray, xix–xx. Malden, Mass.: Blackwell Publishers, 2000.

———. *In Other Worlds: Essays in Cultural Politics.* New York: Methuen, 1987.

Sreenivas, Mytheli. "Emotion, Identity and the Female Subject: Tamil Women's Magazines in Tamil India." *Journal of Women's History* (2003): 59–82.

Srivastava, Sanjay, ed. *Sexual Sites, Seminal Attitudes: Sexualities, Masculinities and Culture in South Asia.* New Delhi: Sage Publications, 2004.

Stansell, Christine. "Women, Children, and Uses of the Streets: Class and Gender Conflict in New York City, 1850–1860." In *Unequal Sisters: A Multicultural Reader in U.S. Women's History,* edited by Vicki Ruiz and Ellen Carol DuBois, 111–27. New York: Routledge, 1994.

Stopes, Marie C. "India and Gandhi." *Birth Control News* 20 (July 1942): 3.

———. "On Some Aspects of Contraception for Indian Women." *Marriage Hygiene* 1 (November 1934): 143–45.

———. "Review of *Self Restraint versus Self-Indulgence* by Mahatma K. Gandhi." *Birth Control News* 9, no. 3 (July 1930): 43–46.

———. *Wise Parenthood.* London: Rendell & Co., 1918.

Szreter, Simon and Kate Fisher. "They Prefer Withdrawal: The Choice of Birth Control Method in Britain, 1918–1950." *Journal of Interdisciplinary History* (2003): 263–91.

Talwar, Vir Bharat. "Feminist Consciousness in Women's Journals in Hindi." In *Recasting Women: Essays in Colonial History,* edited by Kumkum Sangari and Sudesh Vaid, 204–32. New Delhi: Kali For Women, 1989.

Tarlo, Emma. *Unsettling Memories: Narratives of the Emergency in Delhi.* Berkeley: California University Press, 2003.

Thapar, Romila. "Imagined Religious Communities? Ancient History and the Modern Search for a Hindu Identity." *Modern Asian Studies* 23 (1989): 209–31.

Thatcher, Ulrich Laurel. *A Midwife's Tale: The Life of Martha Ballard, Based on Her Diary, 1785–1812.* New York: Alfred A. Knopf, 1990.

Thomas, Lynn M. *Politics of the Womb: Women, Reproduction, and the State in Kenya.* Berkeley: University of California Press, 2003.

Thomas, Nicholas. *Colonialism's Culture: Anthropology, Travel and Government.* Princeton, N.J.: Princeton University Press, 1994.

Thompson, Elizabeth. *Colonial Citizens: Republican Rights, Paternal Privilege, and Gender in French Syria and Lebanon.* New York: Columbia University Press, 1999.

Thursby, G. R. *Hindu-Muslim Relations in British India: A Study of Controversy, Conflict, and Communal Movements in Northern India, 1923–28.* Leiden: E. J. Brill, 1975.

Tong, Rosemarie. *Feminist Approaches to Bioethics: Theoretical Reflections and Practical Applications.* Boulder, Colo.: Westview Press, 1997.

———. *Feminist Thought: A More Comprehensive Introduction.* Boulder, Colo.: Westview Press, 1998.

Tuteja, K. L., and O. P. Grewal. "Emergence of Hindu Communal Ideology in Early Twentieth Century Punjab." *Social Scientist* 20 (July–August 1992): 3–27.

Uberoi, Patricia, ed. *Social Reform, Sexuality and State.* New Delhi: Sage Publications, 1996.

Ulrich, Laurel Thatcher. *A Midwife's Tale: The Life of Martha Ballard, Based On Her Diary, 1785–1812.* New York: Knopf, 1990.

Urla, Jacqueline. "Cultural Politics in an Age of Statistics: Numbers, Nations and the Making of Basque Identity." *American Ethnologist* 20 (1993): 818–43.

Vaidya, Kaviraj Vimla Devi. *Garbh Nirodh* [Birth Control]. New Delhi: Jagath Pustak Bhandar, 1940.

Vance, Carole, ed. *Pleasure and Danger: Exploring Female Sexuality.* Boston: Routledge and Kegan Paul, 1984.

Van Hollen, Cecilia. *Birth on the Threshold: Childbirth and Modernity in South Asia.* Berkeley: University of California Press, 2003.

Vaughan, K. O. "Should the Dai be Trained or Superseded?" *JMMWI*, 5: 9 (February 1916): 16.

Visaria, Leela and Pradip. "Population." In *Cambridge Economic History of India, Volume 2: c. 1757 to c. 1970,* edited by Dharma Kumar and Meghnad Desai, 463–532. Delhi: Orient Longman, 1982.

Vohra, Dharam Bir. "Woman's Revolt against Man: An Analytical Study." *Twentieth Century* 5 (December 1938): 207–27.

Wattal, P. K. *The Population Problem in India: A Census Study.* Bombay: Bennett, Coleman, 1916.

———. *The Population Problem in India: A Census Study,* 2nd ed. Bombay: Bennett, Coleman, 1934.

Weeks, Jeffery. *Sex, Politics, and Society: The Regulation of Sexuality since 1800.* London and New York: Longman, 1989.

———. *Sexuality and Its Discontents: Meanings, Myths and Modern Sexualities.* London: Routledge and Kegan Paul, 1985.

White, Luise. "Colonial State and Civic Virtues in Africa: Essays in Honor of John Lonsdale." *International Journal of African Historical Studies* 37 (2004): 1–11.

Whitehead, Judy. "Modernising the Motherhood Archetype: Public Health Models and the Child Marriage Restraint Act, 1929." *Indian Sociology* 29, nos. 1–2 (January–December 1995): 187–210.

———. "Tropical Medicine and Inscriptions of Stigma: The Lessons of Katherine Mayo's *Mother India*." *The Journal of Canadian Women's Studies* (1991): 41–63.

Wolpert, Stanley. *A New History of India,* 4th ed. New York: Oxford University Press, 1993.

Yadhuvirsingh, Dr. *Gupt Sandesh* [Secret Message], 2nd ed. Lucknow: Ganga Granthagar, 1937.

Young, Ruth. "Medical Women and Conception Control." *Journal of Association of Medical Women in India* 22, no. 2 (May 1934): 5–12.

Zachariah, Benjamin. "British and Indian Ideas of 'Development': Decoding Political Conventions in the Late Colonial State." *Itinerario* 3–4 (1999): 162–209.

Index

abortion: amniocentesis and, 218n39; availability in colonial India, 164; *dais* views of, 160, 179; gender selection of children and, 183, 218n39; health of mother as chief concern, 109; opposition to, 18, 155, 167; tax on large families and, 135; traditional abortifacients as contraceptives, 145; U.S. political debate on, 85

abstinence (as contraceptive): biomedical community advocacy of, 149–50; as economic resistance to birth control trade, 66; Gandhian self-restraint and, 71–72, 92–93, 152–53; opposition to birth control and, 157; psychological harm from, 155. *See also* self-restraint

Abu-Lughod, Lila, 111, 206n101

advertising: for indigenous medical practices, 165–66; magazine advertising for contraceptives, 12–13, 20, 66, 144; "One Is Fun" campaign, 183

Age of Consent Act, 13, 89, 118–20, 141, 201n10, 206n10

ahisma, 101

Ahluwalia, Goplajee, 18, 28–29, 30–32, 61

AIWC. *See* All India Women's Conference

Ali, Begum Hamid: biographical sketch, 90; on contraceptives in Muslim law, 203n34; on *dais,* 177; religious convictions of, 94; support for birth control, 95–96, 98; views on sterilization, 109, 112, 173

Ali, Kamran Asdar, 17–18

All India Population Conference (Lucknow, 1936), 30, 34

All India Trade Union Congress, 36

All India Women's Association, 197–98n54

All India Women's Conference (AIWC), 12, 89–90, 91–92, 200–201n5

Ambedkar, B. R., 62–63, 197n43

American Medical Association, 59

Amiruddin, Begum Sultan Mir, 101

amniocentesis, 218n39

AMWI. *See* Association for Medical Women in India

Anandhi, S., 28

archives, 14–16, 174, 175–76, 189n37, 190n41, 216n7, 216n10–11. *See also* fieldwork; history

Arnold, David, 121–22

Arya Samaj movement, 37, 191–92n17

Association for Medical Women in India (AMWI), 155, 160

Ayurveda, 143, 165, 168–69

baby weeks, 122–23, 207n28

Balfour, Margaret, 158–59, 213n59

Banerjee, Jagdish Chandra, 128–29

Barthes, Roland, 204n59

Basu, Aparna, 7

BCIIC. *See* Birth Control International Information Center

Beadon, Mary O'Brien, 157–58

Beals, Rose, 68

Behar, Ruth, 17–18, 190n41

Belgium, 139

Besant, Annie, 91–92

Bharat Stree Mahamandal (Association/Gathering of Indian Women), 200–201n5

Bhore Committee Report. *See* Health Survey and Development Committee Report

biomedical community. *See* medicalization of birth control; medicine birth control. *See* abstinence; birth control clinics; contraceptive information; contraceptive technology; forced sterilization; sterilization (female); sterilization (male)

birth control clinics: as centers for distributing contraceptive information, 160–61; child welfare and antenatal centers as alternatives to, 159, 162; Girgaum (Bombay), 29; Holloway (London), 54, 66, 159; medicalization of birth control and, 145; responses to famine survey and, 135; traveling clinics, 128; visits by Indian birth control advocates, 6. *See also* contraceptive information; medicine

Birth Control International Information Center (BCIIC), 54, 58, 65–66

Birth Control News, 48–49, 66

Birth Control Review, 29, 31–32

birthing. *See* childbearing

Blacker, C. P., 11, 58, 64, 70

Bock, Gisela, 205n82

body: biomedical colonization of the body, 171–72; bodily integrity as liberal tenet, 88–89; conjugal responsibility and, 103; contraceptives as bodily indulgence, 78; contraceptives as control of sexual body, 39–41; feminine bodily sovereignty, 104–5, 113, 131, 218n40; as object of colonial scrutiny, 118–19; seed/soil sexual metaphors, 46

Bombay Birth Control League, 196–97n36

Bose, Subhas Chandra, 62–63, 197n41

Bradley, Harriet, 176, 216n11

brahmacharya, 71

British Malthusian League, 26, 54

Brown, Judith, 36, 209–10n79

Burton, Antoinette, 5, 141, 189n37

Canada, 129, 206n6

caste system: birth control advocacy and, 35; eugenics and, 25; Gandhian nationalist movement and, 37; Indian feminism and, 98; Mahar movement, 62, 197n43; Rajput caste, 117; upper-caste sexual oppression, 200–201n5. *See also* class; subaltern women

Catholicism, 59, 203–4n53

CBC. *See* Society for Constructive Birth Control and Racial Progress

census. *See* overpopulation; state discourse

cervical caps, 48–49, 61

Chakrabarty, Dipesh, 7

Chakravarty, Uma, 7

Chapaladevi, 167

chastity, 72–73, 78

Chatterjee, Partha, 7, 42

Chatterji, A. N., 147, 150

Chattopadhyaya, Kamaladevi: biographical sketch, 90; on female sexual autonomy, 104, 205n71; nationalist views of, 100; representational agency in, 14–15; support for birth control, 12, 94–95, 96–97, 104–5, 113

Chaudhury, H. K., 145, 148

chemical contraceptives, 151, 160, 163

Chesler, Ellen, 59

childbearing: baby weeks, 122–23, 207n28; birthing positions, 178–79, 214n92; child spacing, 10–11, 68, 160, 162; control of fetal gender, 168; disruption of the feminine body and, 88–89; Gandhi procreative sex theory, 72–84, 173, 215n2; infant mortality, 122–23; maternal mortality, 44, 95–96, 102–3, 108, 204n62; pro-natal birth control views, 155–56; women's emotional satisfaction and, 51

Child Marriage Restraint Act (1929), 118–19, 128, 130–31, 200n1, 206n9

children. *See* childbearing; family

child welfare centers, 159

Chinnathamby, Richard, 110

Choudhry, Prem, 7

Christianity, 59, 93–94, 203–4n53

Clarke, Adele, 213n75

class: access to birth control and, 10–11, 18, 106–8; aristocratic fertility behavior, 40, 136–37, 147; attitudes toward birth control and, 1–2, 39; colonial discourse and, 191n6; Gandhian movement and, 37, 75–76, 79–80, 109; Indian feminism and, 8, 90–91, 98, 112–14; literacy and, 40; Malthusian arguments for contraception and, 32, 34–35; peasant fertility behavior, 39–43, 53, 108–9, 139–40, 152–53, 162, 169–70; socialist movement, 36, 97; universalism and, 61–62, 76, 82–84. *See also* caste system; poverty; subaltern women

Cohn, Bernard, 121, 208n42

coitus interruptus, 47–48

colonialism: Age of Consent Bill and, 120, 206n10; birth control in world colonies, 139–40, 210n89; British vs. Indian economic interests, 36; civilizing burden of Western feminists and, 203–4n53; colonial administrative apparatus, 124–27; colonial government as agent of modernity, 13–14, 20, 120, 207n15; Council of State actions on birth control, 127–33, 208n43; *dais* as symbols for, 117, 217n16; diversity in colonial discourse, 117, 140–41; "foreigners" as eugenics factor, 35; history and, 56, 195n8; native elites appropriation of, 191n6; revolt of 1857, 116–17; sexual liberation and, 80; Western vs. Indian influences on contraceptive policy, 56, 111, 131. *See also* state discourse

Comstock Laws (U.S.), 59, 117, 138, 206n6

condoms, 47–48, 151, 170

consumerism, 110, 112–13

Contrabab, 151

contraceptive information: Balfour contraceptive distribution guidelines, 158–59; Comstock Laws (U.S.) and, 59, 117, 138, 206n6; dissemination by colonial government, 20, 125; dissemination in birth control clinics, 160–61; magazine advertising for contraceptives, 12–13, 20, 144; male control of, 48, 194n106; sex education in schools, 49, 125; "Wives Clinic" presentations, 43–44. *See also* birth control clinics; contraceptive technology

contraceptive sponge, 67–68

contraceptive technology

—issues: "birth control" term, 191n11; competition among contraceptive designs, 61, 196–97n36; feminine sexual bodily sovereignty, 104–5, 113, 218n40; health concerns from contraceptive technologies, 66–67, 93; health concerns from pregnancy and childbirth and, 44, 95–97, 106–8, 119–20, 136, 155–56; homemade contraceptives, 69–70, 170; market concerns about contraceptives, 66, 68, 70; race and class issues, 65–69, 70, 82; Sanger on, 65; seminal energy theories and, 168

—methods: abstinence, 66, 71–72, 92–93, 149–50, 152–53, 155–57; cervical caps, 48–49, 61; *coitus interruptus,* 47–48; condoms, 47–48, 151, 170; homemade contraceptives, 69–70, 170; hormonal contraceptives, 197–98n54, 213n75; male sterilization, 62–63, 180; pessaries, 70, 74, 160, 168, 170; post-coital semen flushing, 170; prolonged lactation, 151, 212n32; rhythm method, 93, 151, 202n23; spermicides, 66, 151, 160, 163, 170; sponge, 67–68. *See also* abstinence; sterilization (female)

Cousins, Margaret, 89–90, 95, 106

Curie, Marie, 203–4n53

dais (midwives): abortion and, 160, 164; colonialism and, 117, 217n16; *dais* kits, 177–79, 217n21; fieldwork with, 16–17; medical stereotypes of, 159–60, 171–72, 176–77; middle-class disdain for, 96; subjectivity of resistance and, 174–75, 216n9; training of, 177–79, 217n23; use by doctors as assistants, 165, 171, 214n92. *See also* indigenous medicine

Darling, Malcolm, 126, 208n40

Datta, Pradip Kumar, 193n61

Davis, Angela, 218n40

demographics. *See* overpopulation; state discourse

Depo-Provera, 197–98n54

developmentalism, 206n101

Devi, Bhura, 17, 183

Devi, Gunda, 17

Devi, Leela, 17, 217n23

Devi, Padma, 17, 217n23

Devi, Rukhma, 17, 179
Devi, Shrimati Chameli, 167
Devi, Vimla, 215n104
Dewey, Clive, 209n78
Dr. DeVilbiss' Powder, 68–69
Dubois, Ellen Carol, 203–4n53
Dufferin fund, 144, 161, 163, 165, 210n1, 213n59, 213n80
Duo-Foam, 67
Duponol foam powder, 68
Dutch Cap, 48–49, 61

Egypt, 17, 114, 206n101
elitism. *See* class
Ellis, Havelock, 6, 64
Emergency, the, 2–3, 187n6
environmentalism: declining middle-class health as environmental concern, 110; fitness of male population and, 32–33; foreign exploitation of resources, 35; Gandhian resource redistribution proposal, 109–10, 146; limited food supply and, 39, 62, 73; underdevelopment of resources, 133. *See also* food supply
eugenics: birth control advocacy and, 18, 31–32, 108, 140; class and, 25, 108; Indian eugenic societies, 28–29; influence on Western birth control advocates, 58; Malthusianism and, 30–35, 173; marriage as "eugenic instrument," 44–45; medical establishment support for, 146–47; nationalism and, 29; origin of, 25; race and, 25, 28–29, 97, 131
Eugenic Society (India), 28–29, 191–92n17
Eugenic Society (United Kingdom), 58

family: antifeminist backlash and, 110–11; baby weeks, 122–23, 207n28; birth control as beneficial for, 49–51, 76, 81, 148–50; birth control as threat to, 93; child marriage, 118–20, 128, 130–31, 134, 201n10, 206n9; collective mothering, 181, 218n34; feminine deference in, 102–4; Indian feminist views on, 99–102; "love marriage" vs. "traditional marriage," 44–45; marital sexuality, 49–51, 103, 148–50, 181–83; maternity as legitimizing role, 87–88; motherhood trope and, 32, 102–3, 152–53, 205n82; platonic vs. procreative marriage, 72, 76, 81, 104; polygamy, 134; "rationalization of marriage," 109; views of ideal family, 183
famine. *See* food supply
Famine Commission Final Report (1945), 13, 115, 133, 136
Female Infanticide Act (1870), 117
Fem-Foam contraceptive foam, 68–69
feminism: alliance with nationalist discourse, 87; history and, 187n1; representation of subaltern women and, 15, 114, 206n101; sovereign vs. relational identity and, 16–17. *See also* women feminism
—Indian feminism: antifeminist backlash, 110–11; birth control debate and, 85–86, 88; class perspective of Indian feminists, 8, 90–91, 98, 112–14; communalization in, 94, 202n33; modernity and, 86, 200n1; nationalism and, 7–9, 56, 86–87, 96–100, 113, 205n77; neglect of subaltern concerns, 90; religious background and, 94; sensitivity to traditional domesticity, 86; Western birth control advocacy and, 85–86; Western vs. Indian influences on, 56, 111
—Western feminism: birth control as feminist issue, 1, 55; civilizing burden of, 203–4n53; class biases in, 10, 188–89n27; gender as analytical category, 10, 61–62; globalist influence on, 57–58; modernity and, 153–54; narrativising strategy in, 5; "universal sisterhood" (Sanger), 76, 82–84, 183–85, 199n100
Ferozuddin, Khadijah Begum, 93, 119
fieldwork: communities studied, 16–17, 174, 217n22; interviews with women medical professionals, 155; native anthropology and, 14, 189n36; use of oral sources, 175–76. *See also* archives; history
Fleischmann, Ellen, 87
foam-powder contraceptives, 67–68
food supply: census commission assessment of, 121–22; Council of State assessment of, 132; Famine Commission Final Report (1945), 13, 115, 133–36; Gandhi on,

79–80; population projections and, 39, 62, 73. *See also* environmentalism; poverty
Forbes, Geraldine, 8, 199n105, 203n34, 212n44
forced sterilization, 2–3, 31–33, 41, 109, 112, 134, 147–48, 156–57, 173. *See also* sterilization
Foucault, Michel, 132, 185, 188n25
France, 93, 129, 139, 203–4n53

Galton, Francis, 25, 28
Gandhi, Mahatma: on abstinence as a contraceptive, 66, 71–72, 92; anti-Malthusian stance of, 173; antimodernism of, 61, 110; civil disobedience movement of, 33, 89; Indian middle-class feminism and, 7–8; nationalist movement of, 37, 56, 80, 86; nonviolence campaign of, 78, 199n105; opposition to birth control, 4, 19, 55, 71–72, 75, 77–78, 138; representational agency in, 14–15, 75–76; resource redistribution agenda of, 109–10, 146; Sanger and, 59, 73, 75–77; suppression of political opposition, 94; views on overpopulation, 79–80; views on sexuality, 71–73, 77–79, 83, 173, 215n2
gender: abstract conceptions of, 10, 61–62; control of fetal gender, 168, 183, 218n39; public vs. private sphere and, 83; tradition as gendered category, 111. *See also* feminism; men; sexuality; women
Ghosh, J. N., 145, 147
Ghoshe, Debendra Nath, 34, 41
globalization: global birth control movement, 11, 55, 85–86, 128–29; globalist influence on feminism, 55–58, 59, 85–86, 110–11, 195n5, 196n11; international conferences, 61; Western Enlightenment paradigm, 15–16; Western nations as cultural models, 131. *See also* feminism—Western feminism
Gokhale, Premila, 163, 165, 171, 214n81, 214n92
Gordon, Linda, 5
Griffith, Edward F., 11, 63–64
Guha, Ranajit, 174, 216n7
Gynomin, 151

hakims, 13, 165–66, 170–71
Hall, Lesley, 41–42
Hallett, M. G., 127, 129–30
Hanssen, Beatrice, 188n25
Hardiman, David, 199n105
Harding, Sandra, 182
Health Survey and Development Committee Report (1946), 13, 133, 135–36
Himes, Norman, 11, 63–64
Hinduism: anti-Brahmanist caste movement, 37, 200–201n5; communalization of, 94; Muslim tension with, 37–40, 94, 203n34; patriarchal structures in, 193n56; Phadke eugenics argument and, 33; teachings on self-restraint, 72–73, 78, 93; teachings on sexuality in, 45
Hindu Mahasabha, 37–38
Hindu-Malthusian League (Madras), 27–28
history: colonialism and, 56, 195n8; feminism and, 87–88, 187n1; gender as analytical category in, 10; malestream nationalism and, 9; mapping of time in, 178, 217n24; nationalist historical narrative, 6; use of diaries, 216n15; use of elite/colonial sources, 14–15, 174, 216n7, 216n9–11; use of oral sources, 157–58. *See also* archives; fieldwork
homemade contraceptives, 69–70, 170
homosexuality, 50
How-Martyn, Edith: as birth control advocate, 19, 54–55; on birth control clinics, 160–61; on contraceptive technology, 65–69; Gandhi and, 71–73; Malthusian affiliations of, 26–27; medicalization of birth control and, 145, 171; racial attitude of, 70; support for Indian contraceptive policy, 4, 11; visit to India, 63, 67, 70–71, 144–45
Hunt, Nancy Rose, 6
Hutton, J. H., 120–24

identity. *See* subjectivity
Imam, Hossain, 127–28, 132
Indian Birth Control Society, 29
Indian Eugenic Society, 28
Indian Medical Board, 80
indigenous medicine: conceptions of

birth control in, 143, 165–69; magazine advertising for contraceptives and, 13, 165–66; study of U.S. midwives, 216n15. See also *dais*

Islam: *ashraf* (upper class) in, 98, 112; Hindu tension with, 37–40, 94, 203n34; medical treatment of Muslims, 165, 214n90; opposition to Child Marriage Restraint act, 128; overpopulation concerns with, 35, 38–40; position on birth control, 93, 202n25, 203n34; teachings on self-restraint, 93

Ittmann, Karl, 210n89

Iyer, T. S. Balasubramania, 148–49

JAMWI. See *Journal of Association of Medical Women in India*

Japan, 60

Jaunpur (Uttaranchal): feminine identity and, 16–17; fieldwork in, 16, 174; reception of state discourse, 183–84; traditional reproductive views in, 181–83

Jayawardena, Kumari, 7–9, 86–87

Jeffries, Lilias M., 155–59

Jhirad, J., 162, 177

Jolly, Margaret, 87

Joshi, Sanjay, 188n26, 190n1, 192n38, 193n73

Journal of Association of Medical Women in India (JAMWI), 155–63, 212n46

kama, 73

Kandiyoti, Deniz, 9, 87

Kanpur, India, 17

Kaplan, Caren, 57

Karve, Dhondo Keshav, 29

Karve, Malati, 29

Karve, Raghunath Dhondo, 18, 28, 37

kavirajs, 166

Kenya, 139

Kishore, Vaidraj Akhil, 166

language: agricultural metaphors for sexuality, 46; animal metaphors for working-class sexuality, 41, 43, 53; birth control booklets in Hindi, 167, 168–69; metaphors for sexual functions, 46, 194n99; in population studies, 30; *sakari bhasha* (government language), 183, 218n37; sterilization procedures and, 180

Lantex Protectives/Paragons, 151

Lebanon, 203–4n53

Lenin, Vladimir, 97

liberalism: feminist reworking of classic individualism, 88–89, 100–102; universalist assumptions in, 61–62, 82–84, 183–85, 199n100; Western Enlightenment paradigm for, 15–16

Linlithgow, Viceroy, 115, 126, 130

literacy, 40

London Eugenic Society, 70

Ludden, David, 191n6

Madhuri, 12, 20, 165–67

Madras Birth Control Bulletin (MBCB), 28, 65–66

Madras Birth Control Review, 19

Madras Neo-Malthusian League, 28

Mahabharata, 45

Mahadevia, G. C., 146

Mahar movement, 62, 197n43

Majumdar, R. C., 56

Majumdar, Vina, 7

Malaviya, Madan Mohan, 37–38

male discourse. See men

Malhotra, Anshu, 7

Malthus, Thomas, 24–25

Malthusianism: antimodernism and, 109–10, 112–13; contraceptive policy and, 3, 18, 31–32, 62; disdain for charity in, 31–32, 34; eugenics and, 30–35, 173; femininity and, 91–92; Gandhi critique of, 79–80; Malthus on population, 24–25, 192n31; in medical writings, 147–48; Neo-Malthusian Leagues in Britain, 26, 58, 91, 191n10; Neo-Malthusian Leagues in India, 26–28; scientific management of sexuality, 33

Mani, Lata, 9

Manusmriti, 37, 193n56

marriage. See family

Marriage Hygiene (journal), 6, 11, 63–65, 66, 82

masturbation, 51, 74

Mayo, Katherine, 217n16

MBCB. See *Madras Birth Control Bulletin*

McCann, Carole, 76, 210–11n4

246   Index

McClintock, Anne, 9, 87
medicalization of birth control: biomedical view of abstinence, 149–50, 210–11n4; contraceptive distribution guidelines and, 135, 158–59; doctors as birth control authorities, 107–8, 142, 171; lack of consensus in medicalization efforts, 171; lack of women doctors and, 130–31, 137; medical training in birth control, 145–46; mistrust of lay public and, 94–95; Sanger initiatives in U.S., 210–11n4. *See also* medicine
medicine: coopting of *dais,* 177–79; eugenics and, 146–47; health concerns from contraceptive technologies, 66–67, 93; health concerns from pregnancy and childbirth and, 44, 95–97, 106–8; Indian medical journals, 12, 144; medical management of epidemics, 210n2; modernity and, 168, 170–71; post-1857 public health initiatives, 117; racial/ethnic discrimination and, 213n80, 214n90; stereotypes of *dais,* 159–60, 171–72, 176–77; treatment of subaltern patients, 180, 218n31; women as medical professionals, 130–31, 137, 144, 154–64, 210n1. *See also* birth control clinics; *dais;* indigenous medicine; medicalization of birth control
men: discourse of male birth control advocates, 7–9, 23–24; Gandhi on male sexuality, 71–73, 77–79, 83, 173, 215n2; "healthy male citizenry" argument for contraception, 32, 42, 53; male contraceptive methods, 47–48; male genitalia, 45–46; male sterilization, 62–63, 147, 180; marital sexuality and, 148–50; natural sexual instincts of, 47, 92, 154; "nervous energy" theory of fertility behavior, 40–41; as partners in family planning, 128; Sanger sexual liberation theory and, 76; seed metaphor for sperm, 46, 194n99; seminal energy theories, 168. *See also* gender
Menon, Lakshmi, 90, 95–96, 108–9, 112
Metcalf, Barbara, 7
Metcalf, Thomas, 116
Mexico, 17

middle class: defined, 40, 190n1; ambiguity toward "improvement," 33; bias and use of contraceptive technology, 136–37; disdain for *dais,* 96; as eugenic ideal, 158, 162; Gandhian nationalism and, 37, 87–88, 99–102; Indian middle-class feminism, 7–9, 85–86, 90–91, 98–114; men's position on birth control, 30, 35, 40–41, 52–53; middle-class health as environmental concern, 110; overpopulation and, 24–25; position on eugenics, 30–31, 108–10; sexuality and, 42–52, 103–5, 162, 169; universalism as Western middle-class value, 61–62; views on subaltern groups, 34–35, 42–43; women's position on birth control, 12, 91–98, 104–8. *See also* class
midwives. See *dais*
Mill, John Stuart, 168
Mil-San, 151
Minault, Gail, 7
Mistry, Jerbanoo, 161–62
modernization: colonial government as agent of modernity, 13–14, 20, 157; consumerism and, 110, 112–13; developmentalism, 206n101; Gandhian antimodernism, 61, 110; gendered traditionalism and, 111; Indian feminism and, 86, 200n1; overpopulation and, 1–2, 30–31; scientific vs. indigenous knowledge, 168, 170–72; *swaraj* and, 35; traditional worldview and, 181–83; Western feminism and, 153–54
mothering. *See* childbearing; family; women
Mudaliar, Murugesa, 27
Mukherjee, Radhakamal, 10–11, 28, 30, 34, 38–39, 41, 52, 124
Mukherji, Santosh, 146–47, 149–51

Naidu, Muthiah, 27
Naidu, V. V., 27
Naiker, Mooneswamy, 27
Narayan, Kirin, 189n36
National Council of Women in India (NCWI), 200–201n5
nationalism: Age of Consent Bill and, 120, 206n10; cultural authenticity and, 111; Gandhi nationalist movement, 37,

56, 78, 80, 199n105; "healthy male citizenry" argument for contraception, 32, 42, 53; historical narrative and, 6; Indian feminism and, 7–9, 56, 86–87, 96–100, 113, 205n77; myth of motherhood and, 102–3, 152–53; nationalist argument for eugenics, 29, 33, 96–97; postindependence access to contraceptives, 17. See also *swaraj*

Nawaz, M. S., 153–54

neem oil, 170

Nehru, Jawaharlal, 73, 203n34

Nehru, Rameshwari: biographical sketch, 89; on nationalism, 99–100; on overpopulation, 109–10, 112–13; position on birth control, 12, 92; representational agency in, 14–15; on traditional domestic gender relations, 86, 102–3

Neo-Malthusian League (India), 26–28

Neo-Malthusian League (United Kingdom), 26, 58, 91, 191n10

Net-en, 197–98n54

Neushul, Peter, 57

Omvedt, Gail, 7–8

Ortho-Gynol, 151, 163

otherness: birth rate strategies and, 123; communalization of demographic issues, 38, 94, 193n61, 202n33, 208–9n52; female other, 45–46; foreignness as other, 111; hypersexuality associated with, 43; silencing of subaltern groups and, 16, 97–98, 106, 173; superstition as the "other" of science, 75; West/Britain as other to nationalist India, 126, 128–29

overpopulation: birth control advocacy and, 23–25, 96, 110, 117–18, 118–19, 121–24; birth rate in world colonies, 139–40; British concern about, 125–26; challenges to overpopulation claims, 130, 133, 208–9n52; economic modernization and, 1–2, 30–31; environmentalist views of, 32–33, 35, 39, 62, 109–10; Gandhi views on, 78–80; infant mortality decline as cause, 122–23; Malthusian views of, 24–25, 27; Mukherjee writings on, 30; state-generated reports on, 13–14, 20, 25–26, 52, 118–19, 121–24, 140, 208n42; as subject in medical journals, 146; Wattal writings on, 29–30, 33–34

Palmer, Eileen: as birth control advocate, 19, 54–55; on birth control clinics, 160–61; globalist perspective of, 55–58, 195n5; support for Indian contraceptive policy, 4, 11; visit to India, 63, 67

Pearson, Gail, 7–8

pessaries, 70, 74, 160, 168, 170

Pethick-Lawrence, Lord, 124–26

Phadke, Narayan Sitaram: anti-Brahmanist caste movement and, 37; birth control advocacy of, 10–11, 18, 23, 28, 29; on contraceptive technology, 48–49, 196–97n36; environmentalist eugenics argument of, 32–33, 35, 44; "nervous energy" theory of male fertility behavior, 40–41; representational agency in, 14–15; Sanger and, 61; writings on sexuality, 39, 42–49

Pillay, Aliyappin Padmanabha: anti-Brahmanist caste movement and, 37; birth control advocacy of, 18, 28; on contraceptive technology, 10–11, 67–68; eugenics advocacy of, 29, 31–32; as *Marriage Hygiene* editor, 6, 11, 63–65, 82; representational agency in, 14–15; "Wives Clinic" conducted by, 43–44; writings on sexuality, 39, 42–51

Planitab, 163

polygamy, 134

population. See overpopulation

Portelli, Alessandro, 176, 216n11

Porter, Roy, 41–42

poverty: birth control as solution for, 30–31, 126, 208n40; child welfare centers, 159; eugenics as solution to, 147; Famine Commission Final Report (1945), 13, 115, 133, 136; resource redistribution as solution to, 109–10, 146; standard-of-living as birth rate factor, 122–23, 134. See also class; food supply; subaltern women

Prakash, Gyan, 168

Prasad, Sir Jagdish, 127, 130, 208–9n52

Pro-Race Cap, 48–49, 70

prostitution, 149

public health, 32

public vs. private sphere, 10; debates on

normative sexuality and, 42, 80–81; gendered divisions of, 83; interrogation of subaltern spaces and, 184, 218n41; oral history as "private" archive, 175–76; surveillance of procreative practices and, 28, 33, 35, 39–41, 118–20
Puerto Rico, 140

race: birth control use by U.S. minorities, 218n40; contraceptive technology and, 68–69, 70; discrimination by medical community, 213n80; eugenics and, 25, 28–29, 31, 97, 131; *Marriage Hygiene* and, 64–65; in medical writings, 146–47; "mother of the race" argument, 32, 152–53; "race suicide" argument for birth control, 139; sexual morality and, 157–58; women's suffrage movement and, 203–4n53
Raina, B. L., 145
Rajwade, Rani Laxmibai: biographical sketch, 90, 202n17; on the nationalist myth of motherhood, 102–3; religious convictions of, 94; support for birth control, 95–96, 108, 113
Ram, Kalpana, 15
Ramabai, Pandita, 200–201n5
Ramayana, 45, 72
Ramusack, Barbara, 5, 7, 191n12, 196n14, 202n25, 207n28, 212n47
Ranadive, B. T., 121
Rangacharlu, Dewan, 27
Rao, Maharaj Sayaji, 60
rape, 147
Ray, Raka, 205n77
Reddi, Muthulaskhmi, 12, 89, 94, 104–5
Rendell, 151
rhythm method, 93, 151, 202n23
Roe, Humphrey Verdon, 54
Rohatgi, Chandrakanta, 163–64, 214n81, 214n90
Rohatgi, Surendra, 164
Roosevelt, Franklin, 59
Roshni, 12, 90, 99, 101

Saheli, 197–98n54
Sahgal, Lakshmi, 163, 214n81
Sangari, Kumkum, 5
Sanger, Margaret: biographical sketch, 191n11; commentary on Phadke's eugenics, 29; on contraceptive technology, 65, 68–70; Gandhi and, 59, 73, 75–77, 94; How-Martyn affiliation with, 26; imprisonment in U.S., 138; international conference involvement, 61; medicalization of birth control and, 145, 171, 210–11n4; on religious opposition to birth control, 94; representational agency in, 14–15, 75–76; Sanger globalist perspective, 55–58, 59, 195n5, 196n11; on sexual liberation, 71–72, 76–77, 80, 83; status in Indian advocacy organizations, 19, 76, 161; support for Indian contraceptive policy, 4, 11; visit to India, 54, 59–61, 63, 71, 144–45, 214n81
Sapru, P. N., 127, 129–32
Saraswati, Dayanand, 37
Sarda Act, 118–19, 130–31, 200n1, 206n9
Sarkar, Sumit, 36, 56
Sarkar, Tanika, 7, 199n105
satyagraha, 78
Satyashodhak movement, 37
Scheper-Hughes, Nancy, 17–18
Scott, Joan, 203–4n53
Self-Respect movement, 37
self-restraint: Gandhi views on, 66, 71–72, 92; Hindu teachings on, 72–73, 78, 93; in indigenous birth control manuals, 169; Islamic teachings on, 93; medical views of, 149–53; Reddi on conjugal self-restraint, 104–5. *See also* abstinence; sexuality
sexology, 49–50, 74–75
sexuality: age of consent, 13, 89, 118–20, 141, 201n10, 206n10; agricultural metaphors for, 46; animal metaphors for, 41, 43, 53; aristocratic fertility behavior, 40, 136–37, 147; dietary recommendations for, 169; Gandhi views on, 71–73, 77–79, 83, 173, 215n2; marital sexuality, 49–51, 76, 103–5, 148–50, 181–83; masturbation, 51, 74; menstruation and, 169; peasant fertility behavior, 39–43, 53, 108–9, 139–40, 152–53, 162, 169–70; procreative sex, 72, 77–78, 81, 104, 149; promotion of "ideal sexual behavior," 42, 45, 155–56, 158; sex education in schools, 49; sexual dysfunctions, 50–51; sexual morality, 157–58; sur-

Index 249

veillance of procreative practices, 28, 33, 35, 39–41, 118–20; working-class sexual practices, 41, 43, 53, 162
SHARE. *See* Society for Health and Rural Education
Shinde, Tarabai, 200–201n5
Sholapur Eugenic Society, 29, 31, 43–44
SIDH. *See* Society for the Integrated Development of the Himalayas
Sinha, Mrinalini: on the Age of Consent Bill, 201n10, 206n10; on feminism as historically bound, 87–88; on historical narrative, 5–6; on Indian feminist modernism, 200n1; on Indian feminist nationalism, 102, 202n33; on middle-class Indian feminism, 9
socialism, 36, 97
Society for Constructive Birth Control and Racial Progress (CBC), 61, 66, 73
Society for Health and Rural Education (SHARE), 174, 179
Society for the Integrated Development of the Himalayas (SIDH), 174, 178, 217n22, 217n30
Soloway, Richard, 57, 58
South Africa, 65, 140
spermicides, 66, 151, 160, 163, 170
Spivak, Gayatri, 16, 215n3
sponge contraceptive, 67–68
Sreenivas, Mytheli, 7
state discourse: access to contraceptive information, 20; approval of chemical contraceptives, 164; birth control as Western influence, 128–29; British government support for birth control, 124–33; "decline of India" argument and, 44, 138, 209–10nn78–79; Government of India Act (1919), 38; localization of decisions on contraceptives, 138; population reports, 13–14, 20, 25–26, 52, 118–19, 121–24, 140, 208n42; post-1857 regulatory reforms, 117; prosecution of Karve, 29; *sakari bhasha* (government language), 183, 218n37; state support for birth control, 114–15, 120–27, 140–41, 208n40; surveillance of procreative practices, 28, 33, 35, 39–41, 118–20; *swaraj* (self-rule), 32, 35
sterilization (female): avoidance of abortion and, 167; "choice" in contraceptive sterilization, 181; miracle drugs for, 166; popularity as contraceptive, 180; women's views of, 217n30. *See also* forced sterilization
sterilization (male), 62–63, 180
Stevens, Mr. (Stella and Company), 67
Stopes, Marie: British birth control advocacy of, 58–59; *Contraception* as medical reference, 146; on contraceptive methods, 65, 69–70, 196–97n36; correspondence with Ahluwalia, 29; Gandhi and, 73–75, 94; globalist perspective of, 55–58, 195n5, 196n11; Holloway birth control clinic and, 54, 66, 159; as Indian birth control authority, 4, 11, 19, 74, 81, 125, 161; medicalization of birth control and, 145, 210–11n4; representational agency in, 14–15; on sexual liberation, 41–42, 71–72, 74–77, 80, 83; visit to Japan, 60
Stree Shakti Sanghatan, 197–98n54
Stri-Darpan, 12, 99
Stri-Dharma, 12, 89–90, 92, 94, 99
subaltern women: biomedical community treatment of, 180, 218n31; birth control advocacy and, 23, 109; communalization of, 106; contraceptive technology and, 65–69; historical study of, 14–16, 174, 216n7, 216n9–10; homemade contraceptives, 69–70, 170; Indian feminism and, 90. *See also* caste system; class
subjectivity: in childbirth, 178–79; "choice" in contraceptive sterilization, 181; "coming to voice" of subalterns, 174; conjugal responsibility and, 103; of ethnographic sources, 176; feminist reworking of liberal individualism, 88–89, 100–102; liberatory telos in birth control, 157, 184–85; in population studies, 30; sovereign vs. relational self, 15–17, 37, 181
Sudha, 12, 20, 165–67
suffrage, 203n53
Sutras, 33
swaraj (self-rule): environmentalist discourse and, 32; feminist discourse and, 99; Indian class structure and, 37; modernism and, 35; opposition of colonial government to, 197n41. *See also* nationalism

Tagore, Rabindranath, 61
Tamta, Savitri, 178, 217n22
Tehri Garhwal District (Uttaranchal). *See* Jaunpur
theosophy, 92
Thomas, Lynn, 40, 139
Thomas, Nicholas, 117
Thompson, Elizabeth, 203–4n53
Tirtha, Rama, 27, 191n15
Tong, Rosemarie, 215n2

Unani, 143
United Kingdom: birth control laws in, 138–39; birth control movement in, 58–59, 61, 63–64, 91; eugenic societies in, 58, 70; global birth control history and, 11, 55; government position on birth control, 124–33; Holloway birth control clinic, 54, 66, 159; population studies in, 38, 93; visits to birth control clinics in, 6
United States: abortion debate, 85; birth control movement in, 61, 63–64; birth control research in, 213n75; Comstock Laws (U.S.), 59, 117, 138, 206n6; global birth control history and, 11, 55; marketing of birth control technology in India, 65; medicalization of birth control in, 210–11n4; opposition to birth control in, 54, 59, 111, 129, 138, 218n40; study of midwives in, 216n15; women's liberation in, 153, 218n40; women's suffrage movement, 203–4n53
universalism, 61–62, 75–76, 82–84, 182, 183–85, 199n100

vaids, 13, 165–67, 170–71
Vaidshastri, Pandit, Chandrashekar, 166
Vaidya, Vimla Devi, 13, 168–70, 179
Van Hollen, Cecilia, 17–18
vasectomy, 62–63
Victorian Memorial Scholarship Fund, 144, 210n1
Vohra, Dharam Bir, 111

Wattal, Pyare Krishan: birth control advocacy of, 18, 28; census commission citation of, 121; on Muslim overpopulation, 38–39; support for access to birth control technology, 10–11; writings on overpopulation, 29–30, 33–34, 52, 124
Wavell, Archibald Percival, Viceroy Lord, 124–26
Western birth control advocacy. *See* globalization
WIA. *See* Women's India Association
Willingdon, Freeman Freeman-Thomas, Marquess of, 124–25, 132
women: abortion of female children, 183, 218n39; as "agents of salvation," 157–58; conjugal responsibility and, 103, 148–50; cures for "women's illnesses," 165–69; female contraceptives, 48–49; female genitalia, 43–44; in Gandhi nationalist movement, 78, 199n105; Gandhi on femininity, 72, 77–78; health concerns from contraceptive technologies, 66–67, 93; health concerns from pregnancy and childbirth and, 44, 95–97, 106–8, 119–20, 136, 155–56; homosexuality and, 50; Malthusian femininity, 91–92; maternal mortality, 44, 95–96, 102–3, 108, 204n62; as medical professionals, 130–31, 137, 143–44, 154–64, 210n1; motherhood trope and, 32, 102–3, 152–53, 205n82; patriarchal structure and, 102, 193n56, 204n59; representation of subaltern women, 14–16; sexual autonomy of, 43, 49–51, 74, 103–4, 204n64; sexual dysfunctions of, 50–51; traditional reproductive destiny, 181, 182–83; "universal sisterhood" (Sanger), 76, 82–84, 183–85, 199n100; "Wives Clinic" presentations, 43–44. *See also* feminism; gender
Women's India Association (WIA), 89–90, 91–92, 200–201n5
Woodhead, Sir John, 133
Workers Birth Control Group, 58

Yadhuvirsingh, 167–68, 170
Young, Ruth, 159–60, 170

Zetland, Lawrence John Lumley Dundas, Marquess of, 124–25, 130

SANJAM AHLUWALIA is an associate professor of history and women's studies at Northern Arizona University. She has contributed to *Confronting the Body: The Politics of Physicality in Colonial and Post-Colonial India,* edited by Jim Mills and Satadru Sen.

The University of Illinois Press
is a founding member of the
Association of American University Presses.

Composed in 10.3/13 Hoefler Text
with Myriad Pro display
by Celia Shapland
at the University of Illinois Press
Manufactured by Cushing-Malloy, Inc.

University of Illinois Press
1325 South Oak Street
Champaign, IL 61820-6903
www.press.uillinois.edu